T0155800

Communications
in Computer and Information Science　　　1804

Editorial Board Members

Joaquim Filipe ⓘ, *Polytechnic Institute of Setúbal, Setúbal, Portugal*
Ashish Ghosh ⓘ, *Indian Statistical Institute, Kolkata, India*
Raquel Oliveira Prates ⓘ, *Federal University of Minas Gerais (UFMG),*
Belo Horizonte, Brazil
Lizhu Zhou, *Tsinghua University, Beijing, China*

Rationale

The CCIS series is devoted to the publication of proceedings of computer science conferences. Its aim is to efficiently disseminate original research results in informatics in printed and electronic form. While the focus is on publication of peer-reviewed full papers presenting mature work, inclusion of reviewed short papers reporting on work in progress is welcome, too. Besides globally relevant meetings with internationally representative program committees guaranteeing a strict peer-reviewing and paper selection process, conferences run by societies or of high regional or national relevance are also considered for publication.

Topics

The topical scope of CCIS spans the entire spectrum of informatics ranging from foundational topics in the theory of computing to information and communications science and technology and a broad variety of interdisciplinary application fields.

Information for Volume Editors and Authors

Publication in CCIS is free of charge. No royalties are paid, however, we offer registered conference participants temporary free access to the online version of the conference proceedings on SpringerLink (http://link.springer.com) by means of an http referrer from the conference website and/or a number of complimentary printed copies, as specified in the official acceptance email of the event.

CCIS proceedings can be published in time for distribution at conferences or as post-proceedings, and delivered in the form of printed books and/or electronically as USBs and/or e-content licenses for accessing proceedings at SpringerLink. Furthermore, CCIS proceedings are included in the CCIS electronic book series hosted in the SpringerLink digital library at http://link.springer.com/bookseries/7899. Conferences publishing in CCIS are allowed to use Online Conference Service (OCS) for managing the whole proceedings lifecycle (from submission and reviewing to preparing for publication) free of charge.

Publication process

The language of publication is exclusively English. Authors publishing in CCIS have to sign the Springer CCIS copyright transfer form, however, they are free to use their material published in CCIS for substantially changed, more elaborate subsequent publications elsewhere. For the preparation of the camera-ready papers/files, authors have to strictly adhere to the Springer CCIS Authors' Instructions and are strongly encouraged to use the CCIS LaTeX style files or templates.

Abstracting/Indexing

CCIS is abstracted/indexed in DBLP, Google Scholar, EI-Compendex, Mathematical Reviews, SCImago, Scopus. CCIS volumes are also submitted for the inclusion in ISI Proceedings.

How to start

To start the evaluation of your proposal for inclusion in the CCIS series, please send an e-mail to ccis@springer.com.

Srikanth Prabhu · Shiva Raj Pokhrel · Gang Li
Editors

Applications and Techniques in Information Security

13th International Conference, ATIS 2022
Manipal, India, December 30–31, 2022
Revised Selected Papers

 Springer

Editors
Srikanth Prabhu 🆔
Manipal Academy of Higher Education
Karnataka, India

Shiva Raj Pokhrel 🆔
Deakin University
Melbourne, VIC, Australia

Gang Li 🆔
Deakin University
Burwood, VIC, Australia

ISSN 1865-0929   ISSN 1865-0937 (electronic)
Communications in Computer and Information Science
ISBN 978-981-99-2263-5   ISBN 978-981-99-2264-2 (eBook)
https://doi.org/10.1007/978-981-99-2264-2

© The Editor(s) (if applicable) and The Author(s), under exclusive license
to Springer Nature Singapore Pte Ltd. 2023
This work is subject to copyright. All rights are reserved by the Publisher, whether the whole or part of the material is concerned, specifically the rights of translation, reprinting, reuse of illustrations, recitation, broadcasting, reproduction on microfilms or in any other physical way, and transmission or information storage and retrieval, electronic adaptation, computer software, or by similar or dissimilar methodology now known or hereafter developed.
The use of general descriptive names, registered names, trademarks, service marks, etc. in this publication does not imply, even in the absence of a specific statement, that such names are exempt from the relevant protective laws and regulations and therefore free for general use.
The publisher, the authors, and the editors are safe to assume that the advice and information in this book are believed to be true and accurate at the date of publication. Neither the publisher nor the authors or the editors give a warranty, expressed or implied, with respect to the material contained herein or for any errors or omissions that may have been made. The publisher remains neutral with regard to jurisdictional claims in published maps and institutional affiliations.

This Springer imprint is published by the registered company Springer Nature Singapore Pte Ltd.
The registered company address is: 152 Beach Road, #21-01/04 Gateway East, Singapore 189721, Singapore

Preface

The 2022 International Conference on Applications and Technologies in Information Security (ATIS) was the 13th event in the ATIS series, which started in 2010. It was held December 30–31, 2022 at Manipal Institute of Technology, Manipal, Karnakata, India. The purpose of ATIS is to provide a forum for the presentation and discussion of innovative ideas, research results, applications, and experiences from around the world. The annual ATIS conference highlights new results in the design and analysis of digital security hardware and software implementations. ATIS provides a valuable connection between the theoretical and implementation communities and attracts participants from industry, academia, and government organizations.

As academic research in information security has developed over the last twenty or so years, applications and techniques have been developed to be of specific use in this area. These include wavelets and their applications in digital forensics, classification algorithms for use in malicious software detection, and genetic algorithms custom-made for the cryptographic community, etc.

ATIS 2022 focused on all aspects of new theories, novel techniques, and innovative applications of Cybersecurity, Machine Learning, IoT, and other related technologies.

ATIS 2022, held at Manipal Institute of Technology (Deemed University), Manipal, Karnataka, India, received a total of 121 papers, of which 23 were accepted. All submitted papers were reviewed under a single-blind review policy with at least 3 reviewers per paper.

February 2023   Editors

Organization

General Chairs

Anil Rana   Manipal Institute of Technology, India
Hai L. Vu   Monash University, Australia

Program Committee Chairs

Srikanth Prabhu   Manipal Institute of Technology, India
Shiva Raj Pokhrel   Deakin University, Australia
Tanweer Ali   Manipal Institute of Technology, India

Steering Committee

Gang Li (Chair)   Deakin University, Australia
Hai L. Vu   Monash University, Australia
Min Yu   Institute of Information Engineering, Chinese
                                 Academy of Sciences, China
Robin Doss   Deakin University, Australia
Bheemarjuna Reddy Tamma   Indian Institute of Technology (IIT) Hyderabad,
                                 India
Shiva Raj Pokhrel (Secretary)   Deakin University, Australia
Heejo Lee   Korea University, Korea
Jiqiang Liu   Beijing Jiaotong University, China
Tsutomu Matsumoto   Yokohama National University, Japan
Wenjia Niu   Institute of Information Engineering, Chinese
                                 Academy of Sciences, China
Yuliang Zheng   University of Alabama at Birmingham, USA

Program Committee

Min Yu   Institute of Information Engineering, Chinese
                                 Academy of Sciences, China
Gaurav Dhiman   Government Bikram College of Commerce
                                 Patiala, India

Jie Kong	Xi'an Shiyou University, China
Veelasha Moonsamy	Radboud University, The Netherlands
Ramji Chalise	IT Infrastructure, Knox City Council, Australia
Sumarga Kumar Sah Tyagi	Zhongyuan University of Technology, China
Yang Cao	Deakin University, Australia
Antony Franklin	Indian Institute of Technology (IIT) Hyderabad, India
Abhinav Kumar	Indian Institute of Technology (IIT) Hyderabad, India
Shashank Vatedka	Indian Institute of Technology (IIT) Hyderabad, India
Niranjan Khakurel	Nepal College of Information Technology, Pokhara University, Nepal
Manjeet Singh	Dr. BR Ambedkar National Institute of Technology Jalandhar, India
Urvashi	Dr. BR Ambedkar National Institute of Technology Jalandhar, India
Satnam Kaur	Thapar Institute of Engineering and Technology, India
Rachit Manchanda	Chandigarh University, India
Diwaker Pant	Tula's Institute, India
Yang Zhao	Nanyang Technological University, Singapore
Mansoor Ali	National University of Computer and Emerging Sciences, Pakistan
Manoj Shokkhya	Nanyang Technological University, Singapore
Tanveer Hussain	Sejong University, Republic of Korea
Noah Oghenefego Ogwara	Auckland University of Technology, New Zealand
Shyam Kumar Shrestha	Fisher & Paykel Healthcare, Australia
Sebastian Alarcon Pinto	DXC Consulting, Australia
Muhammad Baqer Mollah	Nanyang Technological University, Singapore
Zhenshuai Xu	Jilin University, China
Rongxin Xu	Hunan University, China
Sandeep Verma	Dr. BR Ambedkar National Institute of Technology, India
Bahaa Al-Musawi	University of Kufa, Iraq
Sashi Raj Pandey	Kyung Hee University, Republic of Korea
Parshu Pokhrel	Herbert Smith Freehills, Australia
James Elliott Nemecek	Deakin University, Australia
Mohammad Belayet Hossain	Deakin University, Australia
Samman Bhattarai	Charles Sturt University, Australia
Min Yu	Chinese Academy of Sciences, China
Bheemarjuna Reddy Tamma	Indian Institute of Technology (IIT) Hyderabad, India

Rohan de Silva	Central Queensland University, Australia
Xun Yi	RMIT University, Australia
Lei Pan	Deakin University, Australia
Ali Kadhum Idrees	University of Babylon, Iraq
Mohammed Falih	University of Kufa, Iraq
Ali Hilal Ali	University of Kufa, Iraq
Haider AlMosa	University of Kufa, Iraq
Mohammed B. M. Kamel	Furtwangen University, Germany
Wahhab Razzaq Mousa	University of Kufa, Iraq
Nabeel Salih	University of Kufa, Iraq
Yongbin Zhou	Institute of Information Engineering, Chinese Academy of Sciences, China
Yuliang Zheng	University of Alabama at Birmingham, USA
Jinqiao Shi	Institute of Computing Technology, Chinse Academy of Science, China
Kwangjo Kim	Korea Advanced Institute of Science and Technology, Republic of Korea
Wenjia Niu	Institute of Computing Technology, Chinese Academy of Sciences, China
Tianqing Zhu	University of Technology Sydney, Australia
Marilyn Wells	Central Queensland University, Australia
Rafiqul Islam	Charles Sturt University, Australia
Edilson Arenas	Central Queensland University, Australia
Heejo Lee	Korea University, Republic of Korea
Bernard Colbert	Deakin University, Australia
Pramod Kumar (Professor)	Manipal Institute of Technology, India
Vinod K. Joshi	Manipal Institute of Technology, India
M. Sathish Kumar	Manipal Institute of Technology, India
Kumara Shama (Professor)	Manipal Institute of Technology, India
Pallavi R. Mane (Professor)	Manipal Institute of Technology, India
Shounak De	Manipal Institute of Technology, India
Shweta Vincent	Manipal Institute of Technology, India
Krishnaraj Chadaga	Manipal Institute of Technology, India
Poornalatha G.	Manipal Institute of Technology, India
Harish S. V.	Manipal Institute of Technology, India
P. C. Siddhalinga Swamy	Manipal Institute of Technology, India
Renuka A.	Manipal Institute of Technology, India
Krishnamoorthi Makkithaya	Manipal Institute of Technology, India
Mohammad Zuber	Manipal Institute of Technology, India
Sameena Pathan	Manipal Institute of Technology, India
Sanjay Singh	Manipal Institute of Technology, India

Contents

Privacy and Security

Advances in Machine Learning

Cloud, IoT and Computing Technologies

Privacy and Security

Reinforcement Technique for Classifying Quasi and Non-quasi Attributes for Privacy Preservation and Data Protection

Sharath Yaji[1] and Neelima Bayyapu[2(✉)]

[1] Department of Computer Science and Engineering, NMAM Institute of Technology (NMAMIT), Nitte Affiliated to Visvesvaraya Technological University (VTU), Belgavi, Karnataka, India
sharathyaji@nitte.edu.in
[2] Department of Computer Science and Engineering, Manipal Institute of Technology, Manipal Academy of Higher Education (MAHE), Manipal, Karnataka, India
neelima.bayyapu@manipal.edu

Abstract. A quasi attribute refers to a distinct subset of unique attributes that can adequately recognize tuples in a table. Hasty distribution of the quasi attributes will prompt privacy leakage. Choosing private data from a list of attributes is decided by the publisher, and it undoubtedly changes from dataset to dataset. The need for dynamically choosing and informing systems about a quasi and a non-quasi attribute remains a challenging task. Presently, there is no particular automation model for the classification of quasi and non-quasi. It could be a burden when a massive dataset has to be classified, or aggregation of datasets has to be performed.

This research paper considers the need to categorize quasi attributes for a non-expert through a direct attack and proposes a solution through the game theory approach and reinforcement machine learning model. For demonstration, a 2×2 state matrix is considered. The results include case-wise time consumption and comparison among all necessary steps for accurate navigation, between various attributes. Among all the notable cases, the matrix arrangement with a quasi attribute in 00th and 11th position, non-quasi in 01th and 10th position obtained better performance. This reinforcement-based solution helps the automation of the classification of quasi and non-quasi attributes.

Keywords: Personally Identifiable Information · PII · Quasi attributes · Privacy · Reinforcement · Machine learning

1 Introduction

Privacy-preserving data anonymization has considerable attention in recent years as a promising model for sharing helpful information while preserving pri-

Visvesvaraya Technological University, Belagavi.

© The Author(s), under exclusive license to Springer Nature Singapore Pte Ltd. 2023
S. Prabhu et al. (Eds.): ATIS 2022, CCIS 1804, pp. 3–17, 2023.
https://doi.org/10.1007/978-981-99-2264-2_1

vacy issues. In the existing model, an expert classify the Quasi and non-Quasi attributes manually (In this paper Personal Identifiable Information (PII) is considered as Quasi data). It is a burden when massive dataset has to be classified, or aggregation of datasets has to be done. Our proposal gives the solution for this and makes work easier for a data publisher.

In a familiar scenario, data owners' information are collected and stored by a data controller or data publisher (ex: census board). It is known that only after the anonymization of Quasi, personal data are allowed to make it public.

As discussed in [1], most of the attributes, especially set-valued attributes, may or may not be Quasi (or private identifier) by themselves. However, certain values or combinations may be linked to external knowledge to fetch an individual's private information. We refer to this type of attributes as Quasi attributes.

Classifying Quasi and non-Quasi data changes from database table to table. For example, in a sportsman database table, the attribute height can be considered a non-Quasi attribute. However, according to Dwork, Terry Gross, or Turing Gross height is considered as a Quasi attribute [2,3].

The extensive research typically adopts game theory methodology for correctly classifying Quasi, and non-Quasi attributes and effective implementation of the same is shown through the reinforcement learning model. The research article ideologically motivated this research for properly implementing game theory through reinforcement [4–6]. Reinforcement learning has adequately addressed problems in decision making [6].

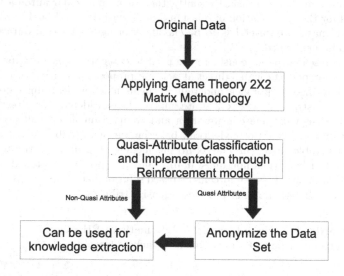

Fig. 1. Quasi attribute classification model with anonymization

The Fig. 1 shows proposed methodology. As shown in the model, the solution is proved by considering a 2×2 matrix with game theory methodology. For demonstration purposes, only two quasi and two non-quasi attributes or identifiers are considered; other combinations such as one quasi and three non-quasi attributes or vice versa can be performed similarly (other cases like quasi and all non-quasi are ignored).

Contributions: The specific objectives of this extensive research are listed as follows:

1. To show the necessity of classification of quasi and non-quasi attributes.
2. To typically make the non-expert (either a machine or a person) learn about classifying in between quasi and non-quasi data.
3. To propose game theory methodology for correctly classifying and properly implementing the process through reinforcement learning.

2 Motivation

This section discusses the motivation of the quasi and non-quasi classification. The classification assists explicitly to share only non-quasi attributes. The demonstration of how an attacker can model and measure privacy risks and perform malicious activity is as follows. The demonstration is about how a potential attacker can efficiently generate his own attribute, for doing malicious activity.

2.1 Dataset Attributes

This section discuss about chosen dataset attibutes. The list of attributes from the chosen dataset has Quasi attributes as *age, education, marital_status, occupation, relationship, race, sex, native_country* and *yearly_earning* and non-quasi attributes as workclass, fnlwgt, *education_num, capital_gain, capital_loss, hours_per_week.*

The Tables 1, 2, 3, and 4 show how a potential attacker makes uses these quasi data for retrieving quasi information. For example, from Table 1, age, marital_status, sex, and relationship are quasi attributes, and a potential attacker can easily generate a Table 2 with a new attribute such as the possibility of staying alone. The possibility of staying alone is retrieved through attributes marital status and relationship, i.e., from the first row of the Table 1, it can be observed that age is 39, he is never married, and he is not in a concerned family. This makes the attacker guess he might be staying alone. It is Yes for the potential attacker's new attribute possibility of staying alone. As another example, let us take the last row, in this table age is 28, married. Now, it is potential "No" in the attacker's new attribute, i.e., the possibility of staying alone. This information helps the attacker to make a physical attack. Similarly, Table 3 discuss another example. As shown, it has essential attributes of work-class, sex, and hours_per_week. A potential attacker can create another table from these personal data as shown in Table 4 and allegedly use it for his malicious activity. From Table 3, it is possible to guess whether the person is rich or poor. i.e., if work hours per week are more then, it can be assumed that person is rich and merely do necessary alterations in his generated Table 4. For example, the first-row person works for the government for 40 h per week, and it can be naturally assumed that he is not poor. A similar type of successful attack known as background knowledge attack is shown by L. Sweeney [7].

Table 1. Original Database

Age	Marital_status	Sex	Relationship
39	Never-married	Male	Not-in-family
50	Married-civ-spouse	Male	Husband
31	Never-married	Female	Not-in-family
28	Married-civ-spouse	Female	Wife

Table 2. Original database with attacker generated set-valued binary data attribute

Age	Sex	Possibility of staying alone
39	Male	Yes
50	Male	No
31	Female	Yes
28	Female	No

Table 3. Original database with single quasi and multiple non-quasi attributes

Work class	Sex	Hours_per_week
State-gov	Male	40
Self-emp-not-inc	Male	13
Private	Female	40
Private	Female	40

Table 4. Original database with attacker generated set-valued binary data attribute

Work class	Sex	Hours_per_week	Rich
State-gov	Male	40	Yes
Self-emp-not-inc	Male	13	No
Private	Female	40	Yes
Private	Female	40	Yes

3   Literature Survey

This section describes literature survey on practical applications of game theory and reinforcement learning.

3.1 Game Theory Applications

Von Neumann and Morgen Stern introduced the critical concept of game theory in their book theory of games and economic behavior. This book properly presents the research framework of game theory [8]. Later in the year 1950, Nash Equilibrium was proposed. This accurately determines the theoretical foundation of the research field of game theory to non-cooperative games and nonzero-sum games. Game theory is suitable for finding solutions for a particular chosen conflict [9]. Game theory deals with three essential parts: 1) Participants 2) The actions initiated by the participants 3) The benefits that participants may receive.

Each participant is allowed to prefer the worthiest action for their maximum benefit and each participant will moreover know those other participants are also choosing the best action to obtain the most encouraging result. The participants preferred strategy must be the best response to the strategy chosen by the other participants. According to a binding agreement between the two parties, game theory can be divided into categories that are called cooperative game and non-cooperative game. Based on whether the sum of the total revenue of both players is zero, game theory can be again categorized into zero-sum game and nonzero sum game. According to the order of decision of the players, game theory can be divided into Static game and Dynamic game.

We model the problem of classifying quasi and non-quasi attribute as a static game problem through sufficiently establishing a set of strategy policies and revenue function for participants. The game sequence is has set of essential attributes that are carefully considered and assumed as all are non-quasi attributes. After applying strategic policies assumed quasi and non-quasi attributes are classified tentatively.

3.2 Reinforcement Applications

In 2002, Lindell and Pinkas introduced a privacy-preserving data-mining algorithm for ID3 decision-tree learning [10]. For K-means clustering and machine learning problems, privately distributed protocols have been proposed by Jagannathan and Wright [11]. Later Gambs et al., proposed privacy-preserving algorithms for Support Vector Machine [12]. Qu et al. demonstrated that fuzzy-based clustering methods could also be used for privacy protection domains [13].

Markov Decision Process (MDP) is utilized for reinforcement learning in our research. Reinforcement learning (RL) can be implemented through MDP. Our proposal uses MDP. MDP consist of states, actions, transitions between states, and reward function. MDP is a tuple <S, A,T, R> in which S is a finite set of states. A is a finite set of actions, T is a transition between states, and R is a reward function. Our proposal is implemented RL through MDP. The MDP scheme in data protection has been successfully proven by Qu et al. to have high privacy effectiveness in social networks and real-time context-aware applications on mobile phones [14]. Qu et al., proposed a private attribute-based privacy model to protect the private or sensitive information of users or data owners"

[13]. Later Qu et al. proved that in big data, privacy-preserving data publishing would continue to be a long-lasting problem in the data publishing domain [13].

3.3   Outcome of Literature

This section discusses quasi, non-quasi, and classification requirements, assumptions and finally presents the existing quasi and non-quasi classification problem for essential attributes.

Quasi, Non-quasi and Classification Requirement. Mainly, there are two significant exposure risks related to the released data. Those are identity disclosure, and attribute necessary disclosure.

Identity disclosure occurs if an individual can be distinguished from revealed data. Attribute disclosure occurs when a quasi attribute is uncovered and can be credited to a person. Identifiers (I) that explicitly recognize record owners' and are normally expelled from the released data, quasi-identifiers (QI) which could be connected with external data to re-distinguish the individual record owners', and sensitive data (S) or quasi data which must be protected. From Tables 1 to 4, it is known that numerous attributes, particularly set-valued attributes, may not be personal or private by themselves, yet certain qualities or their combinations might be connected to outer learning to uncover private data of a person. We carefully considered them as *Quasi* attribute (or quasi characteristics). Typically depending on the situation, possibilities are switching between non-quasi attributes as quasi attributes and vice versa. There are also distinct possibilities that a non-expert may not be able to carefully differentiate or correctly classify between quasi and non-quasi attributes properly. Misleading quasi to non-quasi and vice versa would direct to data breaching. This may typically lead to physical or cyber-attacks. The work proposed in this research makes an attempt to introduce how to classify quasi and non-quasi correctly attributes through game theory and reinforcement learning methods.

Motivation: Classification Problem. A quasi attribute (θ_Q) typically refers to a proper subset of essential attributes in a table that can identify tuples in a dataset. A wrong publication of a quasi-attribute will typically lead to data privacy leakage and an organisation may come under non-compliance.

4   Proposed Methodology

This section discusses the methodology applied in this research.

4.1 Applying Game Theory Strategies

The axiom of the game is considered as follows:

Axiom: The contribution of a player is determined by what is gained Alternatively, lost by withdrawing them from the game. Since our model retains one player strategy with a 2×2 matrix methodology, this research follows mixed strategy equilibrium. In a mixed strategy equilibrium, players randomly navigate two or more actions. In mixed strategy equilibrium, a player will choose the probability, through that he pays each action so that he makes proper navigation in-between states. Our game theory methodology player (player 1) navigates the states (i.e., attributes) only for quasi attributes.

Player 1 does the next navigation P from each case. Those movements are right, left, top, and bottom. Player 1 should choose P so that, $P = 1 - P$ i.e $P = \frac{1}{4}$ for 2×2 model and here $P = N - P$ for NXN model with $P = \frac{1}{N^2}$ states.

Table 5. Player 1 strategy table for navigating

		Player 1	
		Left	Right
Player 1	Top (P)	0, 1	0,0
	Bottom (1-P)	1, 1	0,0

Table 5, discuss the necessary steps to be followed for accurate navigation from S_0 to S_3 is discussed in section *Result discussion*. From top to top (no state navigation) or to typically remain in the same state, zero navigation and from top to left one state is there (so it is 0,1). Similarly, Since S_0 is the initial state and there is no right state available, and hence no navigation is possible (so it is 0,0). One navigation and bottom to top 1 navigation is possible (so it is 1,1). There is no navigation possible from the bottom to the right (so it is 0,0). Game theory methodology gives below key points for this proposed research work as:

- Steps to navigate is considered as 2×2 matrix games.
- Number of active participants, policy, and actions to be efficiently performed for successful implementation.

4.2 Algorithms

There are different approaches available to differentiate quasi and non-quasi carefully. These proposals have their demerits as discussed in a specific section problem analysis Sect. 3.3.

This specific proposal attempted to fill a few loopholes. The proposed algorithm 1 is for a 2×2 matrix. The efficient proposed algorithms are typically based on Divide and Rule principle: Breaking down reinforcement learning process [15]. In the proposal, it is assumed that the machine can carefully navigate in four direction i.e. UP, DOWN, LEFT and RIGHT.

In considered four states (S_0, S_1, S_2, S_3). For variant cases, each state is adopted with randomly chosen attributes from a_1 to a_n. Since, there are four states and those states may typically have $4C_2 = 6$ different cases of quasi and non-quasi attributes. The algorithms are demonstrated merely for two quasi and two non-quasi attributes with below cases.

1. Two quasi $(S_0, S_1)$and two non-quasi$((S_2, S_3)))$.
2. One quasi (S_0), one non-quasi (S_1), one quasi (S_2), and one non-quasi (S_3).
3. One non-quasi (S_0), one quasi (S_1), one non-quasi (S_2), one quasi (S_3).
4. Two non-quasi $(S_0, S_1)$and two quasi (S_2, S_3).
5. One quasi S_0, two non-quasi (S_1, S_2), and one quasi S_3.
6. One non-quasi S_0, two non-quasi (S_1, S_2), and one non-quasi S_3.

Algorithm 1: Quasi and non-quasi learning algorithm

Data: State space S_s, action space A, rewards R, attributes a_0 to a_n, rewards as discussed in table 7
Result: Model learns to classify quasi θ_Q and non-quasi attributes θ_{nQ}
Let $S_s = S_0, S_1, S_2, S_3$// four states for 2X2 matrix Initialize, i=1, s=0;
Initialize, S_0, S_1, S_2, S_3 to chosen a_0, a_1, a_2, a_3 ;
while *not at end of all cases, i.e i¿6* **do**
    for *i* **do**
        i++;
        m=0, n=0;
        // m and n can be maximum 1 ;
        S[m][n]=a[s];
        while *not the end of navigating all states, i.e s¿4* **do**
            navigate to each state from S_0, S_1, S_2, S_3;
            navigation=statenavi(S_s);
            //refer algorithm 2
            modify m and n for navigation;
            reward (r_p or r_n)according to quasi or non-quasi attributes;
            s++;
    the model learns quasi θ_Q and non-quasi attributes θ_{nQ};

Algorithm 1 is based on a set of policies and rewards (positive or negative) laid down for the machine to follow. The training model is a trial and error approaches with the machine uses to train itself. This algorithm trains quasi and non-quasi classified attributes to the model with the help of an expert (who knows well about quasi and non-quasi differentiation). As shown in algorithm 1, the algorithm executes until unless all the considered six cases execute. For state wise rewards for each position are made. According to rewards and penalties, navigation happens. A detailed navigation process is discussed in algorithm 2. After each navigation, rewards, and penalties are assigned. This reward and navigation process continues until the end of all six cases. These steps train the model for quasi and non-quasi attributes. The testing is done using the MDPtoolBox package in R. The obtained results satisfactorily give quasi and non-quasi classification. The classification is measured through navigation results. Algorithm 2, rewards positive r_p or negative r_n as per quasi or non-quasi navigation. The discussion about r_p and r_n is in Table 7. Initially, algorithm 1 starts with state $S0$ and rewards and penalties are assigned to navigate only in quasi attributes

---

Algorithm 2: Navigation process for 2X2 matrix

Data: State space S_s, action space A, rewards R (rewards are as discussed in table 7)
Result: navigation rules
statenavi(S_s) //four states are $S_s = S_0, S_1, S_2, S_3$;
{ NEXTstate = state(S_0);
// OR is logical OR, game starts from the state S_0;
if *(state == state(S_0))* **then**
  action = "down" OR " left";
  if *(action = "down")* **then**
    └ NEXTstate = state(S_1);

  if *(action = "left")* **then**
    └ NEXTstate = state(S_3);

  └ reward;

if *(state == state(S_1))* **then**
  action = "left";
  NEXTstate = state(S_2);
  └ reward;

if *(state == state(S_2))* **then**
  action = "Up" ;
  NEXTstate = state(S_3);
  └ reward;

if *(state == state(S_3))* **then**
  action = "END" ;
  └ NEXTstate = state(S_3);

if *(state == state(S_3))* **then**
  └ state != state(S_3) ;

return(action);
}

(assumptions are discussed in the next Sect. 4.3). The Fig. 2 shows basic version of states from $S0$ to $S3$. All navigation happens from $S0$ to $S3$. The navigation is from $S0$ to $S1$, $S1$ to $S2$, $S2$ to $S3$ and $S3$ to $S0$. This navigation train the model about quasi and non-quasi. In contrast, training rewards and penalties are made for all the state movements. The Algorithm 2 also has steps to move between the states. As shown in the Algorithm 2, the right navigation does not require a 2×2 model.

4.3   Assumptions

We assume that a data provider typically owns a private table with a mixture of quasi (θ_Q) and non-quasi (θ_{nQ}) attributes. To anonymize the essential attributes, there is a specific need to categorize quasi and non-quasi attributes. Here non-expert who does not know can efficiently be either a computer system or a human, who does not have any valuable quasi or sensitive attributes. Initially, expert knowledge is used in classification to help for building the model.

5   Application of Reinforcement Learning

This section adequately explains the demonstration of the proposed methodology. The methodology is adequately implemented through Reinforcement Learning (RL).

5.1   Reinforcement Learning

Implementation is performed by breaking down the process into smaller tasks. The following is required to consider for RL.

- a specific set of the policies laid down for the machine to follow.
- a set of rewards and penalty rules for the machine to assess The step-wise procedure.

The training limit specifies the trial and possible error experiences the machine uses to train itself.

This specific proposal carefully considers a simple game through a 2×2 matrix to make the problem simple. It is assumed that the machine can navigate in 4 directions. Those are up, down, left, and right. From the state S0, the aim is to pass through only quasi-states. The main objective of affirmative action is to move only in quasi attributes, with below conditions

- if the initial state is non-quasi, then move only to quasi attributes.
- there is no movement in non-quasi states.

The demonstration is shown only for two quasi and two non-quasi attributes. The attributes can be arranged in a 2×2 matrix of states in six forms as shown.

In the reinforcement learning model, information is stored in the database and fetched for execution. It uses these data for the classification of quasi and non-quasi through rewards and actions accordingly. To make a machine learn about the navigation, our proposal sets the policies with a set of actions such as UP, DOWN, LEFT and RIGHT. The reward matrix is considered, were taking each step get a small reward and falling into the non-quasi is a penalty and moving from quasi attributes to non-quasi attributes typically has a big reward and big penalty.

In these cases, assigning a minor penalty to each step will be helpful for the machine to minimize the considerable number of necessary steps. Typically assigning a significant potential penalty to quasi to non-quasi should typically make the machine avoid it, and the reward to the goal will attract the machine towards it. This is how the proposal helps to train the machine.

To define the elements of reinforced learning, we have assigned a label to each of the states in the navigation matrix as shown in Fig. 2 (to simplify and demonstration, we will typically take a shot-down 2×2 version of the navigation matrix)

6   Results and Discussion

This section explains about results achieved. The research carefully considers chosen rewards for navigating as follows: The reward is categorized into two parts, i.e., positive r_p and negative reward r_n with a discount 0.5. RL techniques can be used to solve MDPs models. The standard for the discount rate is always rarely than 1.

According to navigation, rewards are typically awarded. In 2×2 matrix, quasi and non-quasi are arranged. The cases are as indicated in Tables 6 and 8.

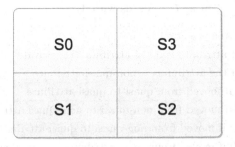

Fig. 2. Proposed quasi-attribute classification model with anonymization

Table 6. Different possible cases with quasi(θ_Q) and non-quasi(θ_{nQ}) attributes

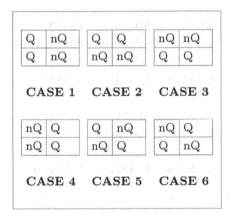

- In the case 1, quasi attributes are in 00th and 10th position. Non-quasi are in 01th and 11th position.
- In the case 2, quasi attributes are in 00th and 01th position, Non-quasi are in 10th and 11th position.
- In the case 3, quasi attribute are in 10th and 11th position. Non-quasi are in 00th and 01th position.
- In the case 4, quasi attribute are in 01th and 11th position, non-quasi are in 00th and 10th position.
- In the case 5, quasi attribute are in 00th and 11th position, non-quasi are in 10th and 01th position.
- In the case 6, quasi attribute are in 01th and 10th position. Non-quasi are in 00th and 11th position.

The navigation rewards and penalties are shown in Table 7. If S_0 is a quasi attribute, then positive reward, r_p is set to be +1. If S_0 is a non-quasi attribute, then the negative reward r_p is set to be −1. It is assumed that there may or may not be direct navigation from S_0 to S_3. While navigating from state to state or attribute to attribute, if navigation occurs from quasi to quasi +10 and non-quasi to non-quasi −10 are awarded. If navigated from non-quasi to quasi +100 and for quasi to non-quasi −100 are awarded.

Table 7. Rewards with discount 0.5

Sl. No	Rewards (r_p or r_n)
1	+1 if attribute is quasi-attribute (i.e. private attribute)
2	−1 if the attributes is non-quasi-attribute
3	+10 if moved from quasi to quasi-attribute
4	−10 if moved from non-quasi to non-Quasi-attribute
5	+100 if moved from non-quasi to quasi-attribute
6	−100 if moved from quasi attribute to non-quasi attribute

Table 8. Different possible cases with states

S0	S2		S0	S1		S2	S3
S1	S3		S2	S3		S0	S1

CASE 1   CASE 2   CASE 3

S2	S0		S0	S3		S2	S1
S3	S1		S2	S1		S0	S3

CASE 4   CASE 5   CASE 6

Table 8, shows different possible cases. For case 1, and the considered matrix is as follows:

$$
\begin{array}{c} & \begin{array}{cccc} 0 & 1 & 2 & 3 \end{array} \\ \begin{array}{c} 0 \\ 1 \\ 2 \\ 3 \end{array} & \begin{pmatrix} +1 & +10 & -100 & -100 \\ +10 & +1 & -100 & -100 \\ +100 & +100 & -1 & -10 \\ +100 & +100 & -10 & -1 \end{pmatrix} \end{array}
$$

Navigation for Case 1: Table 8 shows different possible cases with different states as discussed earlier and Table 6 shows quasi and non-quasi attribute positions for those rare cases. As shown in Table 8 each state is represented with corresponding attributes in the Table 6. This section discusses allotted rewards. The rewards are typically made in such a way to get the final objective, i.e. to train a model or non-expert with the only quasi attribute. To obtain the same, the below assumptions are considered.

1. there will not be navigation if navigation starts with non-quasi and it has consequent two non-quasi attributes
2. if navigation starts with non-quasi, it navigates only to the quasi attribute
3. navigation may happen between the starting state to any state.

Since the example is of 2×2 states, we have 4×4 possible navigation. The matrix values for the same are discussed below row-wise. As shown in the matrix for the case 1, 1st row, trains possibilities in navigation from 0th state to other states (those are 1,2 and 3 from Table 8).

1. 00th position $+1$ reward is for initial state is quasi attribute (i.e. 0 to 0 from Table 8).
2. 01th position is rewarded with $+10$ for quasi to quasi attribute navigation from 00th position to 01th position (i.e. 0 to 1 from Table 8).
3. 02th position is rewarded with -100, for quasi to non-quasi attribute navigation from 10th position to $11th$ position (i.e. 0 to 2 from Table 8).
4. 02th position is rewarded with -100, for quasi to non-quasi attribute navigation from 11th position to 01th position (i.e. 0 to 3 from Table 8).

2nd row, trains possibilities in navigation from 1 to other states (those are 0,2 and 3). Those distinct possibilities of accurate navigation are organized as follows:

1. 10th position $+10$ reward is for quasi to quasi attribute from 11th position to 00th position (i.e. 1 to 0 from Table 8).
2. 11th position is rewarded with $+1$ for no accurate navigation from quasi attribute 10th position (i.e. 1 to 1 from Table 8).
3. 12th position is rewarded with -100, for quasi to non-quasi attribute navigation from 10th position to $01th$ position (i.e. 1 to 2 from Table 8).
4. $13th$ position is rewarded with -100, for quasi to non-quasi attribute navigation from 10th position to 11th position (i.e. 1 to 3 from Table 8).

In 3rd row, that trains possibilities in accurate navigation from 2 to other states (those are 0,1 and 3).

Similarly other cases can be solved. In case 5, quasi attribute in 00th and 11th position, non-quasi in 10th and 01th position is carefully arranged. In this case 1, 2, and 3 had two steps navigation, case 3 and 4 had 1 step navigation, and case 6 had no navigation at all. Since case 6 has all its surroundings with non-quasi attributes, no navigation happened.

7 Conclusions and Future Work

This research proposes an effective method to classify quasi and non-quasi data accurately. The paper considers the game theory methodology and is demonstrated through the reinforcement machine learning model. Initially, an expert in correctly classifying the quasi attribute guides the rewards allotment in-between state movements. The considered non-expert can be either system or human, who does not know about quasi or non-quasi attributes. The research demonstrates for a 2×2 matrices with only two quasi and two non-quasi attributes and its six combinations for simplification. We have shown navigation steps between states in the training model and evaluated the same for the testing model. The experimental observations show that the successful process of classifying quasi and non-quasi attributes using a reinforcement model that adopts game theory.

As future work, this research can be continued for a 3×3 matrix or more combinations to obtain the classification more rapidly properly. Further, this can be made subjectively to different dataset types, and the same learning can be automated through a tool that preserves privacy for general use in preparing public data.

References

1. Shi, P., Xiong, L., Fung, B.C.M.: Anonymizing data with quasi-sensitive attribute values. In: Proceedings of the 19th ACM International Conference on Information and Knowledge Management (CIKM 2010), pp. 1389–1392. Association for Computing Machinery, New York (2010). https://doi.org/10.1145/1871437.1871628
2. Dwork, C., McSherry, F., Nissim, K., Smith, A.: Calibrating noise to sensitivity in private data analysis. In: Halevi, S., Rabin, T. (eds.) TCC 2006. LNCS, vol. 3876, pp. 265–284. Springer, Heidelberg (2006). https://doi.org/10.1007/11681878_14
3. Dwork, C.: A firm foundation for private data analysis. Commun. ACM **54**(1), 86–95 (2011). https://doi.org/10.1145/1866739.1866758
4. Yildiz, Y., Agogino, A., Brat, G.: Predicting pilot behavior in medium-scale scenarios using game theory and reinforcement learning. J. Guid. Control. Dyn. **37**(4), 1335–1343 (2014)
5. Nowé, A., Vrancx, P., De Hauwere, Y.M.: Game theory and multi-agent reinforcement learning. In: Wiering, M., van Otterlo, M. (eds.) Reinforcement Learning. ALO, vol. 12, pp. 441–470. Springer, Heidelberg (2012). https://doi.org/10.1007/978-3-642-27645-3_14
6. Bowling, M., Veloso, M.: An analysis of stochastic game theory for multiagent reinforcement learning. Carnegie-Mellon University Pittsburgh Pa School of Computer Science (2000)
7. Sweeney, L.: K-anonymity: a model for protecting privacy. Int. J. Uncertain. Fuzziness Knowl.-Based Syst. **10**(5), 557–570 (2002). https://doi.org/10.1142/S0218488502001648
8. Von Neumann, J., Morgenstern, O.: 2nd rev. edn. Princeton University Press (1947)
9. Nash, J.F., Jr.: Equilibrium points in n-person games. Proc. Natl. Acad. Sci. **36**(1), 48–49 (1950). https://doi.org/10.1073/pnas.36.1
10. Lindell, P.P., Mining, P.D.: J. Cryptol. **15**, 177–206 (2002). https://doi.org/10.1007/s00145-001-0019-2
11. Jagannathan, G., Wright, R.N.: Privacy-preserving distributed k-means clustering over arbitrarily partitioned data. In: Proceedings of the Eleventh ACM SIGKDD International Conference on Knowledge Discovery in Data Mining (KDD 2005), pp. 593–599. Association for Computing Machinery, New York (2005). https://doi.org/10.1145/1081870.1081942
12. Gambs, S., Kégl, B., Aïmeur, E.: Privacy-preserving boosting. Data Min. Knowl. Disc. **14**, 131–170 (2007). https://doi.org/10.1007/s10618-006-0051-9
13. Qu, Y., Yu, S., Gao, L., Peng, S., Xiang, Y., Xiao, L.: FuzzyDP: fuzzy-based big data publishing against inquiry attacks. In: 2017 IEEE Conference on Computer

Communications Workshops (INFOCOM WKSHPS), pp. 7–12 (2017). https://doi.org/10.1109/INFCOMW.2017.8116344

14. Qu, Y., Yu, S., Zhou, W., Peng, S., Wang, G., Xiao, K.: Privacy of things: emerging challenges and opportunities in wireless internet of things. IEEE Wirel. Commun. **25**(6), 91–97 (2018). https://doi.org/10.1109/MWC.2017.1800112

15. Andre, D., Russell, S.J.: State abstraction for programmable reinforcement learning agents. In: AAAI/IAAI, pp. 119–125 (2002)

Non-malleable Codes from Authenticated Encryption in Split-State Model

Anit Kumar Ghosal$^{(\boxtimes)}$ and Dipanwita Roychowdhury

Department of Computer Science and Engineering, IIT Kharagpur,
Kharagpur, India
anit.ghosal@gmail.com

Abstract. The secret key of any encryption scheme that are stored in secure memory of the hardwired devices can be tampered using fault attacks. The usefulness of tampering attack is to recover the key by altering some regions of the memory. Such attack may also appear when the device is stolen or viruses has been introduced. Non-malleable codes are used to protect the secret information from tampering attacks. The secret key can be encoded using non-malleable codes rather than storing it in plain form. An adversary can apply some arbitrary tampering function on the encoded message but it guarantees that output is either completely unrelated or original message. In this work, we propose a computationally secure non-malleable code from leakage resilient authenticated encryption along with 1-more extractable hash function in split-state model with no common reference string (CRS) based trusted setup. Earlier constructions of non-malleable code cannot handle the situation when an adversary has access to some arbitrary decryption leakage (i.e., during decoding of the codeword) function to get partial information about the codeword. In this scenario, the proposed construction is capable of handling such decryption leakages along with tampering attacks.

Keywords: Authenticated encryption · Non-malleable codes ·
Split-state model · Tamper resilient cryptography

1 Introduction

In cryptography, the security of various primitives like encryption algorithms, message authentication codes (MACs), digital signatures follow a generic template, i.e., the adversary can observe input-output behaviour, and further it can attack the primitives. Usually, the basic assumption is that an adversary is able to learn input-output behaviour only, and the security of cryptographic primitives preserve as long as secret key remains confidential. However, if an adversary gains some partial information about the secret keys, the cryptosystem can be broken easily. The adversary can mount Differential Fault Analysis attack, Template Attack, Timing Attack etc. on the cryptosystem to learn the secret information about keys. In reality, such model does not provide security guarantee when an adversary can tamper the secret key (e.g., flip some bits) and it can

© The Author(s), under exclusive license to Springer Nature Singapore Pte Ltd. 2023
S. Prabhu et al. (Eds.): ATIS 2022, CCIS 1804, pp. 18–33, 2023.
https://doi.org/10.1007/978-981-99-2264-2_2

analyse the behaviour of the cryptosystem on these tampered keys to break it completely [1,5]. Non-malleable codes (NMCs), introduced by Dziembowski et al. [10,21], are used to protect secret message against related tampering, i.e., the adversary cannot tamper the codeword to make another codeword of a related message. More precisely, an adversary can apply the tampering function on the codeword, and the guarantee is that, encoded message either remains completely unchanged or essentially destroyed, i.e., $\perp$. So, the attack on the tampered codeword is now rendered useless and an adversary can not break the security of the cryptosystem. Usually, NMCs are built for the specific classes of tampering functions. Let us consider a secret message d. Non-malleable code is used to encode the message d and it generates the output as Enc(d). An adversary can apply some tampering function $f_{increment}$ on the message encoded by non-malleable code as $f_{increment}(\text{Enc}(d))$. The output of such tampering experiment produces result Enc(d)+1. Further, the adversary decodes the message in the following way Dec(Enc(d)+1). The final result of the experiment is d+1, and it has some relation with the original secret message. Therefore, NMCs can be designed for the specific classes of tampering functions only. The most widely used class of tampering function is the split-state model where the codeword is divided into two different parts and stored into the memory $\mathcal{M}_L$, $\mathcal{M}_R$. Two different functions f_L and f_R act independently but arbitrarily on the codeword [11,13,16,17,19,22,23,25].

Table 1. Comparative results of various multi-bit non-malleable codes in the split-state model [17,22,25].

Scheme	Codeword length	Model	Assumption	Security against leakages
[14]	$\mathcal{O}((|m| + k)^7 \log^7(|m| + k))$	Information theoretic	NA	Encryption leakages
[16]	$\mathcal{O}(max(|m|, k))$	Information theoretic	NA	Encryption leakages
[14] + [19]	$|m| + \mathcal{O}(k^7)$	Computational	Authenticated Encryption	Encryption leakages
[6] + [8] + [11] + [19]	$|m| + \mathcal{O}(k^2)$	Computational, CRS	Leakage resilient PKE + Robust NIZK	Encryption leakages
[17]	$|m| + 18k$	Computational, CRS	One-time leakage resilient AE + KEA	Encryption leakages
[22]	$|m| + 2k$	Computational	Pseudorandom permutation with leakage + Fixed related-key	Encryption leakages
[24]	$|m| + 5k$	Computational	Entropic fixed related-key	Encryption leakages
[25]	$|m| + 2k$	Computational	Related-key + PRP with leakage + Leakage resilient CBC-MAC unforgeability	Encryption leakages
Our work	$|m| + 2k + 2log^2(k)$ [a]	Computational	Leakage resilient AE with decryption leakages + 1-more extractable hash	Encryption + Decryption leakages

[a] k is the security parameter.

Usually, constructions of NMCs can be divided broadly into two domains as information-theoretic [13] and computational [19]. In [14], authors show a construction of non-malleable code of length $\mathcal{O}((|m| + k)^7 log^7(|m| + k))$ in information-theoretic domain, where m and k represent the message length and security parameter respectively. In computational domain, the construction of non-malleable code is shown from public key primitives [8] with robust non interactive Zero knowledge (NIZK) [2] proof [11]. Further, the length of codeword is optimized into $|m| + \mathcal{O}(k^7)$ by combining the idea of [14] and [19]. Subsequently, the size of the codeword is reduced to $|m| + \mathcal{O}(k^2)$ [6,8,11,19]. Usually, non-malleable codes are keyless encoding scheme. Further research work shows that such codeword can be constructed from symmetric-key primitives, i.e., authenticated encryption, block cipher etc. [17,22,25]. In [17], authors show non-malleable codes from one-time leakage-resilient authenticated encryption along with l-more extractable hash function, and the non-standard assumption, called knowledge of exponent assumption (KEA) is used to prove the security in common reference string (CRS) model. The security margin of [17] is extremely high but the construction is based on CRS which should be generated from honest, trusted parties. It is difficult to manage such CRS setup in practical situation. Later, Fehr et al. [22] show NMCs of optimal codeword length from related-key secure block ciphers such as AES [3], SHACAL-2 [4] without any CRS based trusted setup. Unfortunately, their assumptions are not applicable when the tampering function is cipher-dependent. Hence, a better construction [24] is proposed using entropic fixed-related-key security notion but the length of codeword is not optimal. Recently, Ghosal et al. [25] show a construction of non-malleable code of optimal codeword length from a specific authenticated encryption.

Motivation of Our Work. Till now, all of the constructions of NMCs are capable of handling encryption leakages but not the leakage during decryption. An adversary can use arbitrary leakage function during decryption and it can obtain partial information about the codeword that compromises the security of the underlying codeword. Since the codeword length of a non-malleable code is denoted as $|m|^1$ + |security-parameter| and the value of such security-parameter is heavily dependent on the maximum amount of leakage supported by the underlying primitive. The goal of our work is not to optimize the codeword length as already optimal length NMCs are available in the literature [22,25]. Apart from tampering attacks, we want to protect the codeword from encryption and decryption leakages. The main challenge of designing such codeword is to provide security against one-time tampering attack but maintaining the length of codeword optimum as much as possible. In short, the objective of our work is mentioned as follows:

(a) To construct non-malleable codes from authenticated encryption along with 1-more extractable hash function that can handle encryption leakages as well as decryption leakages.
(b) The codeword provides security against one-time tampering attack when an adversary has access to limited bits of leakage.

---

[1] $|m|$, $|k|$ denote the message length and security parameter respectively.

Our Contribution. In this work, we construct a computationally secure non-malleable code from authenticated encryption [20] along with extractable hash function [17] in split-state model. Though NMCs protect message only for tampering attacks but leakage of information from the stored codeword or leakages during encoding and decoding operation, compromises the security of non-malleable code. Our proposed construction is secure against an adversary with access to some arbitrary leakage function during the decoding step, (i.e., decryption leakages) and the adversary cannot gain much useful information from the codeword. The resulting codeword has length of $|m| + 2k + 2log^2k$ compared to other codewords as shown in Table 1.

Organization. The paper is arranged in the following way. The basics of non-malleable code and various definitions are discussed in Sect. 2. There after Sect. 3 illustrates the construction of codeword, while proof of security is explained in Sect. 4. Finally, Sect. 5 concludes our work.

2 Preliminaries

Basic Notations. In split-state model, left and right half of the memories are represented by $\mathcal{M}_L$ and $\mathcal{M}_R$. Two tampering functions f_L and f_R are chosen arbitrarily by an adversary working in $\mathcal{M}_L$ and $\mathcal{M}_R$ respectively. $\mathcal{SK}$ denotes the usable key set. If $\mathcal{SK}$ is the key set, $|\mathcal{SK}|$ is the maximum number of key elements in $\mathcal{SK}$. When sk is uniformly chosen at random from $\mathcal{SK}$, we write $sk \xleftarrow{\$} \mathcal{SK}$. Message set is represented by M whereas $\mathcal{C}$ denotes the codeword set. k is the security parameter. m, e and c denote the plain message, encoded message and codeword $(m, e, c \in \{0,1\}^k)$. m can be broken into small chunks m_1, m_2 etc. and similarly, e. We denote m^1, m^2 as two different messages. v denotes the leakage function. A function $\epsilon(k)$ is called negligible in k if it vanishes faster than the inverse of any polynomial in k.

Definition 2.1 (Coding Scheme and Non-malleable Codes). Let (Enc_{sk}, Dec) be a split-state coding scheme. The encoding algorithm Enc_{sk} takes input a message $m \in M$, key $sk \in \mathcal{SK}$ and it outputs a codeword $c \in \mathcal{C}$, divided into $\mathcal{M}_L$ and $\mathcal{M}_R$ parts of the memory respectively. The decoding algorithm Dec takes input a codeword stored in $\mathcal{M}_R$ and $\mathcal{M}_L$, outputs the plain message $m \in M$. Moreover, let $\mathcal{F}$ be a family of tampering functions. The coding scheme is said to satisfy non-malleability if for each tampering function $f \in \mathcal{F}$ and codeword $c \in \mathcal{C}$, the $Dec(f(c))$ produces m', where m' can be m, $\perp$ or completely unrelated to m. The split-state coding scheme which satisfies the non-malleability property is said to be non-malleable codes.

Definition 2.2 (Strong Non-malleability). Let $\mathcal{F}$ be some family of tampering functions. The tampering experiment for each $f = (f_L, f_R) \in \mathcal{F}$ and $m \in M$ is defined as follows:

$$\textbf{Tamper}_m^f = \left\{ \begin{array}{l} c \leftarrow Enc_{sk}(m), c = \{\mathcal{M}_L, \mathcal{M}_R\} \\ \{\mathcal{M}'_L, \mathcal{M}'_R\} = \{f_L(\mathcal{M}_L), f_R(\mathcal{M}_R)\} \\ c' = \{\mathcal{M}'_L, \mathcal{M}'_R\}, m' = Dec(c') \\ output : same^*, if c' = c, else\ m'. \end{array} \right\},$$

where randomness comes from the encoding algorithm.

We say that the coding scheme (Enc_{sk}, Dec) is strongly non-malleable with respect to some tampering function family $\mathcal{F}$ if the following indistinguishability $\textbf{Tamper}_{m^0}^f(m^0) \underset{c}{\approx} \textbf{Tamper}_{m^1}^f(m^1)$ holds for two arbitrarily chosen messages m^0 and m^1.

Definition 2.3 (Extractable Hash). A hash function H_k is said to be extractable hash [12] if for any PPT algorithm $\mathcal{A}$, there exists a PPT extractor $\mathcal{E}_\mathcal{A}$, such that for all $k \in \mathcal{N}$, for any input $p \in \{0,1\}^k$ and a negligible function $\epsilon(k)$:

$$Pr_{h \leftarrow H_k}[y \leftarrow \mathcal{A}(h,p), \exists x : h(x) = y, x' \leftarrow \mathcal{E}_\mathcal{A}(h,p) \wedge h(x') \neq y] \leq \epsilon(k).$$

Definition 2.4 (1-more Extractable Hash). A hash function H_k is said to be 1-more extractable hash [17] if for any PPT algorithm $\mathcal{A}_v$ and any $p_v \in \{0,1\}^k$, there exists a PPT extractor $\mathcal{E}_v$ and $p_\mathcal{E} \in \{0,1\}^k$, such that for all PPT algorithm $\mathcal{A}_s$, $k \in \mathcal{N}$, for any input message $s \in \{0,1\}^k$ and a negligible function $\epsilon(k)$:

$$Pr_{h_z \leftarrow H_k}[\textbf{Exp}_{\mathcal{A}_v, \mathcal{A}_s, \mathcal{E}_v}^{s, h_z}(1, p_v, p_\mathcal{E}) = 1] \leq \epsilon(k),$$

where $\textbf{Exp}_{\mathcal{A}_v, \mathcal{A}_s, \mathcal{E}_v}^{s, h_z}(1, p_v, p_\mathcal{E})$ should satisfy all the four properties [17] as follows:

- **(Hash computation)** : $(h_1) \leftarrow h_z(sk)$
- **(Hash tampering)** : $(h'_1) \leftarrow \mathcal{A}_v(h_z, h_1, p_v)$
- **(Preimage extraction)** : $(\hat{sk}) \leftarrow \mathcal{E}_v(h_z, h_1, p_\mathcal{E})$
- **(Preimage tampering)** : $(sk') \leftarrow \mathcal{A}_s(h_z, sk)$

If $h_z(sk') = h'_1 \wedge h_z(\hat{sk}) \neq h'_1$, return 1
else, return 0

The experiment $\textbf{Exp}_{\mathcal{A}_v, \mathcal{A}_s, \mathcal{E}_v}^{s, h_z}(1, p_v, p_\mathcal{E})$ works as follows. We use deterministic hash function with no randomness. An adversary $\mathcal{A}_v$ tries to produce a tampered hash h'_1, given a hash value h_1 with auxiliary information p_v. Then, extractor $\mathcal{E}_v$ is used to extract the preimage, given h_1 and auxiliary input $p_\mathcal{E}$. Finally, an adversary $\mathcal{A}_s$ tries to produce preimage of h'_1 with all the information collected in the execution. The experiment outputs 1, if $\mathcal{A}_v$ is able to generate a valid hash h'_1, and $\mathcal{A}_s$ produces a valid preimage of h'_1, while the extractor algorithm fails.

Definition 2.5 (Pseudorandom Function). Let $F : \mathcal{SK} \times M \to \mathcal{T}$ be a deterministic function. We say that F is a pseudorandom function (PRF) if for all (q,t) bounded adversary A, the below advantage holds:

$$Pr[A^{F_{sk}(\cdot)} = 1] - Pr[A^{f(\cdot)} = 1] \leq \epsilon(k),$$

where $sk \xleftarrow{\$} \mathcal{SK}$, $\epsilon(k)$ denotes a negligible function and the function $f : M \to \mathcal{T}$ is chosen uniformly at random.

Definition 2.6 (Strong Pseudorandom Function). Let $F : \mathcal{SK} \times M \to \mathcal{T}$ be a deterministic function. We say that F is a strong pseudorandom function (SPRF) if for all (q, t) bounded adversary A with oracle access to the function and its inverse, the below advantage holds:

$$Pr[A^{F_{sk}(\cdot), F_{sk}^{-1}(\cdot)} = 1] - Pr[A^{f(\cdot), f^{-1}(\cdot)} = 1] \leq \epsilon_F(k),$$

where $sk \xleftarrow{\$} \mathcal{SK}$, $\epsilon_F(k)$ denotes a negligible function and the function $f : M \to \mathcal{T}$ is chosen uniformly at random.

Similarly, a deterministic function F is said to be (q, t, ϵ_F) pseudorandom permutation (PRP) if for all sk, F_{sk} is a permutation, and the above advantage is upper bounded by ϵ_F. The function f is selected among the permutation on $M = \mathcal{T}$ uniformly at random. In case of strong pseudorandom permutation (SPRP), the adversary A has oracle access to the function and its inverse.

Definition 2.7 (Tweakable Pseudorandom Function). Let $F^* : \mathcal{SK} \times \mathcal{TK} \times M \to \mathcal{T}$ be a deterministic function. It is said to be (q, t, ϵ_{F^*}) tweakable pseudorandom function (TPRF) if for all (q, t) bounded adversary A, the below advantage holds:

$$Pr[A^{F_{sk}^{*,(\cdot)}(\cdot)} = 1] - Pr[A^{f^{(\cdot)}(\cdot)} = 1] \leq \epsilon_{F^*(k)},$$

where $sk \xleftarrow{\$} \mathcal{SK}$ is selected uniformly at random and f is chosen from the set of functions $\mathcal{TK} \times M \to \mathcal{T}$ uniformly at random.

Definition 2.8 (Strong Tweakable Pseudorandom Function). Let $F^* : \mathcal{SK} \times \mathcal{TK} \times M \to M$ be a deterministic function. We say that F^* is a (q, t, ϵ_{F^*}) strong tweakable pseudorandom function (STPRF) if for all sk, tweaks $F_{sk}^{*,\mathcal{TK}} : M \to M$ and for all (q, t) bounded adversary A that has oracle access to the function and its inverse, the below advantage holds:

$$Pr[A^{F_{sk}^{*,(\cdot)}(\cdot), F_{sk}^{*,-1,(\cdot)}(\cdot)} = 1] - Pr[A^{f^{(\cdot)}(\cdot), f^{-1,(\cdot)}(\cdot)} = 1] \leq \epsilon_{F^*}(k),$$

where $sk \xleftarrow{\$} \mathcal{SK}$ and $f \xleftarrow{\$} f^{tk}$ is chosen uniformly at random from their domain. Further, f^{tk} is selected from an independent uniformly random permutation on M for each value of tk.

Similarly, we say that F^* is a (q, t, ϵ_{F^*}) strong tweakable pseudorandom permutation (STPRP) if $F_{sk}^{*,tk}$ is a permutation for all sk, tk. Moreover, f^{tk} is a random permutation on $M = \mathcal{T}$ and we select it for each value of tk.

Definition 2.9 (Authenticated Encryption). Let $(\mathcal{SK}, \text{Enc}, \text{Dec})$ be an authenticated encryption (AE) that consists of the following algorithms:

-   Enc : $\mathcal{SK} \times M \rightarrow \mathcal{C}$ algorithm inputs a key $sk \in \mathcal{SK}$ and message $m \in M$. It produces ciphertext $c \in \mathcal{C}$ as output. We denote it as $c \leftarrow \text{Enc}(sk, m)$.
-   Dec : $\mathcal{SK} \times \mathcal{C} \rightarrow M \cup \{\perp\}$ algorithm inputs a key $sk \in \mathcal{SK}$ and ciphertext $c \in \mathcal{C}$. It produces $m \in M$ or $\perp$, if decryption fails. We denote it as $m \leftarrow \text{Dec}(sk, c)$.

Moreover, it should satisfy the correctness property that $\text{Dec}(sk, \text{Enc}(sk, m)) = m$, for all $sk \in \mathcal{SK}$, $m \in M$ and $c \in \mathcal{C}$.

Definition 2.10 (Semantically Secure AE). Let υ be the leakage function that outputs λ bits, i.e., $\upsilon : \{0, 1\}^* \rightarrow \{0, 1\}^\lambda$. An authenticated encryption (AE) scheme is said to satisfy semantically secure property with respect to m and m^1 if $\{\text{Enc}(sk, m), \upsilon(sk)\}$ and $\{\text{Enc}(sk, m^1), \upsilon(sk)\}$ are computationally indistinguishable.

Definition 2.11 (Strong Misuse Resistance of AE). An AE scheme is said to be strong misuse resistance [18], if for every (q, t) bounded adversary A, the below advantage holds:

$$[Pr[A^{\text{Enc}(...),\text{Dec}(...)} = 1] - Pr[A^{R(.),\perp(.)} = 1]] \leq \epsilon(k),$$

where $sk \xleftarrow{\$} \mathcal{SK}$ and $\epsilon(k)$ denotes a negligible function. The function $R(m)$ outputs c and the length of such random bit string is $|\text{Enc}(sk, m)|$. Oracle $\perp(c)$ produces output $\perp$ only if c is generated by $R(m)$ oracle earlier, in that case it returns m.

Definition 2.12 (Encrypt Digest Tag AE). Let $H : \{0, 1\}^k \times \{0, 1\}^* \rightarrow \{0, 1\}^k$ be a collision resistant, range oriented, preimage resistant hash function, $F^* : \{0, 1\}^k \times \{0, 1\} \times \{0, 1\}^k \rightarrow \{0, 1\}^k$ be a strong tweakable pseudorandom function, F_k^* be a leak-free pseudorandom function and F_k be a pseudorandom function which can leak some information. An AE is called encrypt digest tag (EDT) [20], if it combines a tweaked versions of $PSVEnc$ [15] with an "hash-then-MAC" scheme. Further, it can minimize the decryption leakages by giving an invalid ciphertext to restrict the impact of differential power analysis (DPA) attacks on message confidentiality.

Definition 2.13 (Pseudorandom Generator). A deterministic polynomial-time algorithm G is called pseudorandom generator (PRG) [9] against an adversary $\mathcal{A}$ if for all $A \in \mathcal{A}$, there exists a stretching function $l : \mathcal{N} \rightarrow \mathcal{N}$ (domain of l, i.e., $|\mathcal{N}| = 2\lambda$ and codomain of l, i.e., $|\mathcal{N}| = |m| + k$) such that $\{G_k\}_{k \in \mathcal{N}}$ and $\{U_k\}_{k \in \mathcal{N}}$ are computationally indistinguishable:

(a) The probability distribution G_k is defined as the output of G. The length of G_k is $l(k)$ on a uniformly selected seed in $\{0,1\}^k$.
(b) The probability distribution U_k is defined as the uniform distribution on $\{0,1\}^{l(k)}$, $l(k) > k$.

Let U_k be the uniform distribution over $\{0,1\}^k$, we need that for any PPT algorithm A, any positive polynomial $p(.)$, and for all sufficiently large k, it holds that

$$|Pr[A(G(U_k)) = 1] - Pr[A(U_{l(k)})) = 1]| < \frac{1}{p(k)}.$$

3   Code Construction

We propose the construction of non-malleable code from leakage resilient authenticated encryption [20] along with 1-more extractable hash function. Such authenticated encryption can handle encryption leakages as well as decryption leakages. Initially, a pseudorandom generator (PRG) is used to encode the secret key. The pseudorandom generator : $\{0,1\}^{2\lambda} \rightarrow \{0,1\}^{|m|+k}$ of [7] considers secret key $|sk|$ $= 2\lambda/\alpha$, and it can tolerate maximum $\alpha\lambda$ bits of leakage [9], where $\alpha \in [0,1]$ and the value depends on underlying assumption. In our case, we consider the strongest assumption, i.e., $\alpha = 1$ which implies $|sk| = 2\lambda$. The complete encoding and decoding steps are described below:

– **Encoding.** The encoding algorithm takes a message block m, pseudorandom generator with the secret key sk and generates r_1, r_2 as output ($|r_1| = |m|$, $|r_2| = |k|$). The message block m is further divided into small chunks of $m_1, m_2, ..., m_l$ and the randomness r_1 is also broken into $r_1^1, r_1^2, ..., r_1^l$. Then, $PSVEnc_{r_2}(r_1, m)$ [15] is invoked that takes input a message block m, randomness r_1 and secret key r_2, and it generates encoded message $e_1, e_2, ..., e_l$. The $PSVEnc_{r_2}(r_1, m)$ function uses a tweakable leak-free pseudorandom function $F_{k_{i-1}}^{*,tw}(.)$ to generate the master key k_1 and another pseudorandom function $F_k(.)$ that can leak some information, used to generate the remaining keys k_i from the master key, for all $i > 1$. The pseudorandom function is instantiated with AES algorithm. Output of the function is XOR-ed with m_i and r_1^i, and it produces e_i. Next, $Tag_{r_2}(r_1, e)$ is invoked with the encoded message e, randomness r_1 and secret key r_2. Further, the collision resistant hash function H generates a hash value h based on e and r_1. Finally, $F_{r_2}^{*,1}(h)$ returns a tag τ. Apart from that, 1-more extractable hash function h_z is used to generate a hash value for the secret key sk, and the codeword $C = (sk, e, \tau, h_1)$ is stored as $\mathcal{M}_L = \{sk\}$, $\mathcal{M}_R = \{e, \tau, h_1\}$. The encoding steps are illustrated as follows:

Algorithm 1. Function of ExpNMC$_{A,1}^{f,m}()$	**Algorithm 2.** Function of ExpNMC$_{A,2}^{f,m}()$
Input: sk, m	**Input:** sk, m
Output: $same^*$, m'	**Output:** $same^*$, m' or $\perp$

1: $sk \leftarrow \{0,1\}^{2\lambda}$	1: $sk \leftarrow \{0,1\}^{2\lambda}$
2: $(sk, e, \tau, h_1) \leftarrow Enc_{sk}(m)$	2: $(sk, e, \tau, h_1) \leftarrow Enc_{sk}(m)$
3: $c = (sk, e, \tau, h_1)$	3: $c = (sk, e, \tau, h_1)$
4: $\mathcal{M}_L = (sk)$	4: $\mathcal{M}_L = (sk)$
5: $\mathcal{M}_R = (e, \tau, h_1)$	5: $\mathcal{M}_R = (e, \tau, h_1)$
6: $sk' = f_L(sk)$	6: $sk' = f_L(sk)$
7: $(e', \tau', h_1') = f_R(e, \tau, h_1)$	7: $(e', \tau', h_1') = f_R(e, \tau, h_1)$
8: $c' = (sk', e', \tau', h_1')$	8: $c' = (sk', e', \tau', h_1')$
9: **if** $c = c'$ **then**	9: **if** $(h_1, sk, e) = (h_1', sk', e')$ **then**
10: output $same^*$	10: **if** $\tau \neq \tau'$ **then**
11: **else**	11: output $\perp$
12: output $m' = Dec(c')$	12: **else**
13: **end Function**	13: output $same^*$
	14: **else**
	15: output $m' = Dec(c')$
	16: **end Function**

$KeyGen(1^k)$: $sk \leftarrow \{0,1\}^{2\lambda}$

$Enc_{sk}(m)$:

- $(r_1, r_2) \leftarrow PRG(sk)$
- $|r_1| = |m|$, $|r_2| = |k|$
- parse $m = (m_1, m_2, ..., m_l)$
- parse $r_1 = (r_1^1, r_1^2, ..., r_1^l)$
- $e = \{e_1, e_2, ..., e_l\} \leftarrow PSVEnc_{r_2}(r_1, m)$
- $PSVEnc_{r_2}(r_1, m)$
  - $k_1 \leftarrow F_{r_2}^{*,0}(r_1^1)$, also $k_i \leftarrow F_{k_{i-1}}^{*,tw}(p_A)$ and $tw \in \{0,1\}$
  - $e_1 \leftarrow F_{k_1}(p_B) \oplus m_1 \oplus r_1^1$
  - $\forall i = 2$ to l
  - $k_i \leftarrow F_{k_{i-1}}(p_A)$
  - $e_i \leftarrow F_{k_i}(p_B) \oplus m_i \oplus r_1^i$
  - $e = \{e_1, ..., e_l\}$
- $\tau \leftarrow Tag_{r_2}(r_1, e)$
  - $h \leftarrow H(r_1 \| e)$
  - $\tau \leftarrow F_{r_2}^{*,1}(h)$
- $h_z \leftarrow H_k$, $h_1 \leftarrow h_z(sk)$
- return $C = (sk, e, \tau, h_1)$

- **Decoding.** The decoding algorithm first inputs a secret key sk to the PRG and it generates r_1 and r_2. Next, it parses the codeword C. Collision resistant hash function $H(r_1 \| e)$ is invoked that returns a hash value h. Inverse tweakable pseudorandom function $(F_{r_2}^{*,1})^{-1}()$ takes τ as input and produces the hash h^c. Further, h^c is checked with h for consistency, if they are $same$, output of 1-more extractable hash $h_z(sk)$ is compared with h_1. Whenever both the hash values are equal, $PSVEnc_{r_2}(r_1, e)$ returns the message m. Decoding steps are described as follows:

$Dec(C)$:

- Parse $C = (sk, e, \tau, h_1)$
- $(r_1, r_2) \leftarrow PRG(sk)$
- $h \leftarrow H(r_1||e)$
- $h^c \leftarrow (F_{r_2}^{*,1})^{-1}(\tau)$
- If $h \neq h^c$, return $\perp$
- If $h_1 \neq h_z(sk)$, return $\perp$
- $m \leftarrow PSVEnc_{r_2}(r_1, e)$
- return m

Liu et al. [11] observe that an adversary can check the equality between $f_L(\hat{sk})$ and $f_L(sk)$ using the leakage of a universal hash and it generates $log^2 k$ bits as output. Kiayias et al. [17] show that a similar kind of equality check between $f_L(\hat{r}, \hat{sk})$ and $f_L(r, sk)$ can be performed using the leakage of a universal hash that generates $2k + log^2 k$ bits as output, where $|\hat{r}| = 2k$. The proposed split-state non-malleable code is defined as $Enc : m \rightarrow \{sk\}||\{e, \tau, h_1\}$. The length of codeword is $|m| + |\text{security-bits}|$. By setting $\lambda = log^2 k$, we get $|m| + |sk| + |\tau| + |h_1|$, i.e., $|m| + 2k + 2log^2(k)$ (where $|e| = |m|$), assuming the size of $|\tau|$, $|h_1|$ are k bits each. Let $h_z \leftarrow H_k$ be a hash function that is collision resistant, 1-more extractable hash and efficiently samplable as defined in [17]. An adversary chooses $\widetilde{h} \leftarrow \widetilde{H_{\lambda-1}}$ from universal hash function family. The hash function outputs $\lambda - 1$ bits. Let v be the leakage function defined as follows:

$v^{\widetilde{h}}(sk) = (0, \widetilde{h}(f_L(sk)))$ if $(f_L(sk) = sk)$.

else, $v^{\widetilde{h}}(sk) = (1, \widetilde{h}(f_L(sk))), (f_L(sk) \neq sk)$.

The leakage function outputs $\lambda = \beta(logk) + \omega(k)$ bits. Our experiment checks the leaked value instead of the output generated by f_L.

4   Proof of Security

Theorem 1. *Let H_k be 1-more extractable hash function that generates $\omega(k)$ bits as output, where $\omega(k) = poly(k)$, $(\mathcal{SK}, Enc, Dec)$ be a leakage resilient authenticated encryption that can handle λ bits of leakage, where $\lambda = \beta(logk) + \omega(k)$ and k denotes the security parameter. Then, $(KeyGen(1^k), Enc_{sk}(m), Dec(C))$ is strongly non-malleable.*

Proof. We need to show that for the tampering function $f = (f_L, f_R)$ and messages m, m^1, the experiment $Tamper_m^f(m)$ and $Tamper_{m^1}^f(m^1)$ are computationally indistinguishable, i.e., $Tamper_m^f(m) \approx_c Tamper_{m^1}^f(m^1)$. We define the experiment $\mathbf{ExpNMC}_{A,1}^{f,m}()$ (Algorithm 1) and change it incrementally to $\mathbf{ExpNMC}_{A,2}^{f,m}()$, $\mathbf{ExpNMC}_{A,3}^{f,m}()$, $\mathbf{ExpNMC}_{A,4}^{f,m}()$ and show that they are computationally indistinguishable except with negligible probability. Given a message m and tampering function $f = (f_L, f_R) \in \mathcal{F}$, the experiment $\mathbf{ExpNMC}_{A,1}^{f,m}()$ is exactly same as the original tampering experiment, i.e., $Tamper_m^f(m)$.

Algorithm 3. Function of $\mathrm{ExpNMC}_{A,3}^{f,m}()$	**Algorithm 4.** Function of $\mathrm{ExpNMC}_{A,4}^{f,m}()$
Input: sk, m	**Input:** sk, m
Output: $same^*, m'$ **or** $\perp$	**Output:** $same^*, m'$ **or** $\perp$

```
 1:  sk ← {0,1}^{2λ}                         1:  sk ← {0,1}^{2λ}
 2:  (sk,e,τ,h₁) ← Enc_{sk}(m)               2:  (sk,e,τ,h₁) ← Enc_{sk}(m)
 3:  c = (sk,e,τ,h₁)                         3:  c = (sk,e,τ,h₁)
 4:  M_L = (sk)                              4:  M_L = (sk)
 5:  M_R = (e,τ,h₁)                          5:  M_R = (e,τ,h₁)
 6:  sk' = f_L(sk)                           6:  sk' = f_L(sk)
 7:  (e',τ',h₁') = f_R(e,τ,h₁)               7:  (e',τ',h₁') = f_R(e,τ,h₁)
 8:  if (h₁,sk,e) = (h₁',sk',e') then        8:  (b,h₁') ← ṽ^h̃(sk)
 9:     if τ ≠ τ' then                       9:  if (h₁',sk,e) = (h₁',sk',e') then
10:        output ⊥                         10:     if τ = τ' then
11:     else                                11:        output same*
12:        output same*                     12:     else
13:  if h₁ ≠ h₁' then                       13:        output ⊥
14:     ŝk ← E(h_z,h₁)                       14:     ŝk ← E(h_z,h₁)
15:     if sk' = ŝk then                     15:     if h̃(ŝk) ≠ h₁' then
16:        if h₁' = h_z(ŝk) then             16:        if sk' = ŝk then
17:           output m' = Dec(c')            17:           if h₁' = h_z(ŝk) then
18:        else                             18:              output m' = Dec(c')
19:           output ⊥                      19:           else
20:     else                                20:              output ⊥
21:        output ⊥                         21:     else
22:  end Function                           22:        output ⊥
                                            23:  end Function
```

In $\mathbf{ExpNMC}_{A,2}^{f,m}()$ (Algorithm 2), we check whether an adversary has modified the hash value of sk and e. As the hash function H_k is collision resistant, if the adversary does not modify the hash h_1, secret key is not changed at all, i.e., $(h_z(sk) = h_1)$ and the condition $(h_1, sk, e) = (h_1', sk', e')$ should be satisfied. Next, tag is calculated from $Enc_{sk}(m)$. New tag and modified tag are compared and if they are $equal$, output is set to $same^*$. Whenever $(\tau \neq \tau')$ output is set to $\perp$, otherwise, it breaks the authenticity property under leakage. If $(h_1, sk, e) \neq (h_1', sk', e')$, it outputs m' which is same as $\mathbf{ExpNMC}_{A,1}^{f,m}()$.

$\mathbf{ExpNMC}_{A,3}^{f,m}()$ (Algorithm 3) does not use the real decoding procedure but it uses extractor $\mathcal{E}_v$ (i.e., in short $\mathcal{E}$) of 1-more extractable hash function to get preimage of the hash value h_1, i.e., $\hat{sk}$. Using the preimage, it again calculates $h_z(\hat{sk})$ and compares with h_1'. Whenever the condition $(h_1 \neq h_1')$ is satisfied, tampered secret key sk' is compared with $\hat{sk}$, and the new hash value is computed for $\hat{sk}$ to check consistency with h_1'. This part only differs with $\mathbf{ExpNMC}_{A,2}^{f,m}()$ and output m' is generated, otherwise, it returns $\perp$. To illustrate the working strategy of $\mathcal{E}_v$, we define $\mathcal{A}_v$, p_v, with respect to h_z, (e, τ), h_1, and the tampering function $f = (f_L, f_R)$.

- (**Define** $\mathcal{A}_v$) : $\mathcal{A}_v(h_z, h_1, p_v) = ([f_R(h_1, p_v)])$
- (**Auxiliary info for** $\mathcal{A}_v$) : $p_v = (e, \tau)$
- (**Existence of extractor** $\mathcal{E}_v$, **and auxiliary input** $p_{\mathcal{E}}$): Given $\mathcal{A}_v$ and p_v, using 1-more extractability of the hash function H_k, an extractor $\mathcal{E}_v$ can be constructed, with hardwired auxiliary info $p_{\mathcal{E}}$, and it computes $\hat{sk} \leftarrow \mathcal{E}_v(h_z, h_1)$. We denote $\mathcal{E}_v$ as $\mathcal{E}$ for brevity.

In $\mathbf{ExpNMC}_{A,4}^{f,m}()$ (Algorithm 4), we perform consistency check procedure through leakage. Let $\tilde{h} \leftarrow \widetilde{H_{\lambda-1}}$ be selected from universal hash function family.

The underlying hash function generates $\lambda - 1$ bits as output. The leakage function is defined as follows:

$$v^{\widetilde{h}}(sk) = (0, \widetilde{h}(f_L(sk)) \text{ if } (f_L(sk) = sk)$$
$$\text{else, } v^{\widetilde{h}}(sk) = (1, \widetilde{h}(f_L(sk))), (f_L(sk) \neq sk).$$

An adversary has access to the leakage function $v^{\widetilde{h}}(sk)$ to calculate h_1^l. A random variable b is used to store the output, and b is set to 0 if $(f_L(sk) = sk)$. Next, $(h_1^l, sk, e) = (h_1', sk', e')$ is checked. If there is a collision against $\widetilde{h}$, it induces statistical difference only. Since $\widetilde{h}$ is a universal hash function and it is chosen independently for the current experiment, the probability of occurrence is negligible. Further, the tampered tag τ' and the original tag τ are compared and output is set to $same^*$, if they are equal. Whenever $(\widetilde{h}(\hat{sk}) \neq h_1^l)$, it compares tampered secret key sk' with the extracted secret key $\hat{sk}$ and the hash value $(h_1' = h_z(\hat{sk}))$. If it is successful, output $m' = Dec(c')$, otherwise, it outputs $\perp$.

Lastly, we show that $\mathbf{ExpNMC}_{A,4}^{f,m}()$ and $\mathbf{ExpNMC}_{A,4}^{f,m^1}()$ are computationally indistinguishable for any two arbitrarily chosen messages m and m^1.

Lemma 1. *Let H be a collision resistant, range-oriented, preimage resistant hash function, (SK, Enc, Dec) is a leakage resilient authenticated encryption with decryption leakages, $f = (f_L, f_R) \in \mathcal{F}$ be a tampering function and for any message m, $\mathbf{ExpNMC}_{A,1}^{f,m}()$ and $\mathbf{ExpNMC}_{A,2}^{f,m}()$ are computationally indistinguishable.*

Proof. $\mathbf{ExpNMC}_{A,1}^{f,m}()$ and $\mathbf{ExpNMC}_{A,2}^{f,m}()$ are different in the following branch condition:

- $(h_1, sk, e) = (h_1', sk', e') \wedge (\tau \neq \tau')$
- $(h_1, sk, e) = (h_1', sk', e') \wedge (\tau = \tau')$

Let the branch condition $(h_1, sk, e) = (h_1', sk', e') \wedge (\tau \neq \tau')$ be denoted by the event C and $\mathbf{ExpNMC}_{A,2}^{f,m}()$ experiment returns $\perp$ when the event C occurs. So, $\mathbf{ExpNMC}_{A,2}^{f,m}()$ and $\mathbf{ExpNMC}_{A,1}^{f,m}()$ output $same^*$ conditioned on the event $\sim C$. Let F be the event that $(\tau = \tau')$. Now, $Pr[C] = Pr[C \wedge F] + Pr[C \wedge \sim F]$. We have to show that $Pr[C \wedge F]$, $Pr[C \wedge \sim F]$ occurs with negligible probability. Here, we follow proof by contradiction technique. Let us consider $Pr[C \wedge \sim F] > \epsilon(k)$, for some negligible function $\epsilon(k)$. Then, there exists a PPT adversary A which can break the collision resistance property of hash function H. Further, the adversary simulates $\mathbf{ExpNMC}_{A,2}^{f,m}()$ and outputs τ, τ', (sk, e), (sk', e') $(h \leftarrow H(r_1 || e)$ and $\tau \leftarrow F_{r_2}^{*,1}(h))$. The function f is polynomial time computable. So, the running time of the adversary is also polynomial and it wins the event $Pr[C \wedge \sim F]$, where the assumption is that $Pr[C \wedge \sim F] > \epsilon(k)$. Hence, the adversary breaks the collision resistance property of hash function with non-negligible probability. Let us consider that $Pr[C \wedge F] > \epsilon(k)$, for some negligible function $\epsilon(k)$. An adversary with access to tampering function $f = (f_L, f_R)$ with $(e', \tau', h_1') = f_R(e, \tau, h_1)$ breaks the authenticity property under leakage.

Firstly, $Enc_{sk}(m)$ is invoked and the *tag* is recomputed using $h \leftarrow H(r_1||e)$, $\tau \leftarrow F^{*,1}_{r_2}(h)$. Assuming $Pr[C \wedge F] > \epsilon(k)$, the inequality $(\tau \neq \tau')$ generates a valid ciphertext with respect to sk and authenticity property under leakage breaks with non-negligible probability $\epsilon(k)$. Hence, the proof of lemma concludes.

Lemma 2. *Let H_k be 1-more extractable hash function and $f = (f_L, f_R)$ be a tampering function, for any message m, $\mathbf{ExpNMC}^{f,m}_{A,2}()$ and $\mathbf{ExpNMC}^{f,m}_{A,3}()$ are computationally indistinguishable.*

Proof. In $\mathbf{ExpNMC}^{f,m}_{A,3}()$, we do not use real decoding procedure. Here, the role of extractor function in the 1-more extractable hash is used, and $\hat{sk}$ is compared with the tampered key sk' if $(h_1 \neq h'_1)$. This part only differs with $\mathbf{ExpNMC}^{f,m}_{A,2}()$. If $(h'_1 = h_z(\hat{sk}))$ and $(sk' = \hat{sk})$ is true, output of the two experiments are equal. We need to show that two experiments are indistinguishable, i.e., the probability of occurrence of the following two conditions $(sk' \neq \hat{sk}) \wedge (h'_1 = h_z(\hat{sk}))$ and $(sk' = \hat{sk}) \wedge (h'_1 \neq h_z(\hat{sk}))$ are negligible. From the property of 1-more extractable hash function, the probability of occurrence $(sk' = \hat{sk}) \wedge (h'_1 \neq h_z(\hat{sk}))$ is negligible. Let E be the event that $(sk' \neq \hat{sk})$. Consider the below events, denoted as E_1, E_2.

- $E \wedge (h_z(sk') = h_z(\hat{sk}) = h'_1)$: It happens when there is a collision and by the property of hash function used in our scheme $Pr[E_1] \leq \epsilon(k)$.
- $E \wedge (h_z(sk') = h'_1 \wedge h_z(\hat{sk}) \neq h'_1)$: Since the hash function is 1-more extractable [11], we can conclude that $Pr[E_2] \leq \epsilon(k)$. Now, we can relate $\mathbf{ExpNMC}^{f,m}_{A,3}()$ with $Exp^{s,h_z}_{A_v,A_s,\mathcal{E}_v}(1,p_v,p_\mathcal{E})$, for some message m', algorithm $\mathcal{A}_v$, $\mathcal{A}_s$, extractor $\mathcal{E}_v$ and inputs p_v, $p_\mathcal{E}$.

Therefore, we get $Pr[E_1] + Pr[E_2] \leq \epsilon(k)$. Hence, $\mathbf{ExpNMC}^{f,m}_{A,2}()$ and $\mathbf{ExpNMC}^{f,m}_{A,3}()$ are computationally indistinguishable. This concludes the proof of lemma.

Lemma 3. *Let H be a collision resistant, range-oriented, preimage resistant hash function, $\widetilde{h} \leftarrow \widetilde{H_{\lambda-1}}$ is chosen from universal hash function family that generates $\lambda - 1$ bits as output, where $\lambda = \beta(logk)$, for any message m, $\mathbf{ExpNMC}^{f,m}_{A,3}()$ and $\mathbf{ExpNMC}^{f,m}_{A,4}()$ are computationally indistinguishable.*

Proof. In $\mathbf{ExpNMC}^{f,m}_{A,4}()$, we present h_1 as leakage over sk and such thing does not make any statistical difference. $\widetilde{h} \leftarrow \widetilde{H_{\lambda-1}}$ is chosen from universal hash function family and we compare $(h^l_1, sk, e) = (h'^l_1, sk', e')$, whereas in $\mathbf{ExpNMC}^{f,m}_{A,3}()$, we compare $(h_1, sk, e) = (h'_1, sk', e')$. The remaining part $(\tau = \tau')$ is exactly same as previous experiment. If $(h^l_1, sk, e) = (h'^l_1, sk', e')$ and $(\tau = \tau')$ is satisfied, output is set to *same**. The only difference between current and previous experiment is that the calculation of hash value of the secret key over leakage. Let B be the event $(\widetilde{h}(\hat{sk}) = h^l_1) \wedge (sk' \neq \hat{sk})$. It is clear that the statistical difference between the two experiments are upper bounded by $Pr[B]$.

We choose the universal hash function $\tilde{h}$ independently from its input, and the probability of collision is bounded by $\lambda - 1 = \epsilon(k)$. The collision event B is exactly same and we have $Pr[B] \leq \epsilon(k)$. Further, the probability of occurrence of the condition $(h_z(\hat{sk}) \neq h_1') \wedge (sk' = \hat{sk})$, denoted as $B1$, is negligible, i.e., $Pr[B1] \leq \epsilon(k)$, since the hash function is deterministic. Therefore, the proof of lemma completes.

Lemma 4. *Let $(\mathcal{SK}, Enc, Dec)$ be a leakage resilient authenticated encryption scheme, $f = (f_L, f_R)$ be a tampering function and for two arbitrarily chosen messages m and m^1, $\mathbf{ExpNMC}_{A,4}^{f,m}()$ and $\mathbf{ExpNMC}_{A,4}^{f,m^1}()$ are computationally indistinguishable.*

Proof. Here, we use proof by contradiction approach. Let us assume that for the two arbitrarily chosen messages m, m^1, there exists a tampering function $f = (f_L, f_R)$ and PPT distinguisher D such that $|Pr[D(\mathbf{ExpNMC}_{A,4}^{f,m}()) = 1] - Pr[D(\mathbf{ExpNMC}_{A,4}^{f,m^1}()) = 1]| > \epsilon$, where $\epsilon = 1/poly(k)$. The adversary A is able to break the semantic security of encryption scheme (Definition 2.10) under leakage. It picks up the leakage function $v^{\tilde{h}}(sk)$, connect the function with hardware, and performs the experiment $\mathbf{ExpNMC}_{A,4}^{f,m}()$ for two arbitrarily chosen messages m and m^1. It is straightforward to see that A simulates $\mathbf{ExpNMC}_{A,4}^{f,m}()$ and the advantage of breaking semantic security is same as distinguisher D, in distinguishing $\mathbf{ExpNMC}_{A,4}^{f,m}()$ and $\mathbf{ExpNMC}_{A,4}^{f,m^1}()$, which is non-negligible by assumption. Therefore, we arrive at the contradiction and it completes the proof of lemma.

From the above analysis, it is evident that for the tampering function f, two arbitrarily chosen messages m, m^1, $Tamper_m^f(m)$ and $Tamper_{m^1}^f(m^1)$ are computationally indistinguishable, i.e., $Tamper_m^f(m) \approx_c Tamper_{m^1}^f(m^1)$.

5 Conclusion

In this work, we construct a computationally secure non-malleable code from authenticated encryption with 1-more extractable hash function. Our proposed construction removes the requirement of common reference string based trusted setup. The codeword provides security against one-time tampering attack with a limited bits of leakage.

References

1. Boneh, D., DeMillo, R.A., Lipton, R.J.: On the importance of eliminating errors in cryptographic computations. J. Cryptol. **14**(2), 101–119 (2001)
2. De Santis, A., Di Crescenzo, G., Ostrovsky, R., Persiano, G., Sahai, A.: Robust non-interactive zero knowledge. In: Kilian, J. (ed.) CRYPTO 2001. LNCS, vol. 2139, pp. 566–598. Springer, Heidelberg (2001). https://doi.org/10.1007/3-540-44647-8_33

3. Joan, D., Vincent, R.: The Design of Rijndael. Springer, Heidelberg (2002). https:// doi.org/10.1007/978-3-662-60769-5
4. Handschuh, H., Naccache, D.: SHACAL: a family of block ciphers. In: Submission to the NESSIE Project (2002)
5. Agrawal, D., Archambeault, B., Rao, J.R., Rohatgi, P.: The EM side—channel(s): attacks and assessment methodologies. In: Kaliski, B.S., Koç, K., Paar, C. (eds.) CHES 2002. LNCS, vol. 2523, pp. 29–45. Springer, Heidelberg (2003). https://doi. org/10.1007/3-540-36400-5_4
6. Groth, J., Sahai, A.: Efficient non-interactive proof systems for bilinear groups. In: Smart, N. (ed.) EUROCRYPT 2008. LNCS, vol. 4965, pp. 415–432. Springer, Heidelberg (2008). https://doi.org/10.1007/978-3-540-78967-3_24
7. Pietrzak, K.: A leakage-resilient mode of operation. In: Joux, A. (ed.) EURO-CRYPT 2009. LNCS, vol. 5479, pp. 462–482. Springer, Heidelberg (2009). https:// doi.org/10.1007/978-3-642-01001-9_27
8. Naor, M., Segev, G.: Public-key cryptosystems resilient to key leakage. In: Halevi, S. (ed.) CRYPTO 2009. LNCS, vol. 5677, pp. 18–35. Springer, Heidelberg (2009). https://doi.org/10.1007/978-3-642-03356-8_2
9. Standaert, F.-X., Pereira, O., Yu, Y., Quisquater, J.-J., Yung, M., Oswald, E.: Leakage resilient cryptography in practice. In: Sadeghi, AR., Naccache, D. (eds.) Towards Hardware-Intrinsic Security. Information Security and Cryptography, pp. 99–134. Springer, Heidelberg (2010). https://doi.org/10.1007/978-3-642-14452-3_5
10. Dziembowski, S., Pietrzak, K., Wichs, D.: Non-malleable codes. In: Yao, A.C.-C. (ed.) ICS 2010, Beijing, China, 5–7 January 2010, pp. 434–452. Tsinghua University Press (2010)
11. Liu, F.-H., Lysyanskaya, A.: Tamper and leakage resilience in the split-state model. In: Safavi-Naini, R., Canetti, R. (eds.) CRYPTO 2012. LNCS, vol. 7417, pp. 517–532. Springer, Heidelberg (2012). https://doi.org/10.1007/978-3-642-32009-5_30
12. Bitansky, N., Canetti, R., Chiesa, A., Tromer, E.: From extractable collision resistance to succinct non-interactive arguments of knowledge, and back again. In: ITCS, pp. 326–349 (2012)
13. Dziembowski, S., Kazana, T., Obremski, M.: Non-malleable codes from two-source extractors. In: Canetti, R., Garay, J.A. (eds.) CRYPTO 2013. LNCS, vol. 8043, pp. 239–257. Springer, Heidelberg (2013). https://doi.org/10.1007/978-3-642-40084-1_14
14. Aggarwal, D., Dodis, Y., Lovett, S.: Non-malleable codes from additive combinatorics. In: STOC, pp. 774–783 (2014)
15. Pereira, O., Standaert, F.X., Vivek, S.: Leakage-resilient authentication and encryption from symmetric cryptographic primitives. In: ACM CCS 2015. ACM Press (2015)
16. Aggarwal, D., Dodis, Y., Kazana, T., Obremski, M.: Non-malleable reductions and applications. In: Proceedings of the Forty-Seventh Annual ACM on Symposium on Theory of Computing, pp. 459–468. ACM (2015)
17. Kiayias, A., Liu, F.-H., Tselekounis, Y.: Practical non-malleable codes from l-more extractable hash functions. In: CCS, pp. 1317–1328 (2016)
18. Berti, F., Koeune, F., Pereira, O., Peters, T., Standaert, F.X.: Leakage-resilient and misuse-resistant authenticated encryption. Cryptology ePrint Archive, Report 2016/996 (2016)
19. Aggarwal, D., Agrawal, S., Gupta, D., Maji, H.K., Pandey, O., Prabhakaran, M.: Optimal computational split-state non-malleable codes. In: Kushilevitz, E., Malkin, T. (eds.) TCC 2016. LNCS, vol. 9563, pp. 393–417. Springer, Heidelberg (2016). https://doi.org/10.1007/978-3-662-49099-0_15

20. Berti, F., Pereira, O., Peters, T., Standaert, F.X.: On leakage-resilient authenticated encryption with decryption leakages. IACR Trans. Symmetric Cryptol. **3**, 271–293 (2017)
21. Dziembowski, S., Pietrzak, K., Wichs, D.: Non-malleable codes. J. ACM **65**(4), 20:1–20:32 (2018)
22. Fehr, S., Karpman, P., Mennink, B.: Short non-malleable codes from related-key secure block ciphers. IACR Trans. Symmetric Cryptol. 336–352 (2018)
23. Aggarwal, D., Obremski, M.: A constant-rate non-malleable code in the split-state model. In: IEEE 61st Annual Symposium on Foundations of Computer Science, FOCS (2020)
24. Brian, G., Faonio, A., Ribeiro, L., Venturi, D.: Short non-malleable codes from related-key secure block ciphers, revisited. IACR Trans. Symmetric Cryptol. 1–19 (2022)
25. Ghosal, A.K., Ghosh, S., Roychowdhury, D.: Practical non-malleable codes from symmetric-key primitives in 2-split-state model. In: Ge, C., Guo, F. (eds.) ProvSec 2022. Lecture Notes in Computer Science, vol. 13600, pp. 273–281. Springer, Cham (2022). https://doi.org/10.1007/978-3-031-20917-8_18

Continuously Non-malleable Codes from Authenticated Encryptions in 2-Split-State Model

Anit Kumar Ghosal$^{(\boxtimes)}$ ⓘ and Dipanwita Roychowdhury ⓘ

Department of Computer Science and Engineering, IIT Kharagpur, Kharagpur, India
anit.ghosal@gmail.com

Abstract. Tampering attack is the act of deliberately modifying the codeword to produce another codeword of a related message. The main application is to find out the original message from the codeword. Non-malleable codes are introduced to protect the message from such attack. Any tampering attack performed on the message encoded by non-malleable codes, guarantee that output is either completely unrelated or original message. It is useful mainly in the situation when privacy and integrity of the message is important rather than correctness. Unfortunately, standard version of non-malleable codes are used for one-time tampering attack. In literature, we show that it is possible to construct non-malleable codes from authenticated encryptions. But, such construction does not provide security when an adversary tampers the codeword more than once. Later, continuously non-malleable codes are constructed where an attacker can tamper the message for polynomial number of times. In this work, we propose a construction of continuously non-malleable code from authenticated encryption in 2-split-state model. Our construction provides security against polynomial number of tampering attacks and non-malleability property is preserved. The security of proposed continuously non-malleable code reduces to the security of underlying leakage resilient storage when tampering experiment triggers self-destruct.

Keywords: Authenticated encryption · Non-malleable codes · 2-Split-State model · Tamper-resilient cryptography

1 Introduction

In the era of digital evaluation, various kind of attacks on the hardware devices are the most threatening aspects for the crypto designers. The adversary wants to exploit the weakness of physical implementation mechanism by injecting some faults during runtime of the cryptographic algorithm. Then, it can analyze the faulty and fault free output to get partial information about the internal state of the algorithm. Tampering attack is one of the attack where an adversary modifies the internal state of the device and manipulates some parameters of

ⓒ The Author(s), under exclusive license to Springer Nature Singapore Pte Ltd. 2023
S. Prabhu et al. (Eds.): ATIS 2022, CCIS 1804, pp. 34–45, 2023.
https://doi.org/10.1007/978-981-99-2264-2_3

the underlying algorithm. Such attack can be performed by a fault injection or heating up the device. In case of software platform, a virus in the computer can carry out such tampering attack on the storage device by corrupting some regions of the memory. The ultimate goal of the adversary is to find out the keys so that they can destroy the cryptosystem completely. Boneh et al. [2] show such an devastating attack where an adversary can make a minor modification in the crypto device and the signing key can be recovered completely. A line of research work have focused how to secure any cryptographic implementation from such tampering attacks [4,7,8,10,11,25,26].

Non-malleable codes are introduced by Dziembowski et al. [5] as one of the applications of tamper-resilient cryptography. It ensures with *high probability* that if an adversary tampers any message encoded with non-malleable codes, output is either *completely unrelated* or *original message*, when tampering has no effect. Let k be the secret message, i.e., key of any cryptographic algorithm and f be a tampering function. The secret message is encoded as $\mathsf{Encode}(k)$. An adversary can apply the tampering function f on the encoded message as $f(\mathsf{Encode}(k))$. Then, it tries to decode the message in the following way $\mathsf{Decode}(f(\mathsf{Encode}(k)))$. The property of non-malleability ensures that $\mathsf{Decode}(f(\mathsf{Encode}(k))) = k$ with probability one, when tampering has no effect or in case of successful tampering attempt $\mathsf{Decode}(f(\mathsf{Encode}(k))) = k'$, where k and k' both are computationally independent. Let $f_{increment}$ be a tampering function which tampers the encoded data as $f_{increment}(\mathsf{Encode}(k) + 1)$. After decoding output is $k + 1$, which is highly related to the original secret message. Hence, non-malleable codes can be constructed for some classes of tampering function only. In literature, the most widely used model is 2-split-state where the codeword is split into two different parts of the memory $\mathcal{M}_L, \mathcal{M}_R$ and two different tampering functions $f = (f_1(\mathcal{M}_L), f_2(\mathcal{M}_R))$ modify the codeword in an arbitrary and independent way [13,16]. Standard notion of non-malleability deals with *one time* tampering attack only. It cannot handle the situation when an adversary tampers the codeword *polynomial number of times*. Later, Faust et al. [12] propose a stronger version of non-malleability called *continuous non-malleable codes* $(CNMC)$ where an adversary can perform the tampering attack for *polynomial number of times* and still non-malleability is preserved.

There are various flavours of continuous non-malleability. The original message is denoted as m whereas m' is the decoded tampered message. Moreover, c represents the original codeword and c' represents the tampered codeword in a continuous tampering experiment. Usually, *standard* version of continuous non-malleability refers to the situation where the decoded tampered message m' and the original message m are completely independent but an attacker can create an encoding such that c' is not equal to c but c' decodes to m as discussed in [5]. In case of *strong* continuous non-malleability, when c' is not equal to c, it is guaranteed that both m' and m are independent. The more stronger flavour is *super-strong* continuous non-malleability, where c' is not equal to c implies that c' and c are independent [12,14,15]. We consider *stronger* version of continuous non-malleability. Again, based on the situation that how tampering functions are applied to the codeword, tampering experiment of continuous non-malleability has two versions as shown in [15]. In case of *non-persistent* tampering, the adversary applies the tampering functions on initial encoding of the codeword. In *persistent* version, tampering functions are applied to the previous version of tampered codeword rather than initial encoding. An adversary can tamper two different parts of the memory until decoding error is triggered. Continuously non-malleable code constructions are broadly categorized into two domains as information-theoretic [23] and computational [12,20,22]. Information-theoretic continuous non-malleability is impossible to achieve in 2-split-state model as mentioned in [12] due to the generic attack. Later, Aggarwal et al. [19] show that information-theoretic continuous non-malleability is possible when tampering is persistent in 2-split-state model. Ostrovsky et al. propose a more relaxed version of $CNMC$ from computational assumption in the plain model (i.e., without *common reference string* (CRS) based setup) but it provides weaker security guarantee. To achieve stronger security, it is *necessary* to rely on CRS based setup assumptions as described in [24]. Hence, our construction relies on authenticated encryption, *robust non interactive zero knowledge* (NIZK) [3] proof and a commitment scheme with CRS based setup.

Table 1. Comparative results of various continuously non-malleable codes in the 2-split-state model.

Scheme	Model	Security Assumption	Tampering Attempt	Security against Tampering and Leakage Attacks
[12]	Computational, CRS	NIZK, Collision resistant hash, Leakage resilient storage	Non-persistent with self-destruct	Polynomial number of tampering attacks and bounded leakage attacks
[19]	Information theoretic	NA	Persistent with self-destruct	Unbounded Adversary with polynomial number of tampering attacks and bounded leakage attacks
[20]	Computational, CRS	NIZK, Non-interactive commitment Leakage resilient public key encryption	Non-persistent with self-destruct	Polynomial number of tampering attacks and bounded leakage attacks
[22]	Computational	Only one-to-one one-way function	Non-persistent with self-destruct	Unbounded Adversary with polynomial number of tampering attacks and bounded leakage attacks
Our work	Computational, CRS	NIZK, Non-interactive commitment, Leakage resilient storage	Non-persistent with self-destruct	Polynomial number of tampering attacks and bounded leakage attacks

Motivation of the Construction. The initial construction of non-malleable codes are *keyless* in nature. Further research work shows that such codeword can be constructed from symmetric-key primitives, i.e., Authenticated Encryption (AE) [13,17,18,26], related-key secure cipher [21] etc. Unfortunately, the codeword of [13,18] and [17], [21,26] are secure against *one-time* tampering attack only. It can not provide security when an adversary tampers the codeword more than once. Moreover, an adversary can tamper the right part of a codeword M_1 and produce M_1'. Such attack can create two valid codewords (M_0, M_1) and (M_0, M_1') such that their decoding does not return $\bot$, i.e., $\bot \neq \mathsf{Decode}_k(\alpha, (M_0, M_1)) \neq \mathsf{Decode}_k(\alpha, (M_0, M_1')) \neq \bot$, where $M_1 \neq M_1'$. The goal of the adversary is to produce two valid messages m, m'. Further, the adversary may not activate the *self-destruct* feature and it can leak all the bits of M_1 with the assumption that the underlying tampering function is *non-persistent*. In general, for any continuously non-malleable codes, finding two valid codewords (M_0, M_1) and (M_0, M_1') such that $\mathsf{Decode}_k(\alpha, (M_0, M_1)) \neq$

$\mathsf{Decode}_k(\alpha, (M_0, M_1'))$ should be computationally hard to the adversary. This property is called *message uniqueness* as described in [12]. Our goal is to design non-malleable codes from authenticated encryption (i.e., *Encrypt then MAC*) that is secure against *polynomial number of tampering attempts*. Table 1 shows various constructions of continuous non-malleable codes in 2-split-state model.

Our Contribution. In this work, we propose a continuous version of non-malleable code in 2-split-state model from authenticated encryption (i.e., *Encrypt then MAC*) along with *robust* NIZK proof and a commitment scheme, instantiated with one-to-one one-way function [1]. Initially, the message is encoded into leakage resilient storage (*lrs*) to protect from leakage attacks. Further, it is encoded with authenticated encryption along with robust NIZK and a commitment scheme. The authenticated encryption used in our construction should satisfy the following assumptions:

(a) The output produced by the underlying authenticated encryption should be *strong pseudorandom permutation* (*sprp*).
(b) If the decryption algorithm of an authenticated encryption with a key k succeeds, it should return $\perp$ when decrypted with a different key k', where $k \neq k'$.

Organization. The paper is structured as follows. Section 2 describes some preliminaries whereas Sect. 3 provides a brief description about continuous non-malleability. Code construction, limitations and future enhancements are illustrated in Sect. 4. Finally, we conclude the paper in Sect. 5.

2 Preliminaries

Basic Notations. We describe a summary of notations in Table 2.

Table 2. Summary of notations

Notation	Terminology
m	Original message
M_0, M_1	Left and right half of a codeword
$\mathcal{M}_L, \mathcal{M}_R$	Left and right half of the memory
$\mathcal{O}_{cnmc}^T(.,.)$	Tampering oracle
f_1, f_2	Tampering functions
$\mathcal{K}$	Key set
$k \xleftarrow{\$} \mathcal{K}$	A particular key is selected
n	Security parameter
$\mathcal{O}^l(s)$	Leakage oracle with s as input
α	Common reference string
S_0, S_1	Two simulators
$\epsilon(n)$	A negligible function
$\mathbb{E} \approx_s \mathbb{F}$	Statistical indistinguishability
$\tau()$	Leakage function
λ	Public label
π	Proof of a statement
pk, sk	Public and private key pair
r	Randomness

2.1   Leakage Resilient Storage

The purpose of leakage resilient storage (lrs) scheme is to encode the message in such a way that an adversary with access to some additional leakage information is unable to guess the original message from the encoded one. The security of leakage resilient storage is preserved until some bounded information is available to the adversary [12]. It consists of a pair of algorithms (Enc^{lrs}, Dec^{lrs}) described as follows:

- Enc^{lrs} algorithm inputs a message m and produces the output p_0, p_1.
- Dec^{lrs} algorithm inputs p_0, p_1 and generates m as output.

The leakage experiment is defined below:

$$leak^{\beta}_{A,m} = \left\{ \begin{array}{c} (p_0, p_1) \leftarrow Enc^{lrs}(m); \mathcal{L} \leftarrow A^{\mathcal{O}^l(p_0,.),\mathcal{O}^l(p_1,.)} \\ output : (p_\beta, \mathcal{L}_A), \beta \in \{0,1\} \end{array} \right\}$$

Initially, a counter ctr is initialized to 0. When strings are passed into the oracle $\mathcal{O}^l(p_0,.)$, $\mathcal{O}^l(p_1,.)$, the leakage function $\tau(p_0)$, $\tau(p_1)$ are used to calculate the value and finally, it is added to ctr, until $ctr \leq l$ from each part. Oracle terminates if $ctr > l$, and further query would return $\perp$. The storage scheme is said to be *strong lrs* if an adversary should not be able to distinguish between two arbitrarily chosen messages m and m' except with negligible probability, i.e.,

$\mathbf{Adv}^{strong}_{leak^{\beta}_A}(A) = [Pr[A(leak^{\beta}_{A,m}) = 1] - Pr[A(leak^{\beta}_{A,m'}) = 1]] \leq \epsilon(n)$, where m, $m' \in \{0,1\}^n$ and $\epsilon(n)$ denotes a negligible function.

2.2   Robust Non-interactive Zero Knowledge

Let L be the language with relation $\mathcal{R}$, denoted as $L^{\mathcal{R}} = \{ m : \exists w$ such that $\mathcal{R}(m, w) = 1\}$ and $m \in \mathcal{M}$. *Robust non-interactive zero knowledge* (NIZK) proof system for the language $L^{\mathcal{R}}$ consists of a set of algorithms ($CRSGen, Prove, Vrfy, S = (S_0, S_1), Xtr$), defined as follows. $CRSGen$ algorithm inputs a security parameter 1^n and generates $\alpha \in \{0,1\}^n$ as *common reference string* (CRS). *Prove* algorithm inputs α, a label λ, $(m, w) \in \mathcal{R}$ and produces the proof $\pi = Prove^\lambda(\alpha, m, w)$ as output. The deterministic verification algorithm $Vrfy$ outputs *true* in case of successful statement verification, i.e., $Vrfy^\lambda(\alpha, m, Prove^\lambda(\alpha, m, w)) = 1$. S algorithm consists of two simulators, i.e., S_0 and S_1. The simulator S_0 generates a CRS and the *trapdoor key* whereas S_1 performs simulated game with an adversary A. Xtr outputs the hidden value of the relation $\mathcal{R}(m, w)$. It satisfies all the below properties as mentioned in [3]:

- **Completeness.** For every $m \in L^{\mathcal{R}}$ and all w such that $\mathcal{R}(m, w) = 1$, for all $\alpha \leftarrow CRSGen(1^n)$, we require that $Pr[Vrfy(\alpha, m, Prove(\alpha, w, m)) = 1]$ should be satisfied.
- **Multi-Theorem zero knowledge.** The honestly computed proof does not reveal anything except the validity of the statement. Formally, we can define it as follows. For every PPT adversary A, the real experiment and the simulated

experiment are indistinguishable, i.e., $Real(n) \approx Simulated(n)$. $Real(n)$ and $Simulated(n)$ are described below:

$$Real(n) = \left\{ \begin{array}{c} \alpha \leftarrow CRSGen(1^n); \mathcal{L} \leftarrow A^{Prove(\alpha,.,.)}(\alpha) \\ output : \mathcal{L} \end{array} \right\}$$

$$Simulated(n) = \left\{ \begin{array}{c} (\alpha, pk) \leftarrow S_0(1^n); \mathcal{L} \leftarrow A^{S_1(\alpha,.,pk)}(\alpha) \\ output : \mathcal{L} \end{array} \right\}$$

– **Extractability.** Extractability property describes that for every PPT adversary A, there exists a PPT algorithm Xtr, a negligible function ϵ and a security parameter n such that $Pr[G^{Xtr} = 1] \leq \epsilon(n)$, where G^{Xtr} is described below:

$$G^{Xtr} = \left\{ \begin{array}{c} (\alpha, pk, sk) \leftarrow S_0(1^n) \\ (m, \pi) \leftarrow A^{S_1(\alpha,.,pk)}(\alpha); w \leftarrow Xtr(\alpha, (m, \pi), sk) \\ (m, \pi) \notin \mathcal{Q} \wedge \mathcal{R}(m, w) \neq 1 \wedge Vrfy(\alpha, m, \pi) = 1 \end{array} \right\},$$

The query set $\mathcal{Q}$ stores (m, π) pairs that an adversary A asks to S_1.

Our assumption is that if any statement is modified, proof of verification should be unsuccessful as illustrated in [9,12]. Also, the proof system supports public label λ and this label is appended to the statement m during calculation of all the above properties, i.e., $Prove^\lambda(.,.,.)$, $Vrfy^\lambda(.,.,.)$, $Xtr^\lambda(.,.,.)$, $S_1^\lambda(.,.,.)$ etc.

2.3 Authenticated Encryption

An *authenticated encryption* (AE) scheme[1] consists of following algorithms ($k = \{k_{enc}\|k_{mac}\}$, $Encypt$, $Decrypt$) such that

– *Encrypt* : Encryption algorithm takes a key $k_{enc} \in \mathcal{K}$, message $m \in M$ and produces a ciphertext $c \in \mathcal{C}$. We write it as $c \leftarrow Encrypt(k_{enc}, m)$. Then, it produces tag $\leftarrow Tag(k_{mac}, c)$. Finally, it outputs $(c\|\text{tag})$.
– *Decrypt* : Decryption algorithm checks first the tag. If it matches, the plaintext is retrieved as $m \leftarrow Decrypt(k_{enc}, c)$ or $\perp$ if decryption fails.

Moreover, the *correctness* property $Decrypt(k, Encrypt(k, m)) = m$, for all $k \in \mathcal{K}$, $m \in M$ and $c \in \mathcal{C}$ should be satisfied.

2.4 Non-interactive Commitment Scheme

A Non-interactive Commitment Scheme consists of two algorithms, i.e., $CRSGen$ and $Commit$. $CRSGen$ takes input security parameter 1^n and generates $\alpha \in \{0, 1\}^n$ as a commitment key. $Commit$ algorithm takes the commitment key α, message $m \in \{0, 1\}^n$, randomness $r \in \{0, 1\}^n$ and generates γ as output. It satisfies the following properties:

---

[1] We refer only *Encrypt then MAC* scheme.

- **Computationally hiding.** A Non-interactive Commitment Scheme is said to satisfy computationally hiding property if for messages $m^0, m^1 \in \{0,1\}^n$, the equation $Commit(\alpha, m^0) \approx_s Commit(\alpha, m^1)$ should be satisfied.
- **Statistically binding.** The commitment scheme is said to satisfy statistically binding property if there does not exist messages $m^0, m^1 \in \{0,1\}^n$ such that $m^0 \neq m^1$ and pair (m^0, r_0), (m^1, r_1) produces $Commit(\alpha, m^0, r_0) = Commit(\alpha, m^1, r_1)$.

3   Continuously Non-malleable Codes

Leakage Oracle. The purpose of stateful leakage oracle $\mathcal{O}^l(.)$ is to calculate the total leakage through arbitrary leakage function $\tau()$. The complete leakage experiment is defined in Algorithm 1. Initially, the value of counter ctr is initialized to 0. When a new string is passed through the oracle, leakage value is calculated and the result is added with the ctr, until $ctr \leq l$. Otherwise, it returns $\bot$.

Algorithm 1. Leakage Oracle $\mathcal{O}^l(s, .)$

1: Set $ctr = 0$
2: Apply leakage function $\tau()$ on s and calculate leakage
3: Update $ctr = ctr + |\tau(s)|$
4: **if** $ctr \leq l$ **then**
5:     return ctr
6: **else**
7:     return $\bot$
8: **end if**

Tampering Oracle. The tampering Oracle $\mathcal{O}^T_{cnmc}(.,.)$ in 2-split-state model is a stateful oracle that takes input two codewords M_0, M_1 and tampering function $f = (f_0, f_1) \in \mathcal{F}$ with initial $state = alive$. The tampering oracle experiment is defined in Algorithm 2.

Coding Scheme. Let $CNMC = (\mathsf{CRSGen}, \mathsf{Encode}_k, \mathsf{Decode}_k)$ be a split-state coding scheme in the CRS model.

- *CRSGen algorithm takes security parameter 1^n as input and generates output $\alpha \in \{0,1\}^n$ as CRS.*
- *Encode$_k$ algorithm takes key $k \in \mathcal{K}$, CRS α, message $m \in \mathcal{M}$ and produces the codeword (M_0, M_1).*
- *Decode$_k$ algorithm takes the codeword (M_0, M_1), key $k \in \mathcal{K}$, CRS α and generates message m or special symbol $\bot$.*

Algorithm 2. Tampering Oracle $\mathcal{O}_{cnmc}^T((M_0, M_1), (f_0, f_1))$

1: **if** $state = self\text{-}destruct$ **then**
2:   return $\perp$
3: **end if**
4: $(M_0', M_1') = (f_0(M_0), f_1(M_1))$
5: **if** $(M_0, M_1) = (M_0', M_1')$ **then**
6:   return $same^*$
7: **end if**
8: **if** $\text{Decode}_k(\alpha, (M_0', M_1')) = \perp$ **then**
9:   set $state = self\text{-}destruct$ and return $\perp$
10: **else**
11:   return $\text{Decode}_k(\alpha, (M_0', M_1'))$
12: **end if**

Continuous Non-malleability. The coding scheme $CNMC$ is said to be l leakage resilient, q continuously non-malleable code in split-state model if for all messages $m, m' \in \{0,1\}^n$ and for all *probabilistic polynomial-time* adversaries A, $\textbf{Tamper}_{cnmc}^{A,m}$ and $\textbf{Tamper}_{cnmc}^{A,m'}$ are computationally indistinguishable, i.e.,

$$\textbf{Adv}_{Tamper_{cnmc}^A}^{Strong}(A) = [Pr[A(\textbf{Tamper}_{cnmc}^{A,m}) = 1] - Pr[A(\textbf{Tamper}_{cnmc}^{A,m'}) = 1]] \leq$$
$\epsilon(n)$, where $m, m' \in \{0,1\}^n$ and

$$\textbf{Tamper}_{cnmc}^{A,m} = \left\{ \begin{array}{c} \alpha \leftarrow CRSGen(1^n); i = 0; (M_0, M_1) \leftarrow Enc_k(\alpha, m) \\ while\ i \leq q \\ \mathcal{L}_A^i \leftarrow A^{\mathcal{O}^l(M_0^i), \mathcal{O}^l(M_1^i), \mathcal{O}_{cnmc}^T(M_0^i, M_1^i)} \\ i = i+1 \\ end\ while \\ output : \mathcal{L}_A^i. \end{array} \right\},$$

The complete view of an adversary is stored into $\mathcal{L}_A^i$ with two parameters μ and δ, where i denotes the number of tampering queries ($i \leq q$). The array μ captures the value of all leakage queries ($\mu \leq 2l$) whereas δ array stores the value of tampering queries ($\delta \leq q$) from $\mathcal{O}_{cnmc}^T()$. In case, the value $i = 1$ denotes that the codeword can handle *one-time* tampering attack only. Further, the value $i = 0$ denotes that the codeword is capable of handling *leakage* attacks [6].

Message Uniqueness. Let $CNMC = (\text{CRSGen}, \text{Encode}_k, \text{Decode}_k)$ be a 2-split-state (l, q) continuously non-malleable code. The codeword is said to satisfy message uniqueness property if there does not exist a valid pair (M_0, M_1), (M_0, M_1') such that $\perp \neq \text{Decode}_k(\alpha, (M_0, M_1)) \neq \text{Decode}_k(\alpha, (M_0, M_1')) \neq \perp$, where $M_1 \neq M_1'$ and the experiment produces two valid messages m, m'. A continuously non-malleable code should not violate uniqueness property as mentioned in [12].

4 Code Construction

To construct continuously non-malleable codes, we use authenticated encryption along with robust NIZK and a commitment scheme. The complete codeword construction is described as follows:

1. $CRSGen(1^n)$. The CRS generation algorithm inputs 1^n as a security parameter and produces the common reference string α as output.

2. $Encode_k(\alpha, m)$. To encode the message $m \in \mathcal{M}$, a uniformly random key $k \in \mathcal{K}$ ($k = \{k_{enc} || k_{mac}\}$) is selected with CRS α. The algorithm first computes $(p_0, p_1) \leftarrow Enc^{lrs}(m||r)$ with some randomness $r \leftarrow \{0,1\}^n$. Further, p_0, p_1 (i.e., $c_0 \leftarrow Encrypt(k_{enc}, p_0)$, $c_1 \leftarrow Encrypt(k_{enc}, p_1)$) are encrypted by encryption algorithm of the authenticated encryption. The tag_{p_0} and tag_{p_1} are generated as $\mathsf{tag}_{p_0} \leftarrow tag(k_{mac}, c_0)$, $\mathsf{tag}_{p_1} \leftarrow tag(k_{mac}, c_1)$. Commitment scheme is used to check uniqueness of the key $k = \{k_{enc}, k_{mac}\}$, i.e., $com = commit(\alpha, k; r)$. The next step is to calculate the proof of statement, i.e., $\pi_0 = Prove^{c_1}(\alpha, k, (com, c_0))$, $\pi_1 = Prove^{c_0}(\alpha, k, c_1)$. Finally, the codeword $(M_0, M_1) = ((k, p_0, (\mathsf{tag}_{p_1}, com, c_1), \pi_0, \pi_1), (k, p_1, (\mathsf{tag}_{p_0}, c_0), \pi_0, \pi_1))$ is stored into $\mathcal{M}_L$ and $\mathcal{M}_R$ respectively.

3. $Decode_k(\alpha, (M_0, M_1))$. To decode the codeword, π_0, π_1 are parsed and the following steps are performed:
   (a) *Left & Right verification.*   If   the   verification   algorithm $Vrfy^{c_1}(\alpha, (com, c_0), \pi_0)$ and $Vrfy^{c_0}(\alpha, c_1, \pi_1)$ return *false* in (M_0, M_1), output $\perp$. Otherwise, go to the next step.
   (b) *Uniqueness check.* If $com = commit(\alpha, k; r)$, go to the next step. Otherwise, return $\perp$.
   (c) *Cross check & Decode.* If tag_{p_0} and tag_{p_1} are not matched, return $\perp$. Otherwise, compare $p_0 \neq Decrypt(k_{enc}, c_0)$, $p_1 \neq Decrypt(k_{enc}, c_1)$. Whenever the following proofs π_0, π_1 are not matched, return $\perp$. Finally, the equality of p_0, p_1 are checked in M_0 and M_1, if it is satisfied, call decode $Dec^{lrs}(p_0, p_1)$.

Lemma 1. $CNMC = (CRSGen, Encode_k, Decode_k)$ *satisfies message uniqueness property if implemented with a commitment scheme.*

Proof. The binding property of the commitment scheme implies message uniqueness. Let us consider an adversary A has the capability to generate a pair (M_0, M_1), (M_0, M_1') such that both are valid and $M_1 \neq M_1'$. Therefore, the adversary is able to generate the following equation: $\perp \neq \mathsf{Decode}_k(\alpha, (M_0, M_1)) \neq \mathsf{Decode}_k(\alpha, (M_0, M_1')) \neq \perp$. It is only possible if an adversary generates a valid key pair (k, k') in such a way that satisfies $commit(\alpha, k, r) = com = commit(\alpha, k', r)$, where $k \neq k'$. Unfortunately, such equation violates the binding property of the commitment scheme. Hence, $commit(\alpha, k, r) = com \neq commit(\alpha, k', r)$. Therefore, we can conclude that integrity of the key is violated and decoding should return $\perp$.

Correctness and Security. To prove the security of the proposed construction, we need to use reduction. Informally, we can say that when the tampering experiment triggers *self-destruct*, the security of continuously non-malleable code reduces to the security of underlying leakage resilient storage. Alternatively, we can say that if the underlying leakage resilient storage is secure, the proposed continuously non-malleable code is secure. Our future work is to analyse the proof in detail.

Application to Tamper-Resilient Cryptography. In cryptography, the main assumption is that an adversary only has black-box view of the cryptosystem. Further, it can only observe the input-output behavior to the system. Unfortunately, such model does not provide security when an adversary has physical access to the cryptosystem. It can attack the hardware or software module where the actual implementation of the algorithm is present. An adversary can have some arbitrary leakage function to get partial information about the cryptosystem (i.e., using timing, radiation, heating, power consumption etc. of the device). The other way, it can physically tamper the device by heating up to introduce some random errors in the memory or cut the wires. The goal of an adversary is to learn the secret key. Our proposed codeword can be used to protect sensitive information against both leakage and tampering attacks against *polynomial number of* times until *self-destruct* occurs. The codeword takes any *secret key* $< K >$ and converts into $< K^{encoded} >$, i.e., key encoded with continuously non-malleable codes secured against leakage and tampering attacks.

Limitations and Future Directions. Our codeword provides security against *non-persistent* tampering attacks only until *self-destruct* state is triggered. The proposed construction is capable of handling *polynomial number of tampering attacks* in computational domain. The future work is to design continuously non-malleable codes for *persistent* tampering attacks with *self-destruct* feature from authenticated encryptions (i.e., *Encrypt then MAC* and others generic AE scheme) in *common reference string* model or plain model. Also it is not known whether continuously non-malleable codes can be designed from authenticated encryption for *persistent* tampering attacks in information-theoretic domain for computationally unbounded adversary.

5   Conclusion

In this work, we show a construction of continuously non-malleable code from authenticated encryption (i.e., *Encrypt then MAC*) in *common reference string* model. The codeword is capable of handing *non-persistent* tampering attacks with *self-destruct* feature only. To the best of our knowledge, this work is the first one that considers authenticated encryption to design continuously non-malleable codes and handles polynomial number of tampering attacks.

References

1. Goldreich, O., Micali, S., Wigderson, A.: Proofs that yield nothing but their validity for all languages in NP have zero-knowledge proof systems. J. ACM **38**(3), 691–729 (1991)
2. Boneh, D., DeMillo, R.A., Lipton, R.J.: On the importance of eliminating errors in cryptographic computations. J. Cryptol. **14**(2), 101–119 (2001)
3. De Santis, A., Di Crescenzo, G., Ostrovsky, R., Persiano, G., Sahai, A.: Robust noninteractive zero knowledge. In: Kilian, J. (ed.) CRYPTO 2001. LNCS, vol. 2139, pp. 566–598. Springer, Heidelberg (2001). https://doi.org/10.1007/3-540-44647-8_33
4. Bellare, M., Kohno, T.: A theoretical treatment of related-key attacks: RKA-PRPs, RKA-PRFs, and applications. In: Biham, E. (ed.) EUROCRYPT 2003. LNCS, vol. 2656, pp. 491–506. Springer, Heidelberg (2003). https://doi.org/10.1007/3-540-39200-9_31
5. Dziembowski, S., Pietrzak, K., Wichs, D.: Non-malleable codes. In: Yao, A.C.-C. (ed.) ICS 2010, Beijing, China, January 5–7, pp. 434–452. Tsinghua University Press (2010)
6. Davì, F., Dziembowski, S., Venturi, D.: Leakage-resilient storage. In: Garay, J.A., De Prisco, R. (eds.) SCN 2010. LNCS, vol. 6280, pp. 121–137. Springer, Heidelberg (2010). https://doi.org/10.1007/978-3-642-15317-4_9
7. Bellare, M., Cash, D., Miller, R.: Cryptography secure against related-key attacks and tampering. In: Lee, D.H., Wang, X. (eds.) ASIACRYPT 2011. LNCS, vol. 7073, pp. 486–503. Springer, Heidelberg (2011). https://doi.org/10.1007/978-3-642-25385-0_26
8. Kalai, Y.T., Kanukurthi, B., Sahai, A.: Cryptography with tamperable and leaky memory. In: Rogaway, P. (ed.) CRYPTO 2011. LNCS, vol. 6841, pp. 373–390. Springer, Heidelberg (2011). https://doi.org/10.1007/978-3-642-22792-9_21
9. Liu, F.-H., Lysyanskaya, A.: Tamper and leakage resilience in the split-state model. In: Safavi-Naini, R., Canetti, R. (eds.) CRYPTO 2012. LNCS, vol. 7417, pp. 517–532. Springer, Heidelberg (2012). https://doi.org/10.1007/978-3-642-32009-5_30
10. Bellare, M., Paterson, K.G., Thomson, S.: RKA security beyond the linear barrier: IBE, encryption and signatures. In: Wang, X., Sako, K. (eds.) ASIACRYPT 2012. LNCS, vol. 7658, pp. 331–348. Springer, Heidelberg (2012). https://doi.org/10.1007/978-3-642-34961-4_21
11. Damgård, I., Faust, S., Mukherjee, P., Venturi, D.: Bounded tamper resilience: how to go beyond the algebraic barrier. In: Sako, K., Sarkar, P. (eds.) ASIACRYPT 2013. LNCS, vol. 8270, pp. 140–160. Springer, Heidelberg (2013). https://doi.org/10.1007/978-3-642-42045-0_8
12. Faust, S., Mukherjee, P., Nielsen, J.B., Venturi, D.: Continuous non-malleable codes. In: Lindell, Y. (ed.) TCC 2014. LNCS, vol. 8349, pp. 465–488. Springer, Heidelberg (2014). https://doi.org/10.1007/978-3-642-54242-8_20
13. Aggarwal, D., Dodis, Y., Lovett, S.: Non-malleable codes from additive combinatorics. In: STOC, pp. 774–783 (2014)
14. Faust, S., Mukherjee, P., Venturi, D., Wichs, D.: Efficient non-malleable codes and key-derivation for poly-size tampering circuits. In: EUROCRYPT, pp. 111–128 (2014)
15. Jafargholi, Z., Wichs, D.: Tamper detection and continuous non-malleable codes. In: Dodis, Y., Nielsen, J.B. (eds.) TCC 2015. LNCS, vol. 9014, pp. 451–480. Springer, Heidelberg (2015). https://doi.org/10.1007/978-3-662-46494-6_19

16. Aggarwal, D., Dodis, Y., Kazana, T., Obremski, M.: Non-malleable reductions and applications. In: Proceedings of the Forty-Seventh Annual ACM on Symposium on Theory of Computing, pp. 459–468. ACM (2015)
17. Kiayias, A., Liu, F.H., Tselekounis, Y.: Practical non-malleable codes from l-more extractable hash functions. In: Weippl, E.R., Katzenbeisser, S., Kruegel, C., Myers, A.C., Halevi, S. (eds.) ACM CCS 2016, pp. 1317–1328. ACM Press (2016)
18. Aggarwal, D., Agrawal, S., Gupta, D., Maji, H.K., Pandey, O., Prabhakaran, M.: Optimal computational split-state non-malleable codes. In: Kushilevitz, E., Malkin, T. (eds.) TCC 2016. LNCS, vol. 9563, pp. 393–417. Springer, Heidelberg (2016). https://doi.org/10.1007/978-3-662-49099-0_15
19. Aggarwal, D., Kazana, T., Obremski, M.: Inception makes non-malleable codes stronger. In: Kalai, Y., Reyzin, L. (eds.) TCC 2017. LNCS, vol. 10678, pp. 319–343. Springer, Cham (2017). https://doi.org/10.1007/978-3-319-70503-3_10
20. Faonio, A., Nielsen, J.B., Simkin, M., Venturi, D.: Continuously non-malleable codes with split-state refresh. In: Preneel, B., Vercauteren, F. (eds.) ACNS 2018. LNCS, vol. 10892, pp. 121–139. Springer, Cham (2018). https://doi.org/10.1007/978-3-319-93387-0_7
21. Fehr, S., Karpman, P., Mennink, B.: Short Non-Malleable Codes from Related-Key Secure Block Ciphers. IACR Trans. Symmetric Cryptol. 336–352 (2018)
22. Ostrovsky, R., Persiano, G., Venturi, D., Visconti, I.: Continuously non-malleable codes in the split-state model from minimal assumptions. In: Shacham, H., Boldyreva, A. (eds.) CRYPTO 2018. LNCS, vol. 10993, pp. 608–639. Springer, Cham (2018). https://doi.org/10.1007/978-3-319-96878-0_21
23. Aggarwal, D., Döttling, N., Nielsen, J.B., Obremski, M., Purwanto, E.: Continuous non-malleable codes in the 8-split-state model. In: Ishai, Y., Rijmen, V. (eds.) EUROCRYPT 2019. LNCS, vol. 11476, pp. 531–561. Springer, Cham (2019). https://doi.org/10.1007/978-3-030-17653-2_18
24. Dachman-Soled, D., Kulkarni, M.: Upper and lower bounds for continuous non-malleable codes. In: Lin, D., Sako, K. (eds.) PKC 2019. LNCS, vol. 11442, pp. 519–548. Springer, Cham (2019). https://doi.org/10.1007/978-3-030-17253-4_18
25. Chen, B., Chen, Y., Hostáková, K., Mukherjee, P.: Continuous space-bounded non-malleable codes from stronger proofs-of-space. In: Boldyreva, A., Micciancio, D. (eds.) CRYPTO 2019. LNCS, vol. 11692, pp. 467–495. Springer, Cham (2019). https://doi.org/10.1007/978-3-030-26948-7_17
26. Ghosal, A.K., Ghosh, S., Roychowdhury, D.: Practical non-malleable codes from symmetric-key primitives in 2-split-state model. In: Ge, C., Guo, F. (eds.) ProvSec 2022. LNCS, vol. 13600, pp. 273–281. Springer, Cham (2022). https://doi.org/10.1007/978-3-031-20917-8_18

Deep Learning Based Differential Classifier of PRIDE and RC5

Debranjan Pal[✉], Upasana Mandal, Abhijit Das,
and Dipanwita Roy Chowdhury

Crypto Research Lab, IIT Kharagpur, Kharagpur, India
debranjan.crl@gmail.com, mandal.up98@gmail.com,
{abhij,drc}@cse.iitkgp.ac.in

Abstract. Deep learning-based cryptanalysis is one of the emerging trends in recent times. Differential cryptanalysis is one of the most potent approaches to classical cryptanalysis. Researchers are now modeling classical differential cryptanalysis by applying deep learning-based techniques. In this paper, we report deep learning-based differential distinguishers for block cipher PRIDE and RC5, utilizing deep learning models: CNN, LGBM and LSTM. We found distinguishers up to 23 rounds for PRIDE and nine rounds for RC5. To the best of our knowledge this is the first deep learning based differential classifier for cipher PRIDE and RC5.

Keywords: Deep Learning · Block Cipher · Differential Cryptanalysis · Neural Distinguisher · PRIDE · RC5

1 Introduction

Researchers are using deep learning techniques to solve problems from a variety of domains. Nowadays, cryptology researchers are also applying deep learning(DL) mainly for cryptanalysis purposes. Rivest [13] first introduced the relationship between the area of machine learning and cryptography. In the cryptography domain, earlier DL was restricted only to side-channel analysis. In 2019, Aron Gohr [7] first showed a way to find deep learning-based distinguishers. He tries to differentiate between the performance of the classical differential distinguisher and the neural distinguisher. He reveals deep learning-based classifiers perform more efficiently for key recovery of round-reduced SPECK32/64. In 2021, T Yadav et al. [15] use the Ghors approach and reports new neural distinguishers for reduced rounds of SIMON-32 [4], SPECK-32 [4] and GIFT-64 [3]. Baksi et al. [2] proposed a technique by utilizing multiple input differences to generate an ML-based distinguisher. They successfully applied the technique to reduced rounds of Ascon permutation, Chaskey permutation, Knot256/512 permutation, and Gimili permutation/hash/cipher to retrieve the corresponding neural distinguishers. Pal et al. [12] proposes a generic tool for generating deep learning-aided differential distinguishers and applies the strategy to reduced rounds of HIGHT, LEA, SPARX, and SAND64/128. Liu et al. [17] uses Gohr's

© The Author(s), under exclusive license to Springer Nature Singapore Pte Ltd. 2023
S. Prabhu et al. (Eds.): ATIS 2022, CCIS 1804, pp. 46–58, 2023.
https://doi.org/10.1007/978-981-99-2264-2_4

approach and found improved distinguishers for PRESENT, DES, and Chaskey. In 2022 Gohr et al. [8] report a new approach applying multiple ciphertext pairs. They found new distinguishers for SKINNY, Katan, and ChaCha and improved distinguishers for PRESENT, SIMON, and SPECK. Zezhou et al. [9] uses neural distinguishers to recover the last subkey of 11 and 13 rounds of SIMON32. Here our objectives are as follows,

- Searching deep learning based differential distinguishers for the cipher PRIDE and RC5.
- Applying different different deep learning models to get more accuracy for neural distinguishers.
- Increasing number of rounds for the neural distinguishers.

1.1 Our Contribution

In this paper, we introduce differential distinguishers for block cipher PRIDE [1] and RC5 [14] utilizing deep learning-based techniques. We found neural-based classifiers up to 23 rounds for PRIDE and distinguishers up to nine rounds for RC5.

1.2 Organization of the Paper

We organize the rest of this paper in the following manner. Section 2 explains the backgrounds and preliminaries. Here we describe the specifications of PRIDE and RC5 in brief, the description of deep learning models used and a literature review on differential cryptanalysis attacks on PRIDE and RC5. In Sect. 3, we present our approach to finding neural classifiers. The experimental results are shown in Sect. 4. Section 5 concludes the paper.

2 Background

In this subsection we describe the background and preliminaries of our work.

2.1 Short Description of PRIDE

PRIDE follows SPN structure with block size 64 bits and 128 bits key size. The 128 bit master key K is divided into two parts, k_0 and k_1, each of 64 bits. The first part, k_0, is applied as a whitening key for both pre-whitening and post-whitening. The last part, k_1, is again divided into eight bytes, which are used for generating the round keys. It iterates a total of 20 rounds. Each round of PRIDE is mainly composed of three operations:

- **AddRoundKey** Exor the state with the round key.
- **Substitution Operation** After key Exoring the state is applied to 16 parallel SBox(see Table 1).
- **Linear Layer** PRIDE uses a linear layer L, which consists of three parts: first, a permutation layer P is used, then a constant matrix M is multiplied with the state and finally, the inverse of the first permutation P^{-1} is applied. The values for M, P, P^{-1} is provided in specification of PRIDE [1].

Table 1. PRIDE SBbox

x	0	1	2	3	4	5	6	7	8	9	A	B	C	D	E	F
S(x)	0	4	8	F	1	5	E	9	2	7	A	C	B	D	6	3

Algorithm 1. Key Expansion of RC5

1: **procedure** KEY_EXPANSION(K,S,rounds)
2:     b ← 16
3:     w ← 32
4:     u = w/8
5:     c = b/u
6:     t = 2*(rounds + 1)
7:     P ← 0xb7e15163
8:     Q ← 0x9e3779b9
9:     S[0] = P
10:    **for** i = 1 to t **do**
11:        $S[i] = (S[i-1] + Q) \mod 2^{32}$
12:    **end for**
13:    **for** i = b-1 to 0 **do**
14:        $L[i/u] = ((L[int(i/u)] << 8) + K[i]) \mod 2^{32}$
15:    **end for**
16:    $i = j = X = Y = 0$
17:    **for** k = 0 to 3t - 1 **do**
18:        $X = S[i] = ROTL((S[i] + ((X+Y) \mod 2^{32})) \mod 2^{32}, 3)$
19:        $Y = L[j] = ROTL((L[j]+((X+Y) \mod 2^{32})) \mod 2^{32}(X+Y) \mod 2^{32})$
20:        $i = int((i+1) \mod t)$
21:        $j = int((j+1) \mod c)$
22:    **end for**
23: **end procedure**

2.2   Short Description of RC5

RC5 [14] is a symmetric key block cipher. The plaintext and ciphertext are represented as a two-word block. For word size, the allowable values are 16, 32, and 64. The design parameters of RC5 consist of word size w, number of rounds r, the number of bytes in the secret key K is b, and the secret key K represented as $K = K[0], K[1], \ldots, K[b-1]$. The expanded key is stored in table S. The encryption module of RC5 consists of two parts,

(a) **Key Expansion** The key expansion function helps to expand the main key K, to form a table S. The process for key expansion is provided in Algorithm 1. Here, P and Q are magic constants, $P_w = \text{Odd}((e-2)2^w)$ and $Q_w = \text{Odd}((\phi - 1)2^w)$, where e = 2.71828182 and ϕ = 1.618033988749. The function ROTL(x, y), is the circular rotation of the word x by y bits.

(b) **Encryption** The encryption function works with the help of elements in the key expansion table S. The encryption algorithm is as follows:

$$X = X + S[0]$$

$$Y = Y + S[1]$$

for $i = 1$ to rounds,

$$X = (\text{ROTL}((X \oplus Y), Y) + S[2 * i]) \mod 2^{32}$$

$$Y = (\text{ROTL}((Y \oplus X), X) + S[2 * i + 1]) \mod 2^{32}$$

Here, X and Y are the w-bit words of the input plaintext. After r number of rounds, the X and Y will be the two words of ciphertext i.e. $Z = [X, Y]$.

2.3 Deep Learning Models

For finding the differential distinguishers, we use three models CNN, LSTM, and LGBM. Now we describe about these three models in brief.

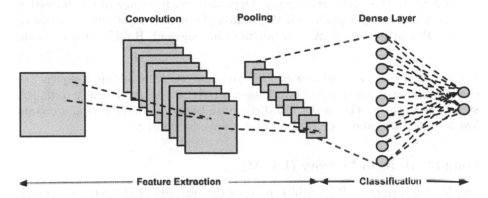

Fig. 1. CNN architecture

Convolutional Neural Network (CNN)

CNN is the most renowned and important Deep Neural Network. The CNN architecture is comparable to the way the neurons are connected in the Human Brain. The emergence of CNN was a motivation by the organization of the visual cortex. Each neuron responds to impulses only in a confined portion of the visual area called the receptive field. A set of such fields overlap to fill the whole visual region. The architecture of a CNN mainly consists of the following layers,

- **Convolution Layer:** The convolution layer has following characteristics,
  i) Unlike the feed-forward network, it follows sparse connectivity. The sparse connectivity reduces the number of parameters in the model.
  ii) Weight sharing is an important property of CNN. The kernel weight needs to be the same for different portions of the same image.

The purpose of the convolution layer is to take out the high-level features, like edges, from an image. The convolution layer in the first level helps to find the low-level features like color, edges, etc. But as the level goes deeper, it grabs a good knowledge of the high-level features and provides a network with a wholesome perception of images in the dataset.

- **Pooling Layer:** The objective of pooling is to decrease the dimension of the feature map that we get from the convolution layer. By dimensionality reduction, it reduces the learning parameters and the computational power which is required to process the data. The pooling layer also helps to fetch the dominant features, which are rotational and positional invariant. Max pooling and average pooling are two types of pooling used in CNN. Max pooling fetches the maximum value from that part that is covered by the kernel. Average pooling computes and returns the average of all the values.
- **Fully Connected Layer:** This layer densely connects all the neurons of the last layer with the next layer. The effect of this layer can be easily calculated by using matrix multiplication and then adding a bias.
- **Non-linear Layer:** A vital layer called activation functions adds non-linearity to the CNN architecture. Depending on the value of the activation function, this layer predicts if the neuron of the next layer will be active or not. Primarily used activation functions are sigmoid, ReLU, softmax, tanh, etc.

Figure 1 depicts a top-level view of CNN architecture. After adding a sequence of convolution layer and pooling layer consecutively, the model is ready to understand the features. The model will distinguish between dominating and certain low-level features and classify them over a series of epochs.

Long Short-Term Memory (LSTM)

LSTM is a variant of RNN which reduces the problem of short-term memory. In RNN, the state s_i records information from the earlier time steps. For each new time instant, the past information gets morphed by the current information as the size of the state is of finite dimension. On the one hand, the information needs to get recorded from all the previous time steps. Still, on the other hand, the memory amount is finite, so it is bound to get overridden. The information will get morphed so much that it will be completely impossible to say the original contribution at step 1 or 2 after 20 or 30-time steps. This is the main problem of RNN, which the LSTM model partially resolves. Figure 2 narrates the architecture of the LSTM model. LSTM resolves the short-term memory problem of RNN. To resolve the problem of short-term memory, three items were included: selective read, selective write, and selective forget.

- **Selective Write** In case of RNN the information of s_{t-1} is being used to compute s_t , $s_t = \sigma(W s_{t-1} + U x_t)$. But here in LSTM, only some portion of the information is passed from the previous state s_{t-1} to the next state s_t. A gate o_{t-1} is introduced, and it is an output gate. Then, an elementwise

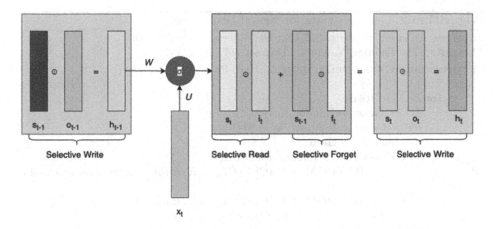

Fig. 2. LSTM architecture

product is performed between the output gate and the cell state s_{t-1}, and the new product is written into h_{t-1}. The output gate o_{t-1} is computed as $o_{t-1} = \sigma(W_o h_{t-1} + U_o x_{t-1} + b_o)$. W_o, U_o are the parameters, and b_o is the bias. The sigmoid function ensures that all the values are between 0 to 1.

- **Selective Read** By using h_{t-1}, the new state at the next time step needs to be computed. From the previously computed h_{t-1} and the new information x_t at the time step t, intermediate state s'_t is computed. s'_t captures all the information from the last state h_{t-1} and the next input x_t. A new gate is introduced as i_t. i_t is computed as $i_t = \sigma(W_i h_{t-1} + U_i x_t + b_i)$. i_t multiplied by s'_t is the selectively read information.
- **Selective Forget** In selective forget, s_{t-1} and s'_t are both combined to get the new state s_t. Before combining, some part of s_{t-1} needs to get forgotten. So, the forget gate f_t is being introduced. $f_t = \sigma(W_f h_{t-1} + U_f x_t + b_f)$. Finally s_t is computed as $s_t = f_t \odot s_{t-1} + i_t \odot s'_t$.

The whole architecture of LSTM using all three above-mentioned items is sketched out in Fig. 2.

Light Gradient Boosting Machine (LGBM)

LGBM is one of the boosting algorithms. Boosting algorithm is an ensemble technique. When there are multiple models such as M_1, M_2, ..., M_n and there is a baseline model M_0, at first M_0 is made, the prediction on a finite set record and whatever errors are achieved from that, the next model is trained with that and so on and so forth it continues. In the end, all the models are combined, and a final model is made. LGBM consists of the following characteristics,

- The training speed is really high. It is very much efficient.
- It can handle large-scale data.
- Memory usage is less.
- LGBM model provides parallel, distributed, and GPU learning.

Algorithm 2. Generate Data for Neural Distinguisher

Inputs: An input differences(Δ_i) for the differential distinguisher
Outputs: The Training/Validation Dataset $DATA_T/DATA_V$

1: **procedure** GENERATEDATASET(Δ_i, Rnd, Itr)
2:     $DATA \leftarrow \{\}$ ▷ Empty set
3:     **for** i = 1 to Itr **do**
4:         $MK \leftarrow$ GenerateRandomKey()
5:         $PT_1 \leftarrow$ GenerateRandomPlaintext()
6:         **if** i mod 2 = 0 **then**
7:             $PT_2 \leftarrow$ GenerateRandomPlaintext()
8:             $CT_1 \leftarrow$ RANDOM_ORACLE(PT_1, MK, Rnd) ▷ Encryption oracle of a
    cipher
9:             $CT_2 \leftarrow$ RANDOM_ORACLE(PT_2, MK, Rnd)
10:             $DATA \leftarrow DATA \cup (CT_1, CT_2, CT_1 \oplus CT_2, 0)$
11:         **else**
12:             $PT_2 = PT_1 \oplus \Delta_i$
13:             $CT_1 \leftarrow$ RANDOM_ORACLE(PT_1, MK, Rnd)
14:             $CT_2 \leftarrow$ RANDOM_ORACLE(PT_2, MK, Rnd)
15:             $DATA \leftarrow DATA \cup (CT_1, CT_2, CT_1 \oplus CT_2, 1)$
16:         **end if**
17:     **end for**
18:     Return $DATA$
19: **end procedure**

2.4   Differential Cryptanalysis of PRIDE and RC5

Differential cryptanalysis [5] is a chosen-plaintext attack that, by speculating on a key establishes a probabilistic relationship between the second last round state difference and the ciphertext difference.

Let (P, P') represent the plaintext pair and (C_m, C'_m) represent the ciphertext pair after m^{th} round. The conditional probability $Pr(\Delta C_m = \beta \mid \Delta P = \alpha)$ is then used to calculate the differential likelihood of an m-round differential $\alpha \to \beta$, where $\Delta P = P \oplus P'$ and $\Delta C_m = C_m \oplus C'_m$ and the sub-keys $K_1, \ldots, K_m$ are independent and uniformly random. The attacker determines the differential probability for each round in preparation for mounting an attack.

PRIDE. Utilizing the shortcomings of the SBox and linear layer of PRIDE [1], Zhao [18] introduce 16 alternative two round differential trails and found multiple 15-round differential characteristics. They mount a differential attack on the 18-round PRIDE based on one of these differentials. They use 2^{60} chosen plaintexts. Applying an automatic tool Yang et al. [16] reports 56 differential characteristics, where also exists 24 one-round differential trails. With the help of three of them, they create a 15-round differential before launching a differential attack on the 19-round PRIDE, with data complexity 2^{62}.

RC5. Kaliski Jr et al. [10] mount differential attack on nine-round RC5(64-bit block size), using 2^{45} chosen plaintext pairs. For 12-round RC5 they need 2^{62}

Algorithm 3. Training Algorithm for Neural Distinguisher
___
Inputs: Training Data $DATA_T$

Outputs: Training accuracy AC_T

1: **procedure** TRAINNEURALDISTINGUISHER($DATA_T$)
2:     Generate the DL model DL_{Δ_i}.
3:     Perform training for DL_{Δ_i} with dataset $DATA_T$.
4:     Let AC_T be the training accuracy that the training algorithm returns.
5:     **if** $AC_T > 0.5$ **then**
6:         Generate new dataset $DATA_V$ for validation algorithm.
7:         Call $ValidationNeuralDistinguisher(ML_{\Delta_i}, DATA_V)$
8:     **else**
9:         Return "Distinguisher can't be identified"
10:    **end if**
11:    Return AC_T
12: **end procedure**

___

pairs. Alex Biryukov et al. [6] uses partial differential technique and improve the 12-round attack for RC5 with 32-bit block size. They needs only 2^{44} chosen pairs. Knudsen [11] demonstrates the shortcomings of Kaliski [10] proposed differential analysis. They improved the complexity of the differential attacks by a factor of up to 512. Additionally, they demonstrate that RC5 has a lot of weak keys in terms of differential attacks.

Algorithm 4. Validation Algorithm for Neural Distinguisher
___
Inputs: Validation Data $DATA_V$ and the pre-trained model DL_{Δ_i}

Outputs: Validation Accuracy AC_V

1: **procedure** VALIDATIONNEURALDISTINGUISHER($DL_{\Delta_i}, DATA_V$)
2:     Run the pretrained model DL_{Δ_i}.
3:     Perform validation for DL_{δ_i} by applying the validation data $DATA_V$.
4:     Let AC_V be the validation accuracy.
5:     **if** $AC_V > 0.5$ **then**
6:         Distinguisher identified.
7:     **else**
8:         Return "Distinguisher can't identified"
9:     **end if**
10:    Return AC_V
11: **end procedure**

___

3   Deep Learning to Model Classical Differential Cryptanalysis

In Gohr's algorithm, the input is a plaintext difference Δ_i. Let (PT_1, PT_2) be a plaintext pair, and the corresponding ciphertext pair after Rnd rounds is (CT_1, CT_2). Now for each plaintext and ciphertext pair, create an output label L such that,

$$\begin{cases} L = 0 & \text{if } PT_1 \oplus PT_2 \neq \Delta_i \\ L = 1 & \text{if } PT_1 \oplus PT_2 = \Delta_i \end{cases}$$

Classifying the real ciphertext pairs from random ciphertext pairs is the primary intention behind this. Following this idea, we create the dataset by choosing the appropriate plaintext difference for a cipher with a predetermined round. Next, we construct a deep learning model and train the model by applying the dataset. Check the training accuracy if it exceeds 50%, then generate the validation dataset applying the same plaintext difference. If the validation accuracy is greater than 50% then we conclude that a differential classifier is found for the corresponding cipher with given rounds.

Table 2. Performance of DL-based distinguishers for cipher PRIDE

DL Technique	No of Rounds	AC_T	AC_V	TPR	TNR
CNN	3	84.23	84.29	0.822	0.810
	4	54.07	54.51	0.267	0.728
	5	50.21	50.53	0.479	0.520
	6	50.31	50.45	0.181	0.811
LGBM	3	63.6	54.62	0.482	0.611
	4	63.59	50.13	0.584	0.418
	5	63.69	50.00	0.493	0.504
LSTM	3	51.08	50.53	0.813	0.195
	4	50.62	50.67	0.745	0.267

Algorithm 2 explains the process of data generation for training and testing. The input is the plaintext difference Δ_i, the number of data elements Itr(number of iterations), and the round number Rnd up to which we want to find the neural classifier for the given cipher. Take two plaintexts PT_1 and PT_2 is selected in such a way that $\Delta_i = PT_1 \oplus PT_2$. The pair (PT_1, PT_2) is called real pair. Also consider one random plaintext pair (PT_1', PT_2'). Now encryption is performed using random oracle (with the round number Rnd) to get the ciphertext pair (CT_1, CT_2) from (PT_1, PT_2) and (CT_1', CT_2') from (PT_1', PT_2'). Next store the real ciphertext pair (CT_1, CT_2) with label 1 and the random ciphertext pair (CT_1', CT_2') with label 0. We also store the corresponding ciphertext differences along with the ciphertexts. Repeat this process for random keys for each iteration to generate a training dataset $DATA_T$ or validation dataset $DATA_V$.

Algorithm 3 explains the training process. The input for training is the training data $DATA_T$, and the output is the training accuracy AC_T. We first construct the DL model DL_{Δ_i} and train applying $DATA_T$. Check the training accuracy AC_T. If AC_T is less than 50% distinguisher is not found for the current dataset else, create the validation data $DATA_V$ and call the validation algorithm.

Algorithm 4 describes the validation process after training. The input for the validation algorithm is validation data $DATA_V$, and the output is validation accuracy AC_V. During validation, load the pre-trained model DL_{Δ_i} and run this for validation data $DATA_V$. If validation accuracy AC_V is greater than 50% distinguisher found for $DATA_T$ and $DATA_V$ corresponding to input difference Δ_i. Save the model DL_{Δ_i}. But if AC_V is less than 50%, distinguisher is not possible.

Table 3. Performance of DL based distinguishers for cipher RC5

DL Technique	No of Rounds	AC_T	AC_V	TPR	TNR
CNN	2	81.48	81.36	0.629	0.998
	3	62.96	58.64	0.425	0.704
	4	56.46	51.2	0.513	0.508
	5	59.14	50.33	0.489	0.509
	6	56.30	50.16	0.499	0.504
	7	53.61	50.18	0.463	0.533
LGBM	2	75.48	74.14	0.558	0.922
	3	62.18	54.02	0.290	0.788
	4	64.57	50.02	0.573	0.427
	5	64.95	50.00	0.496	0.498
	6	64.73	50.15	0.585	0.416
LSTM	2	68.30	67.48	0.518	0.833
	3	50.80	51.30	0.324	0.695
	4	50.35	51.33	0.390	0.609

We use the concept of a generic neural classifier proposed by Pal et al. [12]. We search an x round differential trail for the given cipher and use the corresponding output difference as an input difference for the neural classifier. In this context, if the classifier achieves good accuracy up to y rounds, then we found a new neural classifier with $(x + y)$ rounds.

4   Experiments and Observations

We use CNN, LGBM, and LSTM models to generate deep learning-based distinguishers. For all our experiments, we use google colab with installed GPU (Nvidia T4, 16GB of memory, clock size 1.59GHz). For checking each distinguisher we create a total of 10^5 data elements, out of which 50000 are applied for training, and the rest for validation.

During the training of the models setting up the value of the batch size and number of epochs was a challenging task for us to get the appropriate validation accuracy. We use batch size 30, and the number of epochs is set to nine for both CNN and LSTM models.

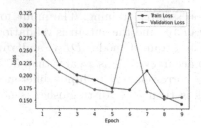

Fig. 3. Epoch Vs Loss for PRIDE (CNN)   **Fig. 4.** Epoch Vs Accuracy for PRIDE (CNN)

4.1 PRIDE

Zaho et al. [18] reports differential characteristics of 15 and 18 for PRIDE. We take the input difference of 18 round distinguisher (08000000) as input to our neural classifier. We achieve good accuracy in up to six rounds, which results in a distinguisher for 23 rounds. The training and validation accuracy with the true positive rate(TPR) and true negative rate(TNR) of these distinguishers for different models are enlisted in Table 2. We are getting distinguishers up to six rounds for CNN, up to five rounds for LGBM, and up to four rounds for LSTM. The change of training and validation accuracy with increasing epochs for CNN and LSTM is depicted in Fig. 4 and 6. The change of training and validation loss with increasing epochs for CNN and LSTM is depicted in Fig. 3 and 5.

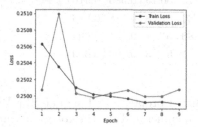

Fig. 5. Epoch Vs Loss for PRIDE (LSTM)   **Fig. 6.** Epoch Vs Accuracy for PRIDE (LSTM)

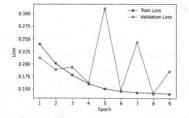

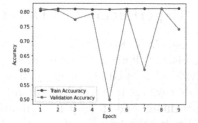

Fig. 7. Epoch Vs Loss for RC5 (CNN)   **Fig. 8.** Epoch Vs accuracy for RC5 (CNN)

4.2 RC5

Birukov et al. [6] propose eight rounds of differential characteristics for RC5. We take the input difference of third round distinguisher (0000080000000000) as input to our neural classifier and achieve good accuracy up to seven rounds, which provides a distinguisher for nine rounds. The training and validation accuracy with the corresponding TPR and TNR of these distinguishers for different models are provided in Table 3. We are getting distinguishers up to seven rounds for CNN, up to six rounds for LGBM, and up to four rounds for LSTM. The training and validation accuracy change with increasing epochs for CNN and LSTM is depicted in Fig. 8 and 10. The change of training and validation loss with increasing epochs for CNN and LSTM is depicted in Fig. 7 and 9.

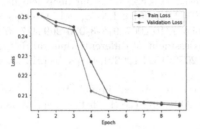
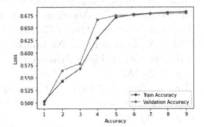

Fig. 9. Epoch Vs Loss for RC5 (LSTM)   **Fig. 10.** Epoch Vs Accuracy for RC5 (LSTM)

5 Conclusion

This paper reports the deep learning-based differential classifiers for PRIDE and RC5. To our knowledge, this is the first deep learning-based distinguisher for PRIDE and RC5. We have applied three deep learning models: CNN, LGBM, and LSTM, for searching neural classifiers. For PRIDE, the classifier works up to 23 rounds; for RC5, it works up to nine rounds, which is better than the existing reported results. CNN performs better with accuracy and distinguishers (with higher rounds) when compared with LGBM and LSTM. In future work, we want to apply partial key recovery attacks for PRIDE and RC5. One can use the techniques for searching neural classifiers to other lightweight block ciphers.

References

1. Albrecht, M.R., Driessen, B., Kavun, E.B., Leander, G., Paar, C., Yalçın, T.: Block ciphers – focus on the linear layer (feat. PRIDE). In: Garay, J.A., Gennaro, R. (eds.) CRYPTO 2014, Part I. LNCS, vol. 8616, pp. 57–76. Springer, Heidelberg (2014). https://doi.org/10.1007/978-3-662-44371-2_4
2. Baksi, A., Breier, J., Chen, Y., Dong, X.: Machine learning assisted differential distinguishers for lightweight ciphers. In: Design, Automation & Test in Europe Conference & Exhibition, DATE 2021, Grenoble, France, 1–5 February 2021, pp. 176–181 (2021). https://doi.org/10.23919/DATE51398.2021.9474092

3. Banik, S., Pandey, S.K., Peyrin, T., Sasaki, Yu., Sim, S.M., Todo, Y.: GIFT: a small present - towards reaching the limit of lightweight encryption. In: Fischer, W., Homma, N. (eds.) CHES 2017. LNCS, vol. 10529, pp. 321–345. Springer, Cham (2017). https://doi.org/10.1007/978-3-319-66787-4_16

4. Beaulieu, R., Shors, D., Smith, J., Treatman-Clark, S., Weeks, B., Wingers, L.: The SIMON and SPECK lightweight block ciphers. In: Proceedings of the 52nd Annual Design Automation Conference, San Francisco, CA, USA, 7–11 June 2015, pp. 175:1–175:6. ACM (2015). https://doi.org/10.1145/2744769.2747946

5. Biham, E., Shamir, A.: Differential Cryptanalysis of the Data Encryption Standard (1993)

6. Biryukov, A., Kushilevitz, E.: Improved cryptanalysis of RC5. In: Nyberg, K. (ed.) EUROCRYPT 1998. LNCS, vol. 1403, pp. 85–99. Springer, Heidelberg (1998). https://doi.org/10.1007/BFb0054119

7. Gohr, A.: Improving attacks on round-reduced speck32/64 using deep learning. In: Boldyreva, A., Micciancio, D. (eds.) CRYPTO 2019. LNCS, vol. 11693, pp. 150–179. Springer, Cham (2019). https://doi.org/10.1007/978-3-030-26951-7_6

8. Gohr, A., Leander, G., Neumann, P.: An assessment of differential-neural distinguishers. Cryptology ePrint Archive, Paper 2022/1521 (2022). https://eprint.iacr.org/2022/1521

9. Hou, Z., Ren, J., Chen, S.: Cryptanalysis of round-reduced simon32 based on deep learning. Cryptology ePrint Archive, Paper 2021/362 (2021). https://eprint.iacr.org/2021/362

10. Kaliski, B.S., Yin, Y.L.: On differential and linear cryptanalysis of the RC5 encryption algorithm. In: Coppersmith, D. (ed.) CRYPTO 1995. LNCS, vol. 963, pp. 171–184. Springer, Heidelberg (1995). https://doi.org/10.1007/3-540-44750-4_14

11. Knudsen, L.R., Meier, W.: Differential cryptanalysis of RC5. Eur. Trans. Telecommun. 8(5), 445–454 (1997)

12. Pal, D., Mandal, U., Chaudhury, M., Das, A., Chowdhury, D.R.: A deep neural differential distinguisher for ARX based block cipher. IACR Cryptol. ePrint Arch., p. 1195 (2022). https://eprint.iacr.org/2022/1195

13. Rivest, R.L.: Cryptography and machine learning. In: Imai, H., Rivest, R.L., Matsumoto, T. (eds.) ASIACRYPT 1991. LNCS, vol. 739, pp. 427–439. Springer, Heidelberg (1993). https://doi.org/10.1007/3-540-57332-1_36

14. Rivest, R.L.: The RC5 encryption algorithm. In: Preneel, B. (ed.) FSE 1994. LNCS, vol. 1008, pp. 86–96. Springer, Heidelberg (1995). https://doi.org/10.1007/3-540-60590-8_7

15. Yadav, T., Kumar, M.: Differential-ML distinguisher: machine learning based generic extension for differential cryptanalysis. In: Longa, P., Ràfols, C. (eds.) LATINCRYPT 2021. LNCS, vol. 12912, pp. 191–212. Springer, Cham (2021). https://doi.org/10.1007/978-3-030-88238-9_10

16. Yang, Q., et al.: Improved differential analysis of block cipher PRIDE. In: Lopez, J., Wu, Y. (eds.) ISPEC 2015. LNCS, vol. 9065, pp. 209–219. Springer, Cham (2015). https://doi.org/10.1007/978-3-319-17533-1_15

17. Zhang, L., Wang, Z.: Improving differential-neural distinguisher model for des, chaskey, and PRESENT. CoRR abs/2204.06341 (2022). https://doi.org/10.48550/arXiv.2204.06341

18. Zhao, J., Wang, X., Wang, M., Dong, X.: Differential analysis on block cipher PRIDE. IACR Cryptol. ePrint Arch., p. 525 (2014). https://eprint.iacr.org/2014/525

A Better MixColumns Matrix to AES Against Differential Fault Analysis Attack

Anit Kumar Ghosal$^{(\boxtimes)}$ (iD)

Department of Computer Science and Engineering, IIT Kharagpur,
Kharagpur, India
anit.ghosal@gmail.com

Abstract. The most widely used block cipher AES, is vulnerable against side channel attacks only. An attacker can mount Differential Fault Analysis attack on AES to find the secret key. In literature, it is shown that AES key can be recovered by forming a system of linear equations with a pair of faulty and fault free ciphertexts with an exhaustive search of 2^{32}, which is further improved to 2^8. Ghosal et al. strengthens the security of AES to 2^{84} with an additional diffusion layer. In this work, we propose two different MixColumns like matrices to the AES block cipher that secures the cipher against Differential Fault Analysis attacks. The attack complexity is increased to 2^{116} with our proposed matrix.

Keywords: AES Rijndael · DFA Attack · Binary Involutive Matrix · SPN cipher

1 Introduction

In the era of digital evaluation, providing security to various cryptographic systems is one of the challenging task. An adversary can perform various cryptanalysis on the hardware or software implementation of the device to break the cryptosystem completely. Advanced Encryption Standard (AES) [4], the global data encryption standard is a popular target of the adversary for cryptanalytic attacks. The adversary can inject fault to the internal state during run time of the algorithm and then analyse the original output and corrupted output. A line of research work shows how to break AES cryptosystem using Differential Fault Analysis (DFA) attacks [2,4–6,8–10]. Giraud et al. [10] show that using a fault in the 9th round of AES with 250 faulty ciphertexts, AES key can be recovered. Later, the same idea has been extended in [8] and 128 faulty ciphertexts are sufficient to retrieve the complete AES-128 key. The attack is further improved in [9] and the adversary can induce a fault between 8th or 9th round of the Mix-Columns and the key can be found with 40 faulty ciphertexts. An adversary can induce byte fault during 8th or 9th round of AES-128 algorithm and the complete AES key can be retrieved with two faulty ciphertexts [6]. Recent literature work [32] shows that Differential Fault Analysis attack on AES-NI removes the support for Software Guard Extension (SGX) in 12th generation Intel Core 11000

© The Author(s), under exclusive license to Springer Nature Singapore Pte Ltd. 2023
S. Prabhu et al. (Eds.): ATIS 2022, CCIS 1804, pp. 59–70, 2023.
https://doi.org/10.1007/978-981-99-2264-2_5

and 12000 processors completely. Our motivation of this work is to protect the AES block cipher against Differential Fault Analysis attacks [15,20,34].

There are various countermeasures proposed so far in the literature to secure AES implementations [23,26,31,33]. Broadly, it can be divided into two categories. One way is to restrict the propagation of fault in the initial place. The other proposal is to use redundancy to eliminate the fault [12,25]. Detection [28] and Infection [22,24,30] countermeasures follow this approach. Alternatively, various masking schemes are proposed to protect AES implementation [7,11,13,17,19,29]. In case of detection-based countermeasure, the algorithm is executed twice times and both the results are compared to find faults. An adversary can inject the same fault in both paths to bypass the comparison. Moreover, there are some attacks on this comparison itself. As the countermeasure does not provide sufficient result [21], infective computation is proposed in place of detection. Unfortunately, some drawbacks are identified in [24]. In literature, it is shown that block ciphers use Maximum Distance Separable (MDS) matrix or near-MDS matrix in MixColumns with some random permutation (e.g., Khazad [3], Midori [27]) in diffusion layer whereas cipher like Present [14] uses bit permutation in the diffusion layer. Ghosal et al. [34] show that adding one extra diffusion layer in the AES algorithm makes the DFA attack costly to the adversary and the end complexity of the exhaustive key search is 2^{84}.

Our Contribution. In this work, we propose two MixColumns like matrices to the AES block cipher. Such matrices protect the cipher against differential fault attacks. The main goal is to restrict the number of linear equations to enlarge the exhaustive key-search space. The best known complexity with such kind of attack is 2^8. With the proposed MixColumns like matrix, the attack complexity is increased to 2^{116}. The underlying matrices are binary, involutive and circulant. Hence, the same matrix can be used for AES encryption and decryption algorithm.

Organization. The paper is structured as follows. Section 2 gives an overview of AES algorithm and the existing attack whereas Sect. 3 illustrates the attack in detail on newly proposed matrices. Results, applications and future works are described in Sect. 4. Finally, Sect. 5 concludes our work.

2 Background

AES-Rijndael. The detailed description of AES-Rijndael algorithm is mentioned in [4]. Here, we consider the AES-128 algorithm. The input of AES is structured as a 4×4 matrix. The algorithm consists of ten rounds and the sub keys at each round are generated from the KeySchedule algorithm. The AES encryption algorithm in each round follows the below steps:

- **SubBytes.** The non-linear step of the cipher. An affine transformation is used with input byte m to produce the output byte $y = Am^{-1} + B$, where A and B both are constant matrices.
- **ShiftRows.** Each row of the state matrix is cyclically shifted into a certain offset.

- **MixColumns.** Each column of the state matrix is multiplied by the following MDS matrix M whose elements belong to $F(2^8)$. Here, the matrix M and its inverse M^{-1} are denoted as follows:

$$M = \begin{pmatrix} 02 \ 03 \ 01 \ 01 \\ 01 \ 02 \ 03 \ 01 \\ 01 \ 01 \ 02 \ 03 \\ 03 \ 01 \ 01 \ 02 \end{pmatrix} \quad M^{-1} = \begin{pmatrix} 0e \ 0b \ 0d \ 09 \\ 09 \ 0e \ 0b \ 0d \\ 0d \ 09 \ 0e \ 0b \\ 0b \ 0d \ 09 \ 0e \end{pmatrix}.$$

- **AddRoundKey.** The state of the AES is XORed with the 128-bit round key generated from the KeySchedule algorithm.

Similarly, the AES decryption algorithm has the following steps: InvShiftRows, InvSubBytes, AddRoundKey, InvMixColumns. The initial nine rounds of encryption algorithm are same except the tenth round that does not perform the MixColumns.

Fault Model of the Attack. This work considers only single byte fault model where a byte b_{ij} is assumed to be faulty. The fault value f_{ij} is used to corrupt the byte $(0 \leq i, j \leq 3)$. The notation $w(f_{ij})$ $(1 \leq w(f_{ij}) \leq 8)$ is used to denote the number of faulty bits in a byte. The fault value should be non-zero and any kind of hardware failure should be discarded.

2.1 Related Research

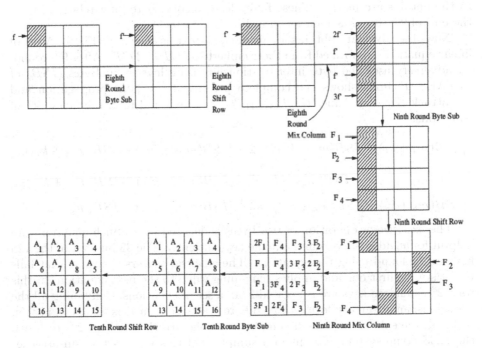

Fig. 1. The propagation of single byte fault in the input of 8th round [15]

The most successful Differential Fault Analysis (DFA) [1] attack is shown in [15] where the AES key can be retrieved with an exhaustive search of 2^{32} using a single byte fault. Later, it is improved to 2^8. An attacker can inject a fault in the intermediate state of the AES cipher to recover the secret key by exploiting the erroneous results. We consider AES-128 only. The 128 bit plaintext matrix is denoted as P, K represents the 128 bit key matrix whereas fault free ciphertext matrix is CT and faulty ciphertext matrix is CT' as shown below:

$$P = \begin{pmatrix} p_1 & p_5 & p_9 & p_{13} \\ p_2 & p_6 & p_{10} & p_{14} \\ p_3 & p_7 & p_{11} & p_{15} \\ p_4 & p_8 & p_{12} & p_{16} \end{pmatrix} K = \begin{pmatrix} k_1 & k_5 & k_9 & k_{13} \\ k_2 & k_6 & k_{10} & k_{14} \\ k_3 & k_7 & k_{11} & k_{15} \\ k_4 & k_8 & k_{12} & k_{16} \end{pmatrix}$$

$$CT = \begin{pmatrix} m_1 & m_5 & m_9 & m_{13} \\ m_2 & m_6 & m_{10} & m_{14} \\ m_3 & m_7 & m_{11} & m_{15} \\ m_4 & m_8 & m_{12} & m_{16} \end{pmatrix} CT' = \begin{pmatrix} m_1' & m_5' & m_9' & m_{13}' \\ m_2' & m_6' & m_{10}' & m_{14}' \\ m_3' & m_7' & m_{11}' & m_{15}' \\ m_4' & m_8' & m_{12}' & m_{16}' \end{pmatrix},$$

where each byte p_i, k_i, m_i, m_i' takes value from $\{0,...,255\}$, $\forall i \in \{1,...,16\}$.

Figure 1 shows the attack strategy. An attacker injects a single byte fault F (or f) at the start of 8th round in $(0,0)^{th}$ location of the state matrix. The MixColumns spreads the fault into entire column of the AES state matrix. The next ShiftRow of 9th round makes one byte of each column faulty as F_1, F_2, F_3 and F_4 respectively. F_1, F_2, F_3 and F_4 denote the fault value at $(0,0)^{th}$, $(1,3)^{th}$, $(2,2)^{th}$ and $(3,1)^{th}$ locations. The next MixColumns spreads the fault to the entire state matrix. These faults lead to some byte inter-relationship at the end of 9th round as mentioned in Fig. 1.

Now, the adversary obtains a pair of ciphertext as shown in [15,16]. A set of linear equations are formed from these ciphertexts CT and CT'. After 9th round, an adversary uses the byte inter-relationship using Inverse SubBytes (ISB) of the AES. Figure 1 shows the complete process of the fault propagation and the attack. The key values $(k_1, k_{14}, k_{11}, k_8)$ can be found from the below set of equations:

$$[ISB(m_1 + k_1) + ISB(m_1' + k_1)] = 2 \times [ISB(m_{14} + k_{14}) + ISB(m_{14}' + k_{14})].$$

$$[ISB(m_{14} + k_{14}) + ISB(m_{14}' + k_{14})] = [ISB(m_{11} + k_{11}) + ISB(m_{11}' + k_{11})].$$

$$[ISB(m_8 + k_8) + ISB(m_8' + k_8)] = 3 \times [ISB(m_{14} + k_{14}) + ISB(m_{14}' + k_{14})].$$

The exclusive-or operation of two bytes is denoted by $+$. Such equations are helpful for an adversary to find out the key efficiently. The 32 bits out of the 128 key can be found using the equations. The adversary filters the value that fails to satisfy the first one and applies remaining value to the next equation. In this way, 2^8 candidate keys are generated from a set of equations. Combining all the equations, an adversary forms three different sets of equations as shown in [15]. In total, the exhaustive search complexity of the attack is $2^{8*4} = 2^{32}$ to break the AES cryptosystem. The main assumption of this work is that an attacker can induce the fault to the specified bit position, i.e., $(0,0)^{th}$ byte of the AES state matrix. When the faulty position is unknown to the adversary, it explores all of the cells of the state matrix. Hence, the attacker performs an exhaustive search of $16*2^{32} = 2^{36}$ and such computation can be easily carried out by latest Intel processors efficiently.

3   MixColumns Like Matrix to AES Diffusion Layer

To strengthen the security of AES against Differential Fault Analysis attacks, we propose two different MixColumns like matrices in AES diffusion layer. It is well known that AES is not secured against fault attack. Since an adversary can inject a single byte fault attack in start of 8th round to find out the key (Fig. 1). Our MixColumns like matrices are binary, involutive, circulant and it provides security against Differential Fault Analysis attack. The two matrices M_1 and M_2 are defined as follows:

$$M_1 = \begin{pmatrix} 01 & 00 & 01 & 01 \\ 00 & 01 & 01 & 01 \\ 01 & 01 & 01 & 00 \\ 01 & 01 & 00 & 01 \end{pmatrix} \quad M_2 = \begin{pmatrix} 00 & 01 & 01 & 01 \\ 01 & 00 & 01 & 01 \\ 01 & 01 & 00 & 01 \\ 01 & 01 & 01 & 00 \end{pmatrix}.$$

3.1   Analysis of DFA with MixColumns Like Matrix M_1

Figure 1 shows the fault propagation in AES with MixColumns matrix M. The adversary can deduce the equations in the same way as described in Fig. 1 except the MixColumns matrix is different, i.e., M_1. The fault propagation in 8th round MixColumns is described as follows:

$$\begin{pmatrix} 01 & 00 & 01 & 01 \\ 00 & 01 & 01 & 01 \\ 01 & 01 & 01 & 00 \\ 01 & 01 & 00 & 01 \end{pmatrix} \times \begin{pmatrix} F & m_5 & m_9 & m_{13} \\ m_2 & m_6 & m_{10} & m_{14} \\ m_3 & m_7 & m_{11} & m_{15} \\ m_4 & m_8 & m_{12} & m_{16} \end{pmatrix} = \begin{pmatrix} F_1 & m_5' & m_9' & m_{13}' \\ m_2 & m_6' & m_{10}' & m_{14}' \\ F_3 & m_7' & m_{11}' & m_{15}' \\ F_4 & m_8 & m_{12} & m_{16}' \end{pmatrix}.$$

The next ShiftRows and MixColumns in 9th round spreads the fault in the following way.

$$\begin{pmatrix} F_1 & m_5' & m_9' & m_{13}' \\ m_6' & m_{10}' & m_{14}' & m_2' \\ m_{11}' & m_{15}' & F_3 & m_7' \\ m_{16}' & F_4 & m_8 & m_{12}' \end{pmatrix} \implies \begin{pmatrix} F_1 & F_4 & F_3 & NF \\ NF & F_4 & F_3 & NF \\ F_1 & NF & F_3 & NF \\ F_1 & F_4 & NF & NF \end{pmatrix}.$$

Three faults F_1, F_3 and F_4 are present in $(0,0)^{th}$, $(2,3)^{th}$, $(3,1)^{th}$ locations (i.e., in case of MixColumns, four bytes are faulty). So, an attacker fails to form any linear equation based on the keys $(k_1, k_{14}, k_{11}, k_8)$:

$$[ISB(m_1 + k_1) + ISB(m_1' + k_1)] = NF \times [ISB(m_{14} + k_{14}) + ISB(m_{14}' + k_{14})].$$

$$\boldsymbol{NF} \times [ISB(m_{14}+k_{14})+ISB(m'_{14}+k_{14})] = [ISB(m_{11}+k_{11})+ISB(m'_{11}+k_{11})].$$

$$[ISB(m_8+k_8)+ISB(m'_8+k_8)] = \boldsymbol{NF} \times [ISB(m_{14}+k_{14})+ISB(m'_{14}+k_{14})].$$

We denote $\boldsymbol{NF}$ as there is no-fault into the cell. Such $\boldsymbol{NF}$ restricts the adversary to form linear equation. Hence, the adversary has to perform an exhaustive search of 2^{32}.

To find the keys (k_9, k_6, k_3, k_{16}), an adversary is able to form two equations and it generates 160 keys approximately after pruning, i.e., $\approx 2^8$. In total, $2^8 \times 2^8 \approx 2^{16}$ candidate keys are generated.

$$[(ISB(m_3+k_3)+ISB(m'_3+k_3)] = [ISB(m_9+k_9)+ISB(m'_9+k_9)].$$

$$[(ISB(m_9+k_9)+ISB(m'_9+k_9)] = \boldsymbol{NF} \times [ISB(m_{16}+k_{16})+ISB(m'_{16}+k_{16})].$$

$$[ISB(m_6+k_6)+ISB(m'_6+k_6)] = [ISB(m_9+k_9)+ISB(m'_9+k_9)].$$

Now in order to obtain $(k_5, k_2, k_{15}, k_{12})$, an attacker fails to form any linear equations:

$$\boldsymbol{NF} \times [ISB(m_{12}+k_{12})+ISB(m'_{12}+k_{12})] = [ISB(m_5+k_5)+ISB(m'_5+k_5)].$$

$$[ISB(m_5+k_5)+ISB(m'_5+k_5)] = \boldsymbol{NF} \times [ISB(m_2+k_2)+ISB(m'_2+k_2)].$$

$$\boldsymbol{NF} \times [ISB(m_{15}+k_{15})+ISB(m'_{15}+k_{15})] = [ISB(m_5+k_5)+ISB(m'_5+k_5)].$$

Hence, the adversary explores all 2^{32} keys. To obtain the keys $(k_{13}, k_{10}, k_7, k_4)$, an attacker uses the following equations:

$$[ISB(m_{10}+k_{10})+ISB(m'_{10}+k_{10})] = \boldsymbol{NF} \times [ISB(m_7+k_7)+ISB(m'_7+k_7)].$$

$$\boldsymbol{NF} \times [ISB(m_7+k_7)+ISB(m'_7+k_7)] = [ISB(m_4+k_4)+ISB(m'_4+k_4)].$$

$$\boldsymbol{NF} \times [ISB(m_{13}+k_{13})+ISB(m'_{13}+k_{13})] = \boldsymbol{NF} \times [ISB(m_7+k_7)+ISB(m'_7+k_7)].$$

Since no equations are formed, the adversary performs an exhaustive search of 2^{32}.

3.2 Analysis of DFA with MixColumns Like Matrix M_2

In this section, we analyse the same equation formation when M_2 is used in the MixColumns layer. After 8th round MixColumns, the fault propagation is described as follows:

$$\begin{pmatrix} 00\ 01\ 01\ 01 \\ 01\ 00\ 01\ 01 \\ 01\ 01\ 00\ 01 \\ 01\ 01\ 01\ 00 \end{pmatrix} \times \begin{pmatrix} F & m_5 & m_9 & m_{13} \\ m_2 & m_6 & m_{10} & m_{14} \\ m_3 & m_7 & m_{11} & m_{15} \\ m_4 & m_8 & m_{12} & m_{16} \end{pmatrix} = \begin{pmatrix} m'_1 & m'_5 & m'_9 & m'_{13} \\ F_2 & m'_6 & m'_{10} & m'_{14} \\ F_3 & m'_7 & m'_{11} & m'_{15} \\ F_4 & m'_8 & m'_{12} & m'_{16} \end{pmatrix}.$$

After 9th round ShiftRows and MixColumns, the state matrix with fault is illustrated below:

$$\begin{pmatrix} m_1' & m_5' & m_9' & m_{13}' \\ m_6' & m_{10}' & m_{14}' & F_2 \\ m_{11}' & m_{15}' & F_3 & m_7' \\ m_{16}' & F_4 & m_8' & m_{12}' \end{pmatrix} \implies \begin{pmatrix} NF & F_4 & F_3 & F_2 \\ NF & F_4 & F_3 & NF \\ NF & F_4 & NF & F_2 \\ NF & NF & F_3 & F_2 \end{pmatrix}.$$

Three faults F_2, F_3 and F_4 are present in $(1,3)^{th}$, $(2,2)^{th}$, $(3,1)^{th}$ locations. NF restricts the adversary to form any linear equations to find out the keys $(k_1, k_{14}, k_{11}, k_8)$:

$$NF \times [ISB(m_1 + k_1) + ISB(m_1' + k_1)] = NF \times [ISB(m_{14} + k_{14}) + ISB(m_{14}' + k_{14})].$$

$$NF \times [ISB(m_{14} + k_{14}) + ISB(m_{14}' + k_{14})] = NF \times [ISB(m_{11} + k_{11}) + ISB(m_{11}' + k_{11})].$$

$$NF \times [ISB(m_8 + k_8) + ISB(m_8' + k_8)] = NF \times [ISB(m_{14} + k_{14}) + ISB(m_{14}' + k_{14})].$$

As NF value is present in the coefficient matrix, no equations are formed. Hence, the adversary uses brute force technique to find the key bytes. In total, an adversary explores $\approx 2^{32}$ candidate keys.

To find the keys (k_9, k_6, k_3, k_{16}), an adversary fails to form one linear equation. The remaining two equations generate $\approx 2^8$ candidate keys. Hence, the following equations generate $\approx 2^{16}$ keys.

$$NF \times [(ISB(m_3 + k_3) + ISB(m_3' + k_3)] = [ISB(m_9 + k_9) + ISB(m_9' + k_9)].$$

$$[(ISB(m_9 + k_9) + ISB(m_9' + k_9)] = [ISB(m_{16} + k_{16}) + ISB(m_{16}' + k_{16})].$$

$$[ISB(m_6 + k_6) + ISB(m_6' + k_6)] = [ISB(m_9 + k_9) + ISB(m_9' + k_9)].$$

In order to obtain $(k_5, k_2, k_{15}, k_{12})$, an attacker uses the following equations:

$$[ISB(m_{12} + k_{12}) + ISB(m_{12}' + k_{12})] = [ISB(m_5 + k_5) + ISB(m_5' + k_5)].$$

$$[ISB(m_5 + k_5) + ISB(m_5' + k_5)] = NF \times [ISB(m_2 + k_2) + ISB(m_2' + k_2)].$$

$$[ISB(m_{15} + k_{15}) + ISB(m_{15}' + k_{15})] = [ISB(m_5 + k_5) + ISB(m_5' + k_5)].$$

From the above system of equations, an adversary generates $\approx 2^{16}$ candidate keys in total. Here, one equation generates 80 keys and the remaining two equations produce 160 keys, i.e., 2^8 candidate keys. The equation that contains NF generates 2^8 candidate keys. To obtain the keys $(k_{13}, k_{10}, k_7, k_4)$, an attacker uses the following equations:

$$[ISB(m_{10} + k_{10}) + ISB(m_{10}' + k_{10})] = [ISB(m_7 + k_7) + ISB(m_7' + k_7)].$$

$$[ISB(m_7 + k_7) + ISB(m_7' + k_7)] = NF \times [ISB(m_4 + k_4) + ISB(m_4' + k_4)].$$

$$[ISB(m_{13} + k_{13}) + ISB(m_{13}' + k_{13})] = [ISB(m_7 + k_7) + ISB(m_7' + k_7)].$$

In this case, an adversary generates $\approx 2^{16}$ candidate keys in total.

4   Results

In literature, the most successful DFA attack complexity of AES is 2^{32}, which is optimized further to 2^8. To protect AES from such attack, we propose Mix-Columns like matrix M_1 and it is shown that the adversary fails to form some linear equations. Our analysis states that an adversary has to explore $2^{32} \times 2^{16} \times 2^{32} \times 2^{32} \approx 2^{112}$ key bits exhaustively when the location of fault is known. In case, the fault location is completely unknown, the adversary explores all 16 possible locations in the state matrix and exhaustive search complexity is $2^4 \times 2^{112} \approx 2^{116}$.

Now, if the matrix M_2 is used in the MixColumns, an adversary has to explore $2^{32} \times 2^{16} \times 2^{16} \times 2^{16} \approx 2^{80}$ candidate keys if the fault location is known earlier. When the adversary does not have any idea on the fault location, it tries all 16 possible locations and attack complexity increases to $2^4 \times 2^{80} \approx 2^{84}$. Table 1 shows the comparative result of DFA on AES with the MixColumns like matrices M_1 and M_2.

Comparison with Ghosal et al. [34]. Recently, an additional diffusion layer MixColumn-Plus is proposed in [34] to protect AES against DFA attack. The end complexity of the attack [15,20] is increased to 2^{84} as claimed in [34]. Our matrices can be used in the MixColumn-Plus layer internally to get better DFA resistance, i.e., 2^{116}. In that case, the order of the MixColumn-Plus matrix coefficients need to be changed only.

Avalanche Effect. We check the avalanche effect in AES with MixColumns matrix M_2 (Table 2) and original AES (Table 3). In this observation, we change one bit of the plaintext at a time in original AES. As a result, more than 60 bits are changed in the ciphertext. When AES is used with MixColumns matrix M_2, 55 to 75 bits are changed on average when one bit is flipped in the plaintext. In this experiment, we consider two different plaintexts and a single bit is modified in the plaintext. The resultant ciphertexts are described in the table for a particular key $K= \{0f\ 15\ 71\ c9\ 47\ d9\ e8\ 59\ 0c\ b7\ ad\ d6\ af\ 7f\ 67\ 98\}$.

Real World Deployment and Applications. When it comes to developing embedded IoT devices, such matrices can be incorporated to protect the cipher against Differential Fault Analysis attack. In software library such as OpenSSL crypto library (libcrypto), Libgcrypt, Crypto++, cryptlib etc., we can incorporate the proposed matrices rather than original AES MixColumns matrix to protect against DFA attacks.

Limitations and Future Work. The major limitation of this work is that we only check the avalanche effect as a security measure. Also, the branch number of the proposed matrices are 4 whereas the original AES matrix has branch number of 5. Though the branch number is reduced, the security against DFA attack is increased. Our further research work is to perform various cryptanalysis,

Table 1. DFA Attack results on original AES and AES with matrices M_1, M_2 against DFA

Fault Attack Scheme	AES version	Fault Injection Round	Original AES Exhaustive Search key	AES with M_1 Matrix Exhaustive Search key	AES with M_2 Matrix Exhaustive Search key
Byte Fault [15]	AES-128	Before 8th or 9th MixColumns	2^{36}	2^{116}	2^{84}
Diagonal Fault [16]	AES-128	Before 8th SubBytes faulty diagonal	2^{34}	2^{116}	2^{84}
DFA on SPN cipher [6]	AES-128	Before 8th SubBytes or 9th SubBytes	2^{40}	2^{90} or more	2^{70} or more
DFA on AES using byte fault [20]	AES-128	Before 8th or 9th MixColumns	2^{8}	2^{116}	2^{84}
DFA on AES-192 AES-256 [18]	AES-192	Before 8th or 9th MixColumns	2^{32}, 2^{8}	2^{90}, 2^{90} or more	2^{70}, 2^{70} or more
DFA on AES-192 AES-256 [18]	AES-256	Before 8th or 9th MixColumns	2^{32}	2^{90} or more	2^{70} or more

Table 2. The result of avalanche effect on AES with MixColumns M_2 matrix

Plaintext of size 128 bit	Faulty bit in a byte of the plaintext	Ciphertext of size 128 bit
02 23 45 67 99 ab cd ef fe dc ba 98 76 54 32 10	Original plaintext	77 35 dc f2 c1 1e 5a 45 0e 80 c6 c1 be 26 cb 8d
12 23 45 67 99 ab cd ef fe dc ba 98 76 54 32 10	4th bit from MSB	48 ab ee a9 2d 47 da 4c d3 0b 49 21 7c d5 af dd
02 33 45 66 99 ab cd ef fe dc ba 98 76 54 32 10	12th bit from MSB	e9 be c8 9a 86 c2 73 27 98 49 06 cb 8e 4f 9d 18
01 23 55 67 95 ab cd ef fe dc ba 98 76 54 32 10	20th bit from MSB	a4 9b b5 1e f3 20 c3 2b 9b 53 e9 48 e4 09 50 1f
02 00 00 00 00 03 00 00 00 00 05 00 00 00 00 07	Original plaintext	75 d0 72 e6 a4 9d 28 d2 3d bc 76 bf 99 9e 7f 4f
02 00 01 00 00 03 00 00 00 00 05 00 00 00 00 07	24th bit from MSB	84 01 7f 89 60 8b 40 c9 58 55 b2 e6 81 1e cd 5b

i.e., Differential Cryptanalysis, Linear Cryptanalysis on the AES with the proposed MixColumns matrices M_1 and M_2. To deploy it in the practical scenario, we need to perform an analysis to measure the energy, delays in hardware applications.

68   A. K. Ghosal

Table 3. The result of avalanche effect on original AES

Plaintext of size 128 bit	Faulty bit in a byte of the plaintext	Ciphertext of size 128 bit
02 23 45 67 99 ab cd ef	Original	d7 6f 6f 02 73 be f9 ec
fe dc ba 98 76 54 32 10	plaintext	7d cc 32 9c 3a 4d 82 d7
12 23 45 67 99 ab cd ef	4th bit	0a 59 3c fa 74 61 e1 e7
fe dc ba 98 76 54 32 10	from MSB	72 3b dd 57 ff 60 40 09
02 33 45 66 99 ab cd ef	12th bit	31 f0 f8 ba db 66 a2 e9
fe dc ba 98 76 54 32 10	from MSB	72 17 b7 14 4c 1f ab e3
01 23 55 67 95 ab cd ef	20th bit	c6 c7 7b eb c6 08 5a 41
fe dc ba 98 76 54 32 10	from MSB	33 29 69 26 a9 b6 f6 73
02 00 00 00 00 03 00 00	Original	7f 85 58 26 5a 01 c0 a8
00 00 05 00 00 00 00 07	plaintext	19 62 67 61 ba 02 85 46
02 00 01 00 00 03 00 00	24th bit	59 a0 fc 74 8e 78 39 13
00 00 05 00 00 00 00 07	from MSB	17 b2 86 d4 4b 61 44 57

5 Conclusion

In this work, we propose new diffusion matrices to the AES block cipher. The main goal of our work is to protect the AES against DFA attacks. Such matrices make the DFA attack costly to the adversary. The proposed M_1 matrix increases the attack complexity to 2^{116}.

References

1. Biham, E., Shamir, A.: Differential fault analysis of secret key cryptosystems. In: Kaliski, B.S. (ed.) CRYPTO 1997. LNCS, vol. 1294, pp. 513–525. Springer, Heidelberg (1997). https://doi.org/10.1007/BFb0052259
2. Boneh, D., DeMillo, R.A., Lipton, R.J.: On the importance of checking cryptographic protocols for faults. In: Fumy, W. (ed.) EUROCRYPT 1997. LNCS, vol. 1233, pp. 37–51. Springer, Heidelberg (1997). https://doi.org/10.1007/3-540-69053-0_4
3. Barreto, P.S.L.M., Rijmen, V.: The Khazad legacy-level block cipher. Primitive submitted to NESSIE (2000)
4. Joan, D., Vincent, R.: The Design of Rijndael. Springer, New York (2002). https://doi.org/10.1007/978-3-662-04722-4
5. Skorobogatov, S.P., Anderson, R.J.: Optical fault induction attacks. In: Kaliski, B.S., Koç, K., Paar, C. (eds.) CHES 2002. LNCS, vol. 2523, pp. 2–12. Springer, Heidelberg (2003). https://doi.org/10.1007/3-540-36400-5_2
6. Piret, G., Quisquater, J.-J.: A differential fault attack technique against SPN structures, with application to the AES and KHAZAD. In: Walter, C.D., Koç, Ç.K., Paar, C. (eds.) CHES 2003. LNCS, vol. 2779, pp. 77–88. Springer, Heidelberg (2003). https://doi.org/10.1007/978-3-540-45238-6_7

7. Golić, J.D., Tymen, C.: Multiplicative masking and power analysis of AES. In: Kaliski, B.S., Koç, K., Paar, C. (eds.) CHES 2002. LNCS, vol. 2523, pp. 198–212. Springer, Heidelberg (2003). https://doi.org/10.1007/3-540-36400-5_16
8. Blömer, J., Seifert, J.-P.: Fault based cryptanalysis of the advanced encryption standard (AES). In: Wright, R.N. (ed.) FC 2003. LNCS, vol. 2742, pp. 162–181. Springer, Heidelberg (2003). https://doi.org/10.1007/978-3-540-45126-6_12
9. Dusart, P., Letourneux, G., Vivolo, O.: Differential fault analysis on A.E.S. In: Zhou, J., Yung, M., Han, Y. (eds.) ACNS 2003. LNCS, vol. 2846, pp. 293–306. Springer, Heidelberg (2003). https://doi.org/10.1007/978-3-540-45203-4_23
10. Giraud, C.: DFA on AES. In: Dobbertin, H., Rijmen, V., Sowa, A. (eds.) AES 2004. LNCS, vol. 3373, pp. 27–41. Springer, Heidelberg (2005). https://doi.org/10.1007/11506447_4
11. Herbst, C., Oswald, E., Mangard, S.: An AES smart card implementation resistant to power analysis attacks. In: Zhou, J., Yung, M., Bao, F. (eds.) ACNS 2006. LNCS, vol. 3989, pp. 239–252. Springer, Heidelberg (2006). https://doi.org/10.1007/11767480_16
12. Bar-El, H., Choukri, H., Naccache, D., Tunstall, M., Whelan, C.: The sorcerer's apprentice guide to fault attacks. Proc. IEEE 94(2), 370–382 (2006)
13. Schramm, K., Paar, C.: Higher order masking of the AES. In: Pointcheval, D. (ed.) CT-RSA 2006. LNCS, vol. 3860, pp. 208–225. Springer, Heidelberg (2006). https://doi.org/10.1007/11605805_14
14. Bogdanov, A., et al.: PRESENT: an ultra-lightweight block cipher. In: Paillier, P., Verbauwhede, I. (eds.) CHES 2007. LNCS, vol. 4727, pp. 450–466. Springer, Heidelberg (2007). https://doi.org/10.1007/978-3-540-74735-2_31
15. Mukhopadhyay, D.: An improved fault based attack of the advanced encryption standard. In: Preneel, B. (ed.) AFRICACRYPT 2009. LNCS, vol. 5580, pp. 421–434. Springer, Heidelberg (2009). https://doi.org/10.1007/978-3-642-02384-2_26
16. Saha, D., Mukhopadhyay, D., RoyChowdhury, D.: A Diagonal Fault Attack on the Advanced Encryption Standard, Cryptology ePrint Archive, Report 2009/581 (2009)
17. Medwed, M., Standaert, F.-X., Großschädl, J., Regazzoni, F.: Fresh re-keying: security against side channel and fault attacks for low cost devices. In: Bernstein, D.J., Lange, T. (eds.) AFRICACRYPT 2010. LNCS, vol. 6055, pp. 279–296. Springer, Heidelberg (2010). https://doi.org/10.1007/978-3-642-12678-9_17
18. Kim, C.H.: Differential fault analysis against AES-192 and AES-256 with minimal faults. In: 2010 Workshop on Fault Diagnosis and Tolerance in Cryptography (FDTC), pp. 3–9. IEEE (2010)
19. Rivain, M., Prouff, E.: Provably secure higher-order masking of AES. In: Mangard, S., Standaert, F.-X. (eds.) CHES 2010. LNCS, vol. 6225, pp. 413–427. Springer, Heidelberg (2010). https://doi.org/10.1007/978-3-642-15031-9_28
20. Tunstall, M., Mukhopadhyay, D., Ali, S.: Differential fault analysis of the advanced encryption standard using a single fault. In: Ardagna, C.A., Zhou, J. (eds.) WISTP 2011. LNCS, vol. 6633, pp. 224–233. Springer, Heidelberg (2011). https://doi.org/10.1007/978-3-642-21040-2_15
21. Van Woudenberg, J., Witteman, M., Menarini, F.: Practical optical fault injection on secure microcontrollers. In: 2011 Workshop on Fault Diagnosis and Tolerance in Cryptography (FDTC), pp. 91–99 (2011)
22. Gierlichs, B., Schmidt, J.-M., Tunstall, M.: Infective computation and dummy rounds: fault protection for block ciphers without check-before-output. In: Hevia, A., Neven, G. (eds.) LATINCRYPT 2012. LNCS, vol. 7533, pp. 305–321. Springer, Heidelberg (2012). https://doi.org/10.1007/978-3-642-33481-8_17

23. Lomné, V., Roche, T., Thillard, A.: On the need of randomness in fault attack countermeasures - application to AES. In: Bertoni, G., Gierlichs, B. (eds.) Fault Diagnosis and Tolerance in Cryptography, FDTC 2012, pp. 85–94. IEEE Computer Society (2012)

24. Battistello, A., Giraud, C.: Fault analysis of infective AES computations. In: 2013 Workshop on Fault Diagnosis and Tolerance in Cryptography (FDTC), pp. 101–107 (2013)

25. Moro, N., Heydemann, K., Encrenaz, E., Robisson, B.: Formal verification of a software countermeasure against instruction skip attacks. J. Cryptogr. Eng. 4(3), 145–156 (2014). https://doi.org/10.1007/s13389-014-0077-7

26. Tupsamudre, H., Bisht, S., Mukhopadhyay, D.: Destroying fault invariant with randomization - a countermeasure for AES against differential fault attacks. In: Batina, L., Robshaw, M. (eds.) CHES 2014. LNCS, vol. 8731, pp. 93–111. Springer, Heidelberg (2014). https://doi.org/10.1007/978-3-662-44709-3_6

27. Banik, S., et al.: Midori: a block cipher for low energy. In: Iwata, T., Cheon, J.H. (eds.) ASIACRYPT 2015. LNCS, vol. 9453, pp. 411–436. Springer, Heidelberg (2015). https://doi.org/10.1007/978-3-662-48800-3_17

28. Breier, J., Jap, D., Bhasin, S.: The other side of the coin: analyzing software encoding schemes against fault injection attacks. In: 2016 IEEE International Symposium on Hardware Oriented Security and Trust, HOST 2016, McLean, VA, USA, 3–5 May 2016, pp. 209–216 (2016)

29. Goudarzi, D., Rivain, M.: How fast can higher-order masking be in software? In: Coron, J.S., Nielsen, J. (eds.) [11], pp. 567–597. Springer, Cham (2017)

30. Patranabis, S., Chakraborty, A., Mukhopadhyay, D.: Fault tolerant infective countermeasure for AES. J. Hardware Syst. Secur. 1(1), 3–17 (2017)

31. Zhang, J., Wu, N., Zhou, F., Ge, F., Zhang, X.: Securing the AES cryptographic circuit against both power and fault attacks. J. Electr. Eng. Technol. 14(5), 2171–2180 (2019). https://doi.org/10.1007/s42835-019-00226-6

32. Murdock, K., Oswald, D., Garcia, F.D., Van Bulck, J., Gruss, D., Piessens, F.: Plundervolt: software-based fault injection attacks against Intel SGX. In: 41st IEEE Symposium on Security and Privacy (2020)

33. Gruber, M., et al.: DOMREP-an orthogonal countermeasure for arbitrary order side-channel and fault attack protection. IEEE Trans. Inf. Forensics Secur. 16, 4321–4335 (2021)

34. Ghosal, A.K., Roychowdhury, D.: Strengthening the security of AES against differential fault attack. In: Yuan, X., Bai, G., Alcaraz, C., Majumdar, S. (eds.) Network and System Security, pp. 727–744. Springer, Cham (2022). https://doi.org/10.1007/978-3-031-23020-2_41

Variants of Crypto-Jacking Attacks and Their Detection Techniques

P. Mercy Praise[1], S. Basil Xavier[1](✉), Anoop Jose[1](✉), G. Jaspher W. Kathrine[1](✉), and J. Andrew[2](✉)

[1] Department of CSE, Karunya Institute of Technology and Sciences, Coimbatore, India
{paradisemercy,anoopjose21}@karunya.edu.in, {basilxavier, kathrine}@karunya.edu
[2] Manipal Institute of Technology, Manipal Academy of Higher Education, Manipal, Udupi, Karnataka, India
andrew.j@manipal.edu

Abstract. Crypto Jacking attack is a type of resource spying in which a crypto-currency mining script is run by the attacker on the victim's machine to profit. Since 2017 it has been widely used and was previously the most serious threat to network security. Because of the number of malicious actors has increased there is a recent increase in the value of cryptocurrencies. The availability of bit-coin mining software has grown significantly. Mining for crypto-currency has a high inclination to spread. Malware can unintentionally use resources, harm interests, and cause further genuine damage to assets. Learning and identifying new malware have the traits of still being unique and self-sufficient, and they cannot be acquired adaptively in order to overcome the aforementioned concerns. Recently, other countermeasures have been introduced, each with its own set of features and performance, but each with its unique design. In order to increase the profitability of crypto-jacking, attackers are expanding their reach to browsers, network devices, and even Internet of Things (IoT) devices. Browsers, for example, are a particularly enticing target for attackers looking to obtain sensitive data from victims. The listed methods are intended to safeguard the individual user, network, and outsiders, particularly against insiders. The newness of the paper is a comprehensive overview of bitcoin along with crypto-jacking malware detection is presented in order to analyze various types of systems based on behaviour-based, host-based, network flow-based, and so on methods. The main aim of the analysis is based on the supervised and unsupervised machine learning algorithms and other algorithms used in the detection of crypto-jacking malware. In the proposed paper combination of the decision tree method (based on Behaviour, Executable) and the crying jackpot method (based on Host, Network) are examined to classify the type of which crypto-jacking attack that takes place within the target victim. The uniqueness of the paper is informative with real-world applications for malware recognition and malware categorization to detect a crypto-jacking attack.

Keywords: Crypto-jacking · Behaviour-based · Host-based · Network-based · Crypto-currency

© The Author(s), under exclusive license to Springer Nature Singapore Pte Ltd. 2023
S. Prabhu et al. (Eds.): ATIS 2022, CCIS 1804, pp. 71–87, 2023.
https://doi.org/10.1007/978-981-99-2264-2_6

1   Introduction

Every day, people who are unaware of the notion of cryptocurrencies want a quick and easy strategy to gain some crypto wealth. Cryptocurrency operates a broad range of financial operations on the Internet and is based on mathematical algorithms [1]. It is not reliant on third-party credit institutions and is available to anyone who has agreed to it [2]. Crypto coins often need massive amounts of computing power, with the Bitcoin network. The growing popularity of cryptocurrency inspires crypto jackets, a type of malware used by hackers which are used to mine cryptocurrency on victims' computers for profit [3]. With the help of specific scripts crypto-jacking, or malicious browser-based crypto-mining programs start the background mining process (e.g. JavaScript), which is the most common hijacking method, particularly since the Coin Hive browser miner was released in 2017 [4]. Cybercriminals are refocusing their energies on crypto-jacking a less dangerous but lucrative behaviour. Several ways for openly taking execution cycles from victims have been disclosed. Forking popular GitHub projects and augmenting injection of JavaScript code into high-traffic websites through standard cross-site scripting (XSS) attacks, with crypto-jacking code, and compromise security by launching seemingly harmless android applications are all examples of cyber-attacks to mine cryptocurrencies into Google's Play Store are examples of such methods [5]. As a result, early identification of crypto-jacking malware is critical in order to limit victim losses. Firstly, the uniqueness of the paper describes the life of browser-based mining's revival on the system based along with the overview of bitcoin. It focuses on crypto-jacking (also known as coin jacking and drive-by mining), a phrase invented to describe the invisibility of mining bitcoin using a susceptible user's computer capabilities. In-browser mining is technical, a subset of crypto-jacking. Most people, however, use the term to refer to browser-based mining. When a user visits a website, mining occurs within the client browser, and then different system-based crypto-jacking malware is examined based on behaviour, host, network, and hybrid. Detection techniques of crypto-jacking malware are examined using supervised and unsupervised machine learning and other algorithms in order to reduce crypto-jacking's resource usage and can significantly minimize victim losses.

2   Related Works

2.1   Overview of Bitcoin and Cryptocurrency

It is a digital payment system which is known as crypto-currency that validates transactions without any bank connection. It lets you send and receive money from people all around the world known as a peer-to-peer payment system [6]. Rather than Tangible money that may be exchanged and sold in the real world, cryptocurrency payments are exclusive as digital inputs to an electronic database signaling particular transactions. Transactions involving Bitcoin money are recorded on a public ledger. Digital wallets are where cryptocurrency is kept. A decentralized system, rather than a single authority, uses the term "cryptocurrency" to authenticate transactions and store records for a digital currency called bitcoin through encrypted transactions [7]. To store and transport bitcoin data between wallets and public ledgers, specific programming is necessary.

Privacy and security are provided through encryption. The cryptocurrency was the first currently well-known bitcoin. With speculators driving prices upward on a daily basis, the majority of interest in bitcoin is speculative.

2.2 How Does Cryptocurrency Work?

Blockchain is a decentralized public ledger that records and maintains currency holders with all transactions and is updated. Generating bitcoin units to solve tough mathematical problems with the help of computer power is a way of mining [8]. Currencies that are bought from brokers and users are kept safe in wallets. Blockchain technology and cryptocurrency applications are still relatively new financial terms, with more on the way, even though bitcoin has been in existence since 2009. The technology might be used to trade bonds, shares, and other financial assets in the future.

Hussein Hellani et al. [11] have proposed a new application feature with numerous additional benefits like high reliability, reluctance to change, low latency, and efficiencies, as well as a quiz to assist enterprises in better utilizing the blockchain's potential.

Dejan Vujičić et al. [12] have proposed an overview of the development of digital currency, its theoretical underpinnings, and its two most promising implementations, Bitcoin and Ethereum. As of the 30th of January 2018, 03:00 GMT, there were 1,498 crypto-currencies listed across 8,250 marketplaces, with a total market value of \$556,471.064.589. For the years 2011 to 2018, TR32043 from the Ministry of Education, Science, and Technological Development of the Republic of Serbia granted the detailed work of this application.

Tyler Thomas et al. [15] have proposed many publicly accessible tools that can't discover transactions produced by Hierarchical Deterministic (HD) wallets because of flaws in their address derivation techniques but can be detected by BlockQuery. BlockQuery meets all four specified querying criteria: confidentiality, open source, automatic key representation conversion, and manual derivation depth adjustment.

Hershih et al. [17] have proposed a smart contract-based storage verification architecture as recommended by Ethereum smart contracts, the decentralized blockchain technology that engages in mining location verification and allows users to locate mining locations. They looked into a variety of contract security issues, such as re-entry and TOD.

Xiao Fan Liu et al. [20] have proposed the Data mining techniques used to process bitcoin transactions. Research majorly concentrates on transaction tracing, blockchain address linkage, aggregate user analysis habits, and individual user behaviours and is even used by machine learning techniques to create models that distinguish and identify economic players in a transaction network (crypto-currency exchanges, online wallets, market places, gambling games, and mixing services).

Ahmed Afif Monrat et al. [22] has proposed the use of cryptocurrency, blockchain and risk management, healthcare facilities, and financial and social services are all examples of financial and social services. Blockchain design has challenges with scalability, privacy, interoperability, energy usage, and regulatory considerations. Usage of blockchain with the development of more practical and efficient industrial applications that may completely benefit and achieve the objectives.

Lasse Herskind et al. [23] has proposed that digital currency evolve from electronic cash to crypto-currencies, and highlighted three research areas that will help cryptocurrencies be more private: transaction propagation techniques, thrustless zero-knowledge proofs, and without a trusted setup having a brief ZK proof systems. The methods used in Zero-knowledge systems, which are more powerful than their decoy-based counterparts, are used to achieve anonymity. True anonymity and network propagation with the space of privacy-enhancing methods have the potential to play a critical role in the fight and are the most fertile for future exploration.

Yannan Li et al. [24] have proposed a novel cryptocurrency that balances user privacy and accountability. They provide a comprehensive design for Traceable Monero that includes two mechanisms: Long-term addresses and one-time addresses for money transfers. The security of Traceable Monero's is crucial in confirming transactions and balancing user privacy and responsibility. The proposed architecture achieves correctness, balance, anonymity, and traceability. The proposed system is as efficient as the underlying Monero, according to both the efficiency study and implementation results.

Massimo Bartoletti et al. [25] have proposed an exhaustive analysis of the scientific literature on cryptocurrency scams. They create a homogenous dataset of thousands of records from public sources that detect frauds automatically and evaluate the tool's effectiveness using industry standards metrics of performance. It has made a fraud dataset available that includes 47,075 address-reported frauds (with 163,777 complaints in total) and there were 8,066 URL-reported frauds (with 187,404 snapshots).

Farida Sabry et al. [27] have proposed and examined the use of artificial intelligence techniques to address issues: in the crypto-currency sector, including mining, cybersecurity, anonymity, and privacy. A comparison of different research based on methodology and datasets used was presented for each class and identified potential research gaps for future progress in this highly dynamic field. The survey will be extremely beneficial to scholars interested in applying AL and machine learning approaches to the field of crypto-currency. It also identifies prospective research gaps and areas for development.

Ling Xiong, Fagen Li et al. [29] have proposed an approach to multi-server privacy awareness authentication based on blockchain. Systems with efficient revocation that addresses a variety of security concerns mutual authentication, user anonymity, and perfect forward security are examples of such features. The proposed technique improves communication performance, making it suitable for use in real-world applications.

2.3 Types of Crypto-Currency

Bitcoin: Bitcoin, the coin that started the cryptocurrency era, is still the most people see when they think about digital cash. Satoshi Nakamoto, the currency's enigmatic founder. In 2009 [9], it was launched. It's been a roller-coaster ride since then. Bitcoin, on the other hand, did not enter the public mind until 2017.

Ethereum: The name of the cryptocurrency platform, Ethereum, is the second most common name in the cryptocurrency sector [10]. To conduct a range of things, the smart contract feature of Ethereum contributes to its popularity even when the system allows you to use ether (the currency).

Tether: Tether coins cost one dollar each. This is due to the fact that tether's stablecoin is linked to the value of a single asset, in this case, the US dollar. Tether is commonly used as a bridge currency when traders transfer from one cryptocurrency to another. Instead of paying back the money, they use Tether [11]. Some people are concerned that Tether is not secure because it is not backed by reserves of dollars, but rather by a type of short-term unsecured debt.

BNB: Binance, is one of the world's major cryptocurrency exchanges, issues the cryptocurrency BNB. Binance Coin, which was designed to pay for reduced transaction fees, can now be used to make payments as well as purchase other goods and services.

USD Coin: USD Coin, like Tether, is a stablecoin with a fixed value based on the US dollar [12]. According to the currency's creators, it is backed by wholly reserved assets or assets of the money backed by entirely reserved assets or assets of "equal fair value" held in accounts at recognized US financial institutions, according to its inventors.

XRP: Users of XRP, originally Ripple which was founded in 2012, can accept payments in a variety of real-world currencies. It allows payments, using a thrustless system, which might be advantageous in cross-border transactions with regard to Ripple [13].

Binance USD: Binance USD is a dollar-backed stablecoin developed by Binance in collaboration with Paxos. Binance USD debuted in 2019 and is governed by the Financial Services Department of New York [14]. The Ethereum blockchain serves as the foundation for the BUSD blockchain.

Cardano (ADA): The Cardano cryptocurrency system powers the currency's name ADA. Cardano uses smart contracts to provide identity management and was founded by Ethereum's co-founder.

Solana (SOL): In March 2020 it debuted that Solana is a newer cryptocurrency and claims about the speed with which transactions are performed as well as the general stability of its "web-scale" network. The total number of SOL coins that may be minted is limited to 480 million.

Dogecoin (DOGE): Dogecoin was formed as a joke following the development of Bitcoin and was called after an online meme portraying a Shibu Inu dog. Unlike many other digital currencies, Dogecoin has no restriction on the number of coins that may be issued. It may be used to send and receive money.

Polygon (MATIC): Polygon is a cryptocurrency that scales up the Ethereum cryptocurrency and focuses on being accessible to individuals producing digital apps. It was formerly known as Matic and was founded in 2017, but it changed its name to Polygon in 2021.

Polkadot (DOT): Polkadot, which will be launched in May 2020, is a digital currency that links blockchain technologies from other cryptocurrencies. Polka Dots co-founder is an Ethereum co-founder, and some industry analysts believe Polkadot is attempting to dethrone Ethereum (Fig. 1).

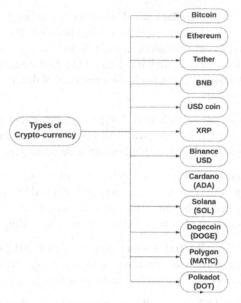

Fig. 1. Different types of crypto-currency

3 Crypto-Jacking

3.1 What is Crypto-Jacking?

Crypto Jacking is a type of cyberattack in which the hacker leverages the processing resources of the victim to mine bitcoin on their behalf. Crypto-jacking can target individual consumers, major organizations, and even industrial control systems [15]. Versions of crypto-jacking malware slow down infected PCs since mining takes precedence over other lawful processes. Crypto-jacking has become a massive global problem, with criminals gaining unauthorized access to computer systems in order to generate money with little risk or effort. Crypto-jacking is becoming more popular, with new ways to steal computer resources and mine for bitcoins emerging. Crypto-jacking malware is increasingly being included on YouTube, where users may easily click and run crypto-mining scripts [16].

3.2 How Does Crypto-Jacking Work?

Cybercriminals breach devices in order to install crypto-jacking software. In the background, the software steals bitcoins from cryptocurrency wallets or mines for them [17]. Unaware victims continue to use their devices on a daily basis, they may, however, detect poor performance or delays. Hackers can mine bitcoins on a victim's device in two ways:

- Crypto mining malware is installed on the machine by tricking the user into clicking on a fraudulent email link.
- When the victim's browser loads JavaScript code that runs and gets executed on their browser to infect a website or online adverts.

3.3 How Do Crypto-Jacking Scripts Spread?

Crypto hackers mine for bitcoin in three ways: they download malware to run crypto mining scripts, they steal IT infrastructure, and they gain access to cloud services.

File-Based Crypto-Jacking: To spread throughout the IT infrastructure malware is downloaded and activated, causing a crypto-mining script [18]. One of the most common methods of crypto jacking is the use of forged emails. An email is sent with a legitimate-looking attachment or link. When a user clicks on the attachment or link, the code that downloads the crypto-mining script is executed on the computer. The script is executed in the background when the user is unaware of it.

Browser-Based Crypto-Jacking: Within a web browser, crypto-jacking attacks can occur instantly, mining for bit-coin with IT infrastructure. Hackers create crypto-mining software in a programming language and insert it into a variety of websites. The code is downloaded to the users' PCs and the script is automatically performed. These malicious scripts may be discovered in advertisements, as well as in outdated and insecure Word Press plug-ins [19]. Crypto-jacking can also occur as a result of a supply chain assault in which crypto-mining code impacts JavaScript libraries.

Cloud-Based Crypto-Jacking: Cloud crypto-jacking is the practice of hackers searching to acquire access to the company's cloud services and search its API keys for code and files. Once allowed access, hackers can use their CPU resources indefinitely resulting in a huge increase in account charges with crypto mining. Using this strategy, hackers may considerably improve their crypto-jacking attempts [20] (Fig. 2).

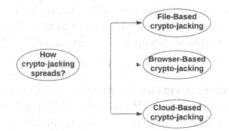

Fig. 2. Distribution of crypto-jacking malware

3.4 Crypto-Jacking Malware Detection

This portion of the study is about the existing crypto-jacking malware detection with various methods. The wide classification of crypto-jacking malware detection is shown in Fig. 3. The classification is done based on the system and on detection techniques [21]. System-based crypto-jacking malware is further defined as being Behaviour-based, Host-based, Network-based, and Hybrid-based systems. It is further divided into Supervised and Unsupervised Machine Learning detections based on the detection of crypto-jacking malware.

3.4.1 Based on Approach

- **Behaviour-based mining systems** are further classified as browser-based and executable-based detection systems. Browser-based mining happens when a user enters the infected website which is executed with JavaScript by crypto-jackets. Executable-based mining launches as an application on infected computers and delivers the payload which means when hackers exploit a vulnerability, a piece of code is executed.

  Dmitry Tanana et al. [3] have proposed a decision tree algorithm with a prototype detection program has been created. Out of 50 samples of crypto-jacking malware, the program was able to identify 41 of them; the remaining nine were undetectable by the decision tree algorithm. The program tested well against a small number of crypto-jacking samples, with an 82% success rate in a controlled virtual machine environment.

  Shayan Eskandari et al. [7] have proposed the current development of crypto-currency in-browser mining. When a user visits a website, JavaScript code is downloaded and executed client-side in the user's browser, then code mine cryptocurrency, generally without the user's knowledge and gathered 105 580 user sessions during the course of the trial, which lasted roughly 3 months, with each session lasting an average of 24 s.

- **Host-based mining systems** are further categorized depending on CPU, memory, network utilization, and the number of processes executing on the host. It analyzes traffic on the corporate network on which it is installed.

  F´abio Gomes et al. [8] have proposed a crypto-jacking detection system that tracks how much CPU each website's visitors use and collects the data 60 times throughout the authorized timeframe, which can range from 15 to 60 s. When no one is using the computer, a crypto miner is run at varying CPU usage rates (20%, 50%, 75%, and 100%), resulting in 240 runs (60 * 4).

- **Network-based mining systems** are further classified in terms of inbound and outbound traffic, packet counts, 80/HTTP, and 443/HTTPS ports [9]. It identifies harmful network flow and to evaluate all traffic, including all unicast traffic, it often needs unrestricted network access.

  Rupesh Raj Karn et al. [21] have proposed an ML-based method for recognizing and categorizing pods in Kubernetes cluster based on an active crypto-mining operation and by monitoring Linux-kernel system calls. SHAP and LIME have the highest system call prediction accuracy of more than 78%, whereas the LSTM autoencoder is the least adaptable owing to lengthier training periods and convergence instability. The tree decision model is the most accurate, with a precision of more than 97%.

- **Hybrid-based mining systems** are further defined as a mix of systems that addresses the drawbacks of behaviour-based, Host-based, and Network-based systems.

Guangquan Xu et al. [1] have proposed that the hybrid CJ Detector is a novel crypto-jacking dynamic detection system and more effective. Malicious mining is detected by monitoring CPU utilization and analyzing function call metadata. CJ Detector has a recognition accuracy of 99.33% Finally, investigated crypto-jacking activity in the real network by testing the web pages in Alexa 50K websites. It has the highest accuracy of 99.33% compared with other individual supervised and Unsupervised Machine Learning detection.

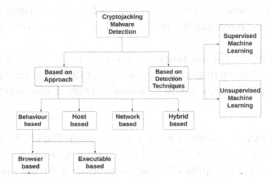

Fig. 3. Overview of crypto-jacking malware detection

3.4.2 Based on Detection Technique

Supervised Machine Learning is the presence of a supervisor functioning as a mentor which is required as the name implies. In essence, supervised learning happens when labeled data is used to teach or train the system. This means that some data has so far been concluded to be accurate. After that, a fresh collection of examples (data) is given by computer so that the supervised learning algorithm may assess the training data (set of training instances) and provide an appropriate result from labeled data. It would be able to identify prior assaults.

- **Random Forest** is a learning technique to resolve classification and regression problems in machine learning and is a popular supervised learning machine learning method that can be used [2]. Which is a technique for integrating several classifiers to solve a complicated issue and enhance model performance based on the notion of ensemble learning [4]. Its expected accuracy by averaging many decision trees of various subsets of a given dataset increases the classifier.

Maurantonio Caprolu et al. [2] have proposed that the Statistics and Machine Learning Toolbox Traffic-classification problems have been solved in MatLab (R2018a). The RF technique was even implemented in MatLab, specifically using the TreeBagger MatLab class. For the ROC of 0.99, it has an outstanding F1-score of 0.96. Many decision tree results are aggregated by the TreeBagger, decreasing overfitting and enhancing generalization.

Giorgio Di Tizio et al. [4] have proposed with the use of case-control research, they have examined crypto-jacking and demonstrated how specific technical aspects of online apps may serve as both positive and negative risk factors. Additionally, from public WWW, they have collected a list of websites in which a keyword or phrase is included in the source code and in the NoCoin6 and the JavaScript Blacklists for Miner-Block7.

- **Cross-sectional data analysis** is the technique of studying a data set at a specific point. Cross-sectional data can be collected using surveys and government databases [10]. The datasets include observations of various factors over time. Financial experts, for example, may wish to compare the financial standing of two companies.

Adam S. Hayes et al. [10] has proposed a mechanism to consistently value bitcoin by comparing the production of bitcoin to that of other digital currencies that are similar to bitcoin. Each cryptocurrency has in common to analyze cross-sectional data on 66 cryptocurrencies.

- **C4.5 algorithm** is a well-known Data Mining approach. The C4.5 algorithm functions as a Decision Tree Classifier. C4.5 is a decision tree-generating data mining method [13]. The C4.5 approach is quite effective for producing a useful judgment based on a sample of data.
- **Deep neural network (DNN)**, A deep net, also known as a high complexity neural network with at least two layers. Deep networks evaluate data in complex ways using advanced math models.

Antonio Pastor et al. [13] has proposed passively identifying such abusive crypto-mining activities in network surveillance. They built a variety of machine and deep learning models, were trained and tested, and a set of 51 characteristics per flow was generated using the Tsat tool, using IETF standard NetFlow/IPFIX metrics the second set of 8 features was captured. Businesses may identify mining activity utilizing Random Forest, C4.5, or fully connected Deep Neural networks.

- **Passive-active flow monitoring:** Active monitoring gives particular information about a situation. Passive monitoring collects data on all interactions [14]. Passive monitors, unlike active monitors, injecting test data into the network to imitate user activity is not permitted. It captures user data from specific network sites. Because passive monitors do not operate as often as active monitors, they may gather and create large volumes of performance data.

Vladimír Veselý et al. [14] have proposed Identifying bitcoin mining within corporate networks. They set up passive-active traffic monitoring (for Business networks) and the sMaSheD catalogue (for mining servers located everywhere on the internet). In contrast to the pure catalogue technique, passive-active detections are false positives, with a false positive rate low enough to allow active verification of the results.

- **Recurrent neural network (RNN)** A neural network that deals with time series or sequential data. Deep learning algorithms are generally employed for ordinal or temporal issues like language translation, natural language processing (NLP), speech recognition, and picture captioning; they may be obtained in popular apps like Siri, voice search, and Google Translate [16].

Abbas Yazdinejad et al. [16] have proposed a unique deep recurrent neural network detecting bitcoin malware risks using a network (RNN) learning model and gathered a real-world dataset with 200 benign and 500 crypto-currency malware samples. They also demonstrated how deep learners (LSTM) outperformed conventional models in dealing with bitcoin malware using classic machine Learning (ML) classifiers. Among the available configurations, the results show that a three-tier setup model has the highest detection accuracy rate of 98%. The findings revealed that it detected their malware family with 98.25% accuracy.

Shuangyu et al. [26] have proposed a practical, useful, and secure crypto-currency system for managing wallets based on semi-trusted social networks. Portable login on many devices, security-enhanced storage, no-password authentication, extendable key delegation, and blind wallet recovery are all part of the proposed solution. According to the results, their proposed systems incur considerable overhead and have minimal time delays, making them acceptable for real-world application (Fig. 4).

Unsupervised Machine Learning is the process of training a computer using unlabeled data and allowing the algorithm to function without the supervision of the data [22]. The machine's purpose in this example is to classify data based on similarities, patterns, and mismatched without any prior data training. Unlike supervised learning, there is no teacher present, suggesting that the machine will not be instructed [23], As a result, the computer's capabilities are restricted to determining the underlying structure of unlabeled data. It would detect unidentified assaults.

- **The Elbow Method** is one of the most well-known methods for obtaining the optimal value of k. A critical component of any unsupervised technique is the appropriate number of clusters into which the data may be grouped.
- **The Silhouette algorithm** is one method for determining the best number of clusters for an unsupervised learning methodology [9]. The number of clusters into which the data may be separated is an important element in an unsupervised learning strategy.
- **The DBSCAN method** is based on the straightforward ideas of "clusters" and "noise." The key premise is that the neighbourhood of a certain radius must contain at least a specific number of points for each cluster point.

Gilberto Gomes et al. [9] have proposed a hybrid strategy to detect crypto-jacking intrusion detection method, with a hybrid dataset that includes host-based and flow-based data. CRYING JACKPOT has been demonstrated to be a trustworthy and adaptable method for crypto-jacking detection. They experimentally assess CRYING JACKPOT, F1-scores of up to 97% with accuracy recall, and F1-scores ranging from 0.92 to 1.

- **Cross-stack Approach** is precisely what cross-platform testing achieves. It is an essential component of software quality assurance. It includes cross-platform browser testing as well as mobile and desktop device testing. This testing approach detects issues in usability, consistency, user interface, and performance on certain devices,

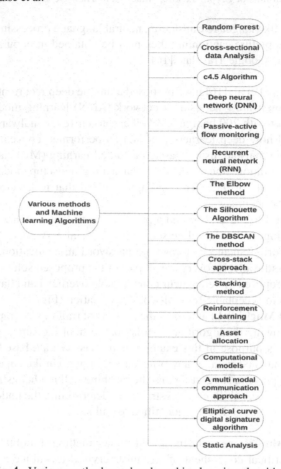

Fig. 4. Various methods used and machine learning algorithms

browser versions, and operating system combinations [5]. If cross-platform testing is not conducted, fully functional apps may fail on numerous browsers or browser versions, as well as different operating systems or versions. Large user bases would be alienated, resulting in decreased traffic, lost money, and unfavourable comments on the product itself.

Abdulrahman Abu Elkhail et al. [5] has proposed a method of dynamically identifying crypto-jacking attempts for finding JavaScript-based preventing web browsers from engaging in crypto-jacking activity and real user applications and workloads from the SPEC CPU2006 suite are tested.

- **Stacking method** is a prominent ensemble machine learning method for predicting multiple nodes to enhance model performance in order to make a new model [6]. It can use stacking to solve similar issues, train numerous models and then combine their output to build a superior-performing model.

Rui Zheng et al. [6] The CMalHunt ensemble learning Framework has been suggested to include the findings of behaviours features, domain knowledge features, and binary bytes characteristics. It illustrates that by combining categorization models with different feature types, CAMel Hunt outperforms the underlying machine learning models. The data collection comprises a small dataset (Lab dataset) as well as a big dataset (Real-world dataset). The datasets were released as part of the 2020 Big Data Security Analysis Competition, and the study provides critical information for practical machine learning applications for malware family classification and detection.

- **Reinforcement Learning** is a Machine Learning approach based on feedback in which an agent learns how to behave in a given environment by carrying out actions and monitoring the results [18].
- **Asset allocation** is a financial technique that attempts to balance risk and return in a portfolio by allocating assets depending on a person's objectives, risk tolerance, and investment horizon.

Zeinab Shahbazi ct al. [18] have proposed Hierarchical Machine learning without supervision and risk parity applied to the bitcoin architecture. The HRP has the best features and desirable diversity, and it provides a substantial alternative to transitory asset allocations and improves the risk management process. To get higher overall performance in a time period of danger control. 10,000 records make up the entire dataset, of which 80% were used for training sets and 20% for testing sets.

- **Computational models** are mathematical models that employ computer simulation to examine the quantitative behaviours of complicated systems [19]. When there are no obvious analytical solutions, a computer model can be used to predict how a system will behave under different situations.
- **A multimodal communication approach** is one in which an individual can communicate in a variety of ways, including speaking words, writing them down, and using a high-tech AAC device. Messages can also be conveyed through drawings, gestures, facial expressions, symbols, images, and other forms of communication.

Mehrnoosh Mirtaheri et al. [19] have proposed and evaluated a computational technique for automatically detecting bomb and dump frauds using information from social media networks. A multimodal technique for predicting the success of certain aspiration efforts. Telegram with adequate precision, and whether the resulting stake will meet the successfully anticipated goal price.

- **The elliptic curve digital signature technique** is used to establish a digital signature (ECDSA). It is almost entirely used by cryptocurrency retailers to authenticate their identification [31]. Certain websites, however, employ this strategy. We explore what makes the ECDSA algorithm unique and suggest potential issues that might make website implementation difficult.

B. Soumya et al. [28] The blockchain architecture and cloud computing technology, when combined, provide numerous approaches for minimizing computational costs in

84   P. M. Praise et al.

identifying anonymous documents delivered by the cloud server. To avoid private data loss, the Hyperledger blockchain's Linear Elliptic Curve Digital Signature (LECDS) was used. The suggested (LECDS) techniques guarantee 91.4% security against different human penetration testing assaults on the system. In this security study, the recommended method LECDS achieves 91.4% security when compared to existing techniques. In the medical blockchain network, MHT has 86.1% security, whereas Auth-Privacy Chain has 84.4%. Compared to previous techniques(500 tps) and AuthPrivacyChain(650 tps), LECDS (700 tps)transactions per second.

- **Static analysis** is a collection of tools for examining software source code or object code in order to learn how it works and develop criteria to ensure its correctness [32]. Static analysis examines source code without running it, exposing features such as model structure, data and control flow, syntax accuracy, and other factors.

Wenjuan Lian et al. [30] have proposed a deep learning model with many inputs and characteristics that accept several modes at the same time with different digital features and different digital dimensions. The static analysis method in their study extracts three separate features: Images in grayscale, byte/entropy histograms, and feature engineering. The model may adaptively learn multi-modal information and predict outcomes. The model's detection rate is 97.01% accurate, with a false alarm rate of only 0.63%.

4   Proposed Methodology

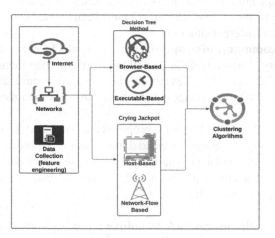

Fig. 5. Architecture Diagram for Crypto-Jacking Detection

This Crypto-Jacking Detection approach aims to spontaneously identify entities host targeted by crypto-jacking attackers by collecting, extracting, combining, and processing a group of data characteristics from the network technology. The data characteristics are gathered based on Behavior, Executable, Host, and Network Flow. Relation to the paper considered the content provided by Task Manager, Windows applications including Render Man, Adobe Photoshop, Blender, CPU, Network Utilization, memory, and running processes from different streams. The use of these data features which are collected within various streams is combined with Decision Tree and Crying-Jackpot methods through the kind of attack that occurred along with related resource consumption contained within the computer network. Even the high increase in Electricity cost, the CPU usage of spikes, Poor performance, shortening the life of the device, and Overheating within the system resembles signs of crypto-jacking attacks and many more. It also evaluates mining coins done from graphic cards (GPU), mining coins done from processing units (CPU), and mining coins done from application-oriented circuits (ASIC).

Examining related resource consumption is done already with previous works. The first step in the proposed approach is Data collection from Cyberspace, secondly Data Extraction with obtained data features within various domains, thirdly Data Clustering with algorithms combined with two. One is the decision Tree method which includes supervised machine learning that explains what input is and what the related output would be, it even tells where data is continuously split according to parameters, It also explains two entities leaves and nodes. The second is the Crying Jackpot method which includes supervised and unsupervised machine learning that explains Elbow, Silhouette, and DBSCAN. In Elbow Algorithm one should choose the number of clusters available so that adding another cluster does not improve the result in a significant way, In Silhouette Algorithm uses two factors cohesion and separation along with coefficients. It is obtained by comparing the similarity between the sample and respective cluster (cohesion) or the similarity between the sample and other clusters (separation), DBSCAN states that density in a community of objects obtained should be high enough in order to get cluster assigned. Analyzing the uniqueness of the proposed method can get better performance by detecting crypto-jacking attacks in cyberspace, which can reduce resource consumption for businesses at early stages (Fig. 5).

5 Conclusion

With the recent growth in the value of cryptocurrencies, the number of malicious actors has increased. The availability of crypto-currency mining software has increased considerably. Crypto-mining is rapidly spreading. Crypto-jacking is a common assault that is both simple to carry out and difficult to detect. It involves taking advantage of users' computing capabilities without their knowledge or agreement in order to get bitcoins. In this research, to assess the rate of crypto-jacking, we will explore several crypto-jacking detection methodologies and machine learning algorithms. It also claims that the detection rate for crypto-jacking detection using several machines learning algorithmic rules is towards the top of the 90th percentile. When compared to other algorithms, Crying-jackpot Detector has the greatest detection rate. Various out-of-date benchmark datasets with a high detection rate are also connected to the datasets used for various crypto-jacking detection activities in real networks. In relation to the uniqueness of the paper analysis of decision tree and crying-jackpot methods with various categorizations of attack based on Host, Network, Behaviour, and Executable is projected and is very enlightening to today's real-world applications to classify malware in order to detect crypto-jacking attack with reduction of resource consumption.

References

1. Xu, G., et al.: A novel crypto jacking covert attack method based on delayed strategy and its detection. Digit. Commun. Netw. (2022)
2. Caprolu, M., Raponi, S., Oligeri, G., Di Pietro, R.: Cryptomining makes noise: detecting cryptojacking via machine learning. Comput. Commun. **171**, 126–139 (2021). https://doi.org/10.1016/j.comcom.2021.02.016
3. Tanana, D.: Behavior-based detection of cryptojacking malware. In: 2020 Ural Symposium on Biomedical Engineering, Radioelectronics and Information Technology (USBEREIT). IEEE (2020)
4. Di Tizio, G., Chan Nam, N.: Are you a favorite target for cryptojacking? A case-control study on the cryptojacking ecosystem. In: 2020 IEEE European Symposium on Security and Privacy Workshops (EuroS&PW). IEEE (2020)
5. Lachtar, N., et al.: A cross-stack approach towards defending against cryptojacking. IEEE Comput. Architect. Lett. **19**(2), 126–129 (2020). https://doi.org/10.1109/LCA.2020.3017457
6. Zheng, R., et al.: Cryptocurrency malware detection in real-world environment: based on multi-results stacking learning. Appl. Soft Comput. **124**, 109044 (2022). https://doi.org/10.1016/j.asoc.2022.109044
7. Eskandari, S., et al.: A first look at browser-based crypto jacking. In: 2018 IEEE European Symposium on Security and Privacy Workshops (EuroS&PW). IEEE (2018)
8. Gomes, F., Correia, M.: Cryptojacking detection with CPU usage metrics. In: 2020 IEEE 19th International Symposium on Network Computing and Applications (NCA). IEEE (2020)
9. Gomes, G., Dias, L., Correia, M.: CryingJackpot: network flows and performance counters against cryptojacking. In: 2020 IEEE 19th International Symposium on Network Computing and Applications (NCA). IEEE (2020)
10. Hayes, A.S.: Cryptocurrency value formation: an empirical study leading to a cost of production model for valuing bitcoin. Telemat. Inform. **34**(7), 1308–1321 (2017)
11. Hellani, H., et al.: On blockchain technology: overview of bitcoin and future insights. In: 2018 IEEE International Multidisciplinary Conference on Engineering Technology (IMCET). IEEE (2018)
12. Vujičić, D., Jagodić, D., Ranđić, S.: Blockchain technology, bitcoin, and Ethereum: a brief overview. In: 2018 17th International Symposium INFOTEH-JAHORINA (INFOTEH). IEEE (2018)
13. Pastor, A., et al.: Detection of encrypted cryptomining malware connections with machine and deep learning. IEEE Access **8**, 158036–158055 (2020). https://doi.org/10.1109/ACCESS.2020.3019658
14. Vladimír, V., Martin, Ž.: How to detect cryptocurrency miners? By traffic forensics! Digit. Investig. **31**, 100884 (2019). https://doi.org/10.1016/j.diin.2019.08.002
15. Thomas, T., Edwards, T., Baggili, I.: BlockQuery: toward forensically sound cryptocurrency investigation. Forensic Sci. Int. Digit. Investig. **40**, 301340 (2022). https://doi.org/10.1016/j.fsidi.2022.301340
16. Yazdinejad, A., et al.: Cryptocurrency malware hunting: a deep recurrent neural network approach. Appl. Soft Comput. **96**, 106630 (2020). https://doi.org/10.1016/j.asoc.2020.106630
17. Shih, D.-H., et al.: Verification of cryptocurrency mining using ethereum. IEEE Access **8**, 120351–120360 (2020). https://doi.org/10.1109/ACCESS.2020.3005523
18. Shahbazi, Z., Byun, Y.-C.: Machine learning-based analysis of cryptocurrency market financial risk management. IEEE Access **10**, 37848–37856 (2022). https://doi.org/10.1109/ACCESS.2022.3162858
19. Mirtaheri, M., et al.: Identifying and analyzing cryptocurrency manipulations in social media. IEEE Trans. Comput. Soc. Syst. **8**(3), 607–617 (2021)

20. Liu, X.F., et al.: Knowledge discovery in cryptocurrency transactions: a survey. IEEE Access **9**, 37229–37254 (2021)
21. Karn, R.R., et al.: Cryptomining detection in container clouds using system calls and explainable machine learning. IEEE Trans. Parallel Distrib. Syst. **32**(3), 674–691 (2020)
22. Monrat, A.A., Schelen, O., Andersson, K.: A survey of blockchain from the perspectives of applications, challenges, and opportunities. IEEE Access **7**, 117134–117151 (2019). https://doi.org/10.1109/ACCESS.2019.2936094
23. Herskind, L., Katsikouli, P., Dragoni, N.: Privacy and cryptocurrencies – a systematic literature review. IEEE Access **8**, 54044–54059 (2020). https://doi.org/10.1109/ACCESS.2020.2980950
24. Li, Y., et al.: Traceable monero: anonymous cryptocurrency with enhanced accountability. IEEE Trans. Depend. Secure Comput. **18**(2), 679–691 (2021). https://doi.org/10.1109/TDSC.2019.2910058
25. Bartoletti, M., et al.: Cryptocurrency scams: analysis and perspectives. IEEE Access **9**, 148353–148373 (2021). https://doi.org/10.1109/ACCESS.2021.3123894
26. He, S.Y., et al.: A social-network-based cryptocurrency wallet-management scheme. IEEE Access **6**, 7654–7663 (2018). https://doi.org/10.1109/ACCESS.2018.2799385
27. Sabry, F., et al.: Cryptocurrencies and artificial intelligence: challenges and opportunities. IEEE Access **8**, 175840–175858 (2020). https://doi.org/10.1109/ACCESS.2020.3025211
28. Sowmiya, B., et al.: Linear elliptical curve digital signature (LECDS) with blockchain approach for enhanced security on cloud server. IEEE Access **9**, 138245–138253 (2021)
29. Xiong, L., et al.: A blockchain-based privacy-awareness authentication scheme with efficient revocation for multi-server architectures. IEEE Access **7**, 125840–125853 (2019). https://doi.org/10.1109/ACCESS.2019.2939368
30. Lian, W.J., et al.: Cryptomining malware detection based on edge computing-oriented multimodal features deep learning. China Commun. **19**(2), 174–185 (2022). https://doi.org/10.23919/JCC.2022.02.014
31. Yuichi Sei, J., Onesimu, A., Ohsuga, A.: Machine learning model generation with copula-based synthetic dataset for local differentially private numerical data. IEEE Access **10**, 101656–101671 (2022). https://doi.org/10.1109/ACCESS.2022.3208715
32. Melvin, A.R., et al.: Dynamic malware attack dataset leveraging virtual machine monitor audit data for the detection of intrusions in cloud. Trans. Emerg. Telecommun. Technol. **33**(4), e4287 (2022)

Comparative Study of Sentiment Analysis on Cyber Security Related Multi-sourced Data in Social Media Platforms

Keshav Kapur(✉), Rajitha Harikrishnan, and S. Raghavendra

Department of Information and Communication Technology,
Manipal Institute of Technology, Manipal Academy of Higher Education,
Manipal 576104, India
{keshav.kapur,rajitha.harikrishnan}@learner.manipal.edu,
raghavendra.s@manipal.edu

Abstract. The comparative study investigates cyber security attitudes and behaviour across time using data gathered from social networking platforms such as Reddit and Twitter. Due to the continuously advancing technology in the modern world, enormous amounts of data are produced every second. The chosen field of study seeks to determine the opinions of people on social media posts. The dataset for the proposed work was a multi-source dataset from the comment or post section of various social networking sites like Twitter, Reddit, etc. Natural Language Processing Techniques were incorporated to perform sentiment analysis on the obtained dataset. The proposed work provides a comparative analysis using various techniques namely ML, DL, and lexicon-based. Naive Bayes Classifier was used as a Machine Learning algorithm, TextBlob is used as the Lexicon-based approach, and the deep-learning algorithm used is BiLSTM. It was observed that BiLSTM model outperforms the other two models with an F1-score of 0.895, accuracy of 0.896, precision of 0.899, and recall of 0.891.

Keywords: Natural Language Processing · Naive Bayes · TextBlob · LSTM · Deep Learning · Sentiment Analysis

1 Introduction

Due to the availability of public data and efficient algorithms, sentiment analysis offers a chance to grasp the subject(s), particularly in the digital era. Public perceptions on cyber security vary widely and are rife with controversy. In order to determine whether cyber security-related content on Twitter and Reddit had a positive, negative, or neutral sentiment, current descriptive investigation assessed the content. The rise of the internet has altered how people now express their ideas and thoughts. In the current world, people tend to express their opinions largely on social networking websites like Twitter, Reddit, etc. Online communities offer interactive media in the form of forums where users can inform and

© The Author(s), under exclusive license to Springer Nature Singapore Pte Ltd. 2023
S. Prabhu et al. (Eds.): ATIS 2022, CCIS 1804, pp. 88–97, 2023.
https://doi.org/10.1007/978-981-99-2264-2_7

persuade others. Furthermore, social media provides businesses with an opportunity by providing a platform for them to communicate with their customers for advertising. The inference of user sentiment can be quite helpful in the field of recommendation systems and personalization to make up for the absence of clear user input on a given service.

Automatic sentiment analysis (SA) is a problem that is becoming popular in the research domain. Sentiment analysis is the process of mining words' contextual meanings to establish a company's social sentiment through Natural Language Processing techniques [1]. It also enables businesses to ascertain whether or not the product they are producing will find a market for it. The process of recognising whether a block of text is positive, negative, or neutral is known as sentiment analysis. Although sentiment analysis has helped in solving many real-world problems and also, has many applications in the current world, there are still many difficulties with natural language processing that are yet to overcome. SA has been used in various domains such as commercial products, feedback systems, social media, etc.

Motivation: In recent years, using social networking platforms for sentiment analysis has been platform specific. In our work, the objective was to understand the divergence and optimality of models trained on data sets sourced from multiple social media platforms. As we are aware that language styles, age demographics, geographical locations vary drastically in all social media platforms, two platforms were chosen with unique identities, i.e., Reddit and Twitter. The user base of these platforms have been found to be non coinciding and due to the nature of communication in these platforms, we were able to continue with our approach with non-overlapping data subsets.

Sentiment analysis is utilised for social media security across a number of security application domains, including fraud detection, outlier detection, etc. A comprehensive study on the various issues related to social media security has been released, covering topics such as the origin of data, lack of trust, e-commerce safety, consumer data breaches, monitoring of markets, credibility, and risk evaluation. The outcomes of several machine learning algorithms are discussed in the current work based on the performance metrics [7].

Contribution: In our work, a short survey of general approaches used for sentiment analysis is described. Three algorithms were considered to select the best classification technique common for all the social media platforms: Naive Bayes Classifier, TextBlob [5] with Random Forest Classifier and a Bidirectional Long Short-Term Memory (BiLSTM) based classifier [2]. The initial two approaches have been a fundamental method for sentiment analysis whereas the custom BiLSTM approach which we have proposed has shown more promising results. The custom BiLSTM model which has performed better than general baseline approaches (TextBlob and Naive-Bayes). This specific model fit very well on the model while being trained on a non-resource intensive platform rendering it useful for training in a fast-paced resource optimised environment. Also, the straightforward approach of the proposed model helps in further modifications while training depending on specific use-case. The comparative study also shows that Lexicon-based models have a higher efficiency than fundamental machine learning models like Naive Bayes Classifier which are mostly used for Sentiment Analysis.

The rest of the paper is organised as follows: In Sect. 2, Literature Survey is presented. Pre-processing is discussed in Sect. 3. Our Proposed Model is discussed in Sect. 4. In Sect. 5, outcomes of the analysis is discussed. Conclusion is discussed in Sect. 6.

2 Literature Survey

Vishal et al. [1] aims to provide a comparative study of various methods on Sentiment Analysis which is similar to what we have done in our work. However, it concentrates only on the twitter data set which helps us to solve a part of our problem statement. The major challenge cited here is it describes the techniques which are very basic and works only on a clean data set. Mickel et al. [2] focuses on identifying both sentiment and aspects using the BERT model and fine-tuning it to a sentence pair classification model. Chen et al. [5] represents a word-based method to obtain the sentiment analysis of the texts. They incorporated a new method called "SOCAL" which out-performs the lexicon based approach. However, as this method is entirely based on the dictionaries and rules, it will be challenging to store dictionaries and to check the rule redundancy. Taboada et al. [6] shows an improved method of Naive Bayes Classifier using feature weighting and Laplace calibration. It was observed that the algorithm fails when the number of categories is greater than 60. Ke et al. [4] proposes a framework that augments sequence classification in low-resource environments by utilising Natural Language explanations as the external knowledge supervision. Bipun et al. [8] explains a method of analysing the tweets and Reddit comments using VADER which is a lexicon-based approach.

It can be noted that most of the papers had used lexicon-based approach [6, 8] while in our work we we able to show a clear differentiation between lexicon-based approach, ML algorithm, and deep learning algorithm. Although some of the references [8, 10] have worked with both the Twitter and Reddit data, they have focused on only one methodology while in our work, we used three different approaches consisting of novel approached which showed outstanding results. Sonal et al. [11] has performed the analysis of the data using rule-based method and Naive Bayes Classifier. In general, the major issue with the rule-based and probabilistic methods is that everything must be defined for performing a particular task while in deep learning algorithms, it is not required. In some references (Luisa et al. [12], Keshav et al. [3]) mainly focusses only on one methodology.

3 Methodology

The block diagram shown in Fig. 1 depicts the methodology proposed for the analysis. The first step was collection of the dataset. The dataset used was obtained from multiple social media platforms to get a heterogeneous collection of data for analysis. The dataset was then pre-processed, which involved taking out URLs, emoticons, hashtags, and mentions. All the models were trained and evaluated on certain performance metrics. Finally, the result was concluded and documented.

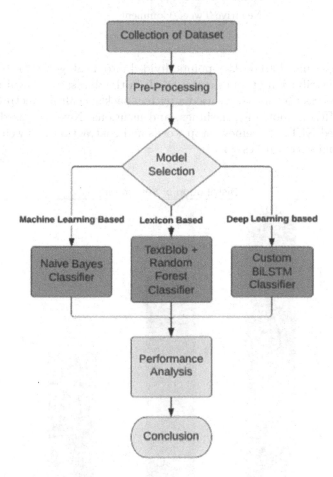

Fig. 1. Block Diagram of Approach

3.1 Pre-processing

The problem statement that this paper currently entails is the classification of tweets (from Twitter) and comments (from Reddit) based on the sentiment observed. The Tweets and Comments were pre-processed using Python re (Regex Library) with a Sentimental Label to each ranging from 1, 0 and −1 as shown in Table 1.

Table 1. Sentiment Labels

Sentiment	Label
Positive Tweet/Comment	1
Neutral Tweet/Comment	0
Negative Tweet/Comment	−1

The dataset has 200118 data points divided into 3 categories (1, 0, −1). The categorical distribution of sentimental labels in the dataset is shown in Fig. 2.

To preprocess the tweets, we used a python package called tweetpreprocessor to remove URLs, emoticons, hashtags, and mentions. Next, we used a python package called NLTK to remove stop words and contractions, as well as special characters and extra spaces. [3]

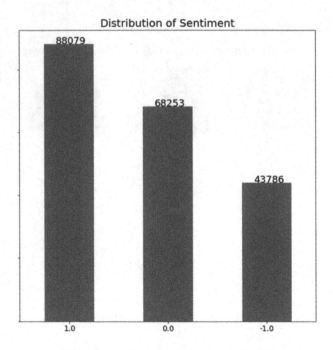

Fig. 2. Distribution of Sentiment Labels

3.2 Proposed Model

The proposed work highlights the differences of using normal NLP techniques, machine learning algorithms, and deep learning techniques. Hence, three main techniques namely TextBlob: a rule-based approach [4] which uses simple NLP technique, Naive Bayes: a probabilistic Machine Learning algorithm, and LSTM: a deep learning algorithm which makes use of RNNs were chosen. Three major techniques for sentiment analysis used on our dataset are:

TextBlob: A Lexicon-Based Method. A Python tool called Textblob is frequently used for Natural Language Processing tasks. It utilizes a lexicon-based approach to gauge sentiment by examining the meaning and intensity of each word in a phrase. This method relies on a dictionary with positive and negative words. A text message is represented as a collection of words, and a score is assigned to each one. The overall sentiment is calculated by taking the average of all these scores.

TextBlob returns two parameters namely polarity and subjectivity. Polarity measures how positive or negative the given problem instance is. Its value lies between $\{-1, 1\}$, -1 indicates a negative statement and 1 indicates a positive statement. Subjectivity quantifies the opinions or perspectives that need to be examined in the context of the problem statement. Its value lies between $[0, 1]$, 1 indicates high subjectivity which means that the text contains personal opinion rather than factual information and 0 indicates low subjectivity. Subjectivity is calculated with the help of another parameter present in TextBlob called intensity which implies if a word modifies the next word.

After obtaining the polarity and subjectivity, a Random Forest Classifier model was used to make the predictions. It is a machine learning algorithm. Decision Trees are the building blocks of Random Forest Classifier. In our model, the predictions are based on 25 Decision Trees which were passed as a hyper parameter for Random Forest Classifier. A predicted class is produced by each individual tree in the random forest classifier. The class with the majority votes becomes our model's prediction.

Naive Bayes Classifier. Naive Bayes classifier is a simple probabilistic classifier based on applying Bayes' theorem with strong (naive) independence assumptions. It is a supervised learning algorithm that can be used to classify a dataset into one of several predefined categories. Assumptions made in Naive Bayes is that each feature can make an equal and independent contribution to the outcome. Pre-processing is performed on the 'text' column of our dataset as there is a need for our text data to convert into numeric type for probability calculations which helps in prediction. The probability of event A occurring, given that event B has occurred, is calculated using Bayes' theorem and the concept of conditional probability. The formula for Bayes' theorem is:

$$P(A|B) = \frac{P(A) \times P(B|A)}{P(B)}$$

Let's consider the probability of event A occurring, given that event B has already happened, denoted as $P(A \mid B)$. Additionally, we have the probability of A occurring regardless of B, referred to as P(A). We can also consider the probability of B happening, given that A has occurred, represented by $P(B \mid A)$. Finally, the probability of B occurring independently of A is represented by P(B). After pre-processing the dataset, a document-term matrix is constructed. Every distinct word in the corpus's lexicon produces a new feature, which causes the document-term matrix to produce a large feature space. To reduce the dimensions and enhance the model performance, we perform the data cleaning steps. TF-IDF method is used to represent a particular text in the form of a vector. N-grams are used to understand the context of the text.

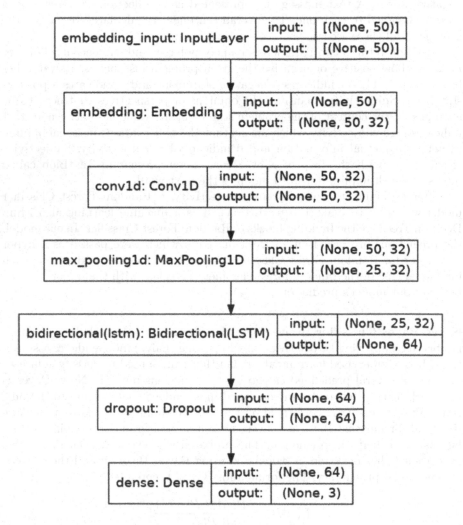

Fig. 3. BiLSTM Model Architecture

Bidirectional Long Short-Term Memory Model (BiLSTM). A Long Short-Term Memory model, or LSTM, is a type of Recurrent Neural Network (RNN) used to process temporal data. Each line has features that furnish context when read in order, which is why choosing a Bidirectional LSTM model is helpful. Before training the model, tokenisation of input sentences into sequences of integers and then padding each sequence to the same length is done. For tokenization, the Keras Tokeniser class was incorporated which creates a vocabulary index based on word frequency and replaces each word corresponding to the vocabulary index integral value. After that, padding the final sequence of integers with '0' was performed. Then splitting the dataset into Training, Validation and Test Data was required.

In this approach, we used a BiLSTM (Bidirectional Long Short-Term Memory) model to improve the training process. The BiLSTM includes two LSTM layers that process the input data sequences in forward and backward directions, respectively. This allows the model to capture contextualized word representations in a clause and better predict the outcome. The purpose of using a BiLSTM model is to capture the intricate semantic and syntactic features of words, as well as the ability of words to have multiple meanings in different contexts (called lexical ambiguity or polysemy). This is achieved by modeling the input data in both forward and backward directions, allowing the model to consider contextual information from both past and future words. This helps the model better handle words with similar pronunciations but different meanings. Our proposed model has the architecture as shown in Fig. 3. We tuned the model with the following hyperparameters: epochs = 20, learning rate = 0.1, momentum = 0.8. To train the model, we used a batch size of 64 and selected the categorical cross entropy loss function with the Stochastic gradient descent optimizer.

4 Performance Evaluation

The dataset has 200118 data points divided into 3 categories (1, 0, −1). The training set and validation set had 130076 and 20011 data points respectively. In the testing phase, we tested over 25% of our dataset which is approximately 50029 data points. Validation data guides the training of our model while the test data is used to check how well our data conforms to our model. The dataset with Tweets and Comments (from Twitter and Reddit Comment Section) were extracted using Twitter and Reddit APIs, i.e., Tweepy and PRAW respectively. The dataset is collected and observed based on multiple features. The two datasets were collected separately where one consisted of Tweets from Twitter with sentiment label and the other from Reddit which consisted of comments with its sentiment label.

The tweets and comments were in context with political discussions occurring over the two platforms. The test results are presented in Table 2, which demonstrates the Accuracy, Precision, Recall, and F1-Score for each model. This research was conducted using Google Colab, with a CPU model of Intel(R) Xeon(R) CPU @ 2.20 GHz dual core processor, 13 GB of memory, and a Tesla K80 GPU with 2496 CUDA cores and 12 GB GDDR5 VRAM.

The evaluation metrics that we have chosen are as follows:

$$Accuracy = \frac{TruePositive(TP) + TrueNegtative(TN)}{TP + TN + FalsePositive(FP) + FalseNegative(FN)}$$

$$Precision = \frac{TP}{TP + FP}$$

$$Recall = \frac{TP}{TP + FN}$$

$$F_1 = 2 * \frac{Precision * Recall}{Precision + Recall}$$

Table 2. Evaluation Scores

Model	Accuracy	Precision	Recall	F1 Score
Naive Bayes	0.6968	0.7220	0.6968	0.6900
TextBlob + Random Forest	0.8159	0.8193	0.8152	0.8106
Custom BiLSTM	0.8963	0.8986	0.8912	0.8949

As seen from Table 2 the custom BiLSTM model performed better than Naive Bayes and TextBlob with an F1 score of 0.8949, followed by TextBlob with a random forest classifier with F1 score 0.8106 and Naive Bayes with F1 score 0.69. It can be noted from the table that accuracy of Custom BiLSTM (0.89) is higher than Naive Bayes and lexicon-based approach (0.69 & 0.82 respectively). In our approach, we used the F1-score as the primary evaluation metric. The F1-score is a balanced metric that considers both precision and recall, and is particularly useful when dealing with imbalanced datasets (i.e., datasets where the number of samples in one class is much smaller than the number of samples in the other class). The F1-score also combines many other metrics into a single value, making it a good overall measure of the performance of the model.

5   Conclusion

In the proposed work, a comparative study of existing techniques for sentiment analysis using lexicon-based approach, machine learning approach and deep learning approach was presented. In the lexicon-based approach, Random Forest Classifier along with TextBlob was used as the dataset was imbalanced and decision trees perform better on such datasets. In the deep learning approach, we have used BiLSTM as each component in the input sequence has information about both the past and present which helps in providing us with more optimal output. Naive Bayes Classifier was used as a machine learning model. It follows a probablistic approach and assumes that all the events are independent of each other. It was observed from the results that TextBlob along with Random Forest Classifier and Custom BiLSTM have performed well. Our future work would involve understanding the data characteristics which affect the performance of Naive Bayes Classifier, and training our model in RoBerta.

References

1. Kharde, V.A., Sonawane, P.S.: Sentiment analysis of twitter data: a survey of techniques. https://doi.org/10.5120/ijca2016908625
2. Hoang, M., Bihorac, O.A., Rouces, J.: Aspect-based sentiment analysis using BERT. In: Proceedings of the 22nd Nordic Conference on Computational Linguistics, pp. 187–196. Linköping University Electronic Press, Turku (2019)
3. Kapur, K., Harikrishnan, R., Singh, S.: MaNLP@SMM4H'22: BERT for classification of twitter posts. In: Proceedings of The Seventh Workshop on Social Media Mining for Health Applications, Workshop & Shared Task, pp. 42–43. Association for Computational Linguistics, Gyeongju (2022)
4. Ke, Z., Sheng, J., Li, Z., Silamu, W., Guo, Q.: Knowledge-guided sentiment analysis via learning from natural language explanations. IEEE Access **9**, 3570–3578 (2021). https://doi.org/10.1109/ACCESS.2020.3048088
5. Chen, H., Hu, S., Hua, R., Zhao, X.: Improved Naive Bayes classification algorithm for traffic risk management. EURASIP J. Adv. Sig. Process. **2021**(1), 1–12 (2021). https://doi.org/10.1186/s13634-021-00742-6
6. Taboada, M., Brooke, J., Tofiloski, M., Voll, K., Stede, M.: Lexicon-based methods for sentiment analysis. Comput. Linguist. **37**, 267–307 (2011)
7. Sharma, S., Jain, A.: Role of sentiment analysis in social media security and analytics. WIREs Data Min. Knowl. Discov. **10**(5), e1366 (2020). https://doi.org/10.1002/widm.1366
8. Thapa, B.: Sentiment analysis of cybersecurity content on Twitter and Reddit (2022). 10.48550/arXiv. 2204.12267
9. Gupta, B., Sharma, S., Chennamaneni, A.: Sentiment analysis: an examination of cybersecurity attitudes and behavior research-in-progress (2017)
10. Shu, K., Sliva, A., Sampson, J., Liu, H.: Understanding cyber attack behaviors with sentiment information on social media. In: Thomson, R., Dancy, C., Hyder, A., Bisgin, H. (eds.) SBP-BRiMS 2018. LNCS, vol. 10899, pp. 377–388. Springer, Cham (2018). https://doi.org/10.1007/978-3-319-93372-6_41
11. Khandelwal, S., Chaudhary, A.: COVID-19 pandemic & cyber security issues: sentiment analysis and topic modeling approach. https://doi.org/10.1080/09720529.2022.2072421
12. Chaparro, L.F.: Sentiment analysis of social network content to characterize the perception of security (2020)

Modified Blowfish Encryption Algorithm for Wireless Body Area Network

S. Divya[1] (ID), K. V. Prema[2]([✉]) (ID), and Balachandra Muniyal[1] (ID)

[1] Department of Information and Communication Technology,
Manipal Institute of Technology, MAHE, Manipal, India
{divya.sharma,bala.chandra}@manipal.edu
[2] Department of Computer Science Engineering,
Manipal Institute of Technology MAHE, Bengaluru, India
prema.kv@manipal.edu

Abstract. Wireless body area network (WBAN) consists of group of wearable devices placed inside or on the human body and wearable device controller. The devices are used to monitor and measure vital parameters, process them, transfer them to the wearable device controller. If an attacker tries to alter the information, the confidentiality of the data is lost and also it could prove fatal to the person to whom the data belongs to. The paper focuses on achieving confidentiality of the data by encrypting using the Modified Blowfish encryption algorithm. It is proved that the proposed method minimizes the encryption time by 50% as compared with Blowfish algorithm. The value calculated for avalanche of the Modified Blowfish is 48.5% and the Blowfish achieved 47.14%. Matlab is used in the research work for performing encryption of the data.

Keywords: Wireless body area network security · Blowfish · Matlab

1 Introduction

It is possible to prevent and detect health threat early by constantly monitoring the health condition of the patients remotely. Since the monitored data plays a major role in diagnosis and treatment, it is highly confidential and providing security and privacy to the data are the challenging issues. Due to this, security and privacy of the data requires special attention in WBANs for Health Care Applications [5,15].

The typical communication in the wireless body area network for healthcare applications is shown in the Fig. 1. The wearable device controller collects the data obtained by the wearable devices attached to the human body. It is then transmitted to the medical server that is monitoring [12]. This transmission takes place over the Internet or a cellular network.

© The Author(s), under exclusive license to Springer Nature Singapore Pte Ltd. 2023
S. Prabhu et al. (Eds.): ATIS 2022, CCIS 1804, pp. 98–108, 2023.
https://doi.org/10.1007/978-981-99-2264-2_8

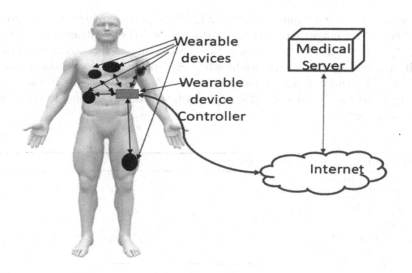

Fig. 1. Typical Wireless Body Area Network

1.1 Security in BAN

Since the private health information of the patient travels from the wearable devices to reach the wearable device controller, securing this data becomes important. If the data that is being communicated was corrupted by an attacker, it could prove life threatening to the patient, since for medical treatment, decisions are to be taken by looking into the information that is received [14]. Therefore, there is a requirement to make the data unreadable for the attacker. One of the methods is to encrypt the data.

The devices in the network has energy constraint due to the placement of the devices on the body of the human being. Encryption and decryption process should perform minimum computations, it should perform minimum exchange of messages and it should also use minimum memory. Therefore, Blowfish encryption algorithm is used which makes use of a symmetric key.

2 Preliminaries

Relevant basic information for understanding the paper in the better way is mentioned in this section.

2.1 Blowfish Encryption and Decryption Algorithm

The algorithm is a symmetric block cipher and makes use of the Feistel network. The encryption of the data is carried out using 16 rounds [4]. Two types of arrays namely, P-array and S-boxes are involved during the encryption process. Eighteen, 32-bit entries are present in P-array and these entries are called sub-keys: P_1 to P_{18}. The S-boxes consist of four S-box and each S-box consists of 256, 32-bit entries. Figure 2 [16] shows blowfish encryption and decryption algorithm and Fig. 3 [16] shows a detailed single round in the Blowfish algorithm.

The following Pseudocode [16] explains how a data can be encrypted using Blowfish algorithm.

Algorithm 1. Blowfish Encryption
___
for $k = 1$ to 16 **do**
    $RE_k = LE_{k-1} \oplus P_k$;
    $LE_k = F[RE_k] \oplus RE_{k-1}$;
end for
$LE_{17} = RE_{16} \oplus P_{18}$;
$RE_{17} = LE_{16} \oplus P_{17}$;

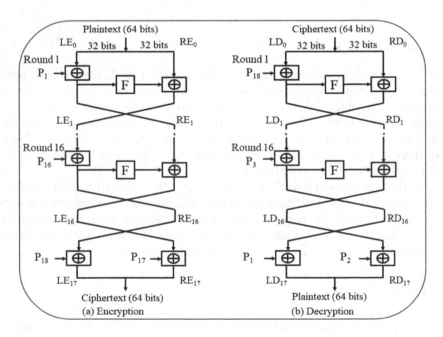

Fig. 2. Blowfish Encryption and Decryption Algorithm

The P-array is used in the reverse order, for performing decryption. The process of decryption is defined by the following Pseudocode [16]:

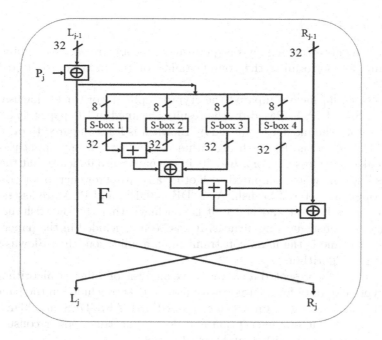

Fig. 3. Details of single Blowfish round

Algorithm 2. Blowfish Decryption

---

for $k = 1$ to 16 **do**
  $RD_k = LD_{k-1} \oplus P_{19-k}$;
  $LD_k = F[RD_k] \oplus RD_{k-1}$;
end for
$LD_{17} = RD_{16} \oplus P_1$;
$RD_{17} = LE_{16} \oplus P_2$;

When security and privacy has to be applied to the data in WBAN, it becomes important to make use of encryption and decryption algorithm scheme that make use of fewer resources and performs minimum computation to achieve the required security. In the Wireless body area network(WBAN), wearable devices are present in the human body, and therefore, they have severe power as well as memory constraints [14].

Therefore, the objective of the research work is to make use of encryption and decryption algorithm that performs less computation and also uses less storage space for the encryption to maintain the confidentiality of the data communicated between the wearable device and wearable device controller.

A literature survey performed for selecting encryption and decryption algorithms are discussed in this section under related work. In Sect. 3, the methodology used for the said objective is indicated. Section 4 indicates the results and analysis of the work. In Sect. 5, the conclusion for the work is indicated.

2.2   Related Work

The following literature survey was performed to compare various cryptographic algorithms for performing the confidentiality of the data transmitted by the devices.

Patil et al. [9] have compared the cryptographic algorithms Blowfish, AES, DES, 3DES, and RSA. Based on the results obtained in the paper, it has been concluded that the memory required by Blowfish is less compared to other algorithms. Therefore, the Blowfish algorithm can be used in any application that has to make use of less memory. Results in the paper also indicate that the Blowfish uses less time when compared with other algorithm for encryption. Based on the entropy parameter, Blowfish, AES, DES, 3DES, and RSA are assessed and Blowfish scores highest and hence, it is concluded that the Blowfish algorithm is strongest against guessing attacks. It has been concluded in the paper that if memory and time is the main constraint in an application, then Blowfish is the best suitable algorithm.

Mota et al. [7] presented a comparative analysis of different algorithms used for encryption of data for secured transmission. It is concluded in the paper that Blowfish is the best algorithm when compared with AES, DES, and 3DES based on the following factors: encryption and decryption time, power consumption, memory usage, latency, jitter, and security level.

Ali Ahmad Milad [1] presented the study and execution of the Blowfish algorithm and Skipjack algorithm in the paper. The performance of both the algorithms was compared by encrypting files with various sizes and contents. The algorithms are implemented using C#. From the results obtained it was concluded that the Blowfish algorithm is faster than Skipjack.

Rajan Patel and Pariza Kamboj [8] projected a scheme to enhance the Blowfish algorithm. In the work, the number of Blowfish rounds performed is skipped using the key called round key. Due to this, Blowfish algorithm security is increased against brute-force attack. It is also discussed that the algorithm uses less encryption and decryption time.

Theda Flare Quilala et al. [11] in the work obtained a modified Blowfish encryption algorithm that makes use of 128 - bits for the block and 128-bit for the key. In this algorithm, the number of rounds used for encryption are reduced. The performance of the algorithm was evaluated using time for encryption, and avalanche. It is indicated in the paper that the modified algorithm is slow when compared with the Blowfish due to difference in the block size. It is also shown that when compared with Twofish algorithm, the modified Blowfish algorithm is faster.

3   Methodology

In this research work, to maintain confidentiality of the transmitted data between wearable device and wearable device controller, the data are encrypted using modified Blowfish algorithm and a symmetric key [2,3,14,18].

Since Blowfish algorithm has certain advantages over other algorithms and also by looking into the constraints of WBAN devices, modified Blowfish algorithm is defined in the work. Where, reduction in the number of computations for encryption is performed by reducing the number of rounds for encryption. The proposed algorithm uses 64- bit data and 128 - bit key.

Following steps were performed for encrypting the data:

1. Generating the subkeys for the modified Blowfish algorithm:

   For Modified Blowfish algorithm, P array and S boxes initialization is same as Blowfish algorithm. It is performed by applying Blowfish algorithm and the encryption key. Following steps are involved:

   (a) In the beginning, P-array is initialized and then the four S-boxes, in order, with a fixed value that comprises of the hexadecimal values of pi: P_1 is initialized to $0 \times 243f6a88$, P_2 is initialized to 0x85a308d3, P_3 is initialized to 0x13198a2e, and so on.

   (b) The small key is converted to a long key. If Q is a 128-bit key, then QQ, QQQ, etc., are the equivalent long keys. P_1 will be XORed with the initial 32-bits from the key, P_2 is XORed with the next 32-bits from the key and the process will be repeated for all bits of the key.

   (c) Next all-zero string is encrypted by making use of the Blowfish algorithm, using the subkeys as mentioned in steps (a) and (b).

   (d) P_1 and P_2 will be replaced with the output from step (c).

   (e) The encryption of the output from step (c) is performed using the Blowfish algorithm and the modified subkeys.

   (f) The output of step (e) is substituted as P_3 and P_4.

   (g) The process is going to be repeated to replace all elements of the P array, and later all the entries of S-boxes in order.

   (h) To obtain all the necessary entries in P array and S boxes, 521 iterations are performed. Applications can store in the memory the P array and S boxes instead of repeating the derivation process several times.

2. Modified Blowfish algorithm:

   John Kelsey developed an attack that was capable of breaking three Blowfish rounds but was proved that it was impossible to break for 8 round and above [17]. In the work, the encryption and decryption are performed by reducing the number of rounds to eight Blowfish rounds.

   For choosing the eight Blowfish rounds from the 16 rounds, following method was adopted.

   If XOR of all the bits of key used for encryption results in Zero, then sub keys P_1, P_2, P_3, P_4, P_5, P_6, P_7, P_8, P_9, P_{10} in P array are used for encryption.

   Else, the sub keys P_{18}, P_{17}, P_{16}, P_{15}, P_{14}, P_{13}, P_{12}, P_{11}, P_{10}, P_9 in P array are used for encryption.

   In total only 8 rounds will be performed. Figure 4 shows Modified Blowfish encryption algorithm.

   Encryption process is defined by the following Pseudo-code:

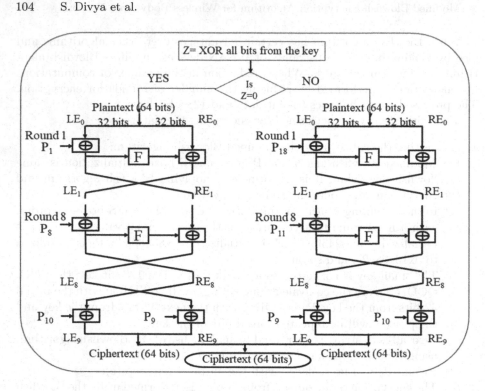

Fig. 4. Modified Blowfish Encryption Algorithm

Algorithm 3. Modified Blowfish Encryption

---
if XOR of individual bits of the key is Zero **then**
    for $k = 1$ to 8 **do**
        $RE_k = LE_{k-1} \oplus P_k$;
        $LE_k = F[RE_k] \oplus RE_{k-1}$;
    end for
    $LE_9 = RE_8 \oplus P_{10}$;
    $RE_9 = LE_8 \oplus P_9$;
else
    for $k = 18$ to 11 **do**
        $RE_{19-k} = LE_{19-k-1} \oplus P_k$;
        $LE_{19-k} = F[RE_{19-k}] \oplus RE_{19-k-1}$;
    end for
    $LE_9 = RE_8 \oplus P_9$;
    $RE_9 = LE_8 \oplus P_{10}$;
end if

For performing decryption, the order of performing the operation remains same as encryption but the keys will be used in the reverse order. Decryption process is defined by the following Pseudo-code:

Algorithm 4. Modified Blowfish Decryption

---

if XOR of individual bits of the key is Zero **then**

    for $k = 9$ to 16 **do**

        $RD_{k-8} = LD_{k-8-1} \oplus P_k$;

        $LD_{k-8} = F[RD_{k-8}] \oplus RD_{k-8-1}$;

    end for

    $LD_9 = RD_8 \oplus P_{18}$;

    $RD_9 = LD_8 \oplus P_{17}$;

else

    for $k = 10$ to 3 **do**

        $RD_{11-k} = LD_{11-k-1} \oplus P_k$;

        $LD_{11-k} = F[RD_{11-k}] \oplus RD_{11-k-1}$;

    end for

    $LD_9 = RD_8 \oplus P_1$;

    $RD_9 = LD_8 \oplus P_2$;

end if

---

4   Result and Analysis

4.1   Comparison of the Proposed Algorithm with Existing Work

Table 1 indicates the comparison of the proposed work based on the operations performed for securing the data with various other similar works.

Table 1. Comparison of the proposed modified Blowfish algorithm with other related work

Work	Block size	Key size	number of rounds	Remarks
Patel and Kamboj [8]	64-bits	16-bits	The number of rounds for encryption depends on the number of ones in the key	Each bit needs to be compared to perform the round
Quilala et al. [11]	128-bits	128-bits	8	Makes use of less memory
Proposed method	64-bits	128-bits	8	Simple XOR operation is used to identify the rounds to be performed

Specification of the processor used is Intel(R) Core(TM) i5-7200U CPU @ 2.50 GHz with RAM of 8.00 GB. Figure 5 shows the plot of encryption time for Blowfish algorithm and modified Blowfish algorithm. It shows that the proposed work make use of less time for encryption.

Figure 6 shows the avalanche percentage. It is observed that Blowfish has 47.14% avalanche, it is at 52.86% in the paper [11] and in the proposed work

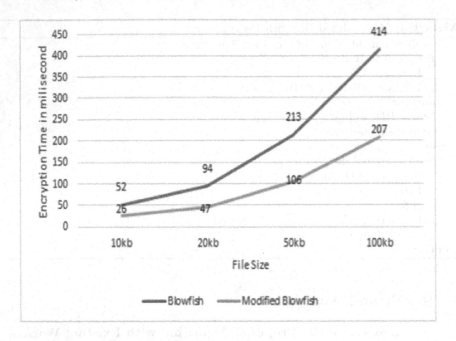

Fig. 5. Modified Blowfish Encryption Algorithm

it is 48.5%. It is indicated in the paper [13] that as the avalanche percentage increases, the security achieved is better. This means that the proposed algorithm has better security than the blowfish algorithm.

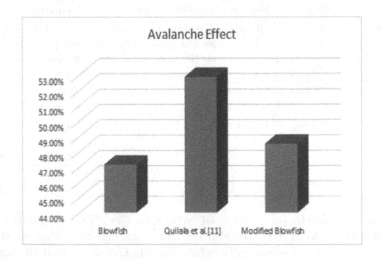

Fig. 6. Avalanche effect

4.2 Details of Security Analysis

Various attacks are discussed in the papers [6,10]. This subsection includes the details of the discussion about how the proposed algorithm can secure the data against multiple attacks so that an adversary cannot attack private patient data.

1. Eavesdropping attack:
   If an attacker is able to read the messages that are transmitted, an eavesdropping attack will take place.
   Since messages transmitted between wearable device controller and wearable devices are encrypted using Modified Blowfish encryption algorithm, eavesdropping attack is eliminated.
2. Message Modification Attack:
   Since encryption is performed on the data that is transmitted, the attacker has to decrypt the message and for performing decryption, the key has to be known. Even if the key is known to the attacker, he should know which rounds are used for encryption. Therefore, it is difficult for this type of attack to take place.

5 Conclusion

In this research work, the data communicated is encrypted using the modified Blowfish encryption algorithm which is proved to be fast as the number of computation is less. In the proposed algorithm, the key size used is 128-bit. It is indicated in [11] that a key with 128-bits has a complexity of 2^{128} or $3.40\ e^{+38}$ and for an encryption algorithm with a key size of 128-bits, performing brute force attack will take around $5e^{+025}$ years. Also since two sets of rounds are used, an attacker has to know which set of rounds are used for encryption.

References

1. Milad, A.A., Muda, Z., Noh, Z.A.B.M., Algaet, M.A.: Comparative study of performance in cryptography algorithms (blowfish and skipjack). J. Comput. Sci. 8(7), 1191–1197 (2012). https://doi.org/10.3844/jcssp.2012.1191.1197,https://www.researchgate.net/publication/250614450. the 6th International Conference on Ambient Systems, Networks and Technologies (ANT-2015), the 5th International Conference on Sustainable Energy Information Technology (SEIT-2015)
2. Ali, A., Khan, F.A.: Key agreement schemes in wireless body area networks: taxonomy and state-of-the-art. J. Med. Syst. 39(10), 1–14 (2015)
3. Das, A.K., Zeadally, S., Wazid, M.: Lightweight authentication protocols for wearable devices. Comput. Electr. Eng. 63, 196–208 (2017)
4. Divya, S., Prema, K., Muniyal, B.: Privacy preservation mechanism for the data used in image authentication. In: 2019 IEEE International Conference on Distributed Computing, VLSI, Electrical Circuits and Robotics (DISCOVER), pp. 1–6. IEEE (2019)

5. González-Valenzuela, S., Liang, X., Cao, H., Chen, M., Leung, V.C.M.: Body Area Networks, pp. 17–37. Springer, Berlin Heidelberg, Berlin, Heidelberg (2013). https://doi.org/10.1007/5346_26,https://doi.org/10.1007/5346_2012_26

6. Masdari, M., Ahmadzadeh, S., Bidaki, M.: Key management in wireless body area network: challenges and issues. J. Netw. Comput. Appl. **91**(Supplement C), 36–51 (2017). https://doi.org/10.1016/j.jnca.2017.04.008, https://www.sciencedirect.com/science/article/pii/S1084804517301492

7. Mota, A.V., Azam, S., Shanmugam, B., Yeo, K.C., Kannoorpatti, K.: Comparative analysis of different techniques of encryption for secured data transmission. In: 2017 IEEE International Conference on Power, Control, Signals and Instrumentation Engineering (ICPCSI), pp. 231–237. IEEE (2017)

8. Patel, R., Kamboj, P.: Security enhancement of blowfish block cipher. In: Unal, A., Nayak, M., Mishra, D.K., Singh, D., Joshi, A. (eds.) SmartCom 2016. CCIS, pp. 231–238. Springer, Singapore (2016). https://doi.org/10.1007/978-981-10-3433-6_28

9. Patil, P., Narayankar, P., Narayan, D.G., Meena, S.M.: A comprehensive evaluation of cryptographic algorithms: DES, 3DES, AES, RSA and blowfish. Proc. Comput. Sci. **78**(Supplement C), 617–624 (2016). https://doi.org/10.1016/j.procs.2016.02.108, https://www.sciencedirect.com/science/article/pii/S1877050916001101. 1st International Conference on Information Security and Privacy 2015

10. Paul, P.C., Loane, J., Regan, G., McCaffery, F.: Analysis of attacks and security requirements for wireless body area networks - a systematic literature review. In: Walker, A., O'Connor, R.V., Messnarz, R. (eds.) EuroSPI 2019. CCIS, vol. 1060, pp. 439–452. Springer, Cham (2019). https://doi.org/10.1007/978-3-030-28005-5_34

11. Quilala, T.F., Sison, A., Medina, R.: Modified blowfish algorithm. Indonesian J. Electr. Eng. Comput. Sci. **12**, 38–45 (10). https://doi.org/10.11591/ijeecs.v12.i1.pp38-45

12. Raazi, S.M., Lee, H., Lee, S., Lee, Y.K.: Bari+: a biometric based distributed key management approach for wireless body area networks. Sensors **10**(4), 3911–3933 (2010)

13. Ross, B.S., Josephraj, V.: Performance enhancement of blowfish encryption using RK blowfish. Int. J. Appl. Eng. Res. **12**(20), 9236–9244 (2017)

14. Sampangi, R.V., Dey, S., Urs, S.R., Sampalli, S.: A security suite for wireless body area networks. arXiv preprint arXiv:1202.2171 (2012)

15. Shen, J., Chang, S., Shen, J., Liu, Q., Sun, X.: A lightweight multi-layer authentication protocol for wireless body area networks. Futur. Gener. Comput. Syst. **78**, 956–963 (2018)

16. Stallings, W.: Cryptography and Network Security Principles and practice. Pearson Education Inc, publishing as Prentice Hall, 3 edn. (2006)

17. Vaudenay, S.: On the weak keys of blowfish. In: Gollmann, D. (ed.) FSE 1996. LNCS, vol. 1039, pp. 27–32. Springer, Heidelberg (1996). https://doi.org/10.1007/3-540-60865-6_39

18. Venkatasubramanian, K.K., Banerjee, A., Gupta, S.K.: EKG-based key agreement in body sensor networks. In: IEEE Infocom Workshops 2008, pp. 1–6. IEEE (2008)

EyeEncrypt: A Cyber-Secured Framework for Retinal Image Segmentation

Govardhan Hegde[1], Shourya Gupta[1(✉)], Gautham Manuru Prabhu[1(✉)], and Sulatha V. Bhandary[2]

[1] Manipal Institute of Technology, Manipal, India
govardhan.hegde@manipal.edu, 13.shourya@gmail.com,
gauthamprabhu9@gmail.com
[2] Kasturba Medical College, Manipal, India
sulatha.bhandary@manipal.edu

Abstract. Concerns in information and data security are addressed based on implementing practices to enhance data security mechanisms and feedbacks. Recent medical data breaches across the globe and rising cybersecurity threats from cyber warfare make research into data privacy more crucial in the system's overall design. The advent of telemedicine and research in the applications of artificial intelligence in the medical domain makes a case for integrating enhanced image analysis inside a secure framework. The proposed modality implements critical principles of "authentication, authorization data integrity, data confidentiality, and the Principle of Least Privilege." The use case chosen for this paper is on a retinal image DRIVE dataset. Retinal images have several applications in the field of medicine, which include the early detection of various diseases such as glaucoma. Characteristics intrinsic to retinal images make the vessel detection process difficult. Our proposed framework EyeEncrypt, aids in effective medical image segmentation on a secure integrated framework.

Keywords: cyber security · information security · data security · cryptography · encryption · image segmentation · computer vision · medical imaging · segmentation

1 Introduction

The recent past has witnessed exponential growth in medical imaging via computed tomography scans, magnetic resonance (MRI) images, X-rays, etc. The volume of patients received and technological advances have elevated the rise of computational medical image analysis, which has been improving with optimization in machine learning techniques. Automated diagnosis systems (ADSs) are vital in the early diagnosis of serious diseases. With increasing growth in medical imaging solutions comes the risk of data misuse. Lack of security leads

© The Author(s), under exclusive license to Springer Nature Singapore Pte Ltd. 2023
S. Prabhu et al. (Eds.): ATIS 2022, CCIS 1804, pp. 109–120, 2023.
https://doi.org/10.1007/978-981-99-2264-2_9

to loss of information and improper storage of images, making improvements in security crucial. One of the commonly used tools to combat security challenges is by employing encryption.

EyeEncrypt is an integrated solution consisting of a vessel segmentation pipeline and a robust security mechanism. The security mechanism ensures that the enhanced medical images are not accessed by unauthorized users. The vessel segmentation pipeline aids the doctor in diagnosing patients by filtering out the noise and applying image processing techniques to segment and enhance the vessels. The framework supports different users, including the Ophthalmologist, Optometrist, and patient.

The Internet of Medical Things (IOMT) consists of sensitive data collected by healthcare institutions. This data helps facilitate early diagnosis, thus facilitating better healthcare. Owing to software vulnerabilities, human error, and lack of implementation of the best security practices, these databases may get accessed by unauthorized users. The unauthorized users can misuse the data resulting in data leaks. Unauthorized users sometimes access these databases. Insider attacks, too, can cause damage to privileged healthcare information. The Healthcare industry is amongst the worst hit by data breaches [1]. Data breaches cost the institution an average of 10.10 million dollars inside the United States of America.

Encryption is a method to protect data from such unauthorized users. The encryption techniques involve the conversion of an original image into a form that is impossible to understand. Symmetric cryptography [2] is a commonly used form of cryptography in which a key is shared to encrypt data between multiple users. Since the shared key is used for encryption and decryption, the method is symmetric. The communicating entities exchange the keys during the decryption process.

Asymmetric cryptography, also called (public key encryption) is a methodology in which the encryption process uses two separate keys for the encryption and decryption process. The private key is not shared, while the public key is shared with the sender. The encryption process happens with the public key. The decryption process happens using the private key. Some popular asymmetric cryptography algorithms include the Rivest-Shamir-Adleman (RSA) [3], Diffie-Hellman [4], ECC [5], El Gamal [6]. Elliptical curve cryptography employs an asymmetric, key-based approach to achieve encryption. The method focuses on pairs of public and private keys. It is considered a safe method since it utilizes the mathematics of the elliptic curves while simultaneously reducing key size. The smaller key size, along with the mathematical approach to encryption, ensures that the algorithm employed is very secure.

To enhance the clarity of the images of the human eye and remove the unwanted noise in the images, fundus imaging [7] is a frequently utilized technique to gather data on the human eye's background to enhance the clarity of the images and remove the unwanted noise in the images. It is employed primarily for detecting medical ailments, including diabetes retinopathy and glaucoma. Medical image analysis generally consists of the following steps. Initially, the raw

images are 'cleaned' before analysis. The preprocessing techniques involve eliminating noise and removing irrelevant information, thus enhancing the image. The
enhanced images are passed through various algorithms and filters to extract the
specific inner anatomical organ required for easy diagnosis. It also helps make
precise surgeries to reach the body's interior organs without causing unnecessary
cuts.

All experiments on the model were run on the DRIVE dataset [8]. The Digital Retinal Images for Vessel Extraction (DRIVE) dataset is a dataset for retinal
vessel segmentation. The dataset was collected from a hospital in the Nether-
lands. It is a commonly used dataset employed in fundus imaging.

2   Literature Review

Yogesh Bala and Amita Malik [9] present a novel biometric-inspired homomorphic encryption algorithm (BIHEA) for secured data/file transmission over a
hybrid cloud environment. The paper proposes encryption of the user data during
run-time by employing a biometric-featured-based one-time password. Ankita
Lathey and Pradeep K. Atrey [10] proposed a cloud-based framework for image
enhancement in an encrypted domain over the cloud. The major limitation of
the proposed framework is the trade-off in applying the masks and filter size.
An IOT based approach is proposed where medical images are stored in an IoT
based system [11]. The integration of IoT, however, increases the execution time,
thus making the solution far from optimal.

Zhen, P., Zhao, G., Min, L. et al. [12] proposed a secure image encryption
algorithm based on logic and spatiotemporal chaos. The paper demonstrates how
the properties of a spatiotemporal system could guarantee structural complexity
by employing the characteristics of RGB images. Lili Liu, Qiang Zhang, and
Xiaopeng Wei [13] method involves a combination of DNA coding and chaotic
mapping to create an RGB encryption algorithm. Grigorios Loukides, John
Liagouris. et al. [14] proposed a method to share health data anonymously. The
approach works by employing disassociation. The disassociation technique frag-
ments medical information into multiple sub-records, thus splitting the framework into independent, well-formulated sub-records.

3   Methodology

EyeEncrypt has been developed using the python library "Streamlit," [15] which
eases the task of efficient deployment and scalability while ensuring security.
Streamlit applications are served using HTTPS Protocol. Data sent to pub-
lic internet is encrypted using 256-bit encryption, and strong ciphers are used.
HTTP Strict Transport Security (HSTS) ensures that browser interaction with
Streamlit apps is carried over HTTPS.

EyeEncrypt gives the user access to three individual roles involved in the
procedural pipeline of an ophthalmological diagnosis, initiating from a patient
visiting an optometrist for retinal imaging until the patient's diagnosis by the

associated Ophthalmologist. The three roles include an "Optometrist," responsible for uploading a concerned patient's retinal fundus images onto the framework; the patient; and the associated Ophthalmologist, evaluating the uploaded retinal images for diagnosis. Apart from the roles, a central administrative authority manages EyeEncrypt's central database. All the user secrets, credentials, and encrypted images get secured in a Cloud-based No-SQL MongoDB database [16] and are stored in collections. A collection in MongoDB is a group of similar documents.

3.1   Optometrist's View of the Framework

The optometrist uses the interactive user interface for logging into the framework by specifying the user credentials such as name, an assigned user id, password, and the role "Optometrist". We have used the Streamlit-Autheticator [17] library for user authentication, a secure authentication module to validate user credentials in a Streamlit application. The credentials are stored in a Cloud-based MongoDB NoSQL database. On logging in, an optometrist is directed to the dashboard, which features a widget to upload a retinal image, along with specifying the associated Opthamologist's and patient's unique user ids and names. After the optometrist uploads the image and specifies the concerned Ophthalmologist and the patient details, they are notified about this activity by the framework through a series of simultaneous API calls. Thus, the associated Ophthalmologist and the patient are informed of the diagnosis pipeline initiation, making the process transparent to the stakeholders involved. On submitting the details and the image, the image encryption pipeline initiates. The pipeline is described in (see Fig. 1), and the Optometrist's dashboard view is displayed in (see Fig. 2).

We have employed the Curve25519 high-speed elliptic curve cryptography algorithm for encryption, using the PyNaCl library [18] to generate the public-private key pairs.

The equation of the Montgomery curve [19] is: $y^2 = x^3 + 486662x^2 + x \bmod(p)$. over Fg prime field where mod (p) is defined by $3 < p <= 2255 - 19$, with a based-point of x = 9.

The equation described above is an elliptic curve employed in elliptic curve cryptography. It, when employed in agreement with the Elliptic Curve Diffie-Hellman scheme, allows two entities, each possessing a public-private key pair, to establish a shared secret passage.

The Diffie-Hellman scheme is described as follows. In a scenario where we possess two private keys, a and b belonging to UserA, and UserB, respectively, and an elliptic curve with generator point G.

$$(a * G) * b = (b * G) * a$$

The equation is described as follows.

$$UserA.pubKey * UserB.privKey = UserB.pubKey * UserA.privKey = secret$$

The ECDH algorithm (Elliptic Curve Diffie-Hellman Key Exchange) is:

1) UserA generates a random ECC key pair: UserA.privKey, UserA.pubKey
2) UserB generates a random ECC key pair: UserB.privKey, UserB.pubKey
3) UserA and UserB exchange their public keys
4) UserA calculates sharedKey = UserB.pubKey * UserA.privKey
5) UserB calculates sharedKey = UserA.pubKey * UserB.privKey

Now both UserA and UserB have the same sharedKey. Here we have considered the Ophthalmologist and the optometrist involved in an ophthalmological case as the two users. The central admin maintains individual pairs of public-private keys for the associated optometrist and the Ophthalmologist for a specific medical case. Hence, each optometrist and Ophthalmologist has different public-private key pairs for each medical case. Thus, whenever an optometrist uploads a retinal image, along with the details of the Ophthalmologist and the patient, a shared secret is created using his public key and the associated Ophthalmologist's private key which are accessed via an API call to the central database. The image is encrypted using the shared secret key, and stored in Database in the "images" collection, and then assigned a unique image id.

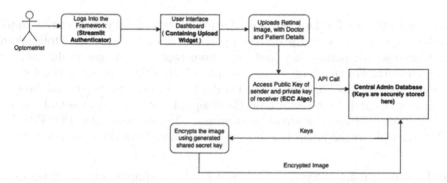

Fig. 1. Sequence Diagram from the Optometrist's point of view.

Further on, the database stores a pentuple consisting of the Optometrist id, the Patient id, the Ophthalmologist id, the image id, and the case Status in the "medcases" collection.

3.2 Opthalmologist's View

Like the optometrist, the Ophthalmologist has access to a user interface for secured logging, using the name, an assigned user id, the user password, and the role "Ophthalmologist." The dashboard presents various medical cases that the doctor is assigned. When the required case is selected, the associated retinal image gets decrypted. An API call to the central database accesses the Ophthalmologist's private key and the related optometrist's public key, which are essential for image decryption. The interactions between these entities is described in (see Fig. 6). These keys reach the doctor via a secure pathway. The Ophthalmologist's Dashboard is displayed in (see Fig. 7).

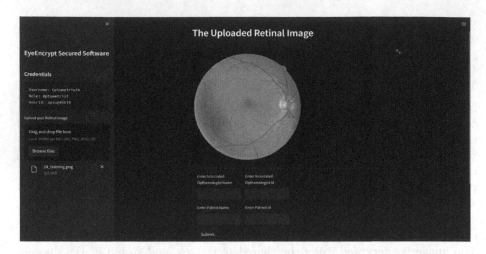

Fig. 2. Optometrist's Dashboard View of the Framework.

Secure Pathway for Decryption. Owing to the critical nature of this step in EyeEncrypt, we propose a procedural pathway to ensure that the Ophthalmologist accesses his private key and the optometrist's public key exclusively and independently. For the same, we have employed a multistep pathway consisting of an email-based One-Time Password(OTP). The API call to the central database generates an email from the admin (the Hospital Authority) to the Ophthalmologist's registered email address, containing a Time-based OTP (TOTP). The OTP available in the email is valid for two minutes from the generation time.

OTP Generation. EyeEncrypt implements a simple way to generate 6-character OTPs consisting of characters and constants using the python libraries, such as math and random [20]. On submitting the OTP, the shared secret key is recreated using the optometrist's obtained public key and the Ophthalmologist's private key. The subsequent steps involve decryption of encrypted image using shared key. The email-based OTP pathway ensures unauthorized users can not access the retinal image. Thus, this secure pathway proliferates the safety aspect of EyeEncrypt. The encrypted image is displayed in (see Fig. 3) and the decrypted image is displayed in (see Fig. 4).

Image Analysis

The framework provides the Ophthalmologist with an interface to perform procedural retinal blood vessel segmentation. We have employed a CLAHE-based pipeline [21].

The pipeline followed for the retinal image segmentation is explained in (see Fig. 5)., The Green channel of the image is first extracted. The green channel of the image contains the greatest light, thus enabling the veins in the eye to be the most visible.

Fig. 3. Encrypted Retinal Image using ECC.

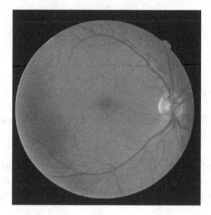

Fig. 4. Decrypted Retinal Image.

Contrast Limited Adaptive Histogram Equalization is employed for the retinal image. This approach is widely used in image enhancement, mainly in the field of ophthalmology. One of the main features in color retinal images is the blood vessel contrast. This method mainly employs the 'contrast' of the image. This is obtained by differentiating the maximum and minimum pixel values. The objective of this phase is to obtain a uniform intensity distribution.

The Gaussian Blur [22] involves passing the kernel through the Gaussian function described below. The pixels of the image get modified after passing through the function, and further analysis is carried out on it.

$$f(x, y) = exp(-(x^2 + y^2)/2 * \sigma^2)$$

where x and y are spatial coordinates of the Gaussian filter and σ is the standard deviation.

The next step involves performing a canny edge detection algorithm [23]. The entire process of the canny edge detection algorithm revolves around the following steps:

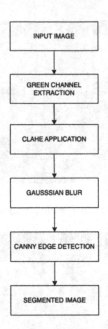

Fig. 5. The followed pipeline for Retinal image segmentation.

1. Smoothen the image using a Gaussian filter to eliminate noise.
2. Compute the change in intensity via computing the gradients of the image.
3. Apply magnitude thresholding to eliminate contrived inputs thus filtering out irrelevant data.
4. Apply a double threshold to determine potential edges
5. Remove all edges that are weakly connected.

Retinal vessel segmentation is generally the first task performed when analyzing retinal fundus images. The Ophthalmologist obtains the segmented image. The segmented image obtained from the framework can be employed in various other medical procedures to predict retinovascular diseases such as glaucoma and diabetes accurately. Finally, the doctor ends the pipeline by submitting a diagnosis report of the patient.

3.3 Patient's View

The patient has access to a dashboard that displays the diagnosis status as "Initiated", "Under Diagnosis", or "Finished", along with the associated Ophthalmologist. Like the other roles, a patient possesses a secured logging system protected by name, the assigned user id, and the user password. The transparency and reliability of the framework assist in efficient diagnosis while ensuring the privacy of the patient's critical medical data.

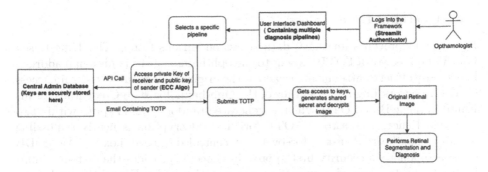

Fig. 6. Sequence Diagram from the Ophthalmologist's point of view.

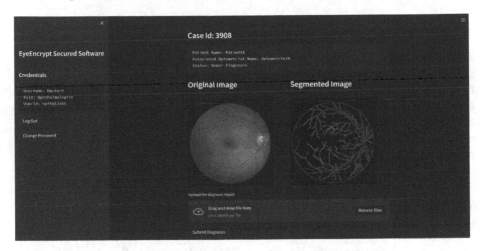

Fig. 7. Ophthalmologist's Dashboard View of the Framework.

4 Results

Eyeencrypt attempts to alleviate cyber attacks targeting critical medical data by employing procedural safety checks and mechanisms for various scenarios, such as contravention of data access by unauthorized users and information leaks during API calls.

4.1 Data Leakage During API Calls

Since Streamlit apps are secured by HTTPS and 256-bit encryption, all the data relayed from the framework to the public internet is safely transported to the destination. Hence, data shared during various API calls, such as keys, encrypted images, and decrypted images, is shared securely. Therefore, any attacker attempting to access data during sharing has to overcome the security checks provided by HTTPS protocol and 256-bit encryption.

4.2   Unethical Data Access

EyeEncrypt prevents unethical data access on various fronts. The Time Based One Time Password(TOTP) is sent to the ophthalmologist via his email address; hence, any attacker attempting to access the original image must first gain access to a) Framework Login Credentials of the Ophthalmologist b) Credentials for his Email c) Time Based OTP, which is generated randomly and expires within two minutes. Hence, access to the OTP for image decryption is nearly impossible for any unauthorized user. Moreover, the central database, i.e., the MongoDB database, follows a security-first approach, hence, it provides the system administrators greater control over resource access. Hence, EyeEncrypt provides the users an improved interface with enhanced information security.

4.3   Framework Time Complexity

All experiments were run on a 1.1 GHz Quad-Core Intel Core i5 machine and a stable internet connection of 78Mbps speed to test the running time of the ECC-based encryption and decryption mechanisms proposed by the framework. On average, the encryption pipeline takes 31.18 ms, while the decryption pipeline takes 8.33 ms. The fast and efficient methodology implemented in the framework ensures an enriching experience for the user while ensuring security. Table 1 displays the time taken for the encryption and decryption process over five experiments.

Table 1. Table showing the running time of the framework for encryption and decryption.

Experiment No	Encryption (in ms)	Decryption (in ms)
1	46.40	9.97
2	21.20	11.48
3	23.70	4.24
4	34.80	9.00
5	29.80	6.95
Average	31.18	8.33

5   Conclusion

The proposed mechanism is a two-step process in which the encryption happens using a shared secret key created by a pair of public and private keys generated using the ECC algorithm. The authentication step happens via an email-based OTP. Data abstraction is implemented by the framework, as only the relevant doctor can access the encrypted enhanced image. The system allows the doctor to perform analysis on the de-encrypted image. Other users will not be able to access the encrypted images, thus incorporating the best practices of security and implementation of Object Oriented Programming concepts such as data abstraction by incorporating different levels of privileged access. The decryption happens using the shared secret key, and the decrypted image is enhanced to facilitate vessel segmentation. The retinal image vessels get effectively segmented, and only the privileged users can access them. After conducting multiple surveys on the existing literature and testing various algorithms, EyeEncrypt incorporates the best practices from multiple domains.

6   Future Scope

The project primarily relies on using the classical asymmetric encryption RSA algorithm; with advances in quantum cryptography, we can integrate the framework with quantum cryptography algorithms. Quantum cryptography would be more secure mainly because it relies on the fundamental laws of physics and not the mathematical computations used today. The use case of our current framework is vessel segmentation. Future enhancements to the project could be scaling up the framework to integrate multiple use cases to optimize medical image diagnosis on a secure framework. Future use cases include an inexhaustive list containing but not limited to, early detection of diseases and surgical optimizations.

References

1. Seh, A.H., et al.: Healthcare data breaches: insights and implications. In: Healthcare, vol. 8, p. 133. Multidisciplinary Digital Publishing Institute (2020)
2. Zia, U., et al.: Survey on image encryption techniques using chaotic maps in spatial, transform and spatiotemporal domains. Int. J. Inf. Secur. **21**, 1–19 (2022)
3. Shand, M., Vuillemin, J.: Fast implementations of RSA cryptography. In: Proceedings of IEEE 11th Symposium on Computer Arithmetic, pp. 252–259. IEEE (1993)
4. Li, N.: Research on Diffie-Hellman key exchange protocol. In: 2010 2nd International Conference on Computer Engineering and Technology, vol. 4, pp. V4-634. IEEE (2010)
5. Hankerson, D., Menezes, A.J., Vanstone, S.: Guide to Elliptic Curve Cryptography. Springer, New York (2006). https://doi.org/10.1007/b97644
6. Tsiounis, Y., Yung, M.: On the security of ElGamal based encryption. In: Imai, H., Zheng, Y. (eds.) PKC 1998. LNCS, vol. 1431, pp. 117–134. Springer, Heidelberg (1998). https://doi.org/10.1007/BFb0054019
7. Perumal, S., Velmurugan, T.: Preprocessing by contrast enhancement techniques for medical images. Int. J. Pure Appl. Math. **118**(18), 3681–3688 (2018)
8. Staal, J., Abramoff, M.D., Niemeijer, M., Viergever, M.A., van Ginneken, B.: Ridge-based vessel segmentation in color images of the retina. IEEE Trans. Med. Imaging **23**(4), 501–509 (2004)

120   G. Hegde et al.

9. Bala, Y., Malik, A.: Biometric inspired homomorphic encryption algorithm for secured cloud computing. In: Panigrahi, B.K., Hoda, M.N., Sharma, V., Goel, S. (eds.) Nature Inspired Computing. AISC, vol. 652, pp. 13–21. Springer, Singapore (2018). https://doi.org/10.1007/978-981-10-6747-1_2
10. Lathey, A., Atrey, P.K.: Image enhancement in encrypted domain over cloud. ACM Trans. Multimedia Comput. Commun. Appl. **11**(3), 1–24 (2015)
11. Sarosh, P., Parah, S.A., Bhat, G.M.: An efficient image encryption scheme for healthcare applications. Multimedia Tools Appl. **81**, 1–18 (2022). https://doi.org/10.1007/s11042-021-11812-0
12. Zhen, P., Zhao, G., Min, L., Jin, X.: Chaos-based image encryption scheme combining DNA coding and entropy. Multimedia Tools Appl. **75**(11), 6303–6319 (2016)
13. Liu, L., Zhang, Q., Wei, X.: A RGB image encryption algorithm based on DNA encoding and chaos map. Comput. Electr. Eng. **38**(5), 1240–1248 (2012)
14. Loukides, G., Liagouris, J., Gkoulalas-Divanis, A., Terrovitis, M.: Disassociation for electronic health record privacy. J. Biomed. Inform. **50**, 46–61 (2014)
15. https://docs.streamlit.io/
16. https://www.mongodb.com/docs/
17. https://pypi.org/project/streamlit-authenticator/
18. https://pypi.org/project/PyNaCl/
19. Costello, C., Smith, B.: Montgomery curves and their arithmetic. J. Cryptogr. Eng. **8**(3), 227–240 (2018)
20. Van Rossum, G.: The Python Library Reference, release 3.8.2. Python Software Foundation (2020)
21. Ooi, A.Z.H., et al.: Interactive blood vessel segmentation from retinal fundus image based on canny edge detector. Sensors **21**(19), 6380 (2021)
22. Hummel, R.A., Kimia, B., Zucker, S.W.: Deblurring gaussian blur. Comput. Vis. Graph. Image Process. **38**(1), 66–80 (1987)
23. Xu, Z., Baojie, X., Guoxin, W.: Canny edge detection based on Open CV. In: 2017 13th IEEE International Conference on Electronic Measurement & Instruments (ICEMI), pp. 53–56 (2017)

Cosine Similarity Based Group Movie Recommendation Scheme Considering Privacy of Users

C. Tripti[1]([envelope]), R. Manoj[2]([envelope]), P. B. Rinsha[1], Megha Suresh[1], Niya Jain[1], and Tanya Sunish[1]

[1] Department of CSE, Rajagiri School of Engineering and Technology, Rajagiri Valley, Kakkanad, Cochin, India
triptic@rajagiritech.edu.in, meghasuresh122@gmail.com
[2] Department of CSE, Manipal Institute of Technology, Manipal Academy of Higher Education (MAHE), Udupi, Manipal, India
manoj.r@manipal.edu

Abstract. The system that can recommend movies for individuals based on their interest has received high popularity. The schemes fail to provide recommendations for a family with people involving different age groups and different interests. Therefore a content based filtering scheme with cosine similarity based recommendation, considering interest of a group of people is proposed here. The system also ensures privacy of the users by generating hash code of the interest provided by the group. The proposed scheme performs well with a prediction accuracy of 83% for a maximum of four users with TMDB database.

Keywords: Recommendation Systems · Cosine Similarity · Content based Filtering · Hash code

1 Introduction

Recommendation systems are popular and help the people to get an optimal automated decision when multiple solutions are available. The movie recommendation systems are basically done with content based filtering scheme. In the case of content based approach, it utilizes item features to suggest related items based on the user's past behavior. Recommendation schemes for a single person is popular and has less complexity whereas the movie recommendation system for a group of people like a family where people having different age groups and different interests is complex. Dissimilarities will be more. Therefore a scheme to identify interests among different categories of people is proposed in this work and a hybrid recommendation scheme involving content based filtering along with cosine similarity is used to give accurate recommendation. The users privacy is protected by generating hash code for the interest provided by the group.

Section 2 gives the current state of art. Section 3 discusses the proposed scheme followed by Sect. 4 detailing on the performance of the system. Section 5 gives the concluding remarks.

© The Author(s), under exclusive license to Springer Nature Singapore Pte Ltd. 2023
S. Prabhu et al. (Eds.): ATIS 2022, CCIS 1804, pp. 121–129, 2023.
https://doi.org/10.1007/978-981-99-2264-2_10

2 Related Works

Recommendation systems provide automated decisions. Sentiment analysis, collaborative filtering, and content-based filtering are examples of popular techniques that have been investigated in literature. These approaches require prior knowledge about the user access history for generating recommendations. Sentiment analysis for movie recommendation system from microblogging data is discussed in [1]. It creates social graphs and recommends movies using sentiment analysis on Twitter data and metadata. Scheme employs a combination of collaborative filtering and content-based filtering. The above mentioned techniques are applied with sentiment analysis of tweets from microblogging sites. A weighted score fusion is applied on the result for movie recommendations. In [2], machine learning approach is used for movie recommendation using cosine similarity to recommend similar type of movies already seen by the user. The Naive Bayes classifier and support vector machine classifier is used to improve the accuracy of the system. In order to categorize the information points, the support vector classifier locates hyperplanes in an N-dimensional space. The Naive Bayes scheme predicts the badge of a text. The probability of each badge is calculated for a given sample and the one that has the highest probability is chosen. Scheme discussed in [3] is based on a collaborative approach that computes connections between different clients, relying on their ratings and recommending movies. The scheme uses the K-means clustering algorithm. To recommend the movies, a collaborative approach combines the ratings of different users with similar interests. Whereas single user's past history and rating are considered to recommend movies for the content-based approach. In [4], the collaborative filtering approach is discussed and the recommended movie list sorted as per the ratings of previous user is presented. The system uses keywords to describe the items and a user profile is built to indicate the interest of the user. Collaborative filtering predicts unknown preferences of user using already known preferences of many users. In [5] analysis of movie recommendation systems with and without considering the low rated movies is discussed. It discusses the effect of ignoring the movies with less rating using Movie-Lens-100k dataset. In the scheme initially the similarities were identified using Pearson correlation coefficient taking all the movies in the database. Then, the low rated movies were ignored and the predictions were done. These recommendations were compared and the changes in the predictions are found to be negligible. The low rated movies do not have a significant contribution in rating prediction.

Cosine similarity scheme along with content based filtering is considered for identifying similarity and popularity based sorting scheme is applied on the result for generating recommendation. Privacy preservation of users is done using hash code.

3   System Architecture

Figure 1 depicts the architecture of the proposed scheme. A website application, in which each user in a group can give a movie name and genre of their interest as inputs, and the system will analyze movies with similar contents. So, using this system people in a group with different interests in movies can watch a single movie together that combines the elements of all the inputs.

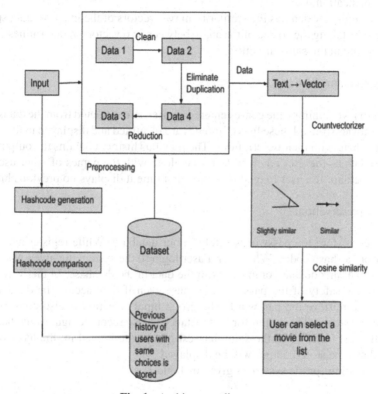

Fig. 1. Architecture diagram

The system includes the following processes:

a   Data pre-processing:

Data pre-processing mainly consists of 3 steps: data cleaning, duplicate, elimination and data reduction. Data cleaning consists of handling data with missing details and irrelevant information. For missing data, ignore the tuples with missing data if the dataset is only large or fill the missing values manually. For noisy data, it is handled using regression or clustering. Duplicate elimination is done to eliminate repeating data. This helps the model to better generalize to the full dataset. Through data cleaning and duplicate elimination, the unwanted data is removed. Data reduction increases the storage efficiency and reduces analysis cost.

b   Count Vectorization and Cosine Similarity:

A document is a collection of thousands of attributes with measure of frequency of a word or phrase in the document. Therefore, the document is an object, which can be represented as a count frequency vector. The text is converted to vector using count vectorizer. Using cosine similarity, these vectors are compared based on the angle between these vectors. The vectors that have minimum angle between them come under the recommendation list.

Cosine similarity denotes the similarity in two vectors of the inner product space. It is indicated by taking the cosine of the angle between two vectors. It determines whether two vectors are in the same direction.

c   Movie recommendation:

The movies containing the genres entered by users are extracted from the dataset. The common movies from all these lists of movies are identified and displayed in the order of popularity along with their descriptions. The previous history contains the output movie recommendations the user received last time along with the names of other users who were in the group. If a user logged in for the first time it displays no previous history.

d   Privacy preservation:

In order to store the passwords safely in our database. While registering we store the password as hash codes. Whenever a user login to the system the given password is converted to hashcode and compared with the data in the database. In this way system can ensure the safety of the password, because even if they access the database it is impossible to retrieve the password. The group input selection is also converted into hashcode and stored. The output for that instance is also recorded against the hash code generated. Next time, when the same interest groups are logged in, the hashcodes are compared and the stored output will be displayed.

The algorithm for the system is given in Table 1:

Table 1. Algorithm

1. Start
2. Hashcode of the username and password is generated and stored in the database.
3. A hashcode of the group interest is also generated to the database.
4. A soup is created containing required features: keywords, cast, director, genres.
5. Count matrix of the soup is generated.
6. Cosine Similarity matrix which depicts similarity between count matrix is generated.
7. For each user input movie,
1. The row of the input movie in the similarity matrix is converted to a list.
2. List is sorted in descending order of similarity value.
3. The title names of each value in the list is extracted.
8. If the users had specified genres, the list of movies of the same genres is extracted into a list.
9. The list from step (6) is intersected with the list from step (5.3) of each user.
10. The resultant list is sorted in descending order of their popularity.
11. The first 6 movies are shown as recommendations and this value is written against the hashcode of the group interest.
12. While getting the input from the user, the generated hashcode is compared with the group interest hashcode and if a match is found, the previously stored recommendation for the specific interest is displayed.
13. Stop

4 Performance Analysis

The proposed scheme has a web page that permits a maximum of four users to input their choices on movie name and genre. The scheme uses TMDB credits and TMDB movies datasets for the proposed scheme. It has about 5000 records. The fields 'crew' and 'cast' from TMDB credits and used keywords, overview, genres, title, popularity fields from TMDB movies. The web user interface is built using HTML, CSS and JavaScript. The signup page is used to create a new account for a user. The sign-in/login page is used by existing users to login to their accounts. Only one user will represent the group and the credentials of the user will be protected by generating a hashcode. The input page records the number of users and their interested movie name and interested genre. The output movie recommendation is displayed in the corresponding page. The hashcode of the inputs from the group is generated and the recommendation for the interest group is stored against the hashcode so that when the same interest group comes next time, the cached data is displayed.

The back end design is done using Python 3.8 version. The program was coded in Pycharm IDE. The dataset used was TMDB credits, TMDB movies with about 5000 records from kaggle. The model performs data extraction and pre-processing of the movie dataset. Count vectorization and cosine similarity is performed on the preprocessed dataset. The similarity score of the movie names entered by users is obtained. The movies similar to the movie names and genres entered by the user are displayed in the order of their popularity. The corresponding description of each movie is also provided.

The model must process the dataset into a suitable format. That is the required fields must be filtered out from the large dataset and the extracted data must be cleaned (duplicate removal, lowercase conversion, etc.). The model creates a soup containing the director's name, genres, cast and keywords. Count vectorization is performed on this soup and cosine similarity function is applied. The similarity score of each movie name entered by the user to every other movie in the dataset is to be obtained in sorted order.

From the similarity scores of the movies entered by each user, the movies similar to each input movie is obtained. The movies containing the genres entered by users are extracted from the dataset. The common movies from all these lists of movies are identified and displayed in the order of popularity along with their descriptions. The previous history contains the output movie recommendations the user received last time along with the names of other users who were in the group. If a user logged in for the first time it displays no previous history.

The model is designed as a user-friendly web application. In which, each user in a group can give a movie name and genre of their interest as inputs, using the Machine Learning approach such as content based filtering, the system will analyze movies with similar contents. It first consists of a sign in page, in which users can sign in using their name, email, password. Then the user can login using his/her username and password.

The model consists of a register table to store the data of registered users and the history table that stores details of user selected movies in the previous login. After logging in, the user is directed to the number of users page, in which user can select the number of users in the group. The user can select a maximum of four users. After choosing the number of users, the user is directed to a page in which the user can enter the names of other users. Then the next page shows two fields – movie name and genre for each user to enter their interested movie name and genre. Based on Cosine Similarity the system will recommend similar movies to the user.

The output also contains a separate part which shows previous history of the logged in user. So, using this system people in a group with different interests in movies can watch a single movie together that combines the elements of all the inputs.

The required features like cast, crew, keywords and genres are extracted from the dataset into python objects. Figure 2 shows the sample of the extracted features.

0	Avatar	[Sam Worthington, Zoe Saldana, Sigourney Weaver]	James Cameron	[culture clash, future, space war]	[Action, Adventure, Fantasy]
1	Pirates of the Caribbean: At World's End	[Johnny Depp, Orlando Bloom, Keira Knightley]	Gore Verbinski	[ocean, drug abuse, exotic island]	[Adventure, Fantasy, Action]
2	Spectre	[Daniel Craig, Christoph Waltz, Léa Seydoux]	Sam Mendes	[spy, based on novel, secret agent]	[Action, Adventure, Crime]
3	The Dark Knight Rises	[Christian Bale, Michael Caine, Gary Oldman]	Christopher Nolan	[dc comics, crime fighter, terrorist]	[Action, Crime, Drama]
4	John Carter	[Taylor Kitsch, Lynn Collins, Samantha Morton]	Andrew Stanton	[based on novel, mars, medallion]	[Action, Adventure, Science Fiction]

Fig. 2. Sample of extracted features

A soup of the required features is created. A Count Vectorizer is used to generate a matrix of token counts. Matrix denotes the frequency of words in the soup. Figure 3 shows the partial count matrix.

```
(0, 40)       1
(0, 111)      1
(0, 2255)     1
(0, 3421)     1
(0, 3710)     1
(0, 4764)     1
(0, 9443)     1
(0, 9841)     1
(0, 10002)    1
(0, 11495)    1
(1, 40)       1
(1, 111)      1
(1, 2937)     1
(1, 3348)     1
(1, 3421)     1
(1, 4005)     1
(1, 5385)     1
(1, 5879)     1
(1, 7961)     1
(1, 8041)     1
(2, 40)       1
(2, 111)      1
(2, 868)      1
(2, 1930)     1
(2, 2226)     1
```

Fig. 3. Partial count matrix

Thus the textual data is converted into vectors which can be used for computing cosine similarity. A cosine similarity matrix which depicts similarity of each movie to every other movie is shown in Fig. 4.

```
[[1.   0.3 0.2 ... 0.   0.   0.  ]
 [0.3 1.   0.2 ... 0.   0.   0.  ]
 [0.2 0.2 1.   ... 0.   0.   0.  ]
 ...
 [0.   0.   0.   ... 1.   0.   0.  ]
 [0.   0.   0.   ... 0.   1.   0.  ]
 [0.   0.   0.   ... 0.   0.   1.  ]]
```

Fig. 4. Partial similarity matrix

Using these similarity scores, the movies similar to each user's input movie can be obtained, which are intersected with each other and the common genres to obtain the final result which is sorted by popularity. A sample input page is shown in Fig. 5.

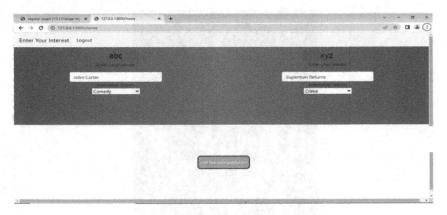

Fig. 5. Input page

The website opens with a signup page which can be used by the user to register himself/herself. Details of the user like username, email, phone number is taken and the user has to set a password. There is also a login page where the user can login using username and password. Followed by which we have the user selection page where the number of users in the group can be selected. For two users, for example, if one user is selecting the interested genre as comedy and movie as John Carter and other user selects crime and Superman Returns, the output include descriptions of movies like Slacker Uprising, Give Me Shelter, This is It, Joe Dirt, etc. For three users, one user selects Batman v Superman: Dawn of Justice, other selects John Carter and the last user selects Superman Returns. Output was Man of Steel, Superman, Superman II, X-men: Days of

Future Past. For four user input movies like John Carter, Titanic, Skyfall, Jakob the Liar and input genres like Thriller, War, Comedy, Animation the output is Outside Providence, Bride & Prejudice, Mean Girls, The Patriot, Failure to Launch. The output page also displays the history of previous recommendations if the group interest is repeated.

5 Conclusion

In the proposed scheme, a web oriented movie recommendation scheme for a family is considered. The scheme accepts multiple movie names as inputs, each family member or friend can input what they want to watch. Using content based filtering the model identifies common traits in the inputs such as genre, director, actor, etc. The model proposes a list of movies that have similar features common to all the inputs. It also does a popularity based sorting to generate an optimal recommendation for the users.

References

1. Kumar, S., De, K., Roy, P.P.: Movie recommendation system using sentiment analysis from microblogging data. IEEE Trans. Comput. Soc. Syst. **7**(4), 915–923 (2020). https://doi.org/10.1109/TCSS.2020.2993585
2. Pavitha, N., et al.: Movie recommendation and sentiment analysis using machine learning. Global Transit. Proc. **3**(1), 279–284 (2022). https://doi.org/10.1016/j.gltp.2022.03.012
3. Furtado, F., Singh, A.: Movie recommendation system using machine learning. Int. J. Res. Ind. Eng. **9**(1), 84–98 (2020)
4. Surendran, A., Kumar Yadav, A., Kumar, A.: Movie recommendation system using machine learning algorithms. Int. Res. J. Eng. Technol. (2020)
5. Reddy, M.M.R., Kanmani, S., Surendiran, B.: Analysis of movie recommendation systems; with and without considering the low rated movies. In: 2020 International Conference on Emerging Trends in Information Technology and Engineering (IC-ETITE), pp. 1–4. IEEE (2020)

Enhancing Face Recognition Accuracy Using the ED-FFP Extraction Method and Ensemble Learning for Forensics and Cyber Security

Pranav Virmani[1], Srikanth Prabhu[2(✉)], and Ramya S.[1(✉)]

[1] Department of Electronics and Communication Engineering, Manipal Institute of Technology (MIT), Manipal Academy of Higher Education (MAHE), Manipal, Udupi, India
`pranav.virmani@learner.manipal.edu, ramya.lokesh@manipal.edu`
[2] Department of Computer Science and Engineering, Manipal Institute of Technology (MIT), Manipal Academy of Higher Education (MAHE), Manipal, Udupi, India
`srikanth.prabhu@manipal.edu`

Abstract. Currently, Face Recognition is the most used biometric to determine an individual's identity due to its natural and unobtrusive nature. This study proposes face recognition and verification of two-dimensional(2D) images by a feature extraction algorithm which involves identifying anthropological facial feature points and calculating the Euclidean Distance (ED) between these points (ED-FFP) as these distances, if required can be used as an objective measure during trials in courts. These measurements are then used as inputs for various classification methods, including Logistic Regression Classifier (LR), Decision Tree (DT), Naive Bayes (NB), and two other classifiers using the Ensemble Learning Model. The method was tested on 2D face image databases (Caltech, Yale, and ORL) and found to be more efficient and accurate for face recognition than other methods, with a maximum accuracy of 85% for predicting distinct faces using the Decision Tree classifier model. The ensemble learning model also had an accuracy of 85%, which could potentially be improved by using more photos for comparison. In future work, the method could be applied to 3D images, which is currently an open challenge in the field.

Keywords: Euclidean Distance · Face Recognition · Logistic Regression · Decision Tree · Naive Bayes · Ensemble Learning

1 Introduction

Automatic face recognition is a biometric technology that uses a database of stored faces to identify or verify individuals in still or moving images. It is a non-intrusive and non-contact form of biometric, unlike methods such as iris or fingerprint recognition which require cooperation from the individual. There are numerous commercial and security applications for face recognition in identity validation and recognition, and it has gained widespread acceptance for use in fields such as law enforcement, security,

© The Author(s), under exclusive license to Springer Nature Singapore Pte Ltd. 2023
S. Prabhu et al. (Eds.): ATIS 2022, CCIS 1804, pp. 130–142, 2023.
https://doi.org/10.1007/978-981-99-2264-2_11

and authentication. Humans also use face recognition to identify people, as the face carries a lot of information about a person's identity.

The development of face recognition technology has attracted researchers from various fields, including computer vision, machine learning, deep learning, neural networks, forensics, and cyber security. Biometric technology, including face recognition, has become increasingly important in facilitating criminal investigations and verifying real human identity through biometric systems. While several biometric traits can be used, such as fingerprints, palm prints, DNA, voice patterns, iris patterns, hand measurements, and facial patterns, face recognition is highly accurate and minimally intrusive, making it a preferred method.

This study aims to develop a face recognition and verification method for forensic examination that can identify and recognize individuals in constrained environments like variations in the pose of the face, expression, occlusion, and illumination. These are some real-life challenges, and the method should be efficient and novel and should be able to differentiate between identical twins and address challenges such as illumination, head pose, and expressions. The steps involved in this process are face detection, feature extraction and training machine learning classifiers using the extracted features. We will test our method on multiple databases. The primary goal of this is to study existing algorithms, analyze their shortcomings, and propose a new technique for forensic investigation in human face verification using a 2D image.

The first section is an Introduction which is a general discussion about the area of work in the present-day scenario. The second section is Related Work. It discusses the already implemented work in the area of face recognition while highlighting the key aspects in which this study differs from the existing literature. The third section is Methodology which includes a detailed explanation of how the work has been carried out. The fourth section is Results where all the experimental results are shown graphically and the final section is Conclusion.

1.1 Face Recognition for Forensics and Face Anthropometry

The face is the front part of the head that in humans extends from the forehead to the chin and includes the mouth, nose, cheeks, and eyes.

Fig. 1. Key anthropometric face landmarks on a face

Forensic photo facial analysis is the method that uses facial images to assist or facilitate human identification. The concept consists of craniofacial identification procedures that use skull and faces i.e., facial approximation and photographic superimposition. This method assists human identification via analysis or generation of facial graphics and is defined as photo facial analysis.

Facial landmarks are defined as the detection and localization of certain key points on the face which have an impact on subsequent tasks focused on the face, like animation, face recognition, gaze detection, face tracking, expression recognition, gesture understanding and more. Table 1 below defines the major landmark points on a human face and Fig. 1 above marks these points on a face.

Table 1. Landmarks Definitions

Anthropometry Landmarks	Definition
Exocanthion(Ex)	The soft tissue point located at the outer commissure of eye fissure
Endocanthion(En)	The soft tissue point located at the inner commissure of eye fissure
Cheilion(Ch)	The point of the mouth corner
Stomion(Sto)	The midpoint of the labial commissure when the lips are closed.
Gnathion(Gn)	The lowest median landmark on the lower border of the mandible
Trichion (Tr)	Anterior hairline at the mid-line
Pogonion(Pg)	The most anterior midpoint of the chin
Glabella(G)	The most prominent midline between eyebrows
Nasion(N)	The midpoint on the soft tissue contour of the base of the nasal root
Subnasale(Sn)	Junction of the inferior portion of the nasal septum and the upper lip
Pronasale(Prn)	The most anterior midpoint of the nasal tip
Pogonion(Pg)	The most anterior midpoint of the chin

2 Related Work

Face recognition has become a popular biometric used by humans in recent decades, with numerous security and forensic applications in both government and industries. It is a non-intrusive and non-contact form of biometric, unlike methods such as fingerprint recognition or iris which require cooperation from the individual. Despite significant progress in face recognition, current systems are not up to the mark, and researchers aim to make them more like the human visual system. The goal of this study is to develop a dependable automated face verification system that is resilient under a range of noise, light, and occlusion conditions and can differentiate between similar-looking individuals, including identical twins.

Facial recognition technology has been widely adopted in security systems in the wake of the 9/11 attacks, particularly in airports and border crossings where facial identification verification is necessary. These systems have the potential to prevent future attacks and help identify criminals or missing persons. Facial recognition is also used in surveillance cameras and on social media platforms like Facebook. However, the effectiveness of these systems depends on the facial recognition algorithms' accuracy and the completeness of the database of faces. Despite this, there are many potential applications for facial recognition technology in a variety of settings.

Since the development of the first computer-based face recognition system by Woody Bledsoe et.al [29] in 1960, the field has advanced significantly and now has many potential applications such as in security and law enforcement. The increasing number of publications and conferences on the topic reflects its current popularity, made possible by the availability of inexpensive cameras and computers. Various algorithms for face recognition and variations have been achieved. Among the algorithms for object detection, the Viola-Jones Algorithm [8] stands out as key research in computer vision for its efficiency and compact size. It implements a well-known algorithm AdaBoost along with a classifier called Haar cascade to detect a face in real-time and has significantly improved detection rates compared to previous algorithms in the field of facial recognition.

Facial recognition and verification using anthropometry for forensic purposes have also been the subject of extensive research, with various algorithms and methods proposed. In 2008, Sohail et al. [9] developed a method for identifying the most crucial 18 feature points on a face for identification using a statistically derived anthropometric facial model. These feature points are typically located near the lips, nose, eyes, and eyebrows, and the model is based on the structural symmetry of the human face. Rachid AHDID et al. [1, 3] subsequently applied and compared the use of Euclidean distance on 5, 10, and 64 facial feature points and found that the 64-point method was the most effective for efficient verification. They used the Gabor Boosted algorithm and tested their method on three different face databases. In 2021, Alsawwaf et al. [15] researched identifying a person's face through ratios and distances between facial feature points for both forensic and general-purpose use, improving the accuracy of identification using various machine learning classifiers.

This study is an evaluation of various ML techniques that are extremely popular in the community like Logistic Regression Classifier (LR), Decision Tree (DT) and Naive Bayes incorporated into an ensemble learning model. These techniques have been applied in past studies for automatic 2D face recognition, with the ability to identify and differentiate between similar-looking, even identical, faces (Rustam, Zuherman et al. [16]). The models presented in these studies have various applications beyond forensics, such as predicting health concerns that affect the facial structure and analyzing facial expressions (Milutinovic, Jovana et al. [13], who used anthropometric models to evaluate facial beauty). In 2021, Gangothri Sanil et al. [7] showed the accuracy of how the golden ratio can be used to identify similar faces using the Dlib's 68-point detector. Her self-created dataset applied on various machine learning classifiers accurately distinguished between look-alike individuals.

The goal of this paper is to design an automatic and robust system for face recognition by extracting the facial feature points and at the same time computing Euclidean Distance (ED) between those points for forensic sciences. Then these measures are given as input to commonly used classifiers like (KNN), (SVM) and a few more using Ensemble learning.

3 Methodology

The process of using an automatic face recognition system starts with pre-processing, followed by the face detection part which is followed by face feature extraction and last is the classification. These here are referred to as the four phases or building blocks. Figure 2 is the process architecture of a face recognition system.

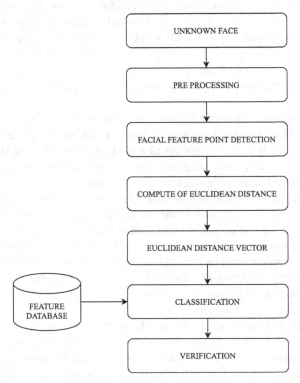

Fig. 2. Methodology Architecture

Pre-processing, which involves removing noise and adjusting illumination and colour, is the initial step. Then, in the input photos, faces should be found, and segmented and the desired facial feature points need to be extracted. This is done with the help of the Dlib library. We have implemented the 68-point landmark detector. The principle this landmark detector works is by implementing a Histogram of Oriented Gradients commonly known as HOG and a Linear Support Vector Machine for training. After the extraction of facial feature points, taking the centroid of the nose as the origin, distances to all the other points were calculated and used to train and classify using the machine learning models in ensemble learning.

3.1 Image Database

The main and primary dataset used is the Caltech Face database [18] which contains 720 facial images of Caltech students and professors. The images are of a resolution of

283 × 327pixels. There are 20 images of each individual and 36 unique individuals in this dataset. Examples of some images are shown in Fig. 3.

Fig. 3. Images from Caltech Face Image Database

To test the robustness of the designed method, we also implement it on the ORL dataset [17] which contains 400 images of 40 individuals and the Yale Face dataset [19] containing 575 images of 25 individuals. These databases are the widely used datasets in the literature and make sure that for a few subjects the images have been taken at different timing while changing the situations like light conditions, different face poses and adding some occlusion.

3.2 Detection of a Face's Feature Points

Accurate detection of feature points of a face is a key part of applications such as face tracking and face identification/verification. Facial landmark is a prominent feature that can play a discriminative role or can serve as anchor points on a face graph. For a face, it can be any point where the intensity varies like eyes, eyebrows, lips etc.

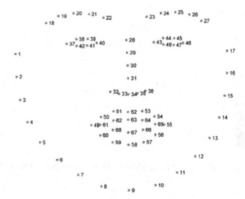

Fig. 4. Visualising the 68 points landmarks coordinates

Here, we extract 68 facial feature points using the Dlib library [20]. This landmark detector is part of the OpenCV library in Python. It extracts the positions of all these 68 points in (x, y) coordinates which can be used to compute the Euclidean distance afterwards. The 68-point detector (shown in Fig. 4) works by first detecting the face with the help of the Histogram of Oriented Gradients commonly known as the HOG algorithm proposed by Navneet Dalal et al., in their paper "Histograms of Oriented Gradients for Human Detection" in 2005 [12]. The HOG method is an algorithm which divides any given image into tiny cells and calculates the gradient, direction and also magnitude for every pixel in each cell. Then a histogram is formed after combining the gradients which represent the shape of the object. After the successful detection of the face and its region of interest (68 facial landmarks points) next comes the feature extraction which is done by a max-margin detector followed by feature classification done by a linear SVM. Figure 5 below is the flow diagram of the entire process.

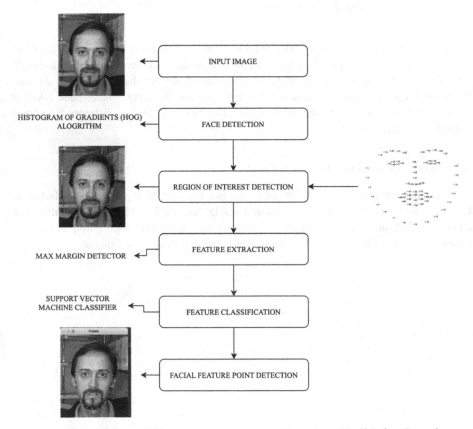

Fig. 5. Flow Diagram of Facial Feature Points Detection using Dlib 68 Points Detection.

3.3 Euclidean Vector

Between two points when one measures a distance, it's called Euclidean distance. It can even be measured with the help of a ruler as well. The ED between two points A and D is equal to the length of the line [AD]. If $A = (a_1, a_2, a_3, a_4, ..., a_n)$ and $D = (d_1, d_2, d_3,$

$d_4, \dots, d_n$) are the two points in Cartesian coordinates then the output distance from A to D or from D to A is:

$$d(A, D) = \sqrt{\sum_{i=1}^{n} (a(i) - d(i))^2} \tag{1}$$

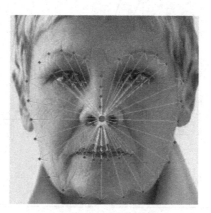

Fig. 6. Example of 68 distance vectors on an image

For the 68 facial feature points detected, we calculated the distance from each point to the centroid of the nose taking it as the reference point. Figure 6 shows how these distance vectors are marked. This results in a total of 68 distances vector for one image, which is stored in an array as shown below and later stored in an excel file. The computation of these distances was done with the help of the NumPy library in Python and the classification is shown next:

$$(Euclidian\,Distance) = \begin{pmatrix} d1 \\ d2 \\ d3 \\ \cdot \\ \cdot \\ \cdot \\ d68 \end{pmatrix} \tag{2}$$

3.4 Classification Using Ensemble Learning

The above Eq. (2) shows that we have computed the Euclidean Distances for all the images. Now the next step is to classify them using some machine learning algorithms. A technique, ensemble learning uses the combined predictions of many different machine learning models together in one single predictive model having the advantage to produce highly accurate predictions. Rather than using any one single model, for the improvement of the performance, algorithms like SVM, Decision Tree, KNN, Logistics Regression

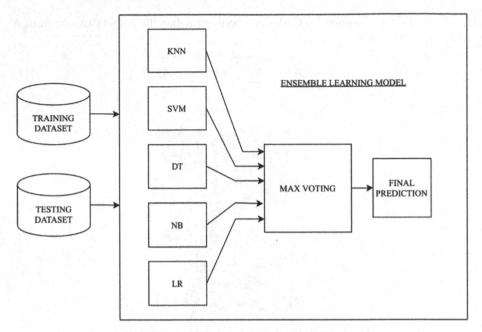

Fig. 7. Ensemble Learning Model Block Diagram

and Naive Bayes are combined to obtain the prediction. Here, Fig. 7 below shows how this is done:

The classification model was implemented using Python 3.7 in PyCharm IDE using the sci-kit-learn library [21]. Here we divide the data into a training set with 80% and a targeting set with a 20% split. This model feeds the input distances and the class labels for each image to learn the patterns in the data and use them to make predictions. Then, we evaluate these predictions by comparing the predicted output labels with true output labels.

4   Results

The steps for both feature extraction and feature classification have been implemented and this section discusses the evaluated results from the algorithms implemented and highlights the extracted output in a tabular/graphical manner.

4.1   Feature Extraction Results

We extracted the facial feature points using the 68-point detector from the Dlib library. On the Caltech face database, out of the 720 images, all of them were detected which yields an accuracy of 100%. For the Yale dataset, out of 575 images, 566 were successfully detected which was 98.44% accurate and for the ORL dataset 345 images were accurately detected from 400 facial images with an accuracy of 86.25%. Figure 8 shows the comparison of detection accuracy on all 3 datasets.

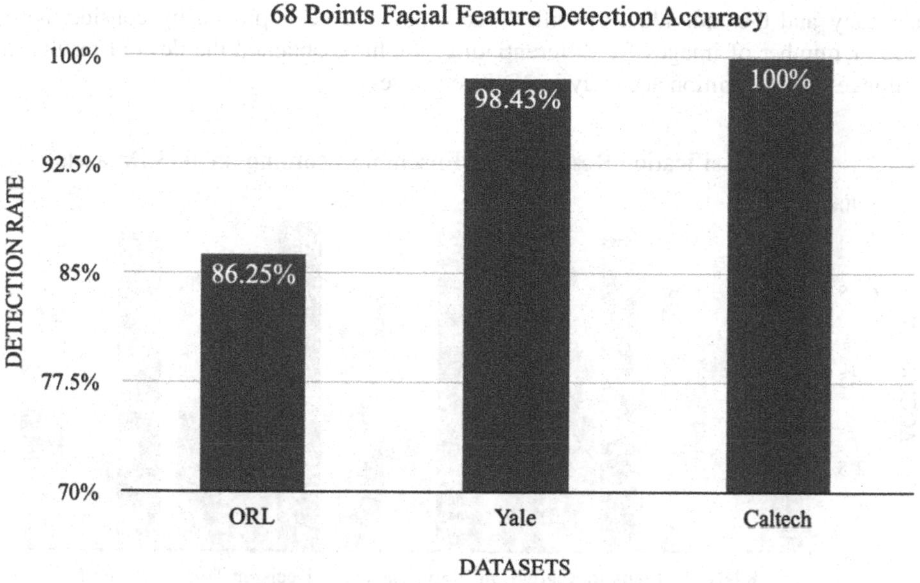

68 Points Facial Feature Detection Accuracy

Fig. 8. Comparison of feature point detection accuracy.

4.2 Classification Results

We classified the input images in all three datasets with ensemble learning. Table 2 below shows the detailed accuracy of every model on each dataset. The model was able to achieve an overall accuracy of 85% for the Caltech face database, 77% for Yale face dataset and 71% for the ORL dataset.

Table 2. Classification Accuracy Comparison

Datasets	KNN	Logistic Regression	Naive Bias	Decision Tree	SVM	Model Ensemble
Caltech	81%	81%	83%	85%	82%	85%
Yale	74%	75%	75%	77%	75%	77%
ORL	69%	70%	68%	71%	62%	71%

Figure 9 below shows the classification accuracy of each machine learning classifier used in the ensemble learning model and highlights that the Decision Tree classifier is the most accurate classification model on all three datasets. The model ensemble accuracy and the individual classifier's accuracy can be improved by considering a greater number of images for differentiating. We have obtained the desired results to enhance the recognition accuracy in 2D face images.

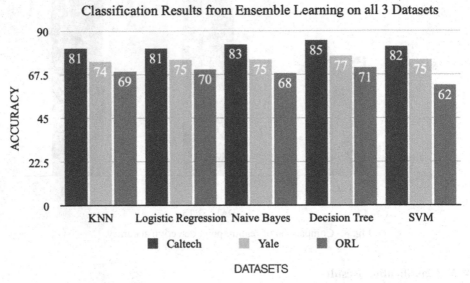

Fig. 9. Classifier-wise comparison of accuracy on all datasets.

5   Conclusions

This paper presented a face recognition system based on Euclidean Distance Facial Feature points. Here, we used 2D images from three renowned face datasets (Caltech, Yale and ORL) and implemented both algorithms for facial feature extraction and classification on the extracted Euclidean distance as these distances can be used as proof in forensic sciences. The feature extraction was done with a Dlib library 68 points detector and the classification by ensemble learning model giving the output accuracy as 85% on the Caltech dataset. This is an improvement over the previous work and shows that the Decision Tree is the most accurate machine learning classifier among the implemented classifiers. These extracted distances can also be used for further work as these labels can be used not only for identification or verification but to detect early-stage diseases which have an impact on an individual's face. Future study is to implement this on 3D images.

References

1. Ahdid, R., Taifi, K., Said, S., Manaut, B.: Euclidean & Geodesic Distance between a Facial Feature Points in Two-Dimensional Face Recognition System (2016)

2. Vukadinovic, D., Pantic, M.: Fully automatic facial feature point detection using Gabor feature based boosted classifiers. In: Conference Proceedings – IEEE International Conference on Systems, Man and Cybernetics, vol. 2, pp. 1692–1698 (2005). https://doi.org/10.1109/ICSMC.2005.1571392
3. Ahdid, R., Taifi, K., Said, S., Manaut, B.: A survey on facial feature points detection techniques and approaches. Int. J. Comput. Electr. Autom. Control Inf. Eng. **10**, 1471–1478 (2016)
4. Amato, G., Falchi, F., Gennaro, C., Vairo, C.: A comparison of face verification with facial landmarks and deep features. In: MMEDIA 2018, The Tenth International Conference on Advances in Multimedia at Athens, Greece (2018)
5. Jafri, R., Arabnia, H.: A survey of face recognition techniques. JIPS **5**, 41–68 (2009). https://doi.org/10.3745/JIPS.2009.5.2.041
6. Lazarini, M.A., Rossi, R., Hirama, K.: A systematic literature review on the accuracy of face recognition algorithms. EAI Endorsed Trans. IoT **8**(30), e5 (2022)
7. Sanil, G., Prakash, K., Prabhu, S., Nayak, V.C.: Effectiveness of the use of golden ratio in identifying similar faces using ensemble learning. In: Pokhrel, S.R., Yu, M., Li, G. (eds.) Applications and Techniques in Information Security: 12th International Conference, ATIS 2021, Virtual Event, December 16–17, 2021, Revised Selected Papers, pp. 62–80. Springer Singapore, Singapore (2022). https://doi.org/10.1007/978-981-19-1166-8_6
8. Viola, P., Jones, M.J.: Robust real-time face detection. Int. J. Comput. Vis. **57**, 137–154 (2004)
9. Abu Sayeed, Md., Sohail, P.B.: Detection of facial feature points using anthropometric face model. In: Damiani, E., Yétongnon, K., Schelkens, P., Dipanda, A., Legrand, L., Chbeir, R. (eds.) Signal Processing for Image Enhancement and Multimedia Processing, pp. 189–200. Springer US, Boston, MA (2008). https://doi.org/10.1007/978-0-387-72500-0_17
10. Kukharev, G.A., Kaziyeva, N.: Digital facial anthropometry: application and implementation. Pattern Recognit. Image Anal. **30**(3), 496–511 (2020). https://doi.org/10.1134/S1054661820030141
11. Quiñones, M.R., Masip, D., Vitrià, J.: Automatic detection of facial feature points via HOGs and geometric prior models. In: Vitrià, J., Sanches, J.M., Hernández, M. (eds.) IbPRIA 2011. LNCS, vol. 6669, pp. 371–378. Springer, Heidelberg (2011). https://doi.org/10.1007/978-3-642-21257-4_46
12. Dalal, N.,, Triggs, B.: Histograms of oriented gradients for human detection. In: 2005 IEEE Computer Society Conference on Computer Vision and Pattern Recognition (CVPR 2005), vol. 1, pp. 886–893 (2005). https://doi.org/10.1109/CVPR.2005.177
13. Milutinovic, J., Zelic, K., Nedeljkovic, N.: Evaluation of facial beauty using anthropometric proportions. Sci. World J. **2014**, 1–8 (2014). https://doi.org/10.1155/2014/428250
14. Ahdid, R., Azougaghe, E., Safi, S., Manaut, B.: Two-dimensional face surface analysis using facial feature points detection approaches. J. Electron. Commerce Org. **16**(1), 57–71 (2018). https://doi.org/10.4018/JECO.2018010105
15. Alsawwaf, M., Chaczko, Z., Kulbacki, M., Sarathy, N.: In your face: person identification through ratios and distances between facial features. Vietnam J. Comput. Sci. **9**(2), 187–202 (2022)
16. Rustam, Z., Faradina, R.: Face recognition to identify look-alike faces using support vector machine. J. Phys. Conf. Ser. **1108**(1) (2018)
17. Database: http://vision.ucsd.edu/datasetsAl
18. Database: https://www.vision.caltech.edu/datasets/caltech_10k_webfaces/
19. Database: http://cvc.cs.yale.edu/cvc/projects/yalefaces/yalefaces.html
20. Dlib library. http://dlib.net/. Accessed 13 Apr 2018
21. Pedregosa et al.: Scikit-learn: machine learning in Python. JMLR **12**, 2825–2830 (2011)

22. Lai, J.H., Yuen, P.C., Chen, W.S., Lao, S., Kawade, M.: Robust facial feature point detection under nonlinear illuminations. In: Proceedings IEEE ICCV Workshop on Recognition, Analysis, and Tracking of Faces and Gestures in Real-Time Systems, pp. 168–174 (2001). https://doi.org/10.1109/RATFG.2001.938927

23. Patil, S., Trivedi, S., Jani, J., Shah, S., Kanani, P.: Digitized railway ticket verification using facial recognition. In: 2021 5th International Conference on Intelligent Computing and Control Systems (ICICCS), pp. 1556–1563 (2021). https://doi.org/10.1109/ICICCS51141.2021.9432371

24. Prayaga, L., Devulapalli, K., Prayaga, C.: Wearable devices data for activity prediction using machine learning algorithms. Int. J. Big Data Analyt. Healthc. 4, 32–46 (2019). https://doi.org/10.4018/IJBDAH.2019010103

25. Brahmbhatt, N.R., Prajapati, H.B., Dabhi, V.K.: Survey and analysis of extraction of human face features. In: 2017 Innovations in Power and Advanced Computing Technologies (i-PACT), pp. 1–8 (2017). https://doi.org/10.1109/IPACT.2017.8245033

26. Jahanbin, A., Rashed, R., Yazdani, R., Shahri, N.M., Kianifar, H.: Evaluation of some facial anthropometric parameters in an Iranian population: infancy through adolescence. J. Craniofac. Surg. 24(3), 941–945 (2013). https://doi.org/10.1097/SCS.0b013e31828dcf4f

27. Ashiba, M.I., Youness, H.A., Ashiba, H.I.: Suggested wavelet transform for cancelable face recognition system. Multimedia Tools Appl. 81(30), 43701–43726 (2022). https://doi.org/10.1007/s11042-022-13070-0

28. Peng, P., Portugal, I., Alencar, P., Cowan, D.: A face recognition software framework based on principal component analysis. PLoS One 16(7), e0254965 (2021). https://doi.org/10.1371/journal.pone.0254965

29. https://en.wikipedia.org/wiki/Facial_recognition_system

Intrusion Detection Using Federated Learning

G. K. Sudhina Kumar [iD], K. Krishna Prakasha[(✉)] [iD],
and Balachandra Muniyal [iD]

Department of Information and Communication Technology,
Manipal Institute of Technology, Manipal Academy of Higher Education,
Manipal, India
sudhina.gk@learner.manipal.edu, {kkp.prakash,bala.chandra}@manipal.edu

Abstract. In the evolving world, the drastic expansion of the internet and the use of smart devices demands a change in existing infrastructure. These rapid changes in the structural level also open new dimensions that are susceptible to cyber-attacks. One of the efficient methods to tackle these situations is to apply intelligence to the systems and detect abnormal behaviours. As privacy plays a vital role, here Federated Learning method is used to detect cyber attacks by analysing the data logs and compared with the non-federated learning techniques on the same data. It is very evident from the experiment that Federated Learning is very effective in detecting these attacks by preserving the privacy of the victim organisations/systems.

Keywords: Federated Learning · Intrusion Detection · Cyber Security · IoT · Deep Learning

1 Introduction

In the modern world, more intelligent devices are taking part in day-to-day activities, and technological advancement effectively minimises the difficulties of achieving complex tasks. As everything gets connected to the more extensive network, it is vital to guard and maintain the integrity of this network to run the system effectively. Researchers are continuously working to create an intelligence which may automatically detect unusual activities and take appropriate actions to maintain the system.

1.1 Intrusion Detection

With time, more devices are getting connected to the network, which opens up new security dimensions that may be prone to attacks such as intrusions. Traditional "Intrusion Detection System" (IDS) are less effective due to the system

© The Author(s), under exclusive license to Springer Nature Singapore Pte Ltd. 2023
S. Prabhu et al. (Eds.): ATIS 2022, CCIS 1804, pp. 143–151, 2023.
https://doi.org/10.1007/978-981-99-2264-2_12

and network structural changes. An efficient and robust intrusion detection system is need of an hour. IDS could be hardware or software that monitors the behaviour in the system [1,2].

IDS records the unusual patterns related to logs, warns the concerned and initiates the necessary action steps if it finds any types of intrusions in the systems, as shown in the Fig. 1.

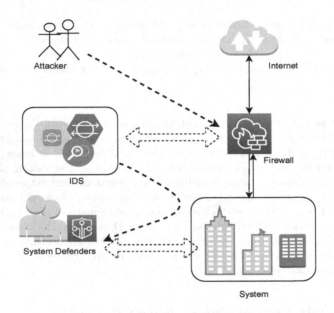

Fig. 1. Overview of an IDS Ecosystem

Majorly used types of IDS [3] are "Host-based intrusion detection systems" and "Network intrusion detection systems". With increased connectivity, other types of IDS are used, such as "Perimeter intrusion detection systems" and "VM-based intrusion detection systems". Most intrusions are commonly detected by signature-based, and anomaly-based detection techniques [4]. Here we are mainly focusing on anomaly-based detection, as signature-based detection cannot find new types of intrusions without knowing attack signatures.

1.2   Federated Learning

Federated Learning (FL) is a particular setting in the Machine Learning method where a group of organisations or people provide the data and collectively train the model as in Fig. 2. Here, the data used are decentralised, and the central server orchestrates the entire process. A model like the "ACH Reference Model" [5] accommodates collaboration between organisations or groups to train the FL models collectively in a privacy preserved manner. FL minimises most of the privacy risks associated with traditional Artificial Intelligence/Machine Learning (AI/ML) usage. Motivated by the widening scope and actual practice, this work embodies FL usage.

FL term was introduced in 2016 by McMahan et al., [6]: "We term our approach Federated Learning since the learning task is solved by a loose federation of participating devices (which we refer to as clients) which are coordinated by a central server". One of the long-standing goals of the active research community is to study, understand and learn from the distributed set of data among different data owners without actually getting/exposing the data.

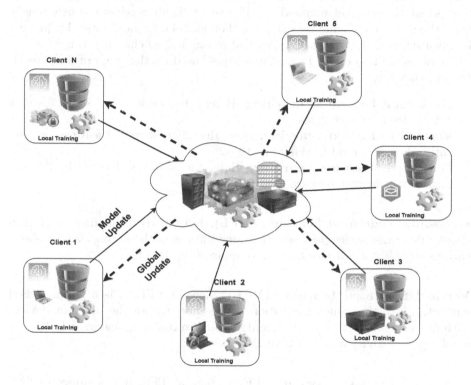

Fig. 2. General Architecture of Federated Learning Technique

FL is the reference for fundamental constraints and risks in traditional applied AI/ML problems on distributed data sets where privacy is the primary concern.

In this work, we have developed a deep-learning auto-encoder model in federated settings for intrusion detection. In addition, we have performed the comparison between FL and centralised learning models for performance metrics to show the suitability of FL in intrusion detection.

2   Background

The primary motivation behind using FL is that it allows the clients to train the global model using decentralized data and it does not demand the clients to share their data, unlike the traditional AI/ML models, where the client must share the data with the centralized server. There are different ways in which the model could be trained over other devices using distributed data over many iterations [7, 8].

FL works in an iterative fashion where in each round, the ML model is trained at the client side, and the weights are sent to the server; this will help the global model to get updated [9]. The set of clients receives the new weight from the global model and uses them in their model over local data; this process is repeated until the threshold is reached or the desired efficiency is achieved.

Generally, FL is divided into three types based on the types of data distribution; they are,

- **Horizontal Federated Learning:** Here, it has an identical set of features with different observations.
- **Vertical Federated Learning:** Here, the different sets of features or even entire domains could be different [10–12].
- **Federated Transfer Learning:** Here, the same devices with different instances or feature sets are used [13, 14].

Horizontal Federated Learning (HFL). Here in HFL, the dataset at each client side or the device possesses the same features with varying sizes or observations. It is like a row vice division of an existing data file.

Vertical Federated Learning (VFL). Here in VFL, it is a feature-based dataset, where the same observation can be noted from the different devices with not matching sets of features and are used to train a global model. It is like a column vice division of an existing dataset.

Federated Transfer Learning (TFL). Here in TFL, It is a subset of VFL where datasets on client devices vary with features and instances; moreover, these different datasets are used to train global models.

3   Methodology

As privacy plays a vital role, training a model on distributed data sets is a crucial research direction. Here we use the IoT-related data set, i.e., "N-BaIoT data-set" from Kaggle [15]. We compartmentalise it into Nine segments, each representing an independent individual IoT device total of nine in number. We then train the "Deep auto-encoder" model over distributed data set using the FL technique. A total of 89 Files are in the data set [15]; These 89 CSV files merged to form nine files based on the nine devices used. These nine files are labelled Device1, Device2 and so on. Different types of "Botnet attacks" are performed on these IoT devices. By analysing the newly formed Data-sets, Here in these nine files, Data from other types of attacks and benign data are distributed, as shown in Fig. 3.

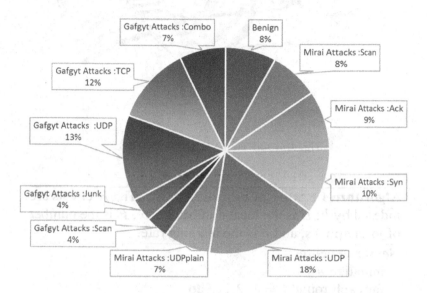

Fig. 3. Attack Types in the N-BaIoT Data-set

Two categories of "Botnet" attacks Five types of attacks in each category are performed on IoT devices, and the details of these attacks as shown in the Fig. 4.

Existing work shows that, when it comes to the matter of anomaly detection, the false alert rate is much lower in "Deep auto-encoder" compared with the mainly used algorithms like: "SVM", "PCA", and "Isolation Forest". Here we are implementing the same using FL and looking into how efficiently it can detect the anomaly.

The primary goal is understanding and implementing the anomaly detection mechanism using FL. Dataset used in this experiment is non-IID and heterogeneous. The aggregation algorithm used is "FedAvg" and "SGD" for the optimization. The FedAvg pseudo code [15] as in Algorithm 1:

"Mean Square Error" is used to find the difference between the actual and estimated values. "Pandas and Numpy" are used for data modification. Pytorch is used for the model building of both the local model and the FL model.

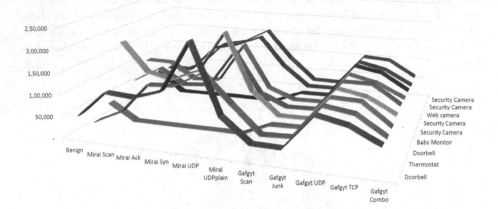

Fig. 4. Total Traffic Data from Devices

Algorithm 1 FederatedAveraging. The K clients are indexed by k; B is the local minibatch size, E is the number of local epochs, and η is the learning rate.

Server executes:
   initialize w_0
   for each round $t = 1, 2, \ldots$ **do**
      $m \leftarrow \max(C \cdot K, 1)$
      $S_t \leftarrow$ (random set of m clients)
      for each client $k \in S_t$ **in parallel do**
         $w_{t+1}^k \leftarrow$ ClientUpdate(k, w_t)
      $w_{t+1} \leftarrow \sum_{k=1}^{K} \frac{n_k}{n} w_{t+1}^k$

ClientUpdate(k, w): // *Run on client k*
   $\mathcal{B} \leftarrow$ (split $\mathcal{P}_k$ into batches of size B)
   for each local epoch i from 1 to E **do**
      for batch $b \in \mathcal{B}$ **do**
         $w \leftarrow w - \eta \nabla \ell(w; b)$
   return w to server

The confusion matrix compares the predicted class to the actual class in anomaly detection and the evaluation metric used are,

- "Recall or TPR: True Positive Rate", "FPR: Fall Out or False Positive Rate", and F1 score.

4   Results

Comparison between FL and Non-FL on different parameters are graphically represented as in the Fig. 5 and Fig. 6.

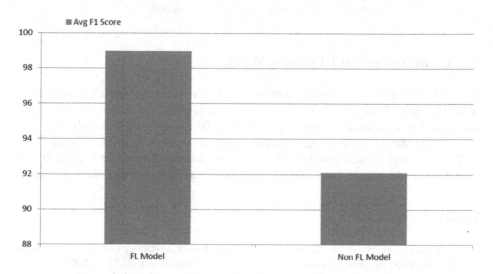

Fig. 5. Average F1 score of FL and Non FL

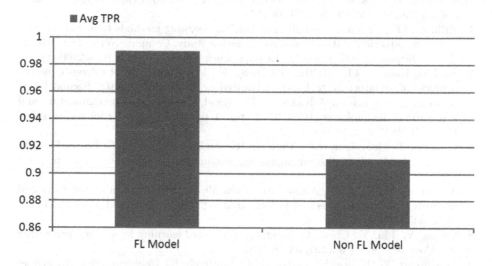

Fig. 6. Avg TPR of FL and Non FL

Experimental understanding shows that the FL technique gives better results in comparison with the Non-FL technique; the practical development is shown in the Table 1.

Table 1. Comparison of FL and Non-FL Results

Model Type	Avg TPR	Avg FPR	Avg F1 score
FL	0.99988	0.026	99.966
Non-FL	0.90076	0.023	93.095

5   Conclusion and Future Work

From the Table 1 in the result section, FL shows better results when compared with the non-FL model. Here data from nine devices are comparatively small compared to real-world scenarios. In future, To know the full potential of FL, we are introducing a more number and variety of devices to generate data. This will help to understand how the FL model can handle diverse data types. It can also use the blockchain for auditing the different models in a distributed fashion.

References

1. Bhattacharya, S., et al.: A novel PCA-firefly based XGBoost classification model for intrusion detection in networks using GPU. Electronics **9**, 219 (2020)
2. Alazab, M., Broadhurst, R.: Spam and criminal activity. Trends Issues Crime Crim. Justice 1–20 (2016)
3. Hindy, H., et al.: A taxonomy of network threats and the effect of current datasets on intrusion detection systems. IEEE Access **8**, 104650–104675 (2020). https://doi.org/10.1109/ACCESS.2020.3000179
4. Kilincer, I.F., Ertam, F., Sengur, A.: Machine learning methods for cyber security intrusion detection: datasets and comparative study. Comput. Netw. **188**, 107840 (2021). https://www.sciencedirect.com/science/article/pii/S1389128621000141
5. Sudhina Kumar, G.K., Krishna Prakasha, K., Muniyal, B.: ACH reference model-a model of architecture to handle advanced cyberattacks. In: 2022 Second International Conference on Advances in Electrical, Computing, Communication and Sustainable Technologies (ICAECT), pp. 1–6 (2022). https://doi.org/10.1109/ICAECT54875.2022.9808076
6. Konecný, J., McMahan, H.B., Yu, F.X., Richtarik, P., Suresh, A.T., Bacon, D.: Federated learning: strategies for improving communication efficiency. arXiv preprint arXiv:1610.05492 (2016)
7. Taheri, R., Shojafar, M., Alazab, M., Tafazolli, R.: FED-IIoT: a robust federated malware detection architecture in industrial IoT. IEEE Trans. Ind. Inform. **17**(12), 8442–8452 (2020)
8. Cheng, Y., Liu, Y., Chen, T., Yang, Q.: Federated learning for privacy-preserving AI. Commun. ACM **63**(12), 33–36 (2020)
9. Mothukuri, V., Khare, P., Parizi, R.M., Pouriyeh, S., Dehghantanha, A., Srivastava, G.: Federated-learning-based anomaly detection for IoT security attacks. IEEE Internet Things J. **9**(4), 2545–2554 (2021)
10. Gadekallu, T.R., Pham, Q.-V., Huynh-The, T., Bhattacharya, S., Maddikunta, P.K.R., Liyanage, M.: Federated learning for big data: a survey on opportunities, applications, and future directions. arXiv preprint arXiv:2110.04160 (2021)

11. Alazab, M., Swarna Priya, R.M., Parimala, M., Maddikunta, P.K.R., Gadekallu, T.R., Pham, Q.-V.: Federated learning for cybersecurity: concepts, challenges, and future directions. IEEE Trans. Ind. Inform. **18**(5), 3501–3509 (2021)
12. Wang, W., et al.: Secure-enhanced federated learning for AI-empowered electric vehicle energy prediction. IEEE Consum. Electron. Mag. **12**(2), 27–34 (2023)
13. Yang, Q., Liu, Y., Chen, T., Tong, Y.: Federated machine learning: concept and applications. ACM Trans. Intell. Syst. Technol. (TIST) **10**(2), 1–19 (2019)
14. Liu, Y., Kang, Y., Xing, C., Chen, T., Yang, Q.: A secure federated transfer learning framework. IEEE Intell. Syst. **35**(4), 70–82 (2020)
15. Naveed, K.: N-BaIoT dataset to detect IoT botnet attacks (2020). https://www.kaggle.com/mkashifn/nbaiot-dataset

Advances in Machine Learning

Analysis of Classification Algorithms for Predicting Parkinson's Disease and Applications in the Field of Cybersecurity

U. Sumalatha[1] , K. Krishna Prakasha[1]([✉]) , Srikanth Prabhu[2]([✉]) ,
and Vinod C. Nayak[3]([✉])

[1] Department of Information and Communication Technology,
Manipal Institute of Technology, Manipal Academy of Higher Education,
Manipal, India
sumalatha.u@learner.manipal.edu, kkp.prakash@manipal.edu
[2] Department of Computer Science and Engineering,
Manipal Institute of Technology, Manipal Academy of Higher Education,
Manipal, India
srikanth.prabhu@manipal.edu
[3] Department of Forensic Medicine, Kasturba Medical College,
Manipal Academy of Higher Education, Manipal, India
vinod.nayak@manipal.edu

Abstract. Parkinson's disease, which affects millions of people worldwide, is a term used to describe a neurological and neurodegenerative movement disorder. Common symptoms include a loss of automatic motions and muscle rigidity, which ultimately result in problems with balance, coordination, and walking. The patient's physical, emotional, and mental health gradually worsens as a result of these symptoms. Before the patient's health worsens, therapeutic care can be given to lower the disease's prognosis. It is possible to predict whether or not a person has Parkinson's disease using machine learning classification algorithms. This can lengthen the lives of older individuals and improve their quality of life when they have Parkinson's. This study suggests a potential technique to identify Parkinson's disease symptoms in their early stages. Based on the speech input parameters, algorithms like Gradient Boosting, XGBoost, Random Forest, and Extra Trees Classification are used to estimate whether the individual is normal or affected by Parkinson's disease. According to this study, the ensemble method Gradient Boosting classification algorithm outperformed other classification algorithms in terms of test accuracy rate (95%). The effectiveness of the approaches was evaluated using a reliable dataset from the UCI Machine Learning library.

Keywords: Gradient Boosting · Machine Learning · Parkinson's dataset · Classification algorithm

© The Author(s), under exclusive license to Springer Nature Singapore Pte Ltd. 2023
S. Prabhu et al. (Eds.): ATIS 2022, CCIS 1804, pp. 155–163, 2023.
https://doi.org/10.1007/978-981-99-2264-2_13

After Alzheimer's disease, Parkinson's disease (PD) is the most common neurodegenerative condition. Debilitating non-motor symptoms of Parkinson's disease include cognitive impairment and dementia, which occur often. At age 60, the occurrence of PD in the population is roughly 1%; by age 80, it is 4%. Tremor, rigidity, and trouble in walking are some of the early signs of PD; later on, cognitive deterioration is also seen [1]. Approximately 30% of PD cases had dementia, according to cross-sectional population studies, and 20–25% of patients had Moderate Cognitive Impairment (MCI) at the time of diagnosis. According to longitudinal research, 50% of PD patients experience dementia within 10 years [2].

Dopamine-producing cells of the substantia nigra, a region of the brain associated with movement, reward, and addiction, are specifically killed off, which is the basic pathology of Parkinson's disease [3]. Dopamine generally causes neurons in the sections to have trouble speaking, writing, walking, or finishing other basic tasks. More than 10 million people globally suffer from PD. There is currently no cure for Parkinson's disease, but research is progressing, and drugs or surgery can frequently significantly alleviate motor symptoms. By 2015, PD had killed roughly 1,17,400 individuals worldwide and affected 6.2 million people. After diagnosis, the typical life expectancy ranges from 7 to 15 years.

The great degree of variability inherent in the disorder, with high inter-individual variance in clinical presentation and progression, makes it difficult to predict cognitive prognosis in PD [4]. Using algorithms that incorporate various indicators for an individual's cognitive outcome prediction could be a way to overcome these difficulties. Large and complicated data sets can be used to extract information using machine learning. It has recently been used to diagnose dementia and determine risk. Genetic testing, cerebrospinal fluid biomarkers, and advanced neuroimaging are just a few examples of information that these models frequently include that is not usually available in clinical practice [5].

Machine learning techniques like Support Vector Machines (SVM), Artificial Neural Network (ANN), K-Nearest Neighbors (KNN), Naive Bayes, Classification and Regression Tree (CART), Decision Tree, Logistic Regression, etc., and novel biomarkers [6] may be adapted in clinical settings to support more precise and informed decision making because their application to clinical as well as non-clinical data of various modalities has frequently resulted in high diagnosis accuracies in human participants.

In order to make a wise choice nowadays, machine learning approaches can detect anomalies, malicious conduct, and data driven patterns of related security issues. The area of cybersecurity data science can be emphasized, where the data is gathered from pertinent cybersecurity sources and the analytics support the most recent data-driven patterns to provide corresponding security solutions [7].

1   Literature Review

Asmae et al. used machine learning classifiers in comparison analysis for effective Parkinson's disease identification from the vocal disorder dysphonia. Using ANN, the system has a 96.7% accuracy rate for separating healthy individuals from a variety of PD patients [8].

Agarwal et al. suggested Extreme Learning Machine that can accurately detect Parkinson's disease using speech samples. The approach can identify between Parkinson's sick cases and healthy subjects with 90.76% accuracy for the training sample and 81.55% for the test data taken from the UCI repository. When compared to other methods like neural networks and support vector machines, the method performed better [9].

Bansal et al. employed different machine learning algorithms including the Random Forest Classifier, the Extreme Gradient Boosting (XGB) Classifier, the Naive-Bayes, the K-NN, and the Decision Tree Classifier. The dataset used in this study was partitioned in a 70:30 ratio followed by tuning of hyperparameters. The f-1 score of 98.00% and accuracy of 96.61% provided by the XGB Classifier were the best results [10].

Mittal et al. provided a technique that divided the dataset into three equal halves and tested two classes (healthy and Parkinson's disease) for each individual set of data using several classifiers depending on acoustic properties. Principal Component Analysis (PCA) was used to enhance the performance of classifying algorithms. The Logistic technique, weighted k-NN classifiers, and SVM with Gaussian were used to achieve classification performance of 74.2%, 85.0%, and 82.1% [11].

Zhao et al. implemented a group of K-nearest neighbors, a way to combat the influence of imbalance on severity level diagnosis. The extracted features are used in the K-NN approach for building the base classifiers. Results indicate that the system can diagnose PD severity levels with an accuracy rate of 95.02% despite an unbalanced distribution of data [12].

Abdulhay et al. proposed an approach to diagnose PD using the gait analysis, which comprises the gait cycle and could be divided into several stages and periods to evaluate normal and abnormal gait. Medium Gaussian SVM yields a diagnosis of PD with an accuracy rate of 92.7%, and tremor assessment is utilized to determine the extent of PD [13].

Surya et al. put out an approach in which the Kaggle data set was assessed using four distinct supervised classification ML models: Random Forest, XGBoost, SVM, and Decision Tree. With an accuracy of 93%, the XGBoost classifier model was shown to be quite effective at accurately classifying PD [14].

Ahmed et al. proposed a method to use human speech signals to categorize Parkinson's disease and to extract crucial elements to simplify the dataset. The intensity and spectrum of human voice signals then are examined for PD patients. The PD patients are then classified using machine learning classifiers based on the features that were retrieved. A 91% accuracy rate for Stochastic Gradient Descent (SGD)-Classifier, a 95% accuracy rate for XGB-Classifier, a 91% accuracy rate for Logistic Regression, a 97% accuracy rate for Random Forest, a 95% accuracy rate for K-NN, and a 95% accuracy rate for Decision Tree is the result [15] (Table 1).

Table 1. Performance of Existing Systems

Reference	Classification Algorithm used	Outcome/s
[8]	ANN	Accuracy = 96.70%
[9]	Extreme Learning Machines	Training accuracy = 90.76% Testing accuracy = 90.76%
[10]	XGB	f1-score-98% Accuracy = 96.61%
[11]	PCA, KNN	Accuracy = 85%
[12]	KNN	Accuracy = 95.02%
[13]	Medium Gaussian SVM	Accuracy = 92.70%
[14]	XGB	Accuracy = 93%
[15]	Random Forest	Accuracy = 97%
[18]	Decision Tree	Accuracy = 85.55%

Sarker et al. spoke about cybersecurity where the information is gathered from pertinent cybersecurity sources and the analytics support the most recent data-driven patterns to deliver more efficient security solutions. A multi-layered system based on machine learning for cybersecurity modeling is designed. Emphasized the use of data-driven, intelligent decision-making to defend systems against cyberattacks [16].

Dutt et al. presented a hybrid system that employs anomaly detection for new assaults and misuse detection for recognized sorts of intrusions. The Chi-square test is utilized for anomaly-based detection. Experiments demonstrate that the intrusion detection system is capable of taking into account both the standard data set and the real-time network traffic to determine the system's effectiveness. By identifying both known assaults from abuse detection systems and new attacks through anomaly detection systems, the proposed system trains itself and improves true positive rates while lowering false negative rates as a result [17].

2   Description of the Dataset and the Classifiers

The machine learning repository at UCI is where the data set was collected. The dataset contains 195 observations and 24 attributes, with "status" as the target or label. The patients are between the ages of 46 and 85. Six phonations on average, ranging in length from 1 to 36 s, were recorded for each patient.

Except for the name, which has an object datatype, and the target variable, which has levels (i.e., 1 if the individual has Parkinson's disease and 0 otherwise), all of the properties are numerical. Table 2 describes the dataset. About 75% of the cases in the data set have Parkinson's disease, while 25% are healthy as shown in Fig. 1 It is clear from the dataset that a patient has Parkinson's disease if

Table 2. Description of the Parkinson dataset:

Attribute	Description
MDVP: F0 (Hz)	Average fundamental frequency of the voice
MDVP: Fhi (Hz)	Maximum fundamental frequency of the voice
MDVP: Flo (Hz)	Minimum fundamental frequency of the voice
MDVP: Jitter (%)	Changes in fundamental frequency (%)
MDVP: Jitter (Abs)	Microseconds of jitter total
MDVP: RAP	Change in Relative Amplitude
MDVP: PPQ	Period Perturbation Quotient in 5 points
Jitter: DDP	When the average period is computed by dividing absolute deviation of variations between cycles
MDVP: Shimmer	Local amplitude disturbance in the shimmer
MDVP: Shimmer(db)	Local amplitude perturbation (decibels)
Shimmer: APQ3	3 point Amplitude Perturbation Quotient
Shimmer: APQ5	5 point Amplitude Perturbation Quotient
MDVP: APQ	11 point Amplitude Perturbation Quotient
Shimmer: DDA	The amplitudes of successive eras' average absolute
NHR	Ratio of Noise to Harmonics
HNR	Ratio of Harmonics to Noise
RPDE	Recurrence Period Density of Entropy
D2	Dimension of Correlation
DFA	Analysis of Detrended Fluctuations
Spread1, Spread2	Variation in fundamental frequency
PPE	Period of pitch entropy

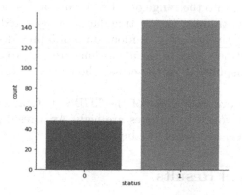

Fig. 1. Counts for two categories in the dataset, 1 for Parkinson's and 0 for healthy

Table 3. The cross-validation scores of various Classification algorithms

Classification Algorithm	Cross-Validation Score
Logistic Regression	0.8651
XGB Classifier	0.9038
Support Vector Classifier	0.8972
Decision Tree Classifier	0.8784
Ada Boost Classifier	0.8972
Bagging Classifier	0.8718
Extra Trees Classifier	0.9163
Gradient Boosting Classifier	0.9103
Random Forest Classifier	0.9103

Table 4. The effectiveness of four machine learning models for predicting parkinson's disease

Classification Techniques	Training Accuracy Rate	Test Accuracy Rate
XGB Classifier	100	92.3077
Extra Trees Classifier	100	89.7436
Gradient Boosting Classifier	100	94.8718
Random Forest Classifier	100	92.3077

they have decreased rates of "HNR," "MDVP:Flo(Hz)," "MDVP:Fhi(Hz)," and "MDVP:Fo(Hz)".

3   Methodologies

We divided the target variables and features in our investigation. The feature variables are brought into the range of -1 to 1, the data is normalized using the minmax scaler. Here, training and testing data are separated into two groups of 80% and 20%, respectively with a random state of 5 provided.

The cross-validation scores of the algorithms are used to evaluate the overall accuracy. Table 3 displays all of the cross-validation results for various classification algorithms.

In this case, the accuracy rates of the XGBoost, Gradient Boosting, Extra Trees, and Random Forest techniques are high. As a result, we'll utilize these methods to fit models and select the best one.

4   Experimental Results

The XGB, Gradient Boosting, Random Forest, and Extra Tree Classification algorithms are used to train the 4 models. The Parkinson dataset's machine

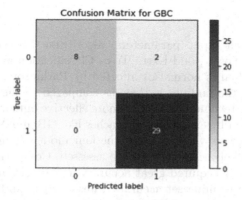

Fig. 2. Confusion Matrix for Gradient Boosting Classifier

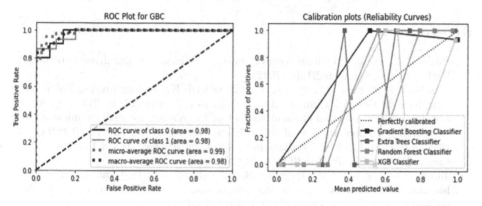

Fig. 3. ROC plot for Gradient Boosting Classifier and Calibration plots for the 4 Classifiers

learning classifiers' findings for determining the presence of the disease is shown in Table 4.

Table 4 shows that the Gradient Boosting Classifier (GBC) achieved the best accuracy of 100% and 95% for the training and test data, respectively, when compared to other machine learning models. The precision, recall, and f1-scores of the algorithm are 100%, 94%, and 97%, respectively. 0.051 is the Mean Squared Error. The confusion matrix for the GBC is shown in Fig. 2. According to the classification report, the model correctly predicted 80% of the individuals who did not have Parkinson's disease and 100% of those who did. Additionally, the confusion matrix reveals that just two values were incorrectly classified. Additionally, Fig. 3 displays the ROC Curve plot demonstrating the excellent performance of the GB classifier on the PD dataset. The calibration plot for Gradient Boosting, XGBoost, Random Forest, and Extra Trees is displayed in Fig. 3. The model is also evaluated by considering input values for 2 cases (healthy and diseased).

5   Conclusion

Based on the speech input parameters, algorithms like Gradient Boosting, XGBoost, Random Forest, and Extra Trees Classification are used to estimate whether the individual is normal or affected by Parkinson's disease. The conclusion drawn from the findings is that, as compared to the base classification algorithm, ensemble techniques produce more effective outcomes. More accurate prediction is provided by ensemble approaches like GB and XGBoost. Based on measures like the accuracy obtained by the four models lying within the range of 89–100%, ensemble learning models are assessed. Comparing Gradient Boost to other algorithms, it acquired great accuracy and precision. It performs with remarkable test and training set accuracy rates of 100% and 95%, respectively. This model might be very useful for early disease diagnosis. The model can be improved through hyperparameter tuning.

References

1. Harvey, J., et al.: Machine learning-based prediction of cognitive outcomes in Parkinson's disease. MedRxiv (2022)
2. Aarsland, D., Creese, B., Politis, M., Chaudhuri, K., Weintraub, D., Ballard, C.: Cognitive decline in Parkinson disease. Nat. Rev. Neurol. **13**(4), 217–231 (2017)
3. Liu, G., et al.: Prediction of cognition in Parkinson's disease with a clinical-genetic score: a longitudinal analysis of nine cohorts. Lancet Neurol. **16**(8), 620–629 (2017)
4. Phongpreecha, T., et al.: Multivariate prediction of dementia in Parkinson's disease. NPJ Parkinson's Dis. **6**(1), 1–10 (2020)
5. James, C., Ranson, J.M., Everson, R., Llewellyn, D.J.: Performance of machine learning algorithms for predicting progression to dementia in memory clinic patients. JAMA Netw. Open **4**(12), e2136553 (2021)
6. Rana, A., Dumka, A., Singh, R., Panda, M.K., Priyadarshi, N., Twala, B.: Imperative role of machine learning algorithm for detection of Parkinson's disease: review, challenges, and recommendations. Diagnostics **12**(8), 2022 (2003)
7. Khraisat, A., Gondal, I., Vamplew, P., Kamruzzaman, J.: Survey of intrusion detection systems: techniques, datasets and challenges. Cybersecurity **2**(1) (2019). Article number: 20. https://doi.org/10.1186/s42400-019-0038-7
8. Asmae, O., Abdelhadi, R., Bouchaib, C., Sara, S., Tajeddine, K.: Parkinson's disease identification using KNN and ANN Algorithms based on Voice Disorder. In: 1st International Conference on Innovative Research in Applied Science, Engineering and Technology (IRASET) (2020)
9. Agarwal, A., Chandrayan, S., Sahu, S.S.: Prediction of Parkinson's disease using speech signal with Extreme Learning Machine. In: International Conference on Electrical, Electronics, and Optimization Techniques (ICEEOT) (2016)
10. Bansal, M., Upali, S.J.R., Sharma, S.: Early Parkinson disease detection using audio signal processing. In: Dutta, P., Chakrabarti, S., Bhattacharya, A., Dutta, S., Piuri, V. (eds.) Emerging Technologies in Data Mining and Information Security. LNNS, vol. 491, pp. 243–250. Springer, Singapore (2023). https://doi.org/10.1007/978-981-19-4193-1_23
11. Mittal, V., Sharma, R.K.: Machine learning approach for classification of Parkinson disease using acoustic features. J. Reliable Intell. Environ. **7**, 233–239 (2021). https://doi.org/10.1007/s40860-021-00141-6

12. Zhao, H., Wang, R., Lei, Y., Liao, W.-H., Cao, H., Cao, J.: Severity level diagnosis of Parkinson's disease by ensemble K-nearest neighbor under imbalanced data. Expert Syst. Appl. **189**, 116113 (2022)
13. Abdulhay, E., Arunkumar, N., Narasimhan, K., Vellaiappan, E., Venkatraman, V.: Gait and tremor investigation using machine learning techniques for the diagnosis of Parkinson disease. Future Gener. Comput. Syst. **83**, 366–373 (2018)
14. Rohit Surya, A.T., Yaswanthram, P., Nair, P.R., Rajendra Prasath, S.S., Akella, S.V.V.S.: Prediction of Parkinson's disease using machine learning models—a classifier analysis. In: Bianchini, M., Piuri, V., Das, S., Shaw, R.N. (eds.) Advanced Computing and Intelligent Technologies. LNNS, vol. 218, pp. 453–460. Springer, Singapore (2022). https://doi.org/10.1007/978-981-16-2164-2_35
15. Ahmed, I., Aljahdali, S., Khan, M.S., Kaddoura, S.: Classification of Parkinson disease based on patient's voice signal using machine learning. Intell. Autom. Soft Comput. **32**(2), 705–722 (2022)
16. Sarker, I.H., Kayes, A.S.M., Badsha, S., Alqahtani, H., Watters, P., Ng, A.: Cybersecurity data science: an overview from machine learning perspective. J. Big Data **7**(1) (2020). Article number: 41. https://doi.org/10.1186/s40537-020-00318-5
17. Dutt, I., Borah, S., Maitra, I.K., Bhowmik, K., Maity, A., Das, S.: Real-time hybrid intrusion detection system using machine learning techniques. In: Bera, R., Sarkar, S.K., Chakraborty, S. (eds.) Advances in Communication, Devices and Networking. LNEE, vol. 462, pp. 885–894. Springer, Singapore (2018). https://doi.org/10.1007/978-981-10-7901-6_95
18. Jeon, H., et al.: Automatic classification of tremor severity in Parkinson's disease using a wearable device. Sensors **17**(9), 2067 (2017)

Optimization of Secured Cluster Based Charging Dynamics and Scheduling of EV Using Deep RNN

Shivanand C. Hiremath[1](✉) and Jayashree D. Mallapur[2](✉)

[1] Department of Electronics and Communication, R. N. Shetty Polytechnic College, Shivbasavnagar, Belagavi 590018, Karnataka, India
shivch612@gmail.com
[2] Department of Electronics and Communication, Basaveshwar Engineering College, Vidyagiri, Bagalkote 587103, Karnataka, India
bdmallapur12@gmail.com

Abstract. In the near future, Electric Vehicles (EVs) are anticipated to develop into fantastic modes of transportation. Due to their limited range and under powered batteries, EVs are crucial for lowering the use of conventional fuel. When the battery charge is about to reach a critical level, it is essential to be aware of local Charging Stations (CS). As a result, we could spot two issues: (1) Secured Cluster based CS allocation and routing to CS (2) Scheduling vehicle at CS based on delay prediction. First, a Cluster based Vacant charging slot is searched in clustered charging stations using cloud and Vehicular Adhoc Network (VANET) model, along with evolutionary Social Ski Driven (SSD) optimized algorithm using Deep Recurrent Neural Network (DRNN) as a new optimal routing for EVs to reach CS based on established fitness function computing distance, battery power and traffic congestion. Second, at CS, vehicle time scheduling is done using the DRNN approach, considering delay-based distance computation. When compared to the stochastic Particle Swarm Optimization (PSO) algorithm for routing, the proposed DRNN-SSD routing algorithm optimizes delay and traffic congestion significantly achieving better successful allocation rate of CS during On-peak and Off-peak hours.

Keywords: CS · DRNN · DRNN-SSD · DRNN-PSO

1 Introduction

The usage of vehicles has dramatically expanded in recent years due to quickly expanding infrastructures and urban modernisation, which has resulted in pollution and global warming difficulties, as well as the lack of supplies and their high floating costs, managing traditional fuels has become more challenging, which has led to the modernization of the automobile industry is looking for affordable and environmentally friendly transportation. In coming days electric vehicles

© The Author(s), under exclusive license to Springer Nature Singapore Pte Ltd. 2023
S. Prabhu et al. (Eds.): ATIS 2022, CCIS 1804, pp. 164–177, 2023.
https://doi.org/10.1007/978-981-99-2264-2_14

have become a great form of transportation in the near future. However, EVs' insufficient battery capacity necessitate regular recharging for travelling over long distances. Many EV manufacturers are building their vehicles with massive battery capacity to go longer distances that weigh between 50 and 400 kgs due to a lack of CS or awareness of its availability and to reduce the time necessary to charge. In the long term, the durability of EVs will be impacted by modest commercial vehicle loads and passenger loads since EVs cannot be instantly recharged like traditional fuels can in emergency situations. In this research work, a cloud assisted VANET model for cluster based vacant charging slot detection is proposed to raise awareness of CS and with the help of a nature-inspired evolutionary optimized SSD routing algorithm, EVs receive assistance to reach CS at its closest proximity based on EV battery power, distance to charging station and traffic congestion across lanes as well as vehicle time scheduling mechanism that is performed using DRNN and made known to EVs using VANET-cloud. In accordance with the utilisation of the requested power configuration at charging stations, EVs are assigned to the vacant charging slots based on priority, notably high for emergency vehicles like ambulances, fire trucks, etc., medium, and low for standard EVs at CS.

2   Motivation

Collaboration of Cloud computing and VANET supports wide variety of applications and in present days finding the CS is a tedious task and reaching to it with minimum battery power are highly needed and also number of CS available for charging EVs are fewer in contrast to the number of EVs that exist and unskillful charging can cause a grievous stress on the power grid and hence, To handle scheduling of time for EV charging to get connected to the required power configurations at CS has become equally essential. A motivation from past research studies led us to introduce A cloud-assisted VANET model uses DRNN that schedules EVs to the vacant slots of CS based on priority option to select high, moderate or low power configurations, and using DRNN-SSD routing algorithm is proposed to select minimum congested route using DRNN based traffic congestion and delay based distance computation.

3   Literature Survey

Due to its affordability and environmental benefits, EV adoption has greatly increased in recent years [1]. Because EVs are being integrated into the power distribution network on such a large scale, the implementation of approved charging schemes is crucial. Decentralized and centralised solutions make up the bulk of the charge control options. While the centralised strategies use a centralised authority to directly regulate the charging process of EVs, the decentralised schemes allow the EVs to conduct regulating of the charging process themselves. Both Vehicle-to-Infrastructure (V2I) and Vehicle-to-Vehicle (V2V) communication are supported by VANETs, which [2–4] enable efficient data gathering from surrounding vehicle nodes and then communicate traffic changes to the Road-Side Units (RSUs) and nearby vehicle nodes. Consequently, real-time traffic-based data may be utilised to administer traffic flow [6]. Many studies have been conducted to develop effective charging scheduling algorithms for EVs in order to suit a variety of needs, including queue time reduction [7], trip energy use reduction [8], overall elapsed time reduction [9]. Due to the costs and limitations of variable rate chargers (VRC) and charging methods, electric vehicles (EVs) are often charged using discrete rate charging (DRC), in which the chargers store a variety of rates, such as binary rates like off/on. DRC reorganises the process of modulating power over a constrained range of rates in general. Therefore, it is important for actual operating conditions [10] that an EV charging approach be compatible with VRC and DRC. The author of [11] proposes SSD routing algorithm for EVs. The author of [12] discusses about efficient routing for EVs using SSD combined with fractional calculus and authors in [13] discusses about cluster based searching for parking also presents a DRL approach for handling user requests for parking.

4   Cluster Based CS Allocation Using VANET- Cloud

VANET is the state-of-the-art in the field of wireless networks where the objective of VANET is to exchange the information or message transfer between the resources. It can be achieved in various ways such as Vehicles to Vehicle (V2V), Vehicle to Infrastructure (V2I) and Vehicle to Road Side Units (RSU) and these RSU's are connected to the cloud platform to form a Cloud-assisted VANET networks that bring forth wide variety of application services. In addition Cloud platform provides storage and computing facilities. Hence, the structural system design of cluster based CS allocation for EV charging using cloud-assisted VANET is presented in Fig. 1. Whenever an EV requests for charging slot using web interface applications gets connected to VANET-cloud the request

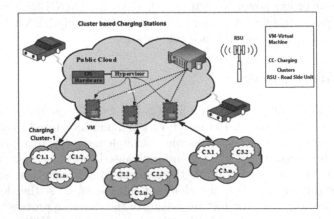

Fig. 1. Cluster based CS allocation for EV Charging

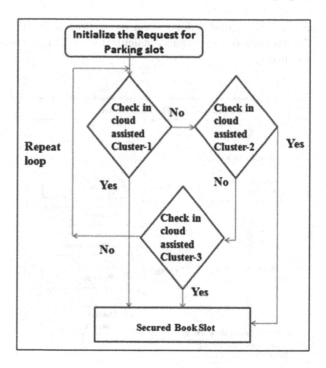

Fig. 2. Workflow of secured Cluster based CS allocation for EV Charging

is searched in multiple clusters consisting of CS are located near to the EV in the range of 1000 m. charging clusters-1 consists of number of CS represented by C1.1 to C1.n, similarly for Charging cluster-2 are C2.1 to C2.n and charging cluster-3 are C3.1 to C3.n. The following flowchart shown in Fig. 2 explains about the searching of vacant slot in cluster based CS allocation model. All clusters having CS consisting of charging ports of high, moderate and low power configurations they gets synchronized with VANET-cloud every 30 min and updates the available vacant charging slots at CS in their respective clusters which helps in determining the vacant charging slots by checking in each nearest cluster from the distance of EV and then second nearest cluster and so on until vacant slot is available then the routing of the EV is done using Social Ski driver routing algorithm.

5   Routing and Scheduling Using DRNN Based System Model

VANET uses V2V and V2I communication to distribute messages. In order to take advantage of the resource management in a specific region, RSU connects with a cloud server and other roadside units in this situation [14, 15]. The data acquired through wireless or cable transmission is processed by the VANET cloud server. Through the cloud, information is acquired from RSU and vehicle units. The cloud then performs centralised calculation and broadcasts the results to the application users.

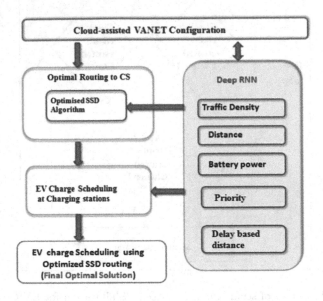

Fig. 3. Routing and Scheduling using DRNN

First, the Proposed Model communicates with electric CS about vacant slots through a cloud interface. The first time an EV requests charging, it sends its vehicle identification number and password to the VANET-cloud model. The corresponding vehicle's private key (V_{pkey}) is generated by the cloud server. To choose the best, quickest, and least congested route for EVs, a cloud server executes the suggested optimised SSD algorithm. To determine the route with the least amount of congestion, Deep RNN is used together with distance, battery power, and traffic density. In the charging station, EVs are secondarily scheduled for charging based on *Priority and delay-based distance prediction* using DRNN. The conceptual diagram is shown in Fig. 3.

5.1 Deep RNN Based Fitness Function Computation

Deep RNN has an infinite number of recurrent concealed levels in its network architecture, and as a result, there is a recurrent relationship between all of these hidden layers [24]. The traffic density, status of EV battery power and distance to CS is given as input because Deep RNN is more adept at managing inputs of various lengths and as a result of continuing to iterate with the data from concealed states, the outcome of the previous state condition is used as input to the subsequent state condition. The output sequences are then mapped using the hidden states that Deep RNN created by drawing the input series to them. Traffic Density signifies number of EVs present in the road lanes of a particular area and is given by

$$T_j = \left[\frac{n+1}{(S_0)\,c} \right] \tag{1}$$

where, c represents the count of road lanes, S_0 signifies the sample road lane length and n specifies count of electric vehicle. Battery status of charge B_s is evaluated using Coulomb's counting method that defines status of charging and discharging current of the battery by integrating values over time is given by

$$B_s = B_s(t-1) + \frac{i(t)}{B_c} \theta t \tag{2}$$

where $B_s(t-1)$ represents initial stage of charge at time '$(t-1)$' and $i(t)$ is the battery current at instant 't' B_c is the battery capacity in ampere hours and θt refers step time.

Hence, The fitness values includes traffic density, battery power and distance is given by

$$f = \frac{1}{2} \left[T_j + \frac{1}{2N} \sum_{m=1}^{N} (1 - B_s) + D_k + (1 - P_i) \right] \tag{3}$$

where T_j represents traffic density at j^{th} time, D_k provides distance travelled by k^{th} EV and B_s refers to battery power of sth EV, P_i refers to priority opted by i^{th} EV and N denotes number of EVs. Hence, optimised DRNN based SSD routing is found by considering the minimum values of fitness function that is given by

$$min(f) \tag{4}$$

5.2   EV Routing Using SSD Algorithm

Numerous metamorphic techniques used to determine the best values for feature selection [25] and also in support vector machines [26] have inspired the social ski driven algorithm [5]. Through a series of collective simulation rounds or iterations, SSD's primary objective is to identify the area where the best possible optimum solutions may be attained from the records of prior data. The mean global solution is produced by averaging all fitness values calculated using Eq. (3). Updated EV positions are obtained by adding the velocity represented as

$$Z_n^{0+1} = Z_n^0 - V_n^0 \tag{5}$$

where Z_n^0 signifies current position of EVs and V_n^0 represents velocity of n^{th}EV at 0th iteration.

$$Z_n^0 = \begin{bmatrix} KSin(\eta 1)(X) + Sin(\gamma 1)(Y); & if\eta 2 \le 0.5 \\ KCos(\eta 1)(X) + Cos(\gamma 1)(Y); & if\eta 2 > 0.5 \end{bmatrix} \tag{6}$$

where

$$X = (A_i^0 - B_i^0)Y = (C_i^0 - B_i^0)$$

where K denotes parameter to stabilizes exploration and exploitation, η_1 and η_2 represents uniformly distributed arbitrary numbers in the range $[0, 1]$. X and Y parameters consists of A_i^0 denotes finest solution of ith EV at 0th iteration, B_i^0 represents current position of ith EV at 0th iteration and C_i^0 denotes mean global solution at 0th iteration for all EVs. To choose optimum charging station to route the EVs is obtained using DRNN based Fitness function to obtain optimal route.

6   Deep RNN Based Vehicle Time Scheduling for Charging

Time scheduling for charging is done by taking into account the fitness function using EV Priority and delay-based distance prediction using Deep RNN to reach the final best solution. Each electric vehicle's request for a charging station is illustrated in the charge station encoding as shown in Fig. 4, which has three charging ports designated as CP1, CP2 and CP3. Here, CP1 are high power with High Priority charging ports that permits speedy recharging at high cost and least time is used for recharging high priority vehicles and for those in need of quick charging service depending on vacancies, etc. Similarly CP2 is having moderate priority and CP3 with Low Priority configurations with moderate and low powers respectively are utilized to charge the EVs at different charging rate, cost and time.

6.1   CS Encoding

An optimized time scheduling of EVs for charging at CS is performed by considering priority, delay prediction using DRNN to reach CS and charging time of EV is based on charging port used by EV and allocation to charging ports defines the response time of EV at CS upon arrival. Emergency vehicles such as ambulances, fire engines, etc. have high priority and routed to CP1 having x slots and other normal EVs requested to get charged are distributed and routed to CP2 and CP3 lines having y and z slots respectively based on their opted charging priorities respectively.

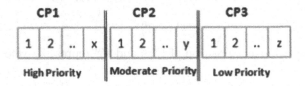

EV Indexes charging requests

Fig. 4. Deep RNN based fitness computation

6.2   EV Time Scheduling for Charging Computation Using DRNN

Priority of charging is opted by EV user such as high, moderate and low based on requirements. The Fig. 5 shows diagram of DRNN the outcome of the previous state condition of traffic data set is used as input to the subsequent state condition. The output sequences are then mapped using the hidden states that Deep RNN created by drawing the input series to them. The optimized fitness function uses minimization function for EV time scheduling to evaluate for delay prediction based on distance considering traffic congestion computation using DRNNis given below.

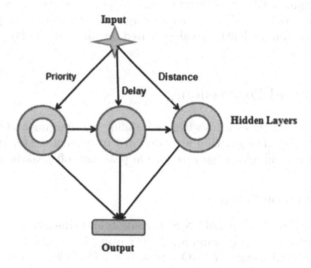

Fig. 5. Deep RNN based fitness computation

$$(min)\,F_{TS} = \frac{\sum_{m=1}^{N}\left[D_t + R_{(i)}\right]}{2} \tag{7}$$

where N stands for the total number of electric cars that will be charged, D_t stands for time delay $R_{(i)}$ stands for the ith EVs minimal response time.

6.3   Delay

Delay is defined as the expected charging time period required based on current EV power available to get charged at CS. minimum delay is considered and computed by Eq. (8).

$$D_t = \left(\frac{EV_{max}.(1 - B_a)}{(CP)_{Pow}}\right) \tag{8}$$

where B_a is the EV's available battery power, $(CP)_{Pow}$ is the charging line power and EV_{max} is the maximum battery capacity of an EV. Response time can be defined as minimum time duration taken by charging station to respond to a request and it is computed using below equation.

$$R_{(i)} = \frac{D_t}{T} \tag{9}$$

where $R_{(i)}$ is the response time and T is the whole time period. Consequently, EVs time scheduling for charging and routing utilising DRNN-SSD Algorithm operates in a cloud server. Where the cloud server initially utilises the EV ID (V_{pkey}) for communication through constant synchronisation, after which all EVs' current locations and velocities are uploaded to assess the most optimal routing and support EV users using Google Maps. As a result, the cloud server assigns the appropriate EV to a vacant charging line according to priority after determining the minimal fitness values based on minimum delay and response time.

7   Results and Discussion

The Performance metrics for EVs time scheduling for charging and routing using optimized DRNN-SSD algorithm are evaluated in percentage for traffic congestion, delay, successful allocation rate for On peak and off peak hours.

7.1   Experimental Setup

The execution of optimized DRNN-SSD routing and time scheduling for charging EVs is performed using windows 10 OS using Intel core i5 processor 6GB Ram and simulated using PYTHON tool. Here, Particle Swarm Optimization (PSO) algorithm is one of the bio-inspired that uses stochastic optimization technique based on the movement and intelligence of swarms is considered as a routing algorithm for comparison with proposed optimized DRNN-SSD routing algorithm.

7.2   % of Traffic Congestion

The proportion of congestion per lane during off-peak hours is seen in Fig. 6. After 50 initial rounds of simulation, the proposed DRNN-SSD is used to calculate traffic congestion, taking previous iterations data into account it yields 31.4%, compared to 33.0% for PSO making 1.6% optimization. After 100 simulation rounds, the proposed DRNN-SSD performs better than PSO, with 25.4% and 28.8%, respectively with 3.4% optimization. The same was true at On peak hours, as seen in Fig. 7. After 50 rounds, the DRNN-SSD and PSO produce 61.4% and 65% percent of congestion, respectively. Finally, after 100 rounds of simulation, DRNN-SSD performs better when picking lanes with the lowest density than PSO, which produces 54.5% and 60.1% of congestion, respectively. Finally making 5.6% optimization in congestion.

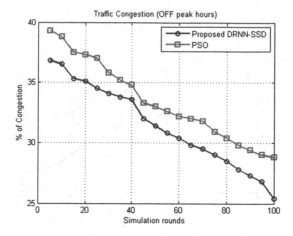

Fig. 6. % of Congestion (Off peak hours)

7.3 % of Delay Prediction to Reach CS

Figure 8 displays the proportion of EV charging delays at CS during on-peak times. The proposed DRNN-SSD outperforms PSO suggesting least delay of 19.2% over 24.1% of PSO after completion of the initial 50 rounds of simulation thereby optimizing delay of 4.9%. This is done in order to compute the delay for expected charging time of EVs at CS while taking previous iterations data into account. PSO gives a result of 29.6% while the proposed DRNN-SSD gives 25.4% after 100 rounds of simulation making a delay optimization of 4.2%. Similar results were obtained during off-peak hours, as shown in Fig. 9. After

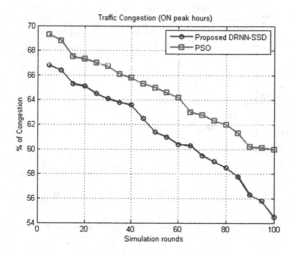

Fig. 7. % of Congestion (On peak hours)

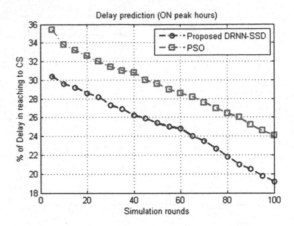

Fig. 8. % of delay (On peak hours)

50 rounds, DRNN-SSD and PSO provided 11.7% and 14.1% with 2.4% optimization in delay, respectively and eventually, after 100 rounds of simulation, DRNN-SSD outperformed PSO, providing 7.2% and 10.3%, respectively making 3.1% of optimization in delay.

7.4   % of Successful Allocation of EVs to CS

The percentage of EVs successfully allocated during On-peak hours is shown in Fig. 10. Unoccupied slots are provided via a cloud-assisted VANET model, and EVs are routed to CS using the DRNN-SSD routing algorithm while taking

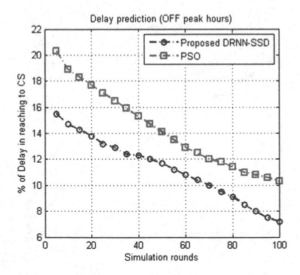

Fig. 9. % of delay (Off peak hours)

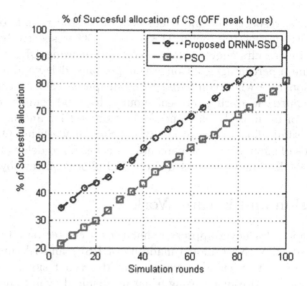

Fig. 10. % of Successful allocation (Off peak hours)

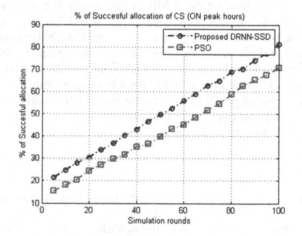

Fig. 11. % of Successful allocation (Off peak hours)

into account the fitness function with minimal delay and least traffic congestion. The recommended solution uses recurrent synchronizations to determine
whether slots are available in nearby CS. The suggested DRNN-SSD takes into
account an improved fitness function computing with least congested route to
reach CS faster than PSO and provides a high success rate for allocating EVs
to charging slots at CS. After the first 50 rounds of simulation, the proposed
DRNN-SSD beats PSO with a score of 49.7% compared to 39.7% after 100
rounds, with scores of 81.3% and 70.7% respectively. During Off peak hours
depicted in Fig. 11, after 50 rounds of simulation, DRNN-SSD and PSO yield

63.6% and 50.3% respectively and eventually, after 100 rounds of simulation, DRNN-SSD outperforms PSO with 93.8% and 81.3% respectively. Hence, The overall simulation results shows better optimization using DRNN approach in choosing minimum percentages of Congestion per lane, delay and maximum successful allocation rate when compared to bio-inspired PSO routing algorithm. With DRNN approach, during off peak hours after 100 rounds of simulations the percentage of optimized delay and congestion is 3.1% and 3.6% leading to increased successful allocation rate by 13.3%. Similarly, during On peak hours after 100 rounds of simulations the percentage of optimized delay and congestion is 4.9% and 3.4% leading to increased successful allocation rate by 10%.

8   Conclusion and Future Work

This study proposed a novel approach that uses a cluster based CS allocation using cloud-assisted VANET model made up of RSUs and EV units as a communication interface to a cloud server to provide vacant slot for charging and evaluation of optimised routing using a nature-inspired evolutionary SSD algorithm while taking into account the minimum fitness values like battery power, distance and the traffic congestion. Additionally, a vehicle time scheduling mechanism based on fitness function is carried out at CS for EVs. Delay prediction and traffic congestion computation is performed using DRNN technique with optimized delays and traffic congestion choosing the route with the least amount of congestion shown the better percentage of EVs successfully allocating to CS during On-peak and Off-peak hours. Here, PSO is outperformed by the proposed DRNN-SSD in terms of performance. In future, further bandwidth parameter has to be considered and comparative performance analysis must be performed with other optimized routing strategies.

References

1. Dow, L., Liu, R., Liu, E.: A survey of PEV impacts on electric utilities, pp. 1–8 (2017)
2. Céspedes, S., Taha, S., Shen, X.: A multihop-authenticated proxy mobile IP scheme for asymmetric VANETs. IEEE Trans. Veh. Technol. **62**(7), 3271–3286 (2013)
3. Tharwat, Liang, H., Zhuang, W.: Efficient on-demand data service delivery to high-speed trains in cellular/info station integrated networks. IEEE J. Sel. Areas Commun. **30**(4), 780–791 (2012)
4. Pierri, E., Cirillo, V., Vietor, T., Sorrentino, M.: Adopting a conversion design approach to maximize the energy density of battery packs in electric vehicles. Energies **14** (2021). https://doi.org/10.3390/en14071939
5. Tharwat, A.: Social Ski-Driver (SSD) optimization algorithm: python code (2019)
6. Leontiadis, I., Marfia, G., Mack, D., Pau, G., Mascolo, C., Gerla, M.: On the effectiveness of an opportunistic traffic management system for vehicular networks. IEEE Trans. Intell. Transp. Syst. **12**(4), 1537–1548 (2011)
7. Liu, A., Li, C., Xia, B., Yue, W., Miao, Z.: G-MACO: a multi-objective route planning algorithm on green wave effect for electric vehicles. In: 2018 IEEE 87th Vehicular Technology Conference (VTC Spring), pp. 1–5 (2018)

8. Pourazarm, S., Cassandras, C.G., Malikopoulos, A.: Optimal routing of electric vehicles in networks with charging nodes: a dynamic programming approach. In: 2014 IEEE International Electric Vehicle Conference (IEVC), pp. 1–7 (2014)

9. Yang, H., Yang, S., Xu, Y., Cao, E., Lai, M., Dong, Z.: Electric vehicle route optimization considering time-of-use electricity price by learnable partheno-genetic algorithm. IEEE Trans. Smart Grid **6**(2), 657–666 (2015)

10. Nimalsiri, N., Smith, D., Ratnam, E., Mediwaththe, C., Halgamuge, S.: A decentralized electric vehicle charge scheduling scheme for tracking power profiles. In: 2020 IEEE Power & Energy Society Innovative Smart Grid Technologies Conference (ISGT), pp. 1–5 (2020)

11. Hiremath, S.C., Mallapur, J.D.: A cloud interfaced social ski driver optimized routing for future electric motor vehicles. In: Tuba, M., Akashe, S., Joshi, A. (eds.) ICT Systems and Sustainability. LNNS, vol. 321, pp. 385–395. Springer, Singapore (2022)

12. Hiremath, S.C., Mallapur, J.D.: Fractional-social ski driver optimization-driven routing protocol for routing electric vehicle under server hosted VANET. Multimed. Tools Appl. **81**, 17437–17456 (2022). https://doi.org/10.1007/s11042-022-12543-6

13. Hiremath, S.C., Mallapur, J.D.: Social SKI driver based efficient parking dynamics and computation using deep reinforcement learning in vehicular cloud. J. Theor. Appl. Inf. Technol. **100**(10), 4615–4627 (2022). ISSN 1992-8645. E-ISSN 1817-3195

Analysis and Prognosis of Water Quality for River Ganga Using Water Quality Index

Yash Bijalwan, Pranav Chaudhari, Om Sharma, and S. Raghavendra[✉]

Department of Information and Communication Technology, Manipal Institute of Technology, Manipal Academy of Higher Education, Manipal 576104, India
raghavendra.s@manipal.edu

Abstract. Due to increased industrialization and human density, the Ganga are becoming one of the most polluted rivers in the world. As a result, the Water Quality Index(WQI) for river water is calculated to check the water quality. The Central Pollution Control Board (CPCB), an Indian organization, built several monitoring stations to keep an eye on the values of the physicochemical parameters under consideration. The Ganga river's water quality index will be developed utilizing eight physicochemical parameters. We have utilized a Linear Regression technique to estimate the trends and quality of the water for the following five years based on the trend observed over the last ten years, from 2011 to 2020. The properties of the provided dataset were then categorized and rated using the Decision Tree Method and Random Forest algorithm. The results of the algorithms were scaled with grades ranging from Excellent (A) to Very Bad (E). Decision trees and random forests are powerful machine-learning algorithms that can be used for regression and classification tasks. Further, we evaluated the two classification algorithms for accuracy-related performance. It can be seen that the two algorithms and the Random Forest algorithm give more accurate results. On the other hand, The Linear Regression algorithm gave alarming results for the river Ganga as water quality was deteriorating over the years. The Ganga river's declining water quality index sparked widespread concern, prompting quick responses from the general public and individuals who had raised their awareness and consciousness.

Keywords: Decision Tree · Random Forest · Linear Regression · Water Quality Index · Physico-chemical Parameters

1 Introduction

The effects of water on the environment and human health are profound. Due to their accessibility, and the development of human societies, rivers have been employed more frequently than other water supply sources [1]. Problems might arise from using alternative water sources like groundwater or the ocean. We rely

© The Author(s), under exclusive license to Springer Nature Singapore Pte Ltd. 2023
S. Prabhu et al. (Eds.): ATIS 2022, CCIS 1804, pp. 178–190, 2023.
https://doi.org/10.1007/978-981-99-2264-2_15

on water for food, health, livelihood, pleasure, and recreation. However, water may also be lethal. Moreover, the lack of water might be even more dangerous. As India expands and urbanizes, its water sources become more polluted. Over 70 percent of India's surface water is reportedly unfit for human consumption. Only a tiny portion of the 40 million liters of effluent that enter rivers and other bodies of water each day is adequately treated. Waterborne infections are widespread nationwide due to open defecation, inadequate washing practices, and inadequate access to sanitary facilities and safe water sources. One of the prominent rivers in India is the River Ganga, often known as The Ganges globally. It is essential to the physical and spiritual survival of millions of people. It drained around one-fourth of Indian land and was designated the "National River of India". The river's water quality has gradually declined due to pollution from numerous points and nonpoint sources brought on by growing living standards, unplanned urbanization, and fast industry [2]. Regardless of the river's carrying capacity, untreated industrial effluents, massive volumes of sewage from the city, agricultural runoff, open defecation, and other debris, including polythenes and dead corpses, are all being dumped into the waterway. Untreated water is nevertheless utilized for a variety of reasons despite the problematic amount of contamination, which might affect human health [3]. Water quality evaluation is crucial as the first step to raising public awareness and assisting planners and government agencies in managing and conserving water bodies [4]. Traditionally, procedures based on monitoring are employed to determine the water quality characteristics. In this study, our primary focus is locating contaminants in the river, determining the water pollution index, and implementing water pollution mitigation measures. The Ganga River canal, which travels through around five states before emptying into the Bay of Bengal, provided water samples for the current study for ten years from 2011 to 2020. Based on this, the Contributions are:

1. Eight distinct physicochemical characteristics, including temperature, power of Hydrogen(pH), dissolved oxygen, conductivity, Biochemical Oxygen Demand(BOD), total coliforms, fecal coliforms, and nitrate-N+nitrite-N, were examined in the samples, and a quality rating was calculated for each of the characteristics.
2. Water Quality Index was computed by using the Quality Ratings and Water Quality Weights for these eight features over a span of ten years. The appropriate rating was in the A-E range (Excellent to Very Bad).
3. To predict how the Ganga River's quality will change over the next five years based on the ratings of the water quality index, we used a linear regression model.
4. The comparison was made between the two classification algorithms, Decision Tree and Random Forest, based on how accurate the outcomes were.

The rest of the paper is organized as follows: Related Works are discussed in Sect. 2. Calculations of the data are presented in Sect. 3. In Sect. 4, the Methodology of analysis is explained. The outcomes of the analysis are discussed in Sect. 5. Conclusions are presented in Sect. 6.

2   Related Works

Rohit et al. [5] calculated the WQI of the Yamuna River in Dehradun, based on monthly measurements of 12 Physico-chemical parameters. The main objective was to predict water pollution trends in the Yamuna River from 2016 to 2024. For discrete parameter values of water parts, the Equipoise Evaluator (EE), a sample distribution-based analytical model, was presented, and the trend analysis using a linear regression model. Shailesh et al. [6] assessed and modeled the water quality of Narmada in Madhya Pradesh using a decision tree algorithm called recursive partitioning. Several data mining methods were implemented in WEKA software. The dataset was created after preprocessing the data and removing the noises. The experiment used five characteristics of water quality data that can affect water accuracy.

Zoltan et al. [7] The potential application of principal component analysis and other multivariate analytic methods to the analysis of data on water quality from natural rivers was investigated in this work. Box Plots, normality checks of the observed values, correlation coefficients, and principal component analysis were used to achieve this. Creating fitting equations (models) for a number of observed water quality characteristics was a secondary goal. To do this, multi-variate polynomial regression was utilized. Al-Akhir et al. [1] Water quality was investigated and predicted using a gradient-boosting model. The study used a gradient-boosting model to narrow the gap between the two groups. This model could detect changes in water composition and use this information to predict water quality. A GMM model was trained on the data and could predict changes in water quality and identify differences between existing water quality and the changes it is undergoing.

Jitha et al. [8] assessed the river water quality using the GRA (Gray relational analysis) approach. The method was devised as a result of a complex and complicated approach using mathematical models and calculus that was used to predict water quality. Cao et al. [9], sought to analyse and describe the river water quality of the Cau River using a combined WQI and PI. To better understand the health of the river's water, cluster analysis was used to organise water monitoring stations into several quality groups. This study showed that, while its single index only displays the present water quality status, a combined analysis of water quality might be an alternative for making decisions regarding water usage. The Cau River's considerable change in water indices between the rainy and dry seasons was assessed using a T-test analysis. To find the significant distinction between upstream, midstream, and downstream, an ANOVA was performed.

Babak et al. [10] for forecasting monthly WQI values at the Lam Tsuen River in Hong Kong, presented an ensemble machine learning model called Extra Tree Regression (ETR). Support Vector Regression (SVR) and Decision Tree Regression, two popular standalone models, were compared with the ETR model's performance (DTR). Several input data combinations were examined and evaluated using graphical comparisons and numerical indices in terms of prediction performance.

Richa et al. [11] The prediction environment was created to categorize water quality according to the Overall Index of Pollution using well-known classification approaches. The learning and testing frameworks of the prediction environment were created using a recurrent k-fold cross-validation approach. Kolli et al. [12] compared standard norms with the Village wise groundwater quality organized around Arc/Info and presented using Arc/View. Taluk-wise groundwater quality maps were prepared. Edza et al. [13] examined the Pucang River's water quality and pollution levels. Purposive sampling, Pollution Indices (PI), shop, street, Phelp, and QUAL2Kw were used to measure the amount of pollution in the river and monitor the river's water quality.

3   Calculations

3.1   Model Parameter

The model has been used to calculate the characteristics indicated in Table 1.

Table 1. Model Parameters with Units

Characteristics	Units
Temperature	°C
Dissolved Oxygen	mg/l
pH	–
Conductivity	umhos/cm
BOD	mg/l
Total Coliform	MPN/100 ml
Fecal Coliform	MPN/100 ml
Nitrate-N + Nitrite-N	mg/l

By using the characteristic Temp, the water temperature is shown. The quantity of dissolved oxygen (DO), particularly non-compound oxygen, is shown in the water. Due to its effect on the aquatic creatures within an ecosystem, it is a crucial factor in determining water quality. The number of basic or acidic compounds in water is measured using the pH. The biological consistency of compounds like vitamins and toxins, as well as the solubility of contaminants, are controlled by water pH. Conductivity is used to gauge how well an electric current can flow through water. To calculate the amount of DO that aerobic bacteria utilize in water, BOD is necessary. This gives a measure to gauge the impact of waste discharges onto the recipient area. Nitrate is what happens when nitrogen is added to oxygen or ozone. However, if the nitrate level rises, it may harm aquatic life.

3.2   Calculations of Water Quality Index

This study's main objective is to quantify and evaluate the significant changes in the Ganga River's water quality. To gauge the changes in the Ganga river's water quality over a ten-year period, a standardized and widely used Water Quality Index (WQI) has been established. Eight physicochemical parameters were examined and evaluated using the usual approach. According to the water quality index (WQI):

$$WQI = \frac{\sum (w_i * q_i)}{\sum w_i} \qquad (1)$$

where q_i stands for a quality rating of the ith water quality parameter, w_i represents the parameter's weight in relation to it. The following equation may be used to obtain the quality rating in this study:

$$q_i = \frac{V_a - V_i}{V_s - V_i} * 100 \qquad (2)$$

The actual and definite value of the quality parameters is shown by V_a their ideal value is indicated by V_i, and their recommended standard value by the WHO is indicated by V_s. The numbers for the unit weight (w_i) used in this investigation were obtained from the following Table 2 [14]:

Table 2. Unit Weights for the characteristics

Analyte	WQI Weight (wi)
Temperature	0.10
Dissolved Oxygen	0.12
pH	0.17
Conductivity	0.10
BOD	0.10
Total Coliform	0.15
Fecal Coliform	0.15
Nitrate-N + Nitrite-N	0.10

After the Water Quality Index was calculated, we concentrated on grading the WQI on a scale from A (Excellent) to E (Very Bad) by comparing it with standard WQI values. Five criteria make up the water quality ranking. The grade following the provided standardized range is displayed in the following Table 3:

4   Methodology

Data mining is used to sort through large data sets to help find patterns to be used in data analysis. Classifying objects in a collection into distinct groups

Table 3. Grading following the standardized range of WQI

Grading	WQI Values	Rating of Water Quality
A	0–25	Excellent
B	26–50	Good
C	51–75	Medium
D	76–100	Bad
E	>100	Very Bad

or classes is a data mining function. To properly anticipate the target class for each sample in the data is the aim of classification. Finding a model that defines and differentiates different data classes and ideas is the process of classification, which is a data analysis activity. Classification and prediction are used to create a model that represents the various data classes and forecasts future data trends, classification and prediction are used. Prediction is figuring out which numerical data for a new observation are unavailable or absent. The degree to which a particular predictor can accurately anticipate the value of a predicted characteristic for new data determines how accurate a prediction is. In this study, we use Linear Regression for making predictions for water quality for the upcoming five years and two classification algorithms, a Decision Tree and Random Forest, for the classification of the dataset with a water quality index and eight different characteristics by putting them on the scale of grades from A (Excellent) to E (Very Bad). The following Fig. 1 depicts the flowchart for the approach that was employed.

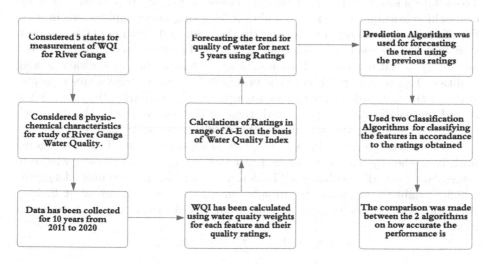

Fig. 1. An Overview of Analysis of Water Quality for River Ganga

4.1 Cyber Security with Data Extraction

The cyber threat landscape requires enterprises to collect and correlate millions of external and internal data points across their infrastructure and users on a continuous basis. This amount of information just cannot be managed by a small group of people. Machine learning excels in this situation because it can rapidly analyse large data sets to find patterns and predict threats. Cyber teams could identify threats more rapidly and pinpoint cases that need more in-depth human investigation by automating the analysis. Traditional phishing detection systems lack the speed and precision required to detect and distinguish between innocent and malicious URLs. The most recent ML algorithm predictive URL categorisation models may detect trends that indicate fraudulent datapoints. To do this, the models are trained on elements such as table headers, body data, punctuation patterns, and other characteristics in order to identify and distinguish the harmful from the harmless.

4.2 Data Cleaning

The dataset from 2011–2020 was loaded into an excel sheet for cleaning. Data were cleaned by removing duplicate or irrelevant observations, fixing the structural error, and filtering unwanted outliers. Missing data were handled with the methods of average binning and replacing with mean or median values of the data.

4.3 Decision Tree

Trees have a significant impact on both classification and regression in a range of machine learning scenarios, in addition to having many applications in daily life. To formally and artistically describe decisions and decision-making, a decision tree can be used in decision analysis. The Decision Tree Algorithm's key advantage is that it is easy to learn and closely resembles human decision-making abilities. To forecast the class of the provided dataset, a decision tree's process starts at the root node and works its way upward. By comparing the values of the record (actual dataset) property with those of the root attribute, this approach follows the branch to the next node. The algorithm confirms the attribute value with the other sub-nodes before going on to the next node. This keeps going until it reaches the tree's leaf node. Entropy is a metric used in data science to assess how "mixed" a column is. To design a decision tree, we must determine which variable(s) or column(s) to split on. In the long run, we want to keep dividing the variables and columns until our mixed target column is no longer mixed.

$$Entropy(T) = -\sum P(x_i) \log_b P(x_i) \tag{3}$$

where 'P(x_i)' is simply the frequentist probability of an element/class 'x' in our data. For a method to observe the entropy shifts on both sides of the divide, the information gain formula is used. It provides us with a number to express how many pieces of knowledge has been acquired after each data split. If the outcome is good, our split has reduced entropy. The greater the outcome, the more entropy has been reduced. The post-split entropy of each set is calculated, weighted by the number of each split's components, and subtracted from the pre-split entropy.

$$Gain = Entropy(T) - \sum_{V \epsilon A} \frac{|T_v|}{T} * Entropy(T_v) \qquad (4)$$

T → Target

A → the variable (column) we are testing

V → each value in A

The entropy and gain was estimated for each of the features using the entropy and gain formula. The attributes with the greatest gain were used as the root node in the calculations, and the leaf nodes served as an evaluation of the water quality using a scale from Excellent to Very Bad (A to E).

4.4   Random Forest

An algorithm for machine learning that is often used to aggregate the output of several decision trees into a single outcome, Random Forest employs the supervised learning method. Its adaptability and usefulness, which may solve classification and regression issues, propel its wide usage. By combining feature randomization and bagging, the random forest technique enhances bagging and produces an uncorrelated forest of decision trees; the larger the forest, the less overfitting and the greater accuracy. The greatest outcomes are obtained when many relatively uncorrelated models (trees) collaborate as a committee. It is built on the idea of ensemble learning, a strategy for merging lots of classifiers to solve complicated issues and enhance model performance. In ensemble learning systems, many classifiers are utilized, and their predictions are combined to identify the result that occurs the most frequently [15]. For random forest algorithms, it is necessary to establish three key hyperparameters before training. Examples of these include the size of the nodes, the number of trees, and the quantity of sampled features. The two premises for a better Random forest classifier are listed below.

- The dataset must have genuine values for the feature variable to forecast actual outcomes rather than just a speculative consequence.
- There must be extremely little connection between the forecasts from each tree.

Here, the training set comprised 70% of the dataset based on randomization. Once the multiple decision tree outputs are finished, we will use the remaining 30% of the dataset as a test set. Each of the eight characteristics from the training set was assigned a grade from A to E and used as the root node of an eight-decision tree classification technique. When the trees' outputs are complete, we compute the average rating of each characteristic for water quality. Then, this Average rating is contrasted with the test data we randomly choose from the dataset.

4.5   Linear Regression

The predictive modeling method known as regression establishes a correlation between dependent and independent variables. There are multiple benefits of using regression analysis. They are as follows:

- The significant correlations between a dependent variable and an independent variable are shown.
- It shows how strongly different independent factors have an effect on a dependent variable.

When the values to be predicted are discrete or quantitative, we use the linear regression concept, which finds the best fit line meaning that the regression line should have a minimum distance from all cluster points [16]. The straight-line equation can be represented as: y = mx + c referred to as the Hypothesis Function for Linear Regression. Here, y is the dependent variable. Most machine learning algorithms make a model, i.e., a Hypothesis, to estimate the dependent variable based on the independent variable. The hypothesis for linear regression is usually represented as follows:

$$h\Theta(x) = \Theta_0 + \Theta_1(x) \tag{5}$$

To calculate the errors in the classifiers, Cost functions are used. It is the sum of all errors (in Layman's terms). We aim to minimize the cost functions. One such function is MSE, Mean Squared Error, to measure the difference between predicted and actual values.

$$MSE = \frac{1}{2}m * \sum(h\Theta(x) - y) \tag{6}$$

Visualization of data is necessary to find any correlation between different parameters. After visualization, the data is usually split into training and test datasets, comprising 80 percent and 20 percent of the given data. Finally, we use the Gradient Descent algorithm to find the minimum of the function.

5   Results and Discussions

The dataset used in this study is taken from an Indian Government Organisation, Central Pollution Control Board (CPCB). National Water Quality Monitoring Programme which is hosted by CPCB maintained a Water Quality Database for many prominent rivers of India [17]. Out of which, River Ganga was taken into consideration for this study. This study was conducted on a laptop with certain specifications of 8-core CPU with 4 performance cores and 4 efficiency cores, 7-core GPU and 16-core Neural Engine.

5.1 Decision Tree

Table 4 displays the confusion matrix along with the predicted class, ratings of the qualities and the proportion of predicted classes that match the one that was successfully predicted. Therefore, we can evaluate the accuracy factor performance of the decision tree technique using the confusion matrix. The Decision Tree Algorithm's accuracy is calculated to be 94.37%, which is a respectable accuracy for the dataset in question. The actual and expected records show large discrepancies, which indicate severe water complex degradation.

Table 4. Decision Tree Confusion Matrix

	True A	True B	True C	True D	True E	Precision
Pred.A	0	0	0	0	0	NA
Pred.B	0	7	3	0	0	70%
Pred.C	0	1	32	2	0	91.43%
Pred.D	0	0	3	25	1	86.21%
Pred.E	0	0	1	1	137	98.56%
Recall	NA	87.50%	82.05%	89.29%	99.28%	94.37%

5.2 Random Forest

The confusion matrix with the predicted class and ratings of the attributes is shown in Table 5 along with the percentage of the predicted class that is really the one that was correctly predicted. So, using the confusion matrix, we can assess the accuracy factor performance of the decision tree method. The Accuracy of the Decision Tree Algorithm is coming out to be 96.24% which comes out to be pretty good accuracy for a given dataset. Significant differences between the actual and projected records point to significant water compound destruction.

Table 5. Random Forest Confusion Matrix

	True A	True B	True C	True D	True E	Precision
Pred.A	0	0	0	0	0	NA
Pred.B	0	7	3	0	0	77.78%
Pred.C	0	1	40	0	0	97.56%
Pred.D	0	0	1	33	1	94.29%
Pred.E	0	0	0	3	125	97.66%
Recall	NA	87.50%	93.02%	91.67%	99.21%	96.24%

5.3   Linear Regression

The model's prediction is detailed in Table 6. We looked at the water quality over a ten-year period based on the Water Quality Index of the eight attributes offered. Using the calculated WQI from the last 10 years, we can predict the quality of water for the following five years, showing that there is a linear increase in the WQI that causes a decline in the quality of water over time. The graph denoting the trendline and the predicted WQI values by the linear regression model is given in Fig. 2.

Table 6. Predicted values of Water Quality Index using Linear Regression

Year	Predicted WQI
2021	241.938
2022	256.685
2023	271.431
2024	286.178
2025	300.925

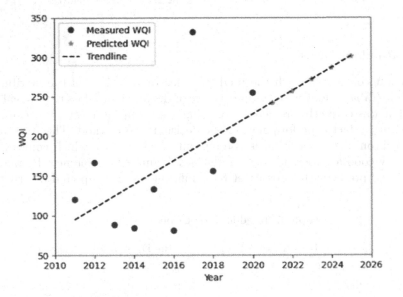

Fig. 2. Water Quality Index Prediction using Linear Regression

Gradient Boosting Model (GBM) model is machine learning technique which is used for classification and forecasting problems [1]. Linear Regression gives more accurate and more realistic results than GBM. For the research, supervised learning models are more suitable, linear regression is best suited for such prediction in comparison to the Principal Component Analysis (PCA) [7].

6   Conclusion

Over the past few decades, pollution-related activities have significantly altered aquatic habitats. The research provided inspiration for the present examination of river water quality, which is determined by factors based on its chemical makeup. And the study makes other connections to river water deterioration. Through the examination of the chemical composition of river water, we have predicted the water quality of river Ganga for five years from 2021 to 2025. The advanced prediction algorithm included in the linear regression model allows it to learn from a real dataset to evaluate water quality and eventually make sensible judgments by forecasting the quality of water in the coming years. The model is able to generate accurate predictions in the face of changes. The model's accuracy is judged to be quite good. Further, the two classification algorithms, Decision Tree and Random Forest were compared. These algorithms categorized the datasets and scaled up each of the eight criteria for the grading from A (Excellent) to E (Very Bad). The random forest method performed better than the decision tree approach in terms of accuracy, scoring 96.24% as opposed to 94.37%. This is because decision trees combine certain decisions, but decision forests combine several decisions, producing more accurate outcomes. Because the random forest approach is able to decrease overfitting without significantly raising a bias-related error, bias-related issues are extremely successfully resolved. Compared to a single decision tree, it is a strong modeling tool that is far more durable. Based on the results of Classification algorithms, it is seen that there is no category with grade A, which is concerned with the river Ganga. Additionally, it serves as a warning for the next generation since the quality of the water in the River Ganga would drastically decline. The Ganga river's declining water quality index caused widespread alarm, which led to quick responses from both the general public and individuals who had increased their awareness and consciousness. Future studies will include researching and studying the water quality of several rivers in India that flow through various states. Using different algorithms, the analysis will be carried out. Finally, the comparison will be made between the rivers to warn the citizens about the water quality so as to take precautionary measures.

References

1. Nayan, A.-A., Kibria, M.G., Rahman, M.O., Saha, J.: River water quality analysis and prediction using GBM. In: 2020 2nd International Conference on Advanced Information and Communication Technology (ICAICT), pp. 219–224. IEEE (2020)
2. Chaudhary, M., Mishra, S., Kumar, A.: Estimation of water pollution and probability of health risk due to imbalanced nutrients in River Ganga, India. Int. J. River Basin Manage. **15**(1), 53–60 (2017)
3. Vega, M., Pardo, R., Barrado, E., Debán, L.: Assessment of seasonal and polluting effects on the quality of river water by exploratory data analysis. Water Res. **32**(12), 3581–3592 (1998)
4. Faisal, M., et al.: Faster R-CNN algorithm for detection of plastic garbage in the ocean: a case for turtle preservation. Math. Probl. Eng. **2022** (2022)

5. Sharma, R., et al.: Analysis of water pollution using different physicochemical parameters: a study of Yamuna river. Front. Environ. Sci. **8**, 581591 (2020)
6. Jaloree, S., Rajput, A., Gour, S.: Decision tree approach to build a model for water quality. Binary J. Data Min. Netw. **4**(1), 25–28 (2014)
7. Horvat, Z., Horvat, M., Pastor, K., Bursić, V., Puvača, N.: Multivariate analysis of water quality measurements on the Danube river. Water **13**(24), 3634 (2021)
8. Nair, J.P., Vijaya, M.S.: Predictive models for river water quality using machine learning and big data techniques-a survey. In: 2021 International Conference on Artificial Intelligence and Smart Systems (ICAIS), pp. 1747–1753. IEEE (2021)
9. Son, C.T., Giang, N.T.H., Thao, T.P., Nui, N.H., Lam, N.T., Cong, V.H.: Assessment of Cau river water quality assessment using a combination of water quality and pollution indices. J. Water Supply: Res. Technol.-Aqua **69**(2), 160–172 (2020)
10. Asadollah, S.B.H.S., Sharafati, A., Motta, D., Yaseen, Z.M.: River water quality index prediction and uncertainty analysis: A comparative study of machine learning models. J. Environ. Chem. Eng. **9**(1), 104599 (2021)
11. Babbar, R., Babbar, S.: Predicting river water quality index using data mining techniques. Environ. Earth Sci. **76**(14), 1–15 (2017)
12. Kolli, K., Seshadri, R.: Ground water quality assessment using data mining techniques. Int. J. Comput. Appl. **76**(15) (2013)
13. Wikurendra, E.A., Syafiuddin, A., Nurika, G., Elisanti, A.D.: Water quality analysis of Pucang river, sidoarjo regency to control water pollution. Environ. Qual. Manage. **32**, 133–144 (2022)
14. Wills, M., Irvine, K.N.: Application of the national sanitation foundation water quality index in Cazenovia Creek, NY, pilot watershed management project. Middle States Geogr. **1996**, 95–104 (1996)
15. Rashu, R.I., Jishan, S.T., Haq, N., Rahman, R.M.: Implementation of optimum binning, ensemble learning and re-sampling techniques to predict student's performance. Int. J. Knowl. Eng. Soft Data Paradigms **5**(1), 1–30 (2015)
16. Kong, L., Zhang, L.: Novel structure-driven features for accurate prediction of protein structural class. Genomics **103**(4), 292–297 (2014)
17. Central Pollution Control Board. National water quality monitoring programme

Detection of Android Ransomware Using Machine Learning Approach

Anoop Jose[1]([⊠]), C. Priyadharsini[1], P. Mercy Praise[1], G. Jaspher W. Kathrine[1]([⊠]),
and J. Andrew[2]([⊠])

[1] Department of CSE, Karunya Institute of Technology and Sciences, Coimbatore, India
{anoopjose21,paradisemercy}@karunya.edu.in, {priyadharsini,
kathrine}@karunya.edu
[2] Senior Scale, Manipal Institute of Technology, Manipal Academy of Higher Education
Manipal, Karnataka, India
andrew.j@manipal.edu

Abstract. The majority of Android smartphone users utilize handheld devices for almost everything in their life, including regular planning, data interchange, correspondence, social interaction, business execution, and financial transactions. The prevalence of cyberattacks on smartphones has drastically increased with people's reliance on smartphone technology. Smartphone applications require permission to access several smartphone features, which might be used by hackers to conduct an attack or implant malware. The main aim of attackers in target cell phones is to obtain victims' personal information for financial benefit. Despite this, as Android has the largest market share among smartphone operating systems, it is frequently attacked by cybercriminals. One such major infestation is Ransomware, which is mainly found on PCs and has the ability to latch onto smartphones. Ransomware encrypts the victim's data and demands for a ransom amount for the decryption key. The present Android ransomware research is deficient in key components and relies on supervised machine-learning techniques. However, these techniques have several drawbacks and early detection and recognition of ransomware in android is required. The main aim of this paper is to examine various machine-learning algorithms used in Android ransomware. The novelty of the paper is to combine Ransom-Droid and concept drift by classifying raw data based on host, network, behaviour, and files. Each data is recognized with the help of static and dynamic analysis based on the type of ransomware detection. The proposed paper is informative with real-world applications in malware identification and categorization.

Keywords: Android Ransomware · Behaviour-based · Host-based · Network-based

1 Introduction

Malware is invasive software that is designed specially to damage and render inoperable computers and computer systems [1]. Malware is an abbreviation for "malicious

© The Author(s), under exclusive license to Springer Nature Singapore Pte Ltd. 2023
S. Prabhu et al. (Eds.): ATIS 2022, CCIS 1804, pp. 191–203, 2023.
https://doi.org/10.1007/978-981-99-2264-2_16

software". Some of the most popular types of malware are worms, Trojan horses, spyware, adware, and ransomware. Malware disrupts or even tampers with an electronic device's operation. Malware has the ability to infect servers, equipment, mobile devices, desktop computers, tablets, and even laptops. The first form of malware ever developed was the computer virus [2]. Android malware is used to attack mobile devices since it is now the most popular mobile operating system worldwide and has the biggest market share, making it a prime target for cybercriminals. Android ransomware is a sort of malicious software (malware) that targets android-powered mobile devices. Android ransomware assaults are similar to kidnappings. Malware can drive toward browser websites or download apps by stealing personal information, forcing victim devices to send SMS messages to services that charge extra for text messaging or installing adware. Passwords, contact information, personal information, location, and other data are all subject to theft. Malware detected on Android smartphones is very similar to attacks that happen on network computers. It can only be used on Android-powered phones and tablets [3]. Programs including trojans, adware, ransomware, spyware, viruses, and phishing apps, which aim to harm a user's device, are examples of mobile malware [4]. Contrary to Apple users, Android users can sideload apps. Users may then download the material directly from the internet or their computer to their smartphone in order to fully avoid the play store [5]. Various traditional sources, such as dubious websites, dubious emails, and links from unknown senders, can also lead to the download of malware [6]. The complexity and expansion of malware threats have been made automated for malware detection research subjects in network security [7]. Ransomware poses a significant danger to cybersecurity because it encrypts consumer data and devices in order to collect money from victims. Payment of a ransom is required by the hacker in order to regain access to personal files [9]. Ransomware has emerged as one of the most serious computer dangers in recent years. As the amount of user data on portable devices has increased, ransomware has become more prevalent on cell phones [10]. The main aim is to evaluate Supervised and Unsupervised Machine learning algorithms and other algorithms which are used to detect Android ransomware. The novelty of the paper is a brief overview of Android Ransomware based on Ransom-Droid and concept-drift methods to detect the ransomware attack within the network.

2   Related Works

This section of the study is about the existing Android ransomware detection with various approaches. The brief classification of Android malware detection is shown in Fig. 1. To categorize the data, the methodology and detection techniques are employed. Additional subcategories of Android ransomware include behaviour-based, host-based, network-based, file-based, and hybrid-based variants. Based on the identification of Android ransomware, it is further divided into machine learning detection of both static and dynamic analysis (supervised and unsupervised).

Behaviour-based methods are done based on before an item may perform its planned activity, it assesses it based on its intended activities. The behaviour of an item, or in certain circumstances its potential behaviours examined for suspicious actions [11]. It is one of the most effective methods of defending against sophisticated threats such as file-less malware, ransomware, and zero-day malware.

Host-based methods are systems that aid organizations in monitoring processes and programs running on devices such as servers and workstations [12]. These monitor registry changes as well as critical system configuration, logs, and content files, alerting users to any unauthorized or unusual activity.

Network-based methods are famously difficult to detect ransomware on a network until it has been thoroughly attacked and encrypted it. This is so that they may compare possible infections using signature-based detection, which is a method used by traditional security systems.

File-based methods run a quick static analysis on files in a specified context. Security platforms and antivirus software can gather data from within an executable to determine if it is ransomware or an authorized executable [13]. Most antivirus software performs this step when searching for harmful infections.

Hybrid-based approaches are further classified to address the shortcomings of behaviour-based, host-based, network-based, and file-based systems, and it is a mix of behaviour-based, host-based, network-based, and file-based systems [14]. Unsupervised machine learning detects unknown attacks using both static and dynamic analysis, whereas supervised machine learning detects known assaults using static analysis.

2.1 Based on Method

Usman Ahmed et al. [9] present a hybrid strategy that takes permissions, text, and images into account. Memory utilization, system call logs, and CPU utilization are all statically and dynamically monitored to provide network-based functionality. An ensemble based on machine learning, a method for detecting ransomware that takes into account multiple applications is presented. It is evaluated online after being offline trained to look into dynamic behaviour. Based on a majority vote, the meta-classifier generated the final prediction. Permission and system call logs were found to be the two most crucial characteristics for recognizing and categorizing android. C4.5, Random Forest, JRip Logistic Regression, SVM, and AdaBoost are among the characteristics. Classifiers are used by both static and dynamic ensemble learners. The results validate their ensemble analyzers for ransomware detection in order to identify Android ransomware successfully, a method that shows promise. By obtaining high accuracy on the supplied data and high precision, recall, and F-measurement, fabricated inputs of 1 bit, 10 bit, 20 bit, 30 bit, and 40 bit.

Burak Filiz et al. [10] Decryption tools have been created by security researchers and practitioners to tackle the rising menace of ransomware. According to the research, several technologies useful for decrypting and recovering damaged data were empirically investigated. These restore encrypted files without charging a fee in an effort to assist victims in getting their data back. Sadly, not much study has been done on the effectiveness of decryption and recovery techniques. The degree to which these methods can really restore lost data is unknown. They found that almost half of the methods are unsuccessful in recovering corrupted data. They compared 61 ransomware samples with 78 technologies created by security companies. Only 55% of the programs tested were able to decrypt all encrypted files completely, 4% gave partial decryption, and 41% failed to decrypt any data at all.

Manabu Hirano et al. [11] ransomware detection systems restarting to use in addition to static features, there are behavioural or dynamic features. While dynamic ransomware detection can detect variants of ransomware, it has the following limitations:

(i) it necessitates ransomware execution; (ii) In the real world, ransomware may behave differently. The brand-new open-source dataset compares storage access patterns from five popular benign software samples and seven well-known ransomware examples. The tests confirmed the average F1 detection rate of 91.4% with 81.8% on a different operating system version and 31.0% on storage devices with full-capacity drive encryption enabled.

The RANSAP dataset, to the best of their knowledge, is one of the only free datasets with dynamic, realistic properties for machine learning training ransomware detection algorithms. Additionally, it contains access patterns for ransomware subtypes, OS iterations, and storage units with full disc encryption turned on. They begin with a hypervisor-based system for tracking storage access patterns, develop and put into practice feature extraction and machine learning models for ransomware detection, and then give a thorough analysis and assessment of the dataset.

Craig Beamana et al. [13] Ransomware is transmitted via a variety of techniques, including phishing and social engineering assaults. They examined current developments in the prevention and detection of ransomware as well as research obstacles and future goals. Cutting-edge ransomware detection algorithms are primarily concerned with honeypots, network traffic analysis, innovative techniques based on machine learning prevention technology, and key management backups. The COVID-19 epidemic has resulted in a significant increase in the frequency of ransomware assaults. Various institutions, including healthcare, finance, and government have been targeted. They have carried out a number of experiments on malware samples, highlighting the need for more intelligent ransomware detection and prevention methods that were discovered through the experiments. According to VirusTotal.com, one of the payloads created was posted, Moreover, the payload was identified as harmful with just only 20 of 72 antivirus engines. Along with that 67 out of 100 people detected Jigsaw's sample was also uploaded. There are 72 engines in total. Both dynamic and static detection can be tested with antivirus software.

Eslam Amer et al. [15] were able to overcome the challenge of significant characteristic size and intricate relationships by grouping similar traits into a few cluster types in their behavioural android malware scent-predicting based on both static and dynamic characteristics. In the suggested design, an LSTM model was used to system call snapshots and categorize newly restructured API in a series that was trained to establish an API and system call sequences using newly generated random snapshots. They validated their approach for defending against typical ransomware attacks. At a particular snapshot size, it was noted that trained LSTM models performed consistently. The design performed admirably when it came to predicting new sequences. They established processes by analyzing random short snapshots, they may be able to foresee dangerous conduct and comparative accuracy measures also demonstrated their model's ability to compete with novel Ransomware samples. As a result, rather than identifying harmful payloads after they were executed, they presented an early warning strategy for preventing them.

As a result, they can save money on future harm. They used a hybrid analysis feature model to analyze malicious Android processes and research Android apps.

Seungkwang Lee et al. [18] presented a block-based model technique for detecting possibly harmful cryptographic activities. Statistical research to discover heuristic rules for distinguishing between regular and encrypted data blocks. With just 13% overhead, many cryptographic operations may be detected. Cryptic can discover cryptographic functions based on their testing results using suspicious blocks that appear to have high entropy in 90% or more of n consecutive blocks. They presented a model technique based on blocks for detecting potentially harmful cryptographic activities. They conduct statistical research in order to discover heuristic rules for distinguishing between regular and encrypted data blocks. The heuristic rule may be applied to the filesystem without changing the kernel by using Filesystem in User Space (FUSE) and defining their filesystem Rcryptect for real-time cryptographic function detection. Before files are destroyed as a result of ransomware hackers' indiscriminate attacks, a basic initial layer of defence is required. In order to identify ransomware cryptographic operations, they finally suggest Rcrypt, a FUSE-based file system that examines block entropy.

Huanran Wang et al. [19] a hybrid malware detection strategy for Android that combines dynamic and static approaches. In order to further detect suspicious programs, extract the RAM heap's object reference associations and use them to build a dynamic feature base. They then provide an improved DAMBA-based state-based method. They distinguish between various permission patterns between malicious and good programs using static analysis and machine learning. This work is limited to what they do not consider deceased objects. More dynamic properties (such as flow information and system load) will be used in future studies. Use a dynamic feature made from an object reference from the RAM heap to better detect suspicious programs. They conducted their experiments using a sizable 12,364 records of real-world datasets. In the experiment verification, there were 9344 innocent samples and 9344 harmful ones. The detection time is less than 2.305 s which is 55% quicker than DAMBA trials, and the detection accuracy is 99.8%. It has the highest accuracy of 99.8% when compared to other individual supervised and unsupervised machine learning identification.

2.2 Based on Detection Technique

- **Based on Supervised Machine Learning**

Timothy McIntosha et al. [3]. In order to drive security metrics, calculate security indicators, and estimate security postures they suggest a dynamic strategy for identifying ransomware-like actions and dynamically controlling access requests. They propose a user-centric dynamic access control decision on files that gathers operating system security indicators. On the Windows desktop platform, Ranacco was shown for protecting user data and monitoring ransomware-like file system activities and to be a workable prototype of an access control framework. To make important security decisions and encourage users Ranacco created a clear warning message. Ranacco enforces UDAC and CBI on specific user files in the user file system for an application-level access control architecture.

Jinting Zhua et al. [4] demonstrated a few shots of a Siamese neural network based on meta-learning that not only identifies but also classifies ransomware attacks. The entropy feature stores fine-grained data associated with various malware signatures that are directly retrieved from ransomware binary files. To provide more accurate weights of unique ransomware samples and to reduce the bias associated with a model trained with a small number of training samples, a pre-trained network like VGG-16 is utilized. When trained with a limited set of training samples, their suggested model produces a weighted F1 score at a rate greater than 86%.

Abdullah Talha et al. [5] extremely efficient The CNN-based Android malware detection framework was created primarily to (i) extract features automatically (ii) offer a one-of-a-kind CNN that operates on one-dimensional data, and (iii) conduct thorough malware analysis and In Addition to the typically used permissions, intents and API calls can be utilized. A created dataset made up of 14,386 applications drawn from de facto standard datasets served as the basis for training and evaluating the suggested system. The suggested framework accuracy was estimated to be as high as .9, exceeding the accuracy obtained from several machine learning methods. The accuracy of the Droid Malware detection testing showed that it could reach .9 which was greater than the industry average. Other seven classifiers are used to determine the detection accuracy using publicly available data. Machine learning algorithms include SVM, Random Forest, KNN, Decision Tree, Naive Bayes, AdaBoost, and MLp.

Alejandro Guerra-Manzanares et al. [6] Using a seven-year data set, proposes and tests a novel strategy for detecting and efficiently addressing idea drift in Android malware detection several timestamps are tested and compared for the performance of their impact on detection. The inner workings of the proposed method are also used to identify concept drift in Android malware. To effectively respond to malware evolution, they proposed a strategy that employs a pool of classifiers trained on recent data and decreases model retraining. In the presence of the idea drift method, delivering high-performance metrics for an application and even system calls can effectively distinguish malware. The proposed solution averaged a 94.65% F1 score, 95.17% precision, and 94.14% accuracy given over a 7-year period. Recall, with 89.49% indicating efficacy in adapting to and responding to idea drift problems affecting Android malware.

Pooja Yadava et al. [7] In this study, Android malware detection is compared with the efficacy of 26 state-of-the-art convolutional neural network (CNN) models. To begin, it extracts bytecode from Android DEX files and feeds it into the efficientNet-B4 network relevant characteristics using image-based malware representations. After passing through a GAP layer, the collected features are sent to a SoftMax classifier. Using SVM, RF-classifiers, stacking, and image-based malware representations of the Android DEX file with the outcomes of large-scale learning are also covered. Conventional techniques demonstrate the efficiency of the proposed RCGU for early crypto-ransomware detection.

Asma Razgallah et al. [16] assess Android and malware detection strategies, emphasizing the benefits and addressing several issues, particularly the malware's evolving nature. They can be used to develop more effective enforcement mechanisms with static and dynamic analysis. They made testing datasets and experiments available. They frequently used different testing datasets and presented different types of metrics (accuracy, precision, recall, and so on) and found it especially difficult to evaluate detection approaches.

Ilker Kara et al. [17] Ransomware and an effective detection analysis strategy presented. The Ransomware threat" Onion ransomware" is detected using a basic assessment of tools and techniques. "VirtualBox 6.1.16 (Free Version)," "FTK Imager 4.2.0 (Free Version)," "Autopsy 4.16.0 (Free Version)," and "Wireshark 3.2.7 (Free Version)" were installed on the workstation and used for analyses. On January 2, 2021, at 10:41:35 UTC, the analysis began. It took about two weeks to complete all of the analyzes.

Alejandro Guerra-Manzanares et al. [21]) Using dynamic detection features which were done from 2011 to 2018 (filesystem calls) was derived from android apps. They compared and contrasted different timestamp options. The results show that idea drift has a negative impact on machine learning classifiers, especially when the timestamp is used. In the android timeline, timestamp appears to be a reliable source of historical app information provided even when different data sets are used with maintaining high-quality service performance detection over time.

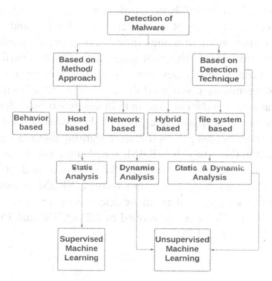

Fig. 1. Overview of android ransomware detection

- **Based on Unsupervised Machine Learning**

Shweta Sharma et al. [1] The Ransom-Droid framework being suggested uses a flexible and probabilistic Gaussian Mixture Model that models the dataset. The two primary steps of the proposed Random-Android system are Android ransomware detection and forensic analysis. Shows how others using unsupervised machine learning techniques are presented with the GMM technique variance threshold and PCA outperforms [23].

This study proposed that it detects Android ransomware in 44 ms with a 98.12% F- score value and 98.08% accuracy rate in Android malware detection.

Syed Ibrahim Imtiaz et al. [2] DeepAMD used a novel approach to defend against real-world Android malware, using deep Artificial Neural Network (ANN) including an efficient comparison of traditional machine learning classifiers with DeepAMD. Deep-AMD is evaluated using a cutting-edge CICAdMal2019 dataset, and testing demonstrates that DeepAMD is the most effective method for Android malware detection and identification on both the static and dynamic levels DeepAMD achieves a maximum accuracy of 92.5% for malware category classification, 93.4% for malware classification and 90% for malware family classification on the static layer. DeepAMD achieves the malware family classification on the Dynamic layer of 59% and the highest accuracy of 80.3% for malware category classification when compared to state-of-the-art approaches.

Alejandro Guerra et al. [8] many benign and malicious data sources are joined to create a data collection with a longer time range and 489 static and dynamic properties. An emulator and a real device are used to address the dynamic features characteristics (i.e. system calls), resulting in two equally featured sub-datasets. The emulator dataset contains 28,745 malicious files, 209 malware family's apps, and 35,246 benign samples. The genuine device data collection contains 41,382 malicious programs from 240 malware families as well as 36,755 benign programs.

Farnood Faghihi et al. [12] Ransomware can identify and eliminate crypto-ransomware in real-time on smartphones in real time using dynamic and lightweight static analysis. Ransomware are detection speed, accuracy, and performance overhead were evaluated on recent smartphones using two datasets of crypto ransomware [24]. The detection of RansomCare discovered the event of an attack with an 8.7% performance overhead that achieves 0% data loss in it. In less than 6.5 s it identifies smartphone crypto ransomware, which is appropriate given its short detection time.

Zhen Liu et al. [20] An unsupervised feature learning method for detecting mobile malware is presented in this study. It is RBM -based and could in unsupervised mobile virus detection to reduce data dimensionality. SRBM is contrasted with RMB, SAE,Agg and PCA. In terms of clustering evaluation metrics, SRBM outperforms alternative approaches in most datasets, particularly in the detection of zero-day malware clustering. RBM's NMI, ACC, and F Score are improved by 6.2%,6.9%, and 15.4%, respectively, across all datasets (Tables 1 and 2).

Table 1. Overview of dynamic analysis

Tool	Algorithm	Features	Dataset	Performance metrics
RansomDroid	Gaussian Mixture Model	2300 APKs, 2000 APKs	RansomProber, AndroZoo	A-98.08% F1--98.12%
DeepAMD	Artificial Neural Network	API calls,logs, packages, log states, battery states etc	CICAdMal2019, CICAndMal2017	A-93.4%
RanSAP	dimensionality reduction algorithm	patterns,OS,storage devices,decoy files etc	RANSAP dataset	F1–96.2%
RansomCare	(AES) with Cipher Block Chaining (CBC)	API calls,Text files,books,audio,videos,images, spreadsheets etc	user file dataset having 2979 files in total	A-87%
Rcryptect	AES-128,RC4,RSA-2048,SHA-256,MD5	text,image,MP3,JPEG,Zip	Reports taken from WannaCry Clop,GandCrab,JSWorm Ransom,PXJ	A-90%
Realtime static & dynamic Hybrid detection	TextCNN	Patterns,Apps,texts,permissions etc	real-world dataset including 12,364 and 9344 benign samples	A-99.8%
Mobile malware detection	Subspace based Restricted BoltzmannMachines (SRBM)	APIcalls,system calls,events permissions. etc	OmniDroid, CIC2019,CIC2020 datasets	F1–0.87
Krono Droid	SHA-256	41,382 malware, belonging to 240 malware families, and 36,755 benign apps	Android dataset with hybrid-features that provides timestamps,(2008–2020)	A-99.4%

3 Proposed Methodology

The proposed Ransomware detection approach automatically recognizes entities host targeted by Ransomware attackers to steal the victim's information through a collection of raw data, pre-processing, and analysis. These attackers would get permission to the victim machine by using supervised and Unsupervised machine learning algorithms to take access to their resources. The data collection is identified through Host-based, Network-based, Behavior-based, and File-based systems. In correspondence to this paper considered data from various windows applications, Android applications, APK tools, permissions, text, images, addresses, timestamps, and signatures. The obtained data features in the paper are combined with Ransom-Droid and Concept Drift methods. When looking into Ransom-Droid is using the Gaussian mixture model which accepts every data point is produced from a combination of a finite number of Gaussian distributions and is flexible with a selective approach. It is even compared with the clustering technique for the detection of ransomware. It detects the malware with different classifications and proceeds to forensic analysis within the data collected by using unsupervised machine learning and then evaluates the ransomware attack within the targeted network. Using Ransom-Droid it is challenging to detect crypto-ransomware. Whereas the concept drift method in machine learning states the statistical properties of selected variables change over time and uses features to statistically distribute and correlate within the legitimate and invalid requests from address, timestamps and signatures by using a supervised machine learning algorithm. It examines applications within the tested timestamps and

Table 2. Overview of static analysis

Tools	Algorithm	Features	Dataset	Performance metrics
few-shot meta-learning	Siamese Neural Network	Binary executables create the Entropy and Images features	VirusShare	F1- > 86%
DroidMalwareDetector	Convolutional Neural Network	14, 386 apps, intent and API calls, images	AndroZoo, Drebin, KuafuDet etc	A- > 0.9
concept drift	trainClassifier Algorithm, Dynamic Ensemble Selection (DES) algorithm:	2,677 samples (i.e., 2,124 genuine apps and 553 malware apps)syscalls	7 year data set from (2012–2020)78,137 Android apps,288 system calls	F1–94.65%, P-95.17%, R-94.14% A-89.49%
EfficientNet-B4 CNN-based model	SVM,RF, CNN	2 million benign and malicious Android apps	R2-D2,Trojan, AdWare, Clicker etc	A-95.7%
Ranacco	MD5	Adobe Acrobat Reader, Microsoft Word, Excel andPowerPoint,WannaCry,Petya etc	Virtual machine, Virushare,Simulation of FTCode	-
hybrid approach Network based	C4.5,Random forest, JRip,Logistic,Regression,SVM, andAdaBoost	permissions, text,monitoring memory usage, system call logs, and CPU usage	Drebin4,RansomProber5, .apk files	P-0.98 R-0.99 F1–0.98
decryption Tools, VirusTotal,ANY-RUN	Full decryption, partial decryption, decryption	78 tools created by 11 security companies against 61 ransomware samples	Alcatraz,Avest,BigBobRoss, GandCrab, GetCrypt, Globev3, Gomasom,InsaneCrypt,etc	-
Dynamic detection with network traffic	Cutting edge ransomware detection algorithm	control data, and key management backups	VirusTotal.com, 20 of 72 Jigsaw's sample 67 out of 100 detected harmful	-

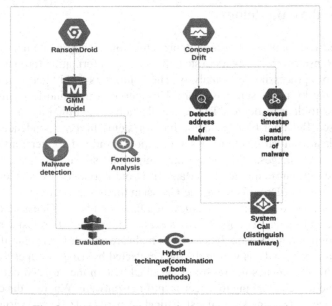

Fig. 2. Architecture diagram for ransom-ware detection

characterizes the data collection with required results and challenges in order to detect any affected ransomware system. Along with this even Ransom forest and K-neighbors machine learning algorithms are used for the classification and regression of the data. Using concept drift is challenging to recognize within the real-time dynamic process. The proposed hybrid Ransomware detection helps us to combine both Ransom-droid and concept drift with the classification of static and dynamic analysis. The novelty of the paper is done according to the data collection and then examine with a generated evaluation of Ransom-droid and eventually distinguish system call efficiently with the help of idea drift and even included drawbacks of previous works within the concept drift. It helps to acquire a proposed hybrid functioning of ransomware detection by enhancing and providing better accuracy within the information technology (Fig. 2).

4 Conclusion

Android ransomware is a sort of harmful software (malware) that targets Android-based mobile devices. Ransomware assaults on Android are similar to kidnappings. Android malware (viruses, Trojan horses, root-kits, and worms) had been installed on the phones of the victims. By obtaining victim credentials, malware may compel victims to browse websites or download programs. Personal information compels user smartphone to send SMS messages to businesses that demand a fee. A charge for SMS texting or the installation of adware Data thieves can steal passwords. There is contact information, personal information, a map, and other information provided. Crypto ransomware is a sort of ransomware that is typically found on PCs, but it is conceivable that it may attack users' Android smartphones as well. It is important for the target user to get data encrypted and then get a ransom letter asking for money in order to gain the decryption key. The proposed methodology assesses the rate of a ransomware attack and even examines several ransomware detections approaches with machine learning techniques. It also claims by utilizing a variety of machine learning algorithmic methodologies, the detection rate for ransomware is around the top of the 90th percentile. The hybrid Ransomware malware detection technique combines dynamic and static approaches by leveraging Ransom-Droid and concept drift methods. Numerous out-of-date benchmark datasets with a high detection rate are also linked in the proposed methodology used for various ransomware detection processes in actual networks. The novelty of the paper is to detect ransomware proposed methodology by examining various features classified as host-based, network-based, behavior-based, and file-system-based using Ransom-droid and concept drift methods. It also helps to classify malware and distinguish the malware feature to get better accuracy for real-world applications in the online community.

References

1. Sharma, S., Krishna, C.R., Kumar, R.: RansomDroid: forensic analysis and detection of android ransomware using unsupervised machine learning technique. Forensic Sci. Int. Digi. Investi. **37** (2021)
2. Imtiaz, S.I., Rehman, S., Javed, A.R., Jalil, Z., Liu, X., Alnumay, W.S.: DeepAMD: detection and identification of android malware using high-efficient deep artificial neural network. Future Generation Computer Systems **115** (2021)

3. McIntosh, T., Kayes, A.S.M., Phoebe Chen, Y.-P., Ng, A., Watters, P.: Dynamic user-centric access control for detection of ransomware attacks. Computers & Security **111** (2021)
4. Zhu, J., Jang-Jaccard, J., Singh, A., Welch, I., AI-Sahaf, H., Camtepe, S.: A few-shot meta-learning based siamese neural network using entropy features for ransomware classification. Computers & Security **117** (2022)
5. Kabakus, A.T.: DroidMalwareDetector: a novel android malware detection framework based on convolutional neural network. Expert Systems with Applications **206** (2022)
6. Guerra-Manzanares, A., Luckner, M., Bahsi, H.: Android malware concept drift using system calls: detection, characterization and challenges. Expert Systems with Applications **206** (2022)
7. Yadav, P., Menon, N., Ravi, V., Vishvanathan, S., Pham, T.D.: EfficientNet convolutional neural networks-based Android malware detection. Computers & Security **115** (2022)
8. Guerra-Manzanares, A., Bahsi, H., Nõmm, S.: KronoDroid: Time-basedHybrid-feature Dataset for Effective Android Malware Detection and Characterization. Computers & Security **110** (2021)
9. Ahmed, U., Chun-Wei Lin, J., Srivastava, G.: Mitigating adversarial evasion attacks of ransomware using ensemble learning. Computers and Electrical Engineering **100**, 2022
10. Filiz, B., Arief, B., Cetin, O., Hernandez-Castro, J.: On the effectiveness of ransomware decryption tools. Computers & Security **111**, 2021
11. Hirano, M., Hodota, R., Kobayashi, R.: RanSAP: an open dataset of ransomware storage access patterns for training machine learning models. Forensic Science International: Digital Investigation **40** (2022)
12. Faghihi, F., Zulkernine, M.: RansomCare: data-centric detection and mitigation against smartphone crypto-ransomware. Computer Networks **191** (2021)
13. Beaman, C., Barkworth, A., David Akande, T., Hakak, S., Khurram Khan, M.: Ransomware: recent advances, analysis, challenges and future research directions. Computers & Security **111** (2021)
14. Saleh Al-rimy, B.A., et al.: Redundancy coefficient gradual up-weighting-based mutual information feature selection technique for crypto-ransomware early detection. Future Generation Computer Systems **115** (2021)
15. Amer, E., El-Sappagh, S.: Robust deep learning early alarm prediction model based on the behavioral smell for android malware. Computers & Security **116** (2022)
16. Razgallah, A., Khoury, R., Hallé, S., Khanmohammadi, K.: A survey of malware detection in android apps: recommendations and perspectives for future research. Computer Science Review **39** (2021)
17. Kara, I., Aydos, M.: The rise of ransomware: Forensic analysis for windows based ransomware attacks. Expert Systems with Applications **190** (2022)
18. Lee, S., Jho, N.-s., Chung, D., Kang, Y., Kim, M.: Rcryptect: real-time detection of cryptographic function in the user-space filesystem. Computers & Security **112** (2022)
19. Wang, H., Zhang, W., He, Hui.: You are what the permissions told me! android malware detection based on hybrid tactics. J. Info. Sec. Appli. **66** (2022)
20. Liu, Z., Wang, R., Japkowicz, N., Tang, D., Zhang, W., Zhao, J.: Research on unsupervised feature learning for android malware detection based on restricted boltzmann machines. Future Generation Computer Systems **120** (2021)
21. Guerra-Manzanares, A., Luckner, M., Bahsi, H.: Concept drift and cross device behavior: challenges and implications for effective android malware detection. Computers & Security **120** (2022)

22. Bertia, A., Xavier, S.B., Kathrine, G.J.W., Palmer, G.M.: A study about detecting ransomware by using different algorithms. In: 2022 International Conference on Applied Artificial Intelligence and Computing (ICAAIC), pp. 1293–1300 (2022). https://doi.org/10.1109/ICAAIC 53929.2022

23. Andrew, J., Karthikeyan, J., Jebastin, J.: Privacy preserving big data publication on cloud using Mondrian anonymization techniques and deep neural networks. In: 2019 5th international conference on advanced computing & communication systems (ICACCS), pp. 722–727. IEEE 2019, March

Cyber Security and Layering of Medical Data Using Machine Learning Algorithms

Anmol Garg[1], Jay Singhvi[1], Saurav Sabu[1], Rushikesh Sahu[1], Srikanth Prabhu[2], and Arti Pawar[1(✉)]

[1] ICAS, Manipal Academy of Higher Education, Manipal 576104, India
arti.pawar@manipal.edu
[2] MIT, Manipal Academy of Higher Education, Manipal 576104, India

Abstract. For a few years, all industries have felt the magic of technological advancements, and one of the fastest-growing industries has been the healthcare industry. Many technologies have now enabled doctors to diagnose and treat patients more accurately than ever.

The Health Insurance Portability and Accountability Act of 1996 (HIPAA) is a law that was enacted by the 104th United States Congress to protect sensitive information in the healthcare industry from being accessed by cybercriminals. It established guidelines for physical and technical security measures to be put in place, such as workstation security, device and media controls, and facility access controls. Technical safeguards include the use of unique identification numbers, emergency access procedures, automatic logoff, encryption, and decryption. The adoption of healthcare technology can be a complex process, requiring careful planning and implementation. Organizations are spending large amounts of funding to become more integrated and secure but need more time or money to update software.

This paper demonstrates the deployment of data layers on Medical Data. Patient records are kept in a remote server and are accessed only when required by algorithms that show the trends at macro levels. In this paper, we have exhibited the deployment of this layer using a disease prediction model that presents current and possible future trends of the disease occurrence.

Keywords: Cyber Security · Healthcare · Machine learning · Chronic hepatitis C · Diabetes · Logistic Regression · Random Forest Classifier · K Neighbors Classifier · Decision Tree Classifier · Gradient Boosting Classifier · Support Vector Machine · Gaussian Naive Bayes Classifier

1 Introduction

This study takes Disease Prediction as a Use-Case and goes one step further and examines the accuracy of a few machine learning algorithms, namely, SVM (Support Vector Machine), Logistic Regression, Naïve Bayes, and Decision trees.

Machine learning algorithms can analyze large amounts of data and identify patterns that may not be apparent to humans. This can be incredibly useful in medicine, where

© The Author(s), under exclusive license to Springer Nature Singapore Pte Ltd. 2023
S. Prabhu et al. (Eds.): ATIS 2022, CCIS 1804, pp. 204–226, 2023.
https://doi.org/10.1007/978-981-99-2264-2_17

doctors constantly work to identify and treat diseases as quickly and accurately as possible. In diabetes, by using data from blood tests, machine learning algorithms can be trained to detect the signs of diabetes with high accuracy.

Hepatitis C is a viral infection that affects the liver. It is caused by the hepatitis C virus (HCV), a blood-borne virus. There is no vaccine for HCV, so preventing infection is essentially a matter of avoiding risky behaviors that can lead to exposure to the virus, such as sharing needles or other drug-injection equipment or getting a tattoo or piercing with unsterilized tools [1].

In predicting who is at risk of developing hepatitis C, certain factors can increase a person's likelihood of becoming infected. These include having a history of intravenous drug use, receiving a blood transfusion or organ transplant before 1992 (when widespread blood supply screening began), being on dialysis for an extended period, or being born to a mother with hepatitis C.

Additionally, specific populations are at higher risk of hepatitis C, such as people who have HIV, those who work in healthcare settings, and those who have been incarcerated.

Since 2000, diabetes has entered the top 10 causes of death charts, following a significant increase of 70% [2]. Currently, even though about 422 million people worldwide have diabetes [3] but over the years, it has become easy to detect it by using various machine algorithms which help us to take in different consideration parameters like age, sex, cholesterol, etc. which can be one of the many causes of diabetes.

2   Background

2.1   An Overview of Related Work

Several scholars have used different machine learning models and compared their accuracy which helped them to reach a conclusion about which model is most accurate.

The Pima Indian Diabetes dataset (PIDD) was utilized Alam, T.M. et al. to evaluate ANN, RF, and K-Means Clustering. The findings show that the accuracy of the random forest approach was 74.7%, that of the ANN was 75.7%, and that of the K-means clustering method was 73.6%. From this, ANN performs better than all other models and that BMI and glucose have a substantial correlation with diabetes [4].

The Pima Indian Diabetes dataset and hospital physical examination data from Luzhou, China were both used by Zou et al. (PIDD). Using this, they used Principal Component Analysis (PCA) and Minimum Redundancy Maximum Relevance (mRMR) approaches to reduce the number of features before applying Random Forest, Decision Tree, and ANN as the classification algorithm on PIDD. Additionally, they discovered that while employing mRMR produces better results, PCA may have superior accuracy. Additionally, there aren't many differences between random forests, decision trees, and neural networks, yet in some cases, random forests are unquestionably superior to the other classifiers. The best result for the Luzhou dataset is 0.8084, and the best performance for Pima Indians is 0.7721, indicating that machine learning can be used for predicting diabetes, but finding suitable attributes, classifiers, and data mining methods are essential [5].

The trials are carried out using WEKA software, and Antony et al. forecast diabetes using medical data. Diabetes is diagnosed using naive Bayes (NB) and decision tree-based random forests (RF) machine learning techniques. According to the findings, naive Bayes had a higher average accuracy than other algorithms [6].

Additionally, Khanam et al. use the Pima Indian Diabetes dataset (PIDD). Even the performance analysis of the diabetes dataset was done using WEKA. They employed Decision Trees (DT), K-Nearest Neighbor (KNN), Random Forest (RF), Naive Bayes (NB), Logistic Regression (LR), and Support Vector Machines, among other machine learning methods (SVM). Results show that logistic regression (78.8571%), naive bayes (78.2857%), random forest (77.3429%), ANN (88.57%), and SVM (77%–78%) have the highest accuracy rates [7].

The research of Sisodia et al. concentrated on diabetes in expectant mothers. They employed Naive Bayes, SVM, and Decision Trees machine learning techniques to evaluate their work on the PIDD dataset. According to their findings, the Naive Bayes classifier, which had an accuracy of 76.30%, was the most accurate of the three methods [8].

A Hep-Pred model was proposed to check liver health. The dataset for simulation was collected from a UCI repository donated in 2019. A fine Gaussian SVM learning algorithm is used for training the model. The model gives us 97.9% accurate results in 5 cross validations [9].

2.2 Dataset Description

This Project utilizes two unique datasets for each listed disease (Figs. 1 and 2):

1. Hepatitis C Virus Dataset taken from the UCI (University of California Irvine) Machine Learning Repository. The dataset comprises 615 reports or rows and 13 attributes or columns. The dataset consists of several medical predictor variables such as their ALB levels, ALP levels, ALT levels, AST levels and one target variable, Outcome (Table 1).

Table 1. Brief Description of the HCV Dataset Attributes

Age	Age of Person
Sex	Sex of a Person
ALB	Albumin Blood Test
ALP	Alkaline Phosphatase
ALT	Alkaline Transaminase
AST	Aspartate Transaminase

(*continued*)

Table 1. (*continued*)

BIL	Bilirubin
CHE	Acetylcholinesterase
CHOL	Cholesterol
CREA	Creatinine Blood Test
GGT	Gamma-Glutamyl Transferase Blood Test
PROT	Protein
Outcome	Diagnosis of Hepatitis C Value 1 = yes Value 0 = no

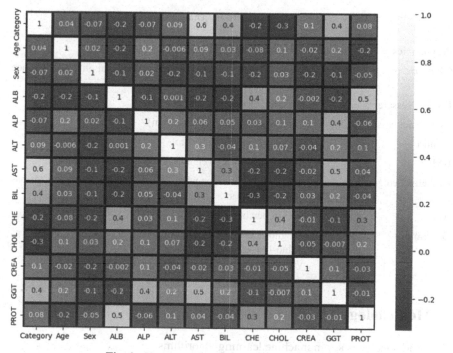

Fig. 1. Heatmap of the HCV Dataset Attributes

2. Diabetes Dataset taken from the National Institute of Diabetes and Digestive and Kidney Diseases repository. The dataset comprises 768 rows and 9 columns or attributes. The dataset consists of several medical predictor variables such as the number of pregnancies the patient has had, glucose levels, Blood Pressure levels, skin thickness BMI, Insulin levels, age, and diabetes pedigree function, and one target variable, Outcome (Table 2 and Figs. 3 and 4).

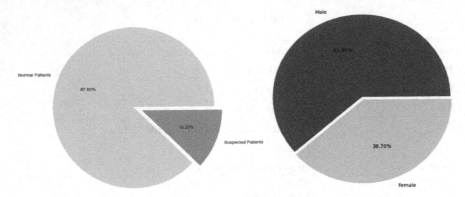

Fig. 2. Distribution of the Target Attribute and Patients based on gender

Table 2. Brief Description of the Diabetes Dataset Attribute

Pregnancies	Number of times pregnant
Glucose	Plasma glucose concentration 2 h in an oral glucose tolerance test
Blood Pressure	Diastolic blood pressure (mm Hg)
Skin Thickness	Triceps skin fold thickness (mm)
Insulin	2-h serum insulin (mu U/ml)
BMI	Body mass index (weight in kg/ (height in m)^2)
Diabetes Pedigree Function	Indicates the function which scores likelihood of diabetes based on family history
Age	Age of person
Outcome	Diagnosis of diabetes or not Value 1 = yes Value 0 = no

3   Methodology

This study analyzes seven machine learning algorithms:

1. Logistic Regression
2. Decision Tree Classifier
3. Random Forest Classifier
4. K Neighbors Classifier
5. Gradient Boosting Classifier
6. Support Vector Machine
7. Gaussian Naive Bayes Classifier

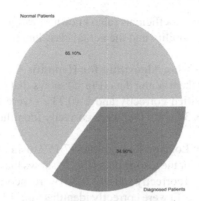

Fig. 3. Patient distribution

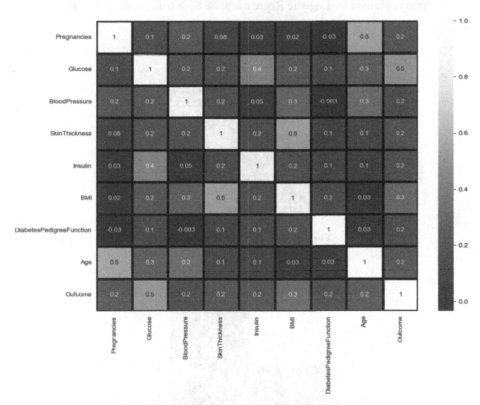

Fig. 4. Heatmap of the diabetes dataset

3.1 Logistic Regression

Logistic regression is a statistical model that is used for binary classification. It is used to predict the probability that an instance belongs to a particular class. The goal of logistic regression is to find the best coefficients (also known as weights) that minimize the error between the predicted probability and the actual class label.

Applying Logistic Regression Algorithm for Hepatitis C

The confusion matrix for the training data (Fig. 5) shows that of the 441 healthy Patients 440 (99.77%) were classified correctly and 1 (0.23%) were incorrectly classified. Of the 51 diagnosed patients 38 (74.51%) were correctly identified and 13 (25.49%) were incorrectly identified.

Accuracy obtained by Logistic Regression: 97.15% using training dataset.

The confusion matrix for the testing data (Fig. 6) shows that of the 99 healthy Patients 97 (97.98%) were classified correctly and 2 (2.02%) were incorrectly classified. Of the 24 diagnosed patients 12 (50.0%) were correctly identified and 12 (50.0%) were incorrectly identified.

Accuracy obtained by Logistic Regression: 88.62% using testing dataset.

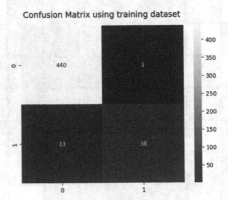

Fig. 5. Logistic Regression (training)

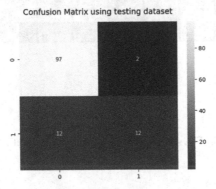

Fig. 6. Logistic Regression (testing)

Applying Logistic Regression Algorithm for Diabetes

The confusion matrix for the training data (Fig. 7) shows that of the 401 healthy Patients 354(88.28%) were classified correctly and only 47(11.72%) were incorrectly classified.

Of the 213 diagnosed patients 120(56.34%) were correctly identified and 93(43.66%) were incorrectly identified.

The accuracy obtained by Logistic Regression model: 77.19869706840392.

In the confusion matrix for the testing data (Fig. 8), we can see that of the 99 healthy Patients 82(82.83%) were classified correctly and only 17(17.17%) were incorrectly classified.

Of the 55 diagnosed patients 34(61.82%) were correctly identified and 21(38.18%) were incorrectly identified.

The accuracy obtained by Logistic Regression model: 75.32467532467533.

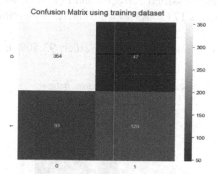

Fig. 7. Logistic Regression (training)

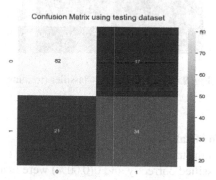

Fig. 8. Logistic Regression (testing)

3.2 Random Forest Classifier

Random forests are a type of ensemble learning method for classification and regression. They work by training many decision trees on different subsets of the training data, and then averaging their predictions to make a final prediction.

Applying Algorithm for Hepatitis C
The confusion matrix for the training data (Fig. 9) shows that of the 441 healthy Patients 441 (100.0%) were classified correctly and 0 (0.0%) were incorrectly classified. Of the 51 diagnosed patients 51 (100.0%) were correctly identified and 0 (0.0%) were incorrectly identified.

Accuracy obtained by Random Forest Classifier: 100.0% using training dataset.

The confusion matrix for the testing data (Fig. 10) shows that of the 99 healthy Patients 98 (98.99%) were classified correctly and 1 (1.01%) were incorrectly classified. Of the 24 diagnosed patients 17 (70.83%) were correctly identified and 7 (29.17%) were incorrectly identified.

Accuracy obtained by Random Forest Classifier: 93.50% using testing dataset.

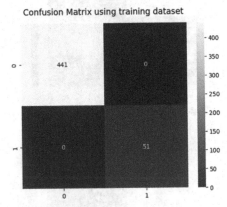

Fig. 9. Random Forest Classifier (training)

Applying Algorithm for Diabetes
The confusion matrix for the training data (Fig. 11) shows that of the 401 healthy Patients 401(100.00%) were classified correctly and 0(0.00%) were incorrectly classified.

Of the 213 diagnosed patients 213(100.00%) were correctly identified and 0(0.00%) were incorrectly identified.

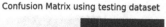

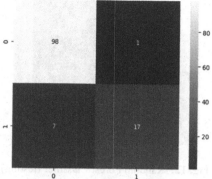

Fig. 10. Random Forest Classifier (testing)

The accuracy obtained by Random Forest Classifier model: 100.0

In the confusion matrix for the testing data (Fig. 12), we can see that of the 99 healthy Patients 78(78.79%) were classified correctly and only 21(21.21%) were incorrectly classified.

Of the 55 diagnosed patients 37(67.27%) were correctly identified and 18(32.73%) were incorrectly identified.

The accuracy obtained by Random Forest Classifier model: 74.67532467532467.

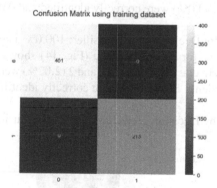

Fig. 11. Random Forest Classifier (training)

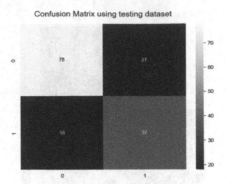

Fig. 12. Random Forest Classifier (testing)

3.3 Decision Tree Classifier

A decision tree is a flowchart-like tree structure that is used to make predictions based on feature values. It works by splitting the training data into smaller and smaller subsets based on the values of the features. The final prediction is made based on which leaf node the instance ends up in.

Applying Algorithm for Hepatitis C

The confusion matrix for the training data (Fig. 13) shows that of the 441 healthy Patients 441 (100.0%) were classified correctly and 0 (0.0%) were incorrectly classified. Of the 51 diagnosed patients 51 (100.0%) were correctly identified and 0 (0.0%) were incorrectly identified.

Accuracy obtained by Decision Tree Classifier: 100.0% using training dataset.

The confusion matrix for the testing data (Fig. 14) shows that of the 99 healthy Patients 97 (97.98%) were classified correctly and 2 (2.02%) were incorrectly classified. Of the 24 diagnosed patients 18 (75.0%) were correctly identified and 6 (25.0%) were incorrectly identified.

Accuracy obtained by Decision Tree Classifier: 93.50% using testing dataset.

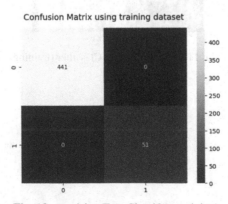

Fig. 13. Decision Tree Classifier (training)

Confusion Matrix using testing dataset

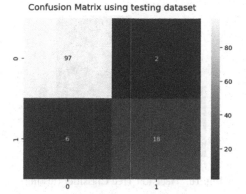

Fig. 14. Decision Tree Classifier (testing)

Applying Algorithm for Diabetes
The confusion matrix for the training data (Fig. 15) shows that of the 401 healthy Patients 401(100.00%) were classified correctly and 0(0.00%) were incorrectly classified.

Of the 213 diagnosed patients 213(100.00%) were correctly identified and 0(0.00%) were incorrectly identified.

The accuracy obtained by Decision Tree Classifier model: 100.0

In the confusion matrix for the testing data (Fig. 16), we can see that of the 99 healthy Patients 75(75.76%) were classified correctly and only 24(24.24%) were incorrectly classified.

Of the 55 diagnosed patients 34(61.82%) were correctly identified and 21(38.18%) were incorrectly identified.

The accuracy obtained by Decision Tree Classifier model: 70.77922077922078.

Confusion Matrix using training dataset

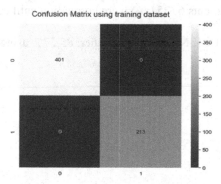

Fig. 15. Decision Tree Classifier (training)

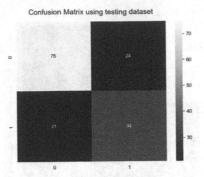

Fig. 16. Decision Tree Classifier (testing)

3.4   K Neighbors Classifier

K-neighbors (k-NN) is a simple, non-parametric classification and regression method. It works by finding the k training examples that are closest (in Euclidean distance) to the test instance, and then classifying the test instance based on the majority class of those neighbors. For regression tasks, the prediction is the average of the values of the k neighbors.

Applying Algorithm for Hepatitis C
The confusion matrix for the training data (Fig. 17) shows that of the 441 healthy Patients 439 (99.55%) were classified correctly and 2 (0.45%) were incorrectly classified. Of the 51 diagnosed patients 32 (62.75%) were correctly identified and 19 (37.25%) were incorrectly identified.

Accuracy obtained by K Neighbors Classifier: 95.73% using training dataset.

The confusion matrix for the testing data (Fig. 18) shows that of the 99 healthy Patients 99 (100.0%) were classified correctly and 0 (0.0%) were incorrectly classified. Of the 24 diagnosed patients 6 (25.0%) were correctly identified and 18 (75.0%) were incorrectly identified.

Accuracy obtained by K Neighbors Classifier: 85.37% using testing dataset.

Confusion Matrix using training dataset

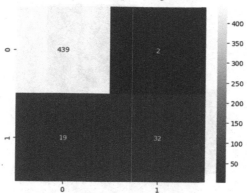

Fig. 17. K Neighbors Classifier (training)

Confusion Matrix using testing dataset

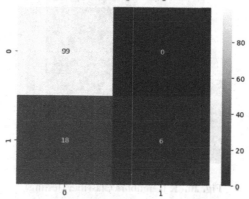

Fig. 18. K Neighbors Classifier (testing)

Applying Algorithm for Diabetes

The confusion matrix for the training data (Fig. 19) shows that of the 401 healthy Patients 359(89.53%) were classified correctly and 42(10.47%) were incorrectly classified.

Of the 213 diagnosed patients 149(69.95%) were correctly identified and 64(30.05%) were incorrectly identified.

The accuracy obtained by K Neighbors Classifier model: 82.73615635179154.

In the confusion matrix for the testing data (Fig. 20), we can see that of the 99 healthy Patients 74(74.75%) were classified correctly and only 25(25.25%) were incorrectly classified.

Of the 55 diagnosed patients 38(69.09%) were correctly identified and 17(30.91%) were incorrectly identified.

The accuracy obtained by K Neighbors Classifier model: 72.72727272727273.

Confusion Matrix using training dataset

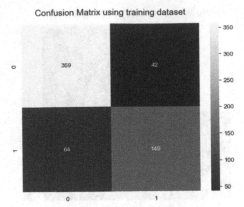

Fig. 19. K Neighbors Classifier (training)

Confusion Matrix using testing dataset

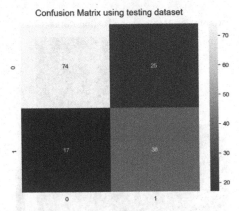

Fig. 20. K Neighbors Classifier (testing)

3.5 Support Vector Machine

Support Vector Machines (SVMs) are a type of supervised learning algorithm that can be used for classification or regression tasks. They work by finding the hyperplane in a high-dimensional space that maximally separates the different classes.

Applying Algorithm for Hepatitis C

The confusion matrix for the training data (Fig. 21) shows that of the 441 healthy Patients 440 (99.77%) were classified correctly and 1 (0.23%) were incorrectly classified. Of the 51 diagnosed patients 43 (84.31%) were correctly identified and 8 (15.69%) were incorrectly identified.

Accuracy obtained by Support Vector Machine: 98.17% using training dataset.

The confusion matrix for the testing data (Fig. 22) shows that of the 99 healthy Patients 96 (96.97%) were classified correctly and 3 (3.03%) were incorrectly classified. Of the 24 diagnosed patients 16 (66.67%) were correctly identified and 8 (33.34%) were incorrectly identified.

Accuracy obtained by Support Vector Machine: 91.06% using testing dataset.

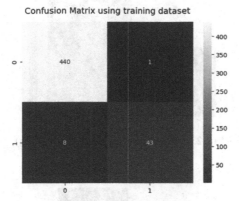

Fig. 21. Support Vector Machine (training)

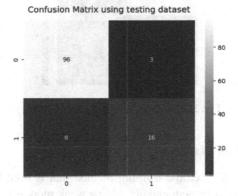

Fig. 22. Support Vector Machine (testing)

Applying Algorithm for Diabetes

The confusion matrix for the training data (Fig. 23) shows that of the 401 healthy Patients 371(92.52%) were classified correctly and only 30(7.48%) were incorrectly classified. Of the 213 diagnosed patients 139(65.26%) were correctly identified and 74(34.74%) were incorrectly identified.

The accuracy obtained by Support Vector Machine model: 83.06188925081433.

In the confusion matrix for the testing data (Fig. 24), we can see that of the 99 healthy Patients 83(83.84%) were classified correctly and only 16(16.16%) were incorrectly classified.

Of the 55 diagnosed patients 32(58.18%) were correctly identified and 23(41.82%) were incorrectly identified.

The accuracy obtained by Support Vector Machine model: 74.67532467532467.

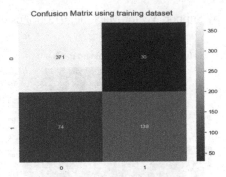

Fig. 23. Support Vector Machine (training)

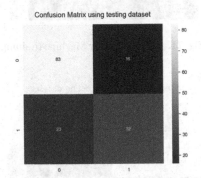

Fig. 24. Support Vector Machine (testing)

3.6 Gradient Boosting Classifier

Gradient boosting is an ensemble learning method that is used for classification and regression tasks. It works by sequentially adding weak models to the ensemble, where each model is trained to correct the errors made by the previous model. The final prediction is made by aggregating the predictions of all the models in the ensemble.

Applying Algorithm for Hepatitis C

The confusion matrix for the training data (Fig. 25) shows that of the 441 healthy Patients 441 (100.0%) were classified correctly and 0 (0.0%) were incorrectly classified. Of the 51 diagnosed patients 51 (100.0%) were correctly identified and 0 (0.0%) were incorrectly identified.

Accuracy obtained by Gradient Boosting Classifier: 100.0% using training dataset.

The confusion matrix for the testing data (Fig. 26) shows that of the 99 healthy Patients 99 (100.0%) were classified correctly and 0 (0.0%) were incorrectly classified. Of the 24 diagnosed patients 17 (70.83%) were correctly identified and 7 (29.17%) were incorrectly identified.

Accuracy obtained by Gradient Boosting Classifier: 94.31% using testing dataset.

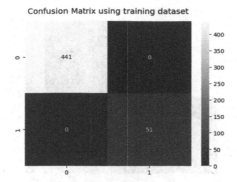

Fig. 25. Gradient Boosting Classifier (training)

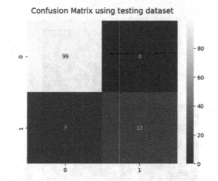

Fig. 26. Gradient Boosting Classifier (testing)

Applying Algorithm for Diabetes

The confusion matrix for the training data (Fig. 27) shows that of the 401 healthy Patients 387(96.51%) were classified correctly and only 14(3.49%) were incorrectly classified.

Of the 213 diagnosed patients 182(85.45%) were correctly identified and 31(14.55%) were incorrectly identified.

The accuracy obtained by Gradient Boosting Classifier model: 92.67100977198697.

In the confusion matrix for the testing data (Fig. 28), we can see that of the 99 healthy Patients 79(79.80%) were classified correctly and only 20(20.20%) were incorrectly classified.

Of the 55 diagnosed patients 38(69.09%) were correctly identified and 17(30.91%) were incorrectly identified.

The accuracy obtained by Gradient Boosting Classifier model: 75.97402597402598.

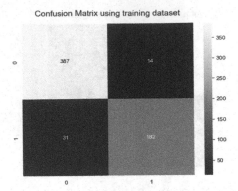

Fig. 27. Gradient Boosting Classifier (training)

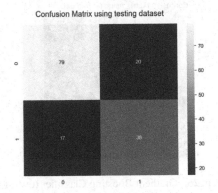

Fig. 28. Gradient Boosting Classifier (testing)

3.7 Gaussian Naive Bayes Classifier

Naive Bayes is a simple, probabilistic classifier based on the idea of applying Bayes' theorem with strong (naive) independence assumptions between the features. It is a popular choice for classification tasks, particularly in the field of natural language processing.

Applying Algorithm for Hepatitis C

The confusion matrix for the training data (Fig. 29) shows that of the 441 healthy Patients 428 (97.05%) were classified correctly and 13 (2.95%) were incorrectly classified. Of the 51 diagnosed patients 37 (72.55%) were correctly identified and 14 (27.45%) were incorrectly identified.

Accuracy obtained by Gaussian Naive Bayes Classifier: 94.51% using training dataset.

The confusion matrix for the testing data (Fig. 30) shows that of the 99 healthy Patients 95 (95.96%) were classified correctly and 4 (4.041%) were incorrectly classified. Of the 24 diagnosed patients 13 (54.17%) were correctly identified and 11 (45.83%) were incorrectly identified.

Accuracy obtained by Gaussian Naive Bayes Classifier: 87.80% using testing dataset.

Confusion Matrix using training dataset

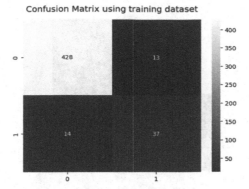

Fig. 29. Gradient Boosting Classifier (training)

Confusion Matrix using testing dataset

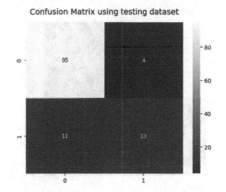

Fig. 30. Gradient Boosting Classifier (testing)

Applying Algorithm for Diabetes

The confusion matrix for the training data (Fig. 31) shows that of the 401 healthy Patients 334(83.29%) were classified correctly and only 67(16.71%) were incorrectly classified.

Of the 213 diagnosed patients 126(59.15%) were correctly identified and 87(40.85%) were incorrectly identified.

The accuracy obtained by Gaussian Naive Bayes Classifier model: 74.9185667752443.

In the confusion matrix for the testing data (Fig. 32), we can see that of the 99 healthy Patients 79(79.80%) were classified correctly and only 20(20.20%) were incorrectly classified.

Of the 55 diagnosed patients 37(67.27%) were correctly identified and 18(32.73%) were incorrectly identified.

The accuracy obtained by Gaussian Naive Bayes Classifier model: 75.324675324675.

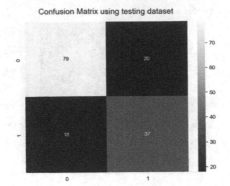

Fig. 31. Gradient Boosting Classifier (training)

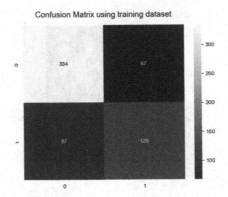

Fig. 32. Gradient Boosting Classifier (testing)

4   Results

We measured the testing and training accuracies for each of the algorithms implemented to examine if the problems of underfitting or overfitting occur. If the training accuracy is very high, the model is facing the problem of overfitting. On the other hand, a high testing accuracy indicates model underfitting. Therefore, an ideal classifier is the one with comparable, testing and training accuracies (Table 3 and Fig. 33).

Table 3. Model Comparison based on Training and Testing accuracies

Machine Learning Algorithms	Hepatitis C Accuracy %		Diabetes Accuracy %	
	Training %	Testing %	Training %	Testing %
Logistic Regression	97.15	88.62	77.19	75.32
Random Forest Classifier	100.0	93.50	100.0	74.67
Decision Tree Classifier	100.0	93.50	100.0	70.77
K Neighbors Classifier	95.73	85.37	82.73	72.72
Support Vector Machine	98.17	91.06	83.06	74.67
Gradient Boosting Classifier	100.0	94.31	92.67	75.97
Gaussian Naive Bayes Classifier	94.51	87.80	74.91	75.32

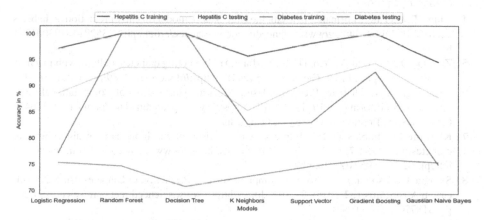

Fig. 33. Accuracy Comparison

5 Conclusion

The liver is a significant organ that performs many essential biological functions, such as detoxifying blood and synthesizing proteins and biochemicals necessary for digestion and growth [10]. Machine learning can improve the accuracy of disease prediction exponentially. In our study, we compared different machine-learning approaches to the prediction of Chronic Hepatitis C in patients. Algorithms like Gradient Boosting Classifier help build effective prediction systems. The dataset for the simulation of the Hepatitis C Virus Dataset was taken from the UCI (University of California Irvine) Machine Learning Repository, and Diabetes Dataset was taken from the National Institute of Diabetes and Digestive and Kidney Diseases repository.

In case of Hepatitis C, A refined Gaussian SVM learning algorithm is used for training the model. The most ideal algorithm was Gradient Boosting Classifier which gave us 94.308% accurate results.

Whereas for Diabetes Dataset, the model's efficiency can be enhanced in the future by adding more patient data.

This method can prove to be instrumental in defining medical data access by adding an extra layer on top of patient files.

References

1. World Health Organization: Hepatitis C. World Health Organization (WHO) (2022). https://web.archive.org/web/20221223120445/ https://www.who.int/news-room/fact-sheets/detail/hepatitis-c
2. The top 10 causes of death (2020, December 9). World Health Organization (WHO). Retrieved 6 December 2022. https://web.archive.org/web/20221223121104/https://www.who.int/news-room/fact-sheets/detail/the-top-10-causes-of-death
3. Fatke, B., Förstl, H., Risse, A.: Diabetologe **9**(6), 475–486 (2013). https://doi.org/10.1007/s11428-013-1109-0
4. Alam, T.M., et al.: Informatics in Medicine Unlocked. A model for early prediction of diabetes **16**, 6 (2019, July 9). https://www.sciencedirect.com/science/article/pii/S2352914819300176#bib29
5. Zou, Q., Qu, K., Luo, Y., Yin, D., Ju, Y., Tang, H.: Predicting diabetes mellitus with machine learning techniques. Front. Genet. **9**, 515 (2018). https://doi.org/10.3389/fgene.2018.00515
6. Danasingh, A.A.: Diabetes Prediction Using Medical Data. Journal of Computational Intelligence in Bioinformatics **10**, 1–8 (2017). https://www.researchgate.net/publication/316432650_Diabetes_Prediction_Using_Medical_Data
7. Khanam, J.J., Foo, S.Y.: ICT Express. A comparison of machine learning algorithms for diabetes prediction **7**(4), 8 (2021, February 20). https://www.sciencedirect.com/science/article/pii/S2405959521000205#b21
8. Sisodia, D., Sisodia, D.S.: Procedia computer science. Prediction of Diabetes using Classification Algorithms **132**(2018), 8 (2018, June). https://www.sciencedirect.com/science/article/pii/S1877050918308548
9. Ghazal, T.M., et al.: Computers, Materials & Continua. Hep-Pred: Hepatitis C Staging Prediction Using Fine Gaussian SVM **10**(2021), 13 (2021, March). https://file.techscience.com/ueditor/files/cmc/TSP_CMC_69-1/TSP_CMC_15436/TSP_CMC_15436.pdf
10. Elias, H., Bengelsdorf, B.: The structure of the liver in vertebrates. Cells Tissues Organs **14**(4), 41 (1952, July 1). https://doi.org/10.1159/000140715

Analysis on Classification of Handwritten Devanagari Characters Using Deep Learning Models

Sai Prashanth Duddela[1,2(✉)], Senthil Kumaran[1], and Priya R. Kamath[3]

[1] Department of CSE, SCSVMV University, Kanchipuram 631561, India
dsaip13@gmail.com, msenthilkumaran@kanchiuniv.ac.in
[2] Department of CSE - AI&ML, Sahyadri College of Engineering and Management, Mangaluru 575007, India
[3] Department of CSE, Sahyadri College of Engineering and Management, Mangaluru 575007, India

Abstract. Handwritten Character Recognition in Indian scripts is a complex problem compared to printed characters. This paper concerns the handwritten isolated Devanagari characters, mainly consonants of 36 classes. The dataset for Devanagari Characters available at UCI library is chosen for this work which consists of 72,000 images for classification. CNN, Alexnet, LeNet and modified LeNet, are used for classification of this dataset. While CNN achieved an accuracy of 98.63% for the training data and 97.71% for unseen data, Alexnet has shown an accuracy of 98.71% accuracy for unseen data and 96.78% for training data. Experiments on LeNet and Modified LeNet have compromised the results with 87.76% maximum. Deep Learning algorithms were analysed with different training and testing data split (80:20, 70:30 and 90:10) with varying combinations of epochs (40, 50, 150).

Keywords: Devanagari Handwritten Character Recognition · Deep Learning · Computer Vision

1 Introduction

Handwritten character recognition is a challenging problem where research has been carried from decades on different scripts in the field of Optical Character Recognition (OCR). Due to large availability of datasets, a lot of literature is available for Latin scripts. Research work is still at its infancy for other scripts like Chinese, Arabic [1] and many Indian scripts [2]. OCR is being done on printed characters and handwritten characters. Many researchers developed segmentation, feature extraction and machine learning-based algorithms for recognizing printed characters and achieving better accuracy. The difficulty of any handwritten character is significant because of the different styles of writing [3].

S. Kumaran and P. R. Kamath—These authors contributed equally to this work.

© The Author(s), under exclusive license to Springer Nature Singapore Pte Ltd. 2023
S. Prabhu et al. (Eds.): ATIS 2022, CCIS 1804, pp. 227–240, 2023.
https://doi.org/10.1007/978-981-99-2264-2_18

Every script has its own set of challenges and issues in recognition. Handwritten characters vary with person, complicating the process. The classification of Devanagari scripts is challenging due to their complex shapes. Research on Handwritten Devanagari Character Recognition (HDCR) has been done over decades, and there is still scope to develop a more robust framework. In this research, handwritten Devanagari isolated characters are considered. Devanagari Script consists of 33 consonants and three combined consonants, i.e., 36 consonants and 13 vowels and ten numerals. In this research, algorithms are developed for recognizing 36 handwritten Devanagari characters offline.

Offline HDCR is a much more complicated than online because of the lack of stroke information. An accuracy of 99% can be achieved to recognize printed characters. This is mainly because the characters' shape and size is the same throughout the document. The feature extraction techniques or recognition algorithms developed on printed characters often fail in HDCR.

In classification, feature extraction and selection are crucial steps. Geometric, statistical and Transformed based feature extraction techniques have shown significant results. These techniques either give low accuracy, or they are limited to a particular data-set. Automatic feature selection from Neural network-based deep learning techniques show high accuracy when compared with feature based classification techniques.

In [4], a novel algorithm using CNN was used to recognize numerals in multiple languages. The accuracy of the classifier increases when the CNN depth rises over time. This was tested with individual language characters and by combining different language numerals. The accuracy achieved by this is 99.26% for separate language databases and an average of 99.32% for particular language character accuracy.

In [5], two pre-trained neural networks are used: Alexnet and Lenet 5. The dataset used is the MNIST digit. The error rate of Alexnet and LeNet5 was 1.03% and 0.95% respectively. ImageNet for numerals is one of the best options for recognizing MNIST numbers.

In [6], Deep CNN was implemented on UCI Devanagari Repository. Hyperparameters are tuned in the CNN for better accuracy, and activation functions used in designing the CNN are ReLU, Linear and tanh. Dropouts were used to avoid overfitting. The maximum accuracy of 96.9% is achieved by CNN with 8 Layers and ReLU activation function.

In [7], developed one of the most extensive data-sets with 240000 Chinese characters covering 3755 classes. They reduced the inference time by multiplying the mid-output layers. The parameters and accuracy are well-adjusted by average pooling.

Deep Convolutional Neural Network and Adaptive Gradient Descents on ISICHAR and V2DMDCHAR datasets was presented in [8]. Architecture with higher accuracy is considered and tested with other optimizers to choose the one with higher accuracy. Six different optimizers - SGS, Adagrad, Adam, AdaDelta, AdaMax, and RMSProp. Out of 6 different architectures, NA-6 gave higher accuracy with adam and RMSProp optimizer 97.3% and 97.65%. By mixing two other datasets, 98% accuracy is achieved.

In [9] extracted projection-based features on each character image and classified them using Multi-Layer Perceptron Neural Network (MLPNN). Number of features used are reduced to reduce the computation cost. A single hidden layer with 64 : 16 : 128 neurons trained over 5000 epochs results in 97% average accuracy. Fivefold validation is adopted.

Benchmark datasets are available for languages like Arabic, Latin, Persian Numbers, and Urdu. The dataset MADBase contains 70000 images collected from 700 volunteers. [10]. MNIST is for Latin numbers, with 70000 images generated with more than 250 participants [11]. Consist of 80000 Persian numbers that were collected from 12000 forms. [12]. PMUdb is an Urdu dataset collected from 170 volunteers [4], For Devanagari, many researchers have developed a dataset of different combinations, with few sets with numerals, few vowels and few consonants. Most of the data generated by the individual groups are not available online, and very few are available on request. Among them, DHCD is one the popular datasets available for Devanagari numerals and consonants with 92,000 images. The same is being used in [13]. The Dataset compromises with numerals and consonants where consonants are considered in this work. Convolution Neural Network has attained the accuracy of 98.63% for training data with loss of 0.03. Alexnet with Dropout values 0.2 and 0.5 are used and gained an accuracy of 98.71% and 98.75% for unseen data, which is better than CNN, where CNN's accuracy for unseen data is 97.71%.

The rest of the sections in this article is organized as follows. Section 2 contains the proposed methodology, where the details of the algorithms used in the report are explained in detail. Section 3 presents the results and discussion of the experiment, including information about the dataset and experimental setup for training different models. Finally, Sect. 4 gives the conclusion and future scope.

2   Proposed Methodology

2.1   Convolution Neural Network

CNN is a deep learning algorithm that can take the whole image as input and classify it based on its features. Two CNN models (Model I and II) are designed to use in this research. The CNN architecture for Model II is shown in Fig. 1. In both models, two convolution layers are there with 32 and 64 kernels of window size $(3,3)$. Convolutions extracts features from the image I using a kernel K as shown in the Eq. 1.

$$C(m,n) = (I * \text{K})(m,n) = \sum_{k} \sum_{l} I(m-p, n-q)\, \text{K}(p,q) \tag{1}$$

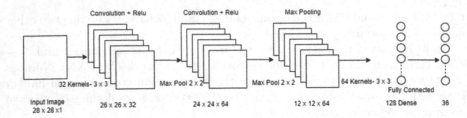

Fig. 1. CNN Architecture

Subsampling is done using max pooling with a pool size of $(2, 2)$. The significant difference in both networks is with dropouts. An analysis is made with CNN Model I, designed using dropout ratio of 25% and 50%, and CNN Model II, with a dropout ratio 20%. Statistical gradient descent (SGD) is used as the optimizer at the different learning rates and chooses the better for this dataset, which is mentioned in the Table 6. The first model uses 1203236 parameters, whereas the second uses 76516. Details of these two models are listed in Tables 1 and 2.

Table 1. CNN Model I

	Image Input	Parameters	Number	Activation Function
1	Convolution	(32, 28, 28)	320	ReLU
2	Convolution	(64, 28, 28)	18496	ReLU
3	Max Pooling	2 × 2 Avg Pooling	-	ReLU
4	Dropout	25 % dropout	-	-
5	Fully Connected	Dense 128	1179776	ReLU
	Dropout	50 % dropout	-	-
6	Fully Connected	Dense 36	4644	Softmax
Total Parameters: 1203236	Trainable: 1203236		Non-Trainable: 0	

Table 2. CNN Model II

	Image Input	Parameters	Number	Activation Function
1	Convolution	(32, 28, 28)	320	ReLU
2	Max Pooling	2 × 2 Avg Pooling	-	
3	Convolution	(64, 28, 28)	18496	ReLU
4	Max Pooling	2 × 2 Avg Pooling	-	
5	Convolution	(64, 28, 28)	36928	ReLU
6	Dropout	20 % dropout	-	-
	Fully Connected	Dense 36	20772	Softmax
Total Parameters: 76516	Trainable: 76516		Non-Trainable: 0	

2.2   LeNet and Modified LeNet

LeNet CNN is made of convolution layer, and subsampling layer. The architecture of the LeNet used is shown in Fig. 2. This LeNet architecture uses 324452 parameters while training. The architecture for LeNet and modified LeNet is shown in the Table 3. While LeNet uses tanh activation function, the modified LeNet makes use of ReLU activation.

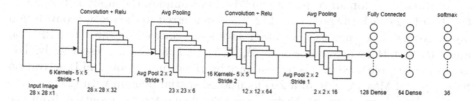

Fig. 2. LeNet Architecture

Table 3. LeNet CNN and Modified LeNet CNN Architecture

	Layer	Image Input	Param	Params	MLenet	Lenet 5
1	'conv1'	Convolution	32 kernel 5 × 5 and input 28 × 28	320	tanh	ReLU
2	'pool1'	Max Pooling	2 × 2	-		
3	'conv2'	Convolution	64 kernel 3 × 3 and input 12 × 12	18496	tanh	ReLU
4	'pool2'	Average Pooling	2 × 2			
5	'fc1'	Fully Connected	Dense 128	295040	tanh	ReLU
6	'fc2'	Fully Connected	Dense 64	8256	tanh	ReLU
7	'fc3'	Fully Connected	Dense 36	2340	Softmax	Softmax
Total Param: 324452			Trainable Params: 324452	Non-Trainable Params: 0		

2.3   Alexnet

Alexnet used in this work is designed with 8 layers consisting of 5 convolution layers and 3 fully connected layers. The first layer of the network takes the input of 28×28 with 28 kernels of size 3×3 for convolution. These are regularized using L2 regularization to omit over-fitting. With this setup, the output obtained is $28 \times 28 \times 28$. The over-fitting reduces by decreasing the weight of the matrices. Lambda optimizes the hyperparameter and controls the degree of penalty. Alexnet was designed in this research with $800,000$ parameters for 36-character classes.

$$\text{Cost Function} = L + \frac{\lambda}{2m} * \sum_{2}^{1} (\text{ target } Oi - \text{ out } 0i)^2 \tag{2}$$

The internal covariant shift problem is solved by using batch normalization. For input is not less than 1, ReLU's gradient is 1. The converging rate is faster for the ReLU activation function when compared with tanh. ReLU activation function is used throughout the network, introducing nonlinearity. The equation for nonlinearity is

$$\text{ReLU}(x) = \max(x, 0) \tag{3}$$

In the spatial domain, especially in 2d - downsamples, the input of $28 \times 28 \times 28$ to $14 \times 14 \times 28$ with the pool size of $(2, 2)$ is transferred to the second convolution layer. Kernels that are used in other layers for convolution are 56, 112, 224, and 448, with the window size of $(3, 3)$, $(5, 5)$, $(7, 7)$ and $(3, 3)$, respectively. The layers in the table used in this network are batch normalization, ReLU activation function and Max Pooling in a 2-Dimensional spatial domain with $(2, 2)$.

The last three layers in Alexnet are fully connected. The output from the convolution layer is 2-dimensional in shape, but the dense layer requires a 1-Dimensional shape. Between the first five layers of convolution and the fully connected layer, flatten function is used to convert from 2-d to 1-d. In these layers, the Dense function is added with parameters of 784,1204 and 36 (number of classes). A dropout of 50% is used to avoid overfitting in the network. In this paper, experiments are done with two different dropout values, one with 50% and the other with 20%. The activation function in the first two fully connected layers is ReLU, softmax is in the final layer, and Adadelta is the optimizer used. Adadelta optimizer helps to reduce the learning rate for frequently occurring features and vice versa. It is an upgraded version of Adagrad. It restricts the window of previous gradients and fixes to a particular size.

$$E\left[g^2\right]_t = \gamma E\left[g^2\right]_{t-1} + (1 - \gamma)g_t^2 \tag{4}$$

3   Experiments Results and Discussion

3.1   Experimental Data

UCI Machine learning repository contains $92,000$ images [13] with $20,000$ images representing Devanagari numerals, and $72,000$ consonants. This data is being used in this research, a sample copies are shown in Table 4. The details of the test and train split used in this work are mentioned in the Table 5.

Table 4. Sample Data of Numerals, Vowels and Consonants

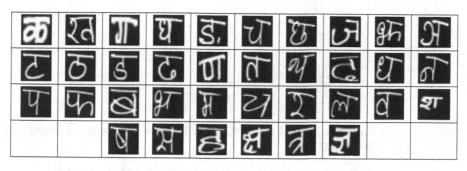

Table 5. Training and Testing Data Splits

Training: Testing	Consonants	
	Training	Testing
90:10	32400	3600
80:20	28800	7200
70:30	25200	10800

3.2 Experimental Analysis

In this research, three different deep learning-based algorithms are implemented in which a modification in its architecture helps yield good results. The distinct architectures that is used in this research are CNN (Models I and II), Alexnet and LeNet with its modification.

CNN model I is trained with different learning rates as shown in Table 6. Figure 3 shows the accuracy for CNN Model I for different epochs at a given learning rate. Based on the accuracy, learning rate of 0.01 is selected with SGD optimizer. Accuracy and Loss of CNN models are shown in Tables 7 and 8. Both models were trained and tested with 50 epochs. The maximum accuracy achieved is 98.63% and 98.64% for the 90:10 ratio in 50 epochs. It is observed that there is no significant difference in accuracy or loss values in models I and II, and the best accuracy and loss values are shown in Fig. 4.

Table 6. Training and Testing CNN Model I

Train & Test Ratio	Learning Rate	Training Accuracy	Training Loss	Testing Accuracy	Testing Loss
80:20	0.01	96.59	0.10	97.53	0.08
80:20	0.001	85.55	0.46	93.41	0.23
80:20	0.0001	48.65	1.84	97.14	1.35

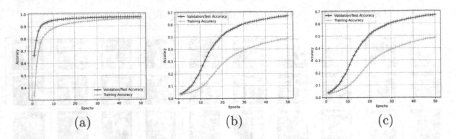

(a)   (b)   (c)

Fig. 3. Accuracy of CNN Model I for 80:20 Train and Test Split with a learning rate of (a) 0.01 (b) 0.001 (c) 0.0001

Table 7. Training and Testing - Accuracy of CNN Model I and II

CNN Model I			CNN Model II		
Training and Testing Accuracies for Consonants 36 Classes with Dropout - 0.25 & 0.5 for 50 Epochs			Training and Testing Accuracies for Consonants 36 Classes with Dropout - 0.2 for 50 Epochs		
Train: Test	Training Accuracy	Testing Accuracy	Train: Test	Training Accuracy	Testing Accuracy
70:30	98.39	97.36	70:30	98.33	97.32
80:20	98.52	97.63	80:20	98.35	97.72
90:10	98.63	97.71	90:10	98.64	97.79

Table 8. Training and Testing - Loss of CNN Model I and II

CNN Model I			CNN Model II		
Training and Testing Loss for Consonants 36 Classes with Dropout - 0.25 & 0.5 for 50 Epochs			Training and Testing Loss for Consonants 36 Classes with Dropout - 0.2 for 50 Epochs		
Train: Test	Training Loss	Testing Loss	Train: Test	Training Loss	Testing Loss
70:30	0.04	0.10	70:30	0.10	0.10
80:20	0.04	0.08	80:20	0.04	0.08
90:10	0.03	0.08	90:10	0.03	0.07

For classification using Alexnet, a detailed analysis is made with different test-train split ratios, epochs and dropout ratios. The accuracy are shown in Table 9 for a dropout ratio of 0.5. From the table, it is observed that a higher accuracy percentage is achieved with higher epochs. The maximum training and testing accuracy and loss for Alexnet for dropout ratio of 0.2 and 0.5 is summarized in Tables 10 and 11. The optimizer used in the Alexnet CNN is Adadelta.

Lenet is designed with tanh activation. This may lead to the problem of universal approximation. To avoid this nonlinearity is introduced into the network

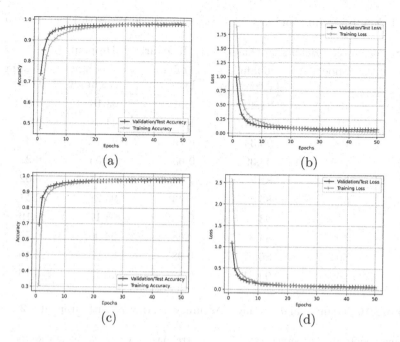

Fig. 4. Accuracy of CNN Model I for 80:20 Train and Test Split with a learning rate of (a) Accuracy of CNN Model I for 90:10 (b) Loss of CNN Model I for 90:10 (c) Accuracy of CNN Model II for 90:10 (d) Loss of CNN Model II for 90:10

using ReLu. Table 12 shows the accuracy achieved by LeNet with the activation function tanh and relu. Using this model in [14], an accuracy of 99.9% was obtained from the dataset of 38,750 images [15]. For the UCI dataset, the maximum accuracy achieved by this model is 87.76% for a 90:10 ratio of training and testing by introducing the Non-Linearity. An accuracy of 85.04% is obtained on using LeNet. The accuracy and loss for LeNet and Modified LeNet is tabulated in Tables 12 and 13.

For UCI dataset, CNN achieves the maximum accuracy of 98.63% for Training data and 97.71% for unseen data. Alexnet, with 0.5 and 0.2 dropout values, gets an accuracy of 98.75% and 98.71% for unseen data and is mentioned in Table 14. There is a drop in accuracy for training data to 94.31% and 96.78%. In [14], Lenet and MLenet have performed well for Devanagari numerals and vowels, which are 10 and 13 classes. Its performance is dropped for consonants with 36 classes.

3.3   Comparison with Other Work on the Same Dataset

In [6], proposed CNN with a combination of different layers, activation functions and dropouts. It has shown a maximum accuracy of 96.9% for the whole dataset

Table 9. Training and Testing - Accuracy of Alexnet with Dropout - 0.5

Accuracies for Consonants 36 Classes with Regularizer (Dropout - 0.5)					
Train: Test	Epochs	Training Accuracy	Training Loss	Testing Accuracy	Testing Loss
70:30	40	81.49	1.21	93.18	0.68
70:30	50	84.44	1.09	94.38	0.57
70:30	100	90.34	0.79	97.17	0.3
70:30	150	93.39	0.65	98.05	0.21
80:20	40	82.9	1.14	93.81	0.62
80:20	50	85.4	1.03	95.28	0.51
80:20	150	93.7	0.62	98.17	0.19
90:10	40	84.35	1.08	94.99	0.54
90:10	50	86.27	0.98	95.95	0.45
90:10	150	94.31	0.59	98.75	0.16

Table 10. Training and Testing - Accuracy of Alexnet with dropout 0.2 & 0.5

Training and Testing Accuracies for Consonants 36 Classes with L Regularizer (Dropout - 0.2)			Training and Testing Accuracies for Consonants 36 Classes with Regularizer (Dropout - 0.5)		
Train: Test	Training Accuracy	Testing Accuracy	Train: Test	Training Accuracy	Testing Accuracy
70:30	95.96	98.23	70:30	93.39	98.05
80:20	96.37	98.54	80:20	93.7	98.17
90:10	96.78	98.71	90:10	94.31	98.75

Table 11. Training and Testing - Loss of Alexnet with dropouts of 0.2 and 0.5

Training and Testing Loss for Consonants 36 Classes with L Regularizer (Dropout - 0.2)			Training and Testing Loss for Consonants 36 Classes with Regularizer (Dropout - 0.5)		
Train: Test	Training Loss	Testing Loss	Train: Test	Training Loss	Testing Loss
70:30	0.55	0.20	70:30	0.65	0.21
80:20	0.52	0.18	80:20	0.62	0.19
90:10	0.49	0.16	90:10	0.59	0.16

consisting of numerals and consonants. In this research, the accuracy attained for training is 98.63% with CNN and 98.75% for unseen data with Alexnet CNN. The experimental results we achieved in this research are satisfactory (Figs.5 and 6).

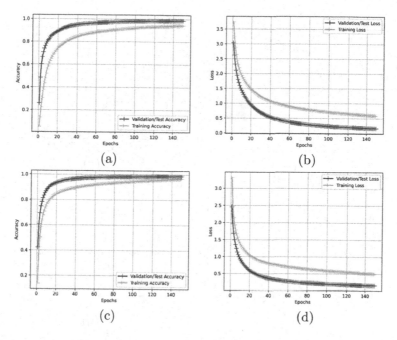

(a)   (b)

(c)   (d)

Fig. 5. Accuracy of Alexnet for 80:20 Train and Test Split with a learning rate of (a) Accuracy of Alexnet with dropout (0.5) for 90:10(b) Loss of Alexnet with dropout (0.5)for 90:10 (c) Accuracy of Alexnet with dropout (0.2) for 90:10 (d) Loss of Alexnet with dropout (0.2) for 90:10

Table 12. Training and Testing - Accuracy of LeNet and Modified LeNet CNN

Training and Testing Accuracies for LeNet			Training and Testing Accuracies for MLeNet		
Train: Test	Training Accuracy	Testing Accuracy	Train: Test	Training Accuracy	Testing Accuracy
70:30	83.07	82.22	70:30	85.03	84.86
80:20	84.64	84.18	80:20	86.36	85.69
90:10	85.04	85.01	90:10	88.03	87.76

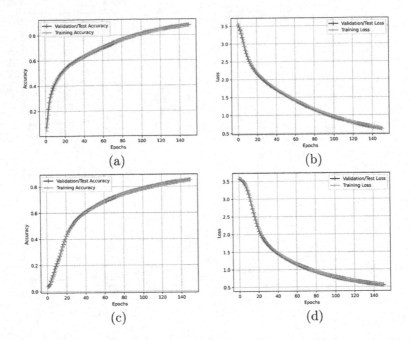

(a)   (b)

(c)   (d)

Fig. 6. Accuracy of LeNet for 80:20 Train and Test Split with a learning rate of (a) Accuracy of Modified LeNet CNN for 90:10 (b) Loss of Modified LeNet CNN for 90:10 (c) Accuracy of LeNet CNN for 90:10 (d) Loss of LeNet CNN for 90:10

Table 13. Training and Testing - Loss of LeNet and Modified LeNet CNN

Training and Testing Loss for LeNet			Training and Testing Loss for MLeNet		
Train: Test	Training Loss	Testing Loss	Train: Test	Training Loss	Testing Loss
70:30	0.60	0.62	70:30	0.76	0.77
80:20	0.55	0.57	80:20	0.68	0.7
90:10	0.53	0.54	90:10	0.61	0.62

Table 14. Top Accuracies in CNN, Alexnet and Lenet

Model	Training Loss	Testing Loss	Training Loss	Testing Loss
CNN	98.63	97.71	0.03	0.08
Alexnet (0.2)	96.78	98.71	0.49	0.16
Alexnet (0.5)	94.31	98.75	0.59	0.16
LeNet	85.04	85.01	0.53	0.54
M Lenet	88.03	87.76	0.61	0.62

4 Conclusion

In this paper, we provided an analysis of implementing CNN, Alexnet and LeNet on the consonants in Devanagari dataset. We used the dataset that is available in the UCI data library. 72, 000 images with 36 different classes are utilized among the numerals and consonants. Two CNN models were designed with different dropout values at 50 epochs and learning rates of 0.01, 0.001 and 0.0001. The training accuracy obtained by the CNN models were greater than 98.33%. Since Alexnet CNN is complex, data is trained with different training and testing ratios like 70:30, 80:20 and 90:10 for 40, 50, and 150 epochs. By considering the accuracy, Alexnet with 150 epochs are selected further and achieves the accuracy greater than 95.96% for unseen data. Whereas LeNet reaches the maximum accuracy of 88.03%.

Acknowledgements. The authors thank the college authorities of SCSVMV University, Sahyadri College of Engineering & Management, Centre of Excellence in AI & ML in Sahyadri College of Engineering & Management, for their support.

Declarations

Conflict of Interests. The authors declare that they have no known competing for financial interests or personal relationships that could have appeared to influence the work reported in this paper.

References

1. Ahmed, R., et al.: Offline Arabic handwriting recognition using deep machine learning: a review of recent advances. In: Ren, J., et al. (eds.) BICS 2019. LNCS (LNAI), vol. 11691, pp. 457–468. Springer, Cham (2020). https://doi.org/10.1007/978-3-030-39431-8_44
2. Yadav, M., Purwar, R.K., Mittal, M.: Handwritten Hindi character recognition: a review. IET Image Proc. **12**(11), 1919–1933 (2018)
3. Kim, I.-J., Xie, X.: Handwritten hangul recognition using deep convolutional neural networks. Int. J. Doc. Anal. Recogn. (IJDAR) **18**(1), 1–13 (2015)
4. Latif, G., Alghazo, J., Alzubaidi, L., Naseer, M.M., Alghazo, Y.: Deep convolutional neural network for recognition of unified multi-language handwritten numerals. In: 2018 IEEE 2nd International Workshop on Arabic and Derived Script Analysis and Recognition (ASAR), pp. 90–95. IEEE (2018)
5. Shima, Y., Nakashima, Y., Yasuda, M.: Handwritten digits recognition by using CNN Alex-Net pre-trained for large-scale object image dataset. In: Proceedings of the 3rd International Conference on Multimedia Systems and Signal Processing, pp. 36–40 (2018)
6. Ram, S., Gupta, S., Agarwal, B.: Devanagri character recognition model using deep convolution neural network. J. Stat. Manag. Syst. **21**(4), 593–599 (2018)
7. Li, Z., Teng, N., Jin, M., Lu, H.: Building efficient CNN architecture for offline handwritten Chinese character recognition. Int. J. Doc. Anal. Recogn. (IJDAR) **21**(4), 233–240 (2018)

8. Jangid, M., Srivastava, S.: Handwritten Devanagari character recognition using layer-wise training of deep convolutional neural networks and adaptive gradient methods. J. Imaging **4**(2), 41 (2018)
9. Rojatkar, D.V., Chinchkhede, K.D., Sarate, G.: Handwritten Devnagari consonants recognition using MLPNN with five fold cross validation. In: 2013 International Conference on Circuits, Power and Computing Technologies (ICCPCT), pp. 1222–1226. IEEE (2013)
10. Abdelazeem, S.: Comparing Arabic and Latin handwritten digits recognition problems. Int. J. Comput. Inf. Eng. **3**(6), 1583–1587 (2009)
11. Deng, L.: The MNIST database of handwritten digit images for machine learning research [best of the web]. IEEE Signal Process. Mag. **29**(6), 141–142 (2012)
12. Khosravi, H., Kabir, E.: Introducing a very large dataset of handwritten Farsi digits and a study on their varieties. Pattern Recogn. Lett. **28**(10), 1133–1141 (2007)
13. Acharya, S., Pant, A.K., Gyawali, P.K.: Deep learning based large scale handwritten Devanagari character recognition. In: 2015 9th International Conference on Software, Knowledge, Information Management and Applications (SKIMA), pp. 1–6. IEEE (2015)
14. Prashanth, D.S., Mehta, R., Ramana, K., Bhaskar, V.: Handwritten Devanagari character recognition using modified LeNet and AlexNet convolution neural networks. Wirel. Pers. Commun. **122**(1), 349–378 (2022)
15. Prashanth, D.S., Mehta, R.V.K., Challa, N.P.: A multi-purpose dataset of Devanagari script comprising of isolated numerals and vowels. Data Brief **40**, 107723 (2022)

Cloud, IoT and Computing Technologies

Analysis and Comparison of Different Frontend Frameworks

Suryaansh Rathinam[(✉)] [iD]

Manipal Institute of Technology, Manipal, Karnataka, India
suryaansh2002@gmail.com

Abstract. A frontend framework is pre-written code that provides the architecture for a project, along with certain features to help with the development process. With the availability of many frameworks, each with its own features and advantages, it is important to understand the difference between the various frameworks and make the right choice of framework for a particular project. This paper elaborates on the features of three popular frameworks: React, Angular and Vue, draws a comparison among them, and provides guidelines on how to make the choice of a suitable framework for a project.

Keywords: Frameworks · React · Angular · Vue · JavaScript

1 Introduction

Over the past couple of decades, the web has grown exponentially, and with it has increased the size and complexity of various web applications and services provided over the web. This has led to developers needing higher-level tools and technologies which cater to the development of complex web applications, handling more user traffic.

To cater to this increasing need, various frontend web-development frameworks such as ReactJS, AngularJS, VueJS, and NextJS, to name a few, were developed. While all these frameworks find their base in JavaScript, each offers developers a different set of features, structures, and options.

The objectives of this paper are as follows-

- To analyze various popular frontend frameworks that have come into use over the last couple of years.
- To do a qualitative comparison between the features and structures of these frameworks.
- To break-down some of the large-scale applications built using particular frameworks.
- To assess how to choose between the vast array of frameworks available.

2 Research Questions

This paper aims to tackle the following questions:

1. What are the different features provided by the various frontend frameworks?
2. How can one choose between various frameworks for a web application?

© The Author(s), under exclusive license to Springer Nature Singapore Pte Ltd. 2023
S. Prabhu et al. (Eds.): ATIS 2022, CCIS 1804, pp. 243–257, 2023.
https://doi.org/10.1007/978-981-99-2264-2_19

3 Contributions

1. A detailed comparison of various frontend frameworks' features, functionality, and structure.
2. Case study analysis of large-scale applications built using particular frontend frameworks
3. Methodology and suggestions in making choices of frameworks for particular projects.

4 Literature Review

Over the past couple of decades, web development, along with its associated technologies, has continuously changed. With the advent of the Web in the 1990s, early web pages, built primarily using HTML and CSS, were text-based websites that did not have to deal with much traffic. As time passed and the size of the web expanded rapidly, so did the need for more complex web applications to provide services to the users.

To simply work for developers and facilitate faster and more efficient development of websites, JavaScript-based frameworks started emerging in the 2000s. The first of these was jQuery [1], launched in 2006. jQuery is referred to as a fast, lightweight, JavaScript library, that uses an API to make tasks like document traversal, manipulation, and event handling simpler [1]. It is referred to as a library and not a framework; for this paper, we will consider JavaScript libraries such as jQuery and ReactJS alongside JavaScript frameworks.

While subtle, the distinction between a library and a framework is essential to understand. A library consists of a reusable package of predefine functions, objects, and methods that the developer can use in the project as and when deemed fit. Some of the popular JavaScript libraries are jQuery, ReactJS, and D3.js.

On the other hand, a JavaScript framework is a pre-written code that provides an architecture for the project. It provides a standardized structure that developers can follow and extend based on the framework's features and the developer's needs. Some of the popular JavaScript frameworks are AngularJS and VueJS.

While there has not been extensive research comparing the various available frameworks, the works of [2] and [3] serves as a basis for me to build upon further in this paper (See Fig. 1).

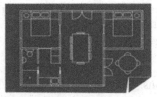

Framework: Blueprint of house   Library: Furniture inside the house

Fig. 1. Depiction of difference between framework and library

After jQuery for developed in 2006, the upcoming years saw the release of many new frontend frameworks and libraries, which helped ease the development process (See Fig. 2).

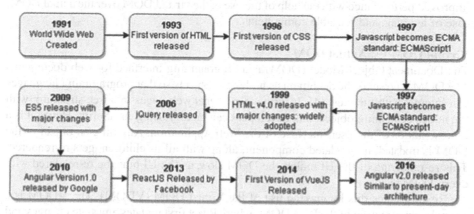

Fig. 2. Advancement in Web-Development over the years

5 Frameworks Analysis

5.1 Methodology

For the purpose of analysis and further comparison, this paper will be focusing on three frameworks in particular namely React, Angular and Vue. While apart from these frameworks there are many more JavaScript frameworks used for frontend development, such as jQuery, Svelte, Ember etc., the popularity of React, Angular and Vue far supersedes that of the other available frameworks [Table 1]. Due to their vast popularity these frameworks have been used for the development of many large-scale applications. Hence, in this section we will focus on each of the individual frameworks, their features and functionality.

According to a survey by JetBrains in 2021 [2], comparing the popularity of JavaScript Frameworks among developers.

Table 1. Popularity of Frameworks among developers

Framework	React	Vue	Angular	-
% of Developers Using Regularly	49%	43%	18%	

5.2 React JS

ReactJS is a JavaScript library developed and maintained by Facebook (now Meta), used to create interactive user-interfaces [3]. React's wide popularity is primarily due to its improved performance with the help of the use of the virtual DOM over the actual DOM, ease of learning, and reusable components.

Virtual DOM Vs. Actual DOM

The Document Object Model (DOM) is a programming interface for web documents. The DOM represents the document as nodes and objects so that programming languages can interact with the page [4]. It further represents web pages in a tree structure, with the nodes containing objects that developers can modify using JavaScript. Hence it is a representation of the user-interface of the Web Application. Any time an object of the DOM is updated, the updated component, along with all its children, gets re-rendered. This re-rendering of the UI makes the DOM slow, as the UI must be re-rendered with every DOM update.

React handles this by making use of the Virtual DOM (VDOM). The VDOM is a virtual representation of the Real DOM, where React first updates any state changes and the affected components, then compares the VDOM obtained with the snapshot of the VDOM before the update occurs. This helps React figure out which objects have been changed, and only those objects are updated in the Real DOM; instead of the entire Real DOM being updated, only the, affected objects are updated.

This greatly helps React improve the performance and memory utilization of the DOM (See Fig. 3).

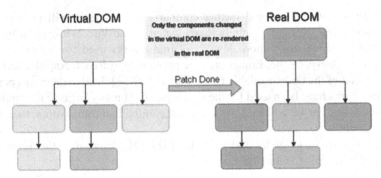

Fig. 3. Use of Virtual DOM to handle updates to the DOM

In addition to the performance optimization offered by React, it is also preferred by developers (Table 1) because it is extremely easy for new developers familiar only with HTML and Vanilla JS (refers to the use of JavaScript without any of its libraries), to adapt to ReactJS. This is because ReactJS allows developers to write code in JSX, a syntactic extension to JavaScript, which allows HTML code to be embedded along with the JavaScript functions [3].

Lastly, Meta (Facebook) also provides browser extensions to simplify the process of debugging React Applications. It allows developers to inspect component hierarchies in React and record the web application's performance [5].

5.3 Angular

Angular is a popular JavaScript frontend framework developed by Google. Angular 1 (also known popularly as AngularJS) was the version released by Google in 2010; however, in 2016, Google released Angular 2, completely rewriting the original version released [6]. While over the years, AngularJS was popular due to a variety of its features, as of January 2022, Google has officially announced the end of support for AngularJS [7]. Hence, for this paper, we shall primarily focus on Angular2 and its subsequent versions, which are currently in wide use among developers, the features offered, and how it differed from its predecessor, AngularJS.

Angular is a development platform built with the help of Typescript, which includes a component-based framework, a collection of libraries, and a set of developer tools to build and test applications [8]. Some of the features of Angular that impact its use among developers are as follows:

Compared to React, which uses a Virtual DOM as discussed previously, Angular directly interacts with the Real DOM, updating the entire DOM tree when any change to the user interface occurs.

Architecture

While AngularJS supported MVC and MVVM Architecture, Angular2, taking inspiration from React, shifted to a Component-based Architecture. In the Angular Framework, Applications consist of Angular Components organized into NgModules. All the components and modules in Angular are classes with associated decorators that provide Angular with the required metadata.

Components have associated templates that define views that Angular can access and modify based on the app's logic. The components also utilize services, providing functionality to the application that may not directly be related to the view; these services are injected into the components and dependencies. The components of an application consist of many views arranged hierarchically.

The template associated with a component works to combine HTML with the Angular markup. Templates have associated directives that provide the program logic. Angular evaluates the program logic and resolves the template's binding (Event and Property Binding) [9] (See Fig. 4).

Data Binding in Angular

Data Binding refers to keeping the UI of the page up to date based on the state of the web application [8]. Angular provides three categories of Data Binding:

- One-way from data source to view target
- One-way from view target to data source
- Two-way (See Figs. 5 and 6)

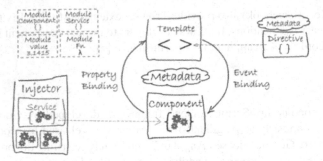

Fig. 4. Angular Architecture (From [8])

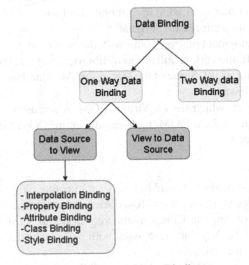

Fig. 5. Types of Data Binding

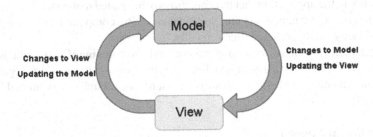

Fig. 6. Two-Way Data Binding

Furthermore, Angular also provides inbuilt support to set up Unit Testing and Integration Testing with the help of the Jasmine testing Framework, an open-source behavior-driven development framework for testing JavaScript code [10], and Karma as the task-runner for tests.

Changes from AngularJS to Angular2+

While the upgrade from AngularJS to Angular2 and then subsequent updates to Angular2 have resulted in many changes in the frameworks, some of the significant differences between the versions are:

- While AngularJS is a JavaScript-based framework, Angular is built using Type-Script, which is statically typed and helps ensure fewer errors and better code understandability.
- Applications made using Angular are also optimized for mobile browsers, whereas AngularJS provides no support for mobile devices.
- While AngularJS has an MVC based architecture, the architecture of Angular is primarily based on Components consisting of templates and directives.
- AngularJS relies on third party tools for testing where as Angular comes support for unit and integration testing based on Jasmine and Karma.

5.4 Vue

VueJS is a JavaScript framework for building a user interface built upon HTML, CSS, and JavaScript [11]. Of all the frameworks analyzed in this paper, Vue is the newest, having been created by Evan You in 2014. Even despite its comparatively late emergence, due to the robust set of features offered by it, it has grown to give competition to similar frameworks like React and Angular.

Architecture

VueJS is based on the MVVM (Model – View – ViewModel) architecture which consists of the following three components:

- Model: Represents the data access and business logic of the application
- View: It represents the UI of the application that the user interacts with.
- View Model: It consists of the logic of the view layer, linking it to the model layer, and processing the interactions between the two.

VueJS primarily focuses on implementing the functionality of the ViewModel layer (See Fig. 7).

VueJS follows a component-based structure similar to both React and Angular. Components help split the user interface into simple, easy-to-understand, and reusable pieces of code. This modularization process helps improve the development and maintainability of web applications.

Since Vue was initially developed by Evan You to take the best features of Angular and make a lightweight custom tool for development, Vue contains some of the primary

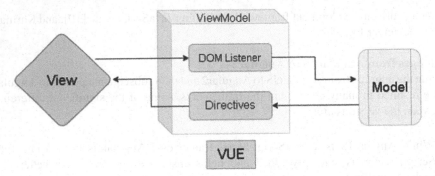

Fig. 7. VueJS Architecture

functions and features of Angular such as templates, views, and directives, as discussed previously.

Rendering Mechanisms

Similar to React JS, Vue, too, uses the Virtual DOM to handle rendering and re-rendering of the user interface, hence improving the performance and memory utilization of the web applications.

VueJS templates are first compiled into render functions that return the VDOM trees. Then, on runtime, the VDOM tree is mounted on the actual DOM, which renders the web application. The render functions are generated to track the dependencies, and in case of any changes, an updated VDOM tree is created. The updated VDOM tree is compared with the older version, and only the particular components that were changed are updated in the actual DOM (See Fig. 8).

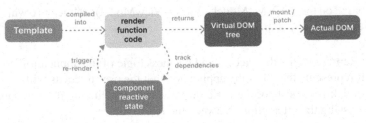

Fig. 8. Rendering pipeline of VueJS using Virtual DOM (From [11])

Overall, the popularity of VueJS has grown over the last couple of years. Despite not being backed by a large corporation like Meta for React and Google for Angular, it has still been able to give them competition and is now widely adopted among developers. Vue JS is maintained primarily by its creator Evan You, and a large open-source community, leading to many libraries such as Vuex, Element, and the Vue CLI being developed. Vue has worked to combine the rich functionality of Angular with the lightweight, fast and easy learning curve of ReactJS.

6 Case Studies

In this section, we will analyze some of the large-scale applications built using the frontend frameworks discussed previously and the advantages of using the particular framework.

6.1 React: Facebook

As ReactJS was developed at Facebook and is maintained by developers at Facebook and a large community of developers, it is no surprise that the Facebook website is developed using ReactJS and the mobile app using React Native.

Facebook is a social networking platform founded in 2004, with over 2.9 billion users now. It allows users to connect with other individuals, share updates and photos of their lives, and direct messaging services. It has also grown to offer additional services such as live streaming, a marketplace, and news feeds.

React is now among the most popular frameworks used among developers. Facebook has been using React to develop their web application as it provides efficiency and optimization with the Virtual DOM and easy SEO optimization, among other features discussed in Subsect. 5.1. Furthermore, since React is developed by Facebook and then used for building their applications, it is easier to fix any issues or work on additional functionality required in React or the Facebook Web Application.

6.2 Angular: Firebase

Since Angular is developed and maintained by Google, many of the internal products used by Google and many public-facing services use Angular as part of their technology; one of the most prominent services of Google built using Angular is Firebase.

Firebase is a Backend-as-a-Solution (BaaS), providing developers with the ability to build and manage their applications' backend; it provides services such as a real-time database, authentication, cloud messaging, and hosting, which developers can easily integrate into their existing applications.

Most of the reasons for Angular's adoption have been discussed in Subsect. 5.2; in addition to its various features, such as in-built testing, two-way data binding, and dependency injection, it offers high-end functionality to developers, as there is no dependency on any third-party libraries and packages, as is with the case React and Vue. Instead, all the functionality needed by developers comes covered within the framework.

6.3 Vue: GitLab

VueJS which was created by Evan You and released in 2014, has fast risen to popularity in the developer community, and has come to be adopted in the development of many large-scale popular applications, such as GitLab.

GitLab is a DevOps software package that offers remote access to GitHub repositories, along with features that simplify the software development life cycle, such as collaborative development, Continuous Integration- Continuous Deployment (CI/CD) pipelines, bug-tracking, and code review.

The primary reason for adopting VueJS for the development of GitLab has been its simplicity and ease of use [12]. It's easy-to-understand source code and documentation, coupled with the robust set of features provided by it, further help to simplify the development process. Hence VueJS provides developers with a balance between the structure and simplicity of the framework and enables them to implement the same functionality and features required with less code [12].

7 Results and Discussion

7.1 Comparison

After an elaborate discussion of the features offered by the various frameworks, this section works on a side-by-side comparison of these frameworks.

Figure 9 Below depicts that over the last 5 years, the popularity of React, and hence the number of its downloads, has been increasing at a rapid pace, while for Angular and Vue, the number of downloads have been increasing, but at a much slower pace compared to that of React. This correlates with the data in Table 1, pertaining to the current popularity of the Framework.

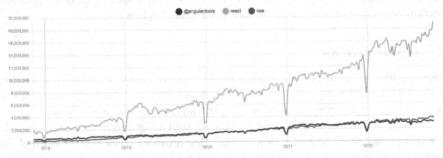

Fig. 9. Comparison of NPM Downloads of the 3 Frameworks over the last five years [13]

Table 2 below depicts the comparison of the GitHub repositories of the three frameworks, which is the open-source popularity of these frameworks, as we have seen in Fig. 9 as well, the React GitHub repository has the most number of stars, forks and watchers, followed by that of Angular and then Vue. The comparatively low number of interactions on Vue's repository can be due to its recent emergence in 2014, compared to that other two frameworks.

The Tables 3, 4 and 5 given below, draw a side-by-side comparison of the differences in the features of Angular, React and Vue, taking two of the frameworks at a time, based on the discussions on these frameworks in Sect. 5.

Table 2. Comparison of GitHub Repositories of the 3 Frameworks

FRAMEWORKS	STARS	FORKS	WATCH	ISSUES
React	197K	40.9K	6.7K	834
Angular	84.7K	22.5K	3.1K	139
Vue	33.5K	6K	752	510

Table 3. Comparison of Angular and React

Angular	React
With a large core library, it reduces any dependencies on external libraries.	It has a small core library with external libraries to provide additional functionality.
It has a steeper learning curve.	It provides an easy learning curve for developers familiar with JS and HTML.
Based on Typescript.	Based on ES6 Syntax and JSX

Table 4. Comparison of Vue and React

Vue	React
Easier to work with for beginners not familiar with JavaScript concepts.	Easy to work with for developers familiar with functional JavaScript
It handles the mutation of data using data objects.	It handles the mutation of data using state objects.
Supports two-way data binding	Supports one-way data binding

7.2 Suggestions

Based on previous discussions, it is evident that for any developer starting work on a project, the dilemma of choosing the suitable framework from a variety of options, each with its own set of features and structures, is always present. Hence, to decide

Table 5. Comparison of Angular and Vue

Angular	Vue
It is a heavy framework suitable for large enterprise-scale applications.	Lightweight framework, suitable for small-scale applications
It has a steep learning curve.	Easy to work with for beginners not familiar with JavaScript concepts.

on a framework based on a project's requirements and the developer's capabilities, the following can be kept in mind.

Suppose the project is one of your first projects, or the developer is relatively inexperienced. In that case, it might be preferable to opt for Vue.js or React, as they are much easier to grasp and start working with compared to Angular, which is more challenging to learn.

If the application to be built is a large, enterprise-scale application, then it is preferable to work with Angular as it is suited for such applications. In contrast, if the application is meant to be a small-scale application with no plans of scaling up, VueJS would be the preferred choice as it is lightweight and, at the same time, provides many of the features that Angular provides.

Lastly, a developer's familiarity with TypeScript can prove advantageous, as using TypeScript helps debug code, resulting in cleaner, easier-to-understand code. Since Angular is based on TypeScript, a developer familiar with TypeScript can also take advantage of the variety of functionality offered in the Angular framework. While both React and Vue also support TypeScript, only HTML and JavaScript knowledge are sufficient to get started with them.

7.3 Performance Comparison

The previous sections of this paper focused on comparing the different features and structures of the frameworks, while this section will elaborate on the quantitative performance comparison between the frameworks.

The tables below are taken from [14] in which a large, randomized table was created using various frameworks on Chrome 104 Browser, and different operations were performed on the table, the speed (in milliseconds) and memory usage (in MB) (with 95% confidence interval) for the frameworks.

Table 6. Memory Usage for different frameworks [14]

Name	angular-v13.0.0	react-v17.0.2	vue-v3.2.37
ready memory Memory usage after page load.	2.0 (1.57)	1.4 (1.14)	1.3 (1.00)
run memory Memory usage after adding 1,000 rows.	5.3 (1.22)	5.6 (1.28)	4.4 (1.00)
update every 10th row for 1krows (5 cycles) Memory usage after clicking update every 10th row 5 times	5.4 (1.22)	6.1 (1.39)	4.4 (1.00)
creating/clearing 1k rows (5 cycles) Memory usage after creating and clearing 1000 rows 5 times	2.7 (1.71)	2.2 (1.39)	1.6 (1.00)
run memory 10k Memory usage after adding 10,000 rows.	32.6 (1.07)	39.5 (1.30)	30.5 (1.00)

Table 6 above depicts the difference in memory usage of the three frameworks at various stages, while Table 7 depicts the speed of different operations being conducted on a table. As is evident from Table 7, React is slightly slower in selecting rows compared to Angular and Vue, whereas both Angular and React are considerably slower than Vue when it comes to swapping rows, and Angular is at a slight disadvantage compared to React and Vue, at clearing table. When it comes to memory usage, there is no major disparity among the three frameworks for this particular test, but the values in Tables 6 and 7, vary with operating systems, browser, browser version and depending on the operations being tested.

Table 7. Speed of Operations done on large randomized table

Name Duration for... Implementation notes	vue- v3.2.37	angular- v13.0.0	react- v17.0.2
create rows creating 1,000 rows (5 warmup runs).	119.3 ±1.2 (1.01)	118.5 ±1.4 (1.00)	126.2 ±1.4 (1.06)
replace all rows updating all 1,000 rows (5 warmup runs).	113.2 ±1.5 (1.00)	130.7 ±1.0 (1.15)	126.7 ±0.9 (1.12)
partial update updating every 10th row for 1,000 rows (3 warmup runs). 16x CPU slowdown.	359.0 ±11.2 (1.05)	343.0 ±6.7 (1.00)	399.5 ±5.4 (1.16)
select row highlighting a selected row. (5 warmup runs). 16x CPU slowdown.	53.7 ±1.2 (1.23)	43.6 ±0.8 (1.00)	105.2 ±3.7 (2.41)
swap rows swap 2 rows for table with 1,000 rows. (5 warmup runs). 4x CPU slowdown.	73.6 ±4.5 (1.00)	512.8 ±3.4 (6.97)	494.1 ±7.7 (6.71)
remove row removing one row. (5 warmup runs).	28.0 ±0.6 (1.09)	25.7 ±0.4 (1.00)	27.8 ±0.5 (1.08)
create many rows creating 10,000 rows. (5 warmup runs with 1k rows).	1,149.2 ± 5.1 (1.00)	1,215.1 ± 11.5 (1.06)	1,488.1 ± 10.2 (1.29)
append rows to large table appending 1,000 to a table of 10,000 rows. 2x CPU slowdown.	268.8 ±7.3 (1.00)	303.2 ±2.8 (1.13)	322.5 ±4.0 (1.20)
clear rows clearing a table with 1,000 rows. 8x CPU slowdown. (5 warmup runs).	90.0 ±2.9 (1.00)	231.0 ±6.8 (2.57)	101.0 ±2.9 (1.12)

8   Conclusion

This paper has analyzed in depth the importance of frontend frameworks and the features provided by three frontend frameworks: React, Angular, and Vue. It then goes on to examine some of the large-scale applications built using these frameworks and understand the reason for their use. Then a qualitative comparison is drawn between the various frameworks based on various features that they offer, and guidelines are provided to developers on selecting a particular framework for projects. Lastly, a quantitative comparison is analyzed among the three frameworks.

References

1. Jquery. [Online]. Available: https://jquery.com/
2. JetBrains. [Online]. Available: https://www.jetbrains.com/lp/devecosystem-2021/javascript/. [Accessed 29 Oct 2022]
3. ReactJS, "React – A JavaScript library for building user interfaces". [Online]. Available: https://reactjs.org/. [Accessed 29 Oct 2022]
4. Introduction to the DOM - Web APIs - MDN Web Docs. [Online]. Available: https://developer.mozilla.org/en-US/docs/Web/API/Document_Object_Model/Introduction. [Accessed 29 Oct 2022]
5. React Developer Tools. [Online]. Available: https://chrome.google.com/webstore/detail/react-developer-tools/fmkadmapgofadopljbjfkapdkoienihi/related?hl=en. [Accessed 31 Oct 2022]
6. Xing, Y.: Research and analysis of the front-end frameworks and libraries in E-business (2019)
7. AngularJS. [Online]. Available: https://docs.angularjs.org/. [Accessed 31 Oct 2022]
8. Angular: Introduction to Angular Docs. [Online]. Available: https://angular.io/docs. [Accessed 31 Oct 2022]
9. Angular: Introduction to Angular Concepts. [Online]. Available: https://angular.io/guide/architecture. [Accessed 1 Nov 2022]
10. Jasmine Documentation. [Online]. Available: https://jasmine.github.io/. [Accessed 1 Nov 2022]
11. Vue.js. [Online]. Available: https://vuejs.org/. [Accessed 1 Nov 2022]
12. Why we chose Vue.js | GitLab, GitLab. [Online]. Available: https://about.gitlab.com/blog/2016/10/20/why-we-chose-vue/. [Accessed 6 Nov 2022]
13. NPM Trends. [Online]. Available: https://npmtrends.com/@angular/core-vs-react-vs-vue. [Accessed 6 Nov 2022]
14. Interactive Results. [Online]. Available: https://krausest.github.io/js-framework-benchmark/2022/table_chrome_104_windows.html. [Accessed 6 Nov 2022]

Lightweight Capability-Based Access Control for Internet of Things (IoT)

S. Deepthi$^{(\boxtimes)}$ ⓘ and Shrey Khandwekar

Department of Computer Science and Engineering, Manipal Institute of Technology, Manipal Academy of Higher Education (MAHE), Manipal, Karnataka 576104, India
deepthi.s@manipal.edu

Abstract. Internet of Things applications encompassed heterogeneous devices that are uninterruptedly exchanging data and being accessed ubiquitously through lossy networks. This raises the need for an elastic, lightweight, and access control mechanism to survive with the pervasive nature of such a global ecosystem, ensuring reliable communications between trusted devices. To address this gap, this paper proposes a capability-based access control system for IoT, which supplies an end-to-end and reliable security mechanism for IoT devices, based on a lightweight authorization mechanism and a novel trust model that has been specially devised for IoT environments. The algorithm has been implemented and evaluated successfully in a real testbed for constrained IoT devices.

Keywords: Access control · capability based · Internet of things

1 Introduction

A growing number of heterogeneous devices are now being able to get connected to the internet, which leads to success of the internet of things. According to Gartner's research [1], the IoT will have a profound impact on the economy facilitating new business models, by transforming many enterprises into digital businesses and, improving efficiency, and increasing employee and customer engagement. IoT can make people's lives simpler and convenient. There are wide application fields in which IoT plays a significant role, including smart city, smart grids, smart industry, smart hospitals and many more. IoT has induced a huge economic value. Now devices can see, hear, and talk to other devices. However, this brings new security challenges. Traditional security techniques are not suitable for IoT as it is computation and memory intensive, to be implemented in resource-constrained devices. Also, devices may be installed in remote places where patches cannot be sent regularly and not available for physical access.

IoT environment should be completely secured, along with using services capable of continuously auditing IoT configurations to ensure that they are following security best practices. Insecure network services running on the edge devices itself, especially those exposed to the internet that compromise the confidentiality, integrity/authenticity, or availability of information or allow unauthorized remote control is the one of the top IoT vulnerability [2]. Hence there is a need for a new security algorithm for IoT.

© The Author(s), under exclusive license to Springer Nature Singapore Pte Ltd. 2023
S. Prabhu et al. (Eds.): ATIS 2022, CCIS 1804, pp. 258–266, 2023.
https://doi.org/10.1007/978-981-99-2264-2_20

In this paper, we discuss the novel algorithm for access control for IoT. Access control is an important security aspect as it prevents unauthorized access to the network. Access control is even more challenging in IoT compared to traditional networks. In IoT, networks are heterogeneous, devices are not basically designed for internet connectivity, for example, refrigerators, have limited memory and low battery life. Power and computation ability is low compared to computers. Devices may be installed in places wherein it is difficult to reach. The data can be small in size and frequent in transmission. The number of devices, or nodes, that are connecting to the network are also greater in IoT than in traditional Personal Computer computing. The nature of devices is heterogeneous. There are not designed to connect to network and/or communicate with each other. In this paper, we propose an access control algorithm that overcomes the drawbacks of traditional access control algorithms and is lightweight.

The remainder of the paper is organized as follows. In Sect. 2 we discuss related work in IoT access control. In Sect. 3 we propose the new access control algorithm. Results are discussed in Sect. 4. Finally, in Sect. 5, we present our conclusion.

2 Related Work

Access control is one of the most critical aspect of IoT system. There are lot of work carried out in the domain. The most common is role based access control(RBAC) [3] where in users can associated with roles and roles are associated with operations. Then there are many versions of RBAC has been deployed on internet of things. Guoping Zhang et al. [4] extends RBAC by using context information to enhance the security for IoT. The algorithm lacks flexibility in generating roles. Attribute Based Access control(ABAC) [5] is another popular access control in which decisions are taken based on attributes, usually represented by a tuple <S,O,P,E> where S is user attributed, O is object attributes, P is permission attributes and E is Environment attributes. Security of data is not guaranteed. Organization based access control (OrBAC) [6] is not completely adapted in IoT because it is difficult to manage collaboration related aspects in IoT.

A capability based access control is being promising technique showing better performance. In capability based access control (CBAC) [7], each subject is associated with its capabilities. And, the subject presents to the guard a capability in order to get access to an object. Initially, capability was represented using access control matrix and access control lists [8]. In the context of IoT, as we are dealing with constrained devices, capability is represented using tokens, tickets or keys. Bayu et al. describes a capability based access control for M2M in which CBAC is used along with key management.

Sergio Gusmeroli et al.[10], implemented CBAC in IoT in sophisticated manner, used XML and SAML/XACML for capability tokens. XML has issue with less powerful devices.

3 Proposed System

In [11], the system is not suitable for low power devices by default – the issuer must verify tokens from all subjects. In our proposed method, we are using MQTT, which uses a publisher-subscriber model. An entity E who requires information from some device D first registers with broker B (a replacement for the issuer), where an entry is made in advance to store its public key. Here we assume that this entry is authenticated or attested by the owner of broker B and device D. Then, every device which can provide information also registers in the same way. The entity subscribes to the broker with some conditions that require contextual information from the device. The device provides data to the broker in a push fashion. The broker then decides if it matches any of the conditions and forwards the information to eligible subscribers. By shifting the authorization and condition verification process from the device to the broker, we are also reducing the load on the device.

There are 2 legs of the information to be transferred. One is the information sent from the device to the broker, and the other from the broker to the entity.

Here, [12], we can apply these principles. Using the device's secret key and receiver's public key, we utilize "public-key authenticated encryption," and this data can only be decrypted using the receiver's secret key and device's public key. The broker provides the receiver's and device's public keys to the other, where it maintains a simple mapping of device and receiver ID to public key. If the device is capable, it can cache the receiver's key for future messages. The encryption is performed with NaCl's crypto_box [13] mechanism that uses a combination of Curve25519 and XSalsa20 which were specifically designed for low power, constrained devices.

Along with this encrypted data, we provide some event information for MQTT's topic system. This can serve as a replacement for the condition fields suggested in [11]. In [11] Fig. 2, contextual information is requested and provided immediately before the PDP verifies any policies. This results in unnecessary computation on the device before the requester is even verified. In our method, the information is provided directly to the PDP, who "pushes" the information to the receiver instead of the receiver requesting it. This can also reduce the load on the constrained devices and the broker since they will not have to deal with spurious and malicious requests, as they are interrupted at the broker itself (Fig. 1).

Steps at the broker:

1) Decrypt message from the device.
2) Use event information to match topics.
3) Encrypt message for all subscribed clients of a topic.
4) Transmit message to all clients.
5) Verify signature of received data.

The key benefits of the publish-subscribe architecture are clear – all data moves in a 'push' fashion, with no device having to deal with spurious requests. This leaves the device open to more computation or processing if required. Here, we are using client-broker encryption since end-to-end encryption will be computationally intensive for a large number of receivers. Depending on the device, it can be selected as an option.

1) Capability request phase

When a device wants to receive data from a resource, it makes a capability request to the device or domain owner of the resource. This capability request is a

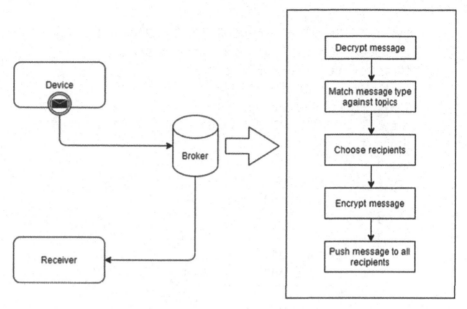

Fig. 1. System Architecture

JSON object that lists the device requesting access, and the conditions under which it wishes to receive data.

2) Capability token provision

The device or domain owner authenticates the request and authorizes access by generating a capability token. The capability token is a JSON object containing fields to identify the issuer, receiver, and the terms of the agreement.

Structure of the capability token:

ID: string – A UUIDv4-generated alphanumeric string to identify the token
Device: string – A unique device path for the issuing device
Not Before: integer – Unix Epoch timestamp before which the token is invalid
Not After: integer – Unix Epoch timestamp after which the token is invalid
To: string – A unique device path for the receiver
Key: string – Public key of the receiver
Conditions: object – Array of conditions required to use the capability token

The conditions object specifies the conditions under which the data is to be transmitted to the receiver. In the example provided, the value generated by the thermostat must be between 35 and 45, and the time must be between 12PM and 12AM.

The generation of the capability token and the communication mechanism between the issuer and receiver is assumed to be secure and its implementation is beyond the scope of this paper.

3) Device registration phase

```
{
    "id": "4a4b7670-02fc-41e5-a74f-df2e4ae3d2b7",
    "device": "home/livingroom/thermostat",
    "not_before": 1641067098,
    "not_after": 1641097098,
    "to": "home/master/rpi",
    "key": "c312144005c3688908a9218e604009969b9e0085",
    "conditions": [
        {
            "resource": "value",
            "condition": "> 35 && < 45"
        },
        {

            "resource": "time",
            "condition": "12:00PM -- 12:00AM"
        }
    ]
}
```

Fig. 2. Capability token format

The issuer and receiver both register themselves with the broker. The issuer provides its public key as a means to decrypt the data sent by it, and the receiver submits the capability token and its public key. The broker stores this capability token.

The verification of the device and device owner is beyond the scope of this paper.

4) Data generation phase

The device generates some data, e.g. A thermostat generates a temperature reading. This reading is packed into a JSON object and is encrypted with the proposed method using the device's private key and the broker's public key. This encrypted message is also signed to ensure that the data is not tampered with. A verifying key for the signature is added to the final message, which is then transmitted to the broker.

5) Broker receiver selection phase

The broker receives the data and verifies the signature with the provided verifying key. If the verification passes, then it decrypts the message using its private key and the device's public key. If the verification fails, then the message has been tampered with and is discarded. After decryption, the broker filters its list of capability tokens by matching the issuer of the token with the transmitter of the data received. The conditions present in each of the capability tokens are verified against the data. If all conditions are matched, then the receiver is marked eligible to receive the data.

6) Data transmission phase

With the list of all eligible receivers, the corresponding public key is extracted from their capability tokens, and the data is encrypted, signed, and transmitted to the receivers using the same mechanism as detailed above. The receiver then verifies and decodes the data and continues processing it (Fig. 3).

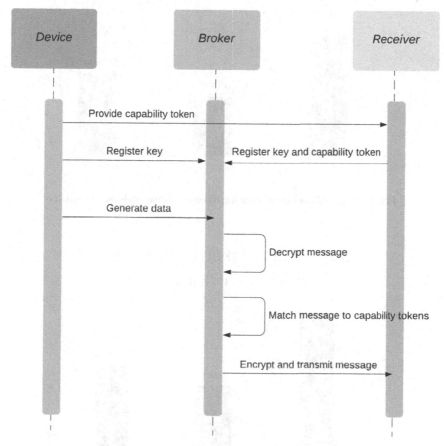

Fig. 3. Sequence diagram of proposed mechanism

4 Results

We are performing some encryption and signing on our device. To keep this lightweight, we are using secure and fast algorithms provided by NaCl or libsodium. XSalsa20 for encryption and Ed25519 for signing. These are modern, open-source algorithms that have been audited by several organizations and researchers around the world for their security and have been tested to do so while requiring less computation power (Figs. 4 and 5).

The figures above present the average time taken by each of the operations over 200 iterations. Each iteration consists of a randomly generated message that is encrypted

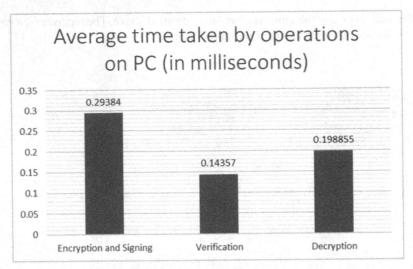

Fig. 4. Principal operations benchmarked in milliseconds on a computer

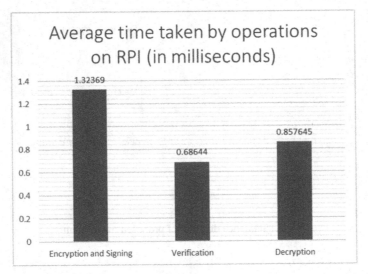

Fig. 5. Principal operations benchmarked in milliseconds on a constrained device

by one device and verified and decrypted at the other device. As shown, encryption is the most computationally intensive task among the three. The next table provides more statistics for the test conducted. As can be seen, the majority of the time is consumed during the encryption process (Table 1).

In comparison with the GetAccess step in [14], our algorithm shows an improvement of 92% on a similar setup. The time needed to communicate with the IOTA blockchain is not considered. BlendCAC [15] added an overhead of 5 ms, and the maximum overhead incurred by devices with equal or more computing power than a Raspberry Pi using

Table 1. Statistics for RPI and PC (milliseconds)

Statistics	Encryption and Signing	Verification	Decryption
Minimum	1.305	0.633	0.799
Maximum	1.674	2.074	2.219
Standard Deviation	0.029	0.198	0.236
Statistics	Encryption and Signing	Verification	Decryption
Minimum	0.25	0.111	0.165
Maximum	0.611	0.307	0.343
Standard Deviation	0.059	0.033	0.04

our method is about 2.7 ms, an improvement of 82%. Our method does not rely on the blockchain for token generation, hence eliminating additional latency and avoiding high gas fees. The large amount of energy consumed to generate a token by mining is saved as well.

5 Conclusion

The experimental results shown in this paper support the efficacy of a push-based communication mechanism with the use of capability tokens. Devices that depend on data from other devices must request it, and no data is forcefully pushed to a device that does not ask for it. This results in several benefits, since unnecessary computation is avoided by the receiving device. It reduces the power consumed by the device and minimizes wasteful packets generated on the network. We have also used modern and secure encryption and signing algorithms specifically designed for use with low power devices, and it is fair to expect further improvement if this method is used with more powerful devices such as smartphones.

References

1. https://www.gartner.com/en/newsroom/press-releases/2021-06-30-gartner-global-govern
   ment-iot-revenue-for-endpoint-electronics-and-communications-to-total-us-dollars-21-bil
   lion-in-2022. Accessed on 12 Jan 2022
2. https://www.networkworld.com/article/3332032/top-10-iot-vulnerabilities.html.   Accessed
   12 Jan 2022
3. Ferraiolo, D., Cugini, J., Kuhn, R.: Role-based access control (RBAC): Features and motivations. In: Proceedings of 11th annual computer security application conference, pp. 241–248 (1995)

4. Zhang, G., Tian J.: An extended role based access control model for the Internet of Things. In: 2010 International Conference on Information, Networking and Automation (ICINA), pp. V1-319–V1-323 (2010). https://doi.org/10.1109/ICINA.2010.5636381
5. Bhatt, S., Sandhu, R.: ABAC-CC: attribute-based access control and communication control for Internet of Things. In: Proceedings of the 25th ACM Symposium on Access Control Models and Technologies (SACMAT'20), pp. 203–212. Association for Computing Machinery, New York, NY, USA (2020). https://doi.org/10.1145/3381991.3395618
6. Bouij-Pasquier, I., Ait Ouahman, A., Abou El Kalam, A., Ouabiba de Montfort, M.: SmartOrBAC security and privacy in the Internet of Things. In: 2015 IEEE/ACS 12th International Conference of Computer Systems and Applications (AICCSA), pp. 1–8 (2015). https://doi.org/10.1109/AICCSA.2015.7507098
7. Anggorojati, B., Prasad, N.R., Prasad, R.: Secure capability-based access control in the M2M local cloud platform. In: 2014 4th International Conference on Wireless Communications, Vehicular Technology, Information Theory and Aerospace & Electronic Systems (VITAE), pp. 1–5 (2014). https://doi.org/10.1109/VITAE.2014.6934469
8. Lampson, B.: Protection, ACM SIGOPS Oper. Syst. Rev. http://dl.acm.org/citation.cfm?id=775268 (1974)
9. Nakamura, S., Enokido, T., Takizawa, M.: A capability token selection algorithm for lightweight information flow control in the IoT. In: Barolli, L., Chen, H.-C., Enokido, T. (eds.) NBiS 2021. LNNS, vol. 313, pp. 23–34. Springer, Cham (2021). https://doi.org/10.1007/978-3-030-84913-9_3
10. Gusmeroli, S., Piccione, S., Rotondi, D.: A capability-based security approach to manage access control in the Internet of Things. Math. Comput. Model. 58(5–6), 1189–1205 (2013). https://doi.org/10.1016/j.mcm.2013.02.006
11. Ramos, J.L.H., Jara, A.J., Marin, L., Gomez, A.F.S.: DCapBac: embedding authorization logic into smart things through ECC optimizations. Int. J. Comput. Math. 93, 345–366 (2016)
12. Pinjala, S.K., Sivalingam, K.M.: DCACI: a decentralized lightweight capability based access control framework using IOTA for Internet of Things. In: 2019 IEEE 5th World Forum on Internet of Things (WF-IoT), pp. 13–18 (2019). https://doi.org/10.1109/WF-IoT.2019.8767356
13. https://cr.yp.to/highspeed/naclcrypto-20090310.pdf. Accessed 10 Dec 2021
14. Xu, R., Chen, Y., Blasch, E., Chen, G.: Blendcac: a smart contract enabled decentralized capability-based access control mechanism for the IoT. Computers 7(3), 39 (2018)

Securing IoT Using Blockchain

S. Deepthi(✉) ⓘ and Apoorva

Department of Computer Science and Engineering, Manipal Institute of Technology, Manipal
Academy of Higher Education (MAHE), Manipal, Karnataka 576104, India
deepthi.s@manipal.edu

Abstract. Over the last few years, IoT progressed exponentially in field of automation by providing M2M communication. With increase in popularity of IoT, number of devices connected to the internet has also increased. These devices share confidential information and are vulnerable to attacks. However, securing the IoT is challenging because of its resource-constrained and heterogeneous environment. This paper discusses about the challenges and implementation of blockchain technology in IoT which can withstand cybercrime and network flaws.

Keywords: Blockchain · Internet of Things · Security

1 Introduction

Over the last decade, technology has been progressing rapidly. The technological invention is reducing the risk, human-error by automating the work, which in turn saves the time and money. Currently, the technology is on cusp of fourth industrial revolution (Industry 4.0) which describes the exponential changes in the field of technology [1]. One such area is internet of things. Internet of things is a network of physical devices (such as sensors, actuators etc.) with unique identity which communicate intelligently. They share information through unified framework across a platform [2]. The development of IoT and rate of adoption to the network is fastest that it has ever been. According to Gartner, by 2020 there would be 26 billion devices which will connect to the network [3]. Cisco.Inc, predicts that IoT market may reach to 50 billion connected devices in 2020. These large numbers of devices share mission-critical data regarding smart-home, smart-healthcare, smear-wearable, smart-irrigation, smart-vehicle and more via internet. Since IoT deals with real world entities, any security related issue may result in destruction of system, life or resources. Considering the fact that internet permits eavesdropper to spy, it is essential to provide privacy, access control, authentication, data-integrity to the user's data. Most basic, 3-layered architecture for IoT is as shown in the Fig. 1. It consists of three layers -Application layer, Transport Layer and Perception Layer.

Perception layer is a physical layer which is the lowest level of the conventional architecture. It aims to collect, filter, process the information from sensors, microcontrollers, and to receive control signal. In transportation layer, the data is communicated between the entities. In application layer, application regarding to domain are built to process the data and to provide user interface to access the data.

© The Author(s), under exclusive license to Springer Nature Singapore Pte Ltd. 2023
S. Prabhu et al. (Eds.): ATIS 2022, CCIS 1804, pp. 267–278, 2023.
https://doi.org/10.1007/978-981-99-2264-2_21

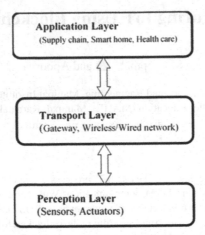

Fig. 1. IoT 3-layered architecture

Another technology which is driving attention of industry and researchers is blockchain. A blockchain is open, distributed ledger that can record transaction between 2 entities efficiently, in a verifiable and permanent way [4]. This technology was conceptualised in 2009 by Satoshi Nakamoto [5]. Originally, blockchain is utilized by the crypto-currency such as Bitcoin, Ethereum etc. to provide decentralized mechanism. Eventually it is gaining the enormous attention from other areas beyond crypto-currency. Now, blockchain's application is not only limited in financial transaction but also in big data, artificial intelligence and other technologies because of its structure and features. Features of blockchain are:

1. Transparent: All the information about transaction is accessible to all the nodes in the network. But identity of sender and receiver is concealed behind strong cryptographic technique.
2. Distributed: There is no centralised authority to control and validate each transaction. All the nodes participate in the computation and information sharing process.
3. Immutability: Once data is written into the blockchain, no one can alter it. Because, all the nodes are interconnected with cryptographically calculated hash values.
4. Security: Blockchain is secured using hash algorithm SHA256. It provides digital signature mechanism i.e., every transaction is digitally signed by sender's private key.

Integrating IoT with blockchain provides tamper proof, decentralised mechanism [6, 7]. But converging blockchain with IoT is challenging due to following reasons:

1. Resource-constrained devices: IoT deals with resource constrained devices which has limited computational resources and power.
2. Heterogeneity: The devices in the network are heterogeneous and need to provide inter-operability among them.

3. Scalability: As the blockchain size increases, it may require larger persistence memory.

This paper aims to solve above problems and deploy blockchain in IoT. As the data-transaction between the devices increase, it might affect the blockchain size and may overload it. So, this paper proposes a method to decrease overload on IoT-gateways.

This paper is documented as follows. Section 1 gives introduction to technology being used. Section 2 covers recent development and background of the related technology. Section 3 deals with methodology and architecture. Section 4 covers implementation details and concludes with Sect. 5.

2 Related Work

In past few years, researchers are working on solving the issues related to IoT. Sehgal et al. [8] discussed about using communication protocol like SNMP and NETCONF which effectively uses constrained device resource and it is suitable for heterogeneous devices. But it doesn't support scalability. Mayzaud et al. [9] discussed about using RPL protocol which is a distance vector routing protocol for low power and lossy network which is suitable for resource constrained environment such as IoT. It is more effective than SNMP protocol and it is also scalable. Disadvantage of these two methods are, they don't provide suitable security mechanism. Abdmeziem et al. [10] proposed method on lightweight key management protocol, a communication protocol. It provides data confidentiality and constrained node authentication. Here, 3rd parties encrypt the randomly splitted secret key generated by the IoT devices. But this method imposes heavy weight cryptographic primitives on the 3rd parties. Chakrabarty et al. [11] discussed on black network, unified registry, trusted SDN controller, key management system to secure basic IoT network of smart-city by providing data privacy, authentication, confidentiality and integrity which mitigates the security attacks although it doesn't discuss about location privacy. Later Yu Zhang et al. [12] proposed a modern IoT e-business model which makes use of ranking algorithm, credit algorithm and Bitcoin blockchain to control and monitor smart-property transaction. Christidis et al. [6] also demonstrated that integrating IOT with blockchain would be powerful, cost effective and time saving. They also discussed about implementing smart contract to automate the contract between 2 parties. Recently, Khan et al. [7] reviewed on security related issues of IoT, effectiveness of integrating IoT with blockchain and challenges that need to be faced. Lunardi et al. [13] proposed a distributed access control mechanism using IoT ledger based architecture on heterogeneous devices. Banerjee et al. [14] also reviewed on various security technique and discussed about facilitating secure sharing of confidential IoT dataset. Wazid et al. [15] proposed a fog network model to provide key management and authentication. It is decentralised, emerging technology to provide security cloud. It would be more efficient when blockchain technology integrated with it.

Studies mentioned above describe the recent development in IoT security. But most of these follow centralised mechanism which is vulnerable to the attacks. So using decentralised mechanism such as blockchain technology could build hurdles for eavesdropper.

3 Methodology

3.1 Basic Architecture

By considering 3-layer architecture model, IoT-ledger architecture can be constructed as follows [13] (Fig. 2).

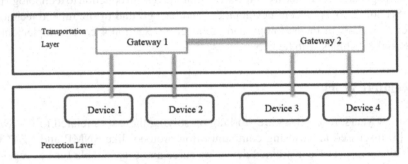

Fig. 2. Architecture

This architecture constituent of following components:

Devices

Device refers to sensors, actuators (such as temperature sensor, GPS, relay etc.) which collect data from real world in real time, periodically. These devices are resource constrained i.e., device with limited processing and storage capabilities. The data gathered from sensors are filtered, processed and sent across internet by microcontrollers (such as arduino, raspberry pi). This model assumes that each device has a private key, a public key and ip-address of any one of the gateway. After processing the required data, they are digitally signed by its private key and sent to gateway along with encrypted message and device's public key(device is addressable in internet via their public key, so they are stored in blockchain). Device and gateway uses MQTT protocol to communicate with each other and communication between them is fully duplex.

Gateway

It lies in transportation layer. These are device with limited storage, processing power and operate interminably. They provide interoperability between the heterogeneous devices. There will be number of interconnected gateways in network and each gateway maintains local copy of the global blockchain i.e., IoT ledger copy. IoT ledger is a data structure which stores the blocks which contains information gathers by sensors. Every gateway has its own private and public to provide digital signature mechanism. In a gateway, one block is maintained for each device and all the data transmitted from that device is stored in that block only. The blocks are stored and connected through linked-list. Gateway creates a block for new devices by linking with previous device hash value. It also calculates hash value of this block which will be used for future. In this model, gateway only calculate hash and add device to blockchain, thus it does the work of miner.

They must ensure consistency in local copy of blockchain with its peers. Local copy of data should be identical and updated.

Block

Block is container of data-structure which stores data from particular device. The architecture of the block [13] is as shown in Fig. 3.

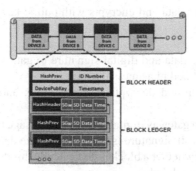

Fig. 3. Block structure

One block is dedicated to one device only. All the data from that device are stored or appended in that block only. The blocks are stored in linked list fashion, where first device is connected to genesis block which is first block in the blockchain. Last block is pointed to null, which will be changed when new device is added to network. They are linked together using cryptographically generated hash value. Each block is sub divided in two parts – Block header and Block ledger.

Block header contains the details about the device like, hash code of previous block, Unique Identification number to access the block, device Public key: public key is made global to facilitate communication. Timestamp contain the time at which block is added to the blockchain. First device contain the hash value of genesis block and genesis block contains predefined hash value.

Block ledger consist of following field:

Hash number: Cryptographically generated hash value for that transaction.
SGw: Digital signature by gateway to for security and to get information about which gateway device connected to.
SD: Digital signature by device.
Data: Data sent by sensors.
Timestamp: Time at which, information is added to the block.

Security Goals

Proposed model provides following three basic services:

– Confidentiality: The information is encrypted using RSA.

– Authentication: Digital signature and SHA-256 provides user authentication.
– Message integrity: It can be achieved using digital signature and SHA-256 mechanism.

Operation

4. Device collects sensor data and encrypts with public key of gateway and digitally
   signs.

It sends the encrypted data and digital signature to gateway using MQTT protocol
along with device pre-defined id as message tuple.

Gateway receives data and decrypts message tuple, and check for validation of
signature.

If signature valid, then gateway digitally signs on message tuple to declare that device
connected to this gateway. If signature is invalid reject the data.

Then gateway checks whether a block is dedicated to this device, if yes then it append
the data to latest data in block ledger.

If there is no block is dedicated to device (i.e., the device is newly registered), create
a block and append to latest block in IOT ledger. Then add data as child.

4 Experimental Evaluation

For the evaluation of experimental setup, temperature sensor and GPS module are used
to obtain sample datasets. Each of them is controlled by Raspberry Pi-2 model B with
8GB SD card and 1GB RAM. Another Raspberry Pi 3 model B with 16GB SD and 1 GB
RAM is used as gateway. Every Raspberry-Pi which is associated with sensors have its
own private key and public key as well as gateway's public key. Similarly, gateway
will have pre knowledge about public key of all devices and its own set of private and
public key. The devices in perception layer has unique id through which it is identified
in network. Sensors collect the real world data and it is encrypted using RSA algorithm
with help of rsa library. Later, hashed encrypted message is digitally signed by device by
its private key. Both cipher test and digital signature are concatenated along with unique
device id to form message tuple which will be communicated to gateway.

MQTT communication between multiple raspberry pi's are achieved using paho-
mqtt library which uses Mosquitto internally. It is a publisher-subscriber model where
publisher publishes the data and subscriber which is already subscribed for it, receives
data from publisher through MQTT broker. In this experiment, an online broker named,
www.eclipse.org is used which connects devices and gateway. Gateway disintegrates
received message and decrypts and checks for validation of digital signature. If the
signature is valid, gateway digitally signs the plaintext and device digital-signature. This
helps in identifying which device is connected to which gateway. Later, it checks whether
block is reserved for that device in blockchain, if yes, message tuple is append inside
block else create new block and add the message tuple as first child.

In blockchain, there are 2 user defined class, block ledger and block header which gives skeleton structure of blockchain. Block header stores device information such unique id for device in blockchain, hash calculated by previous hash, unique id for device in network, time at which the block is created. Block ledger consists of all sensor data obtained from device, which are linked via hash. Block ledger stores data, digital signature by device, digital signature by gateway, time at which data added to blockchain, hash of the previous hash and where previous-hash is previous sensor data hash which will be hash of header for first sensor node (Fig. 4).

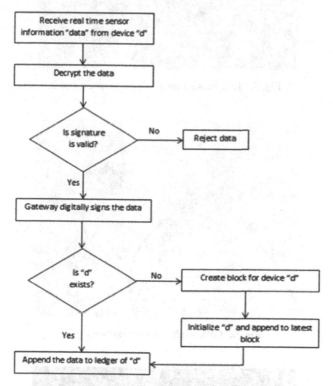

Fig. 4. Flow diagram of uploading message tuple

Experimental setup to obtain temperature is given in Fig. 5. Temperature sensor is directly connected to GPIO pin of Raspberry pi. Temperature data are fetched using Adafruit library. Raspberry pi-2 uses external Wi-Fi adopter to connect to internet.

In the similar way, set-up is made to fetch location details. Location details are processed using gps package. GPS module is connected to Raspberry pi 2 using TTL-USB converter. The experimental setup is shown in Fig. 7. It also uses external Wi-Fi adopter, since raspberry pi 2 doesn't include inbuilt Wi-Fi adopter (Fig. 6).

Figures 7 and 8 shows result of extracted data. And also shows cipher text, digital signature for both temperature and GPS module.

The basic structure of a block is as shown in Fig. 9. It consist of a block of unique ID = 1, and stores 3 temperature sensor data. For every sensor data, ledger information is

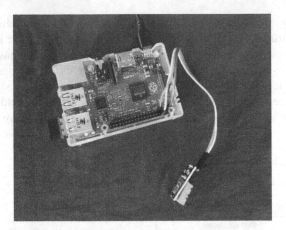

Fig. 5. Temperature sensor with Raspberry pi 2

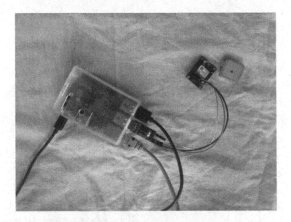

Fig. 6. GPS module with Raspberry pi2

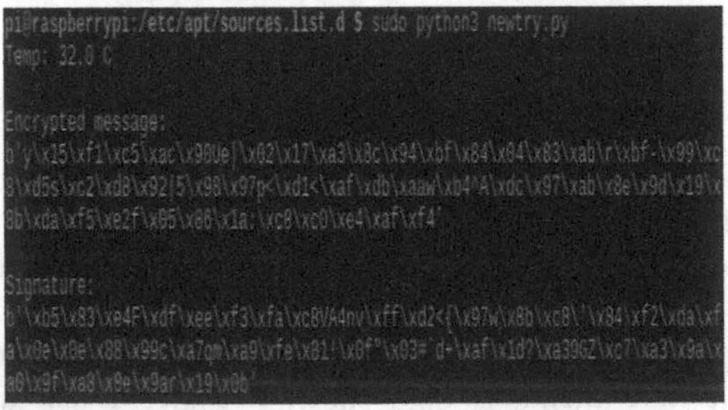

Fig. 7. Temperature data, cipher text and digital signature

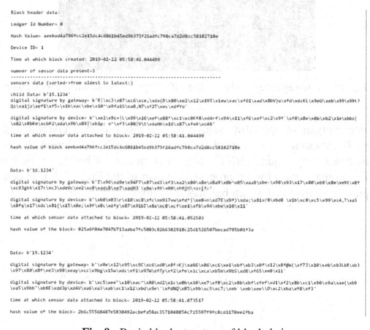

Fig. 8. Location coordinates, cipher text and digital signature

generated and appended to last recent message tuple. Any modification in ledger ripples throughout block hence easy to detect. This happens because hash value for a ledger is calculated by data and previous hash.

Fig. 9. Basic block structure of blockchain

Data received by gateway from temperature sensor as well as GPS sensor is as shown in Fig. 10. In this setup, gateway subscribed to topic "gateway/data" and location and temperature sensor sends the data in name of topic "gateway/data". Gateway identifies the multiple devices using unique id in message tuple sent by device.

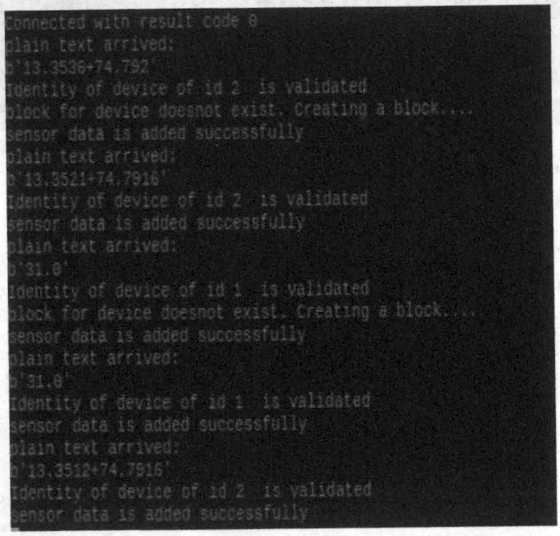

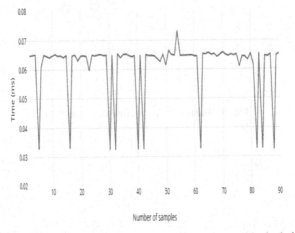

Fig. 10. Gateway receives data using MQTT protocol adds it to block chain

The time analysis of uploading sensor data to blockchain is given in Fig. 11. For experiment 90 data samples are considered which belongs to 2 different blocks. Finding appropriate block may require $O(N)$, where N is number of blocks in the blockchain. The memory consumption by the process is shown in the Fig. 12. For experiment, 55 data samples are considered which belongs to 2 blocks.

Fig. 11. Time required for uploading sensor data to block chain

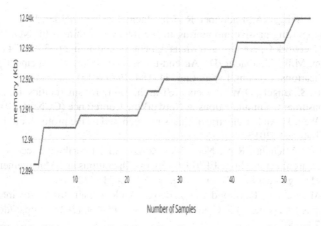

Number of Samples

Fig. 12. Memory required for uploading sensor data to block chain

5 Conclusion

For resource constrained environment such as IoT, deploying blockchain is possible and efficient. By integrating blockchain with IoT would enhance the security features. It can be improved by negotiating changes with its peers to maintain consistency. If data stored in device exceeds the threshold, they need to be store in cloud for making space for new data transaction.

References

1. Marr, B.: The 4rth industrial revolution is here are you ready. https://www.forbes.com/sites/ber nardmarr/2018/08/13/the-4th-industrial-revolution-is-here-are-you-ready/#2ba2805a628b
2. Gubbi, J., Buyya, R., Marusic, S., Palaniswami, M.: Internet of things (IoT): A vision, architectural elements, and future directions. Future Gener. Comput. Syst. **29**(7), 1645–1660 (2013). https://doi.org/10.1016/j.future.2013.01.010
3. Gartner says 6.4 billion connected things will be in use in 2016, up 30 percent from 2015. https://www.gartner.com/newsroom/id/3165317
4. Chakraborty, S., Jaychandran, P.: Blockchain Architecture and design and usecase. https://onlinecourses.nptel.ac.in/noc18_cs47/preview
5. Marr, B.: A very brief history of blockchain technology everyone should read. https://www.forbes.com/sites/bernardmarr/2018/02/16/a-very-brief-history-of-blockchain-technology-everyone-should-read/#2f06b38c7bc4
6. Christidis, K., Devetsikiotis, M.: Blockchains and smart contracts for the internet of things. IEEE Access **4**, 2292–2303 (2016)
7. Khan, M.A., Salah, K.: IoT security: review, block chain solutions, and open challenges. Futur. Gener. Comput. Syst. **82**, 395–411 (2017)
8. Sehgal, A., Perelman, V., Kuryla, S., Schönwälder, J.: Management of resource constrained devices in the internet of things. Commun. Mag. IEEE **50**(12), 144–149 (2012)

9. Mayzaud, A., Sehgal, A., Badonnel, R., Chrisment, I., Schönwälder, J.: Using the RPL protocol for supporting passive monitoring in the internet of things. In: NOMS 2016 – 2016 IEEE/IFIP Network Operations and Management Symposium, pp. 366–374 (2016)
10. Abdmeziem, M.R., Tandjaoui, D.: An end-to-end secure key management protocol for e-health applications. Comput. Electr. Eng. **44**, 184–197 (2015)
11. Chakrabarty, S., Engels, D.W.: A secure IoT architecture for smart cities. In: 2016 13th IEEE Annual Consumer Communications & Networking Conference (CCNC) (2016)
12. Zhang, Y., Wen, J.: An IoT electric business model based on the protocol of bitcoin. In: ICIN. IEEE, pp. 184–191 (2015)
13. Lunardi, R.C., Michelin, R.A., Neu, C.V., Zorzo, A.F.: Distributed access control on IoT ledger-based architecture. In: IEEE/IFIP Network Operations and Management Symposium: Cognitive Management in a Cyber World, NOMS, pp. 1–7 (2018)
14. Banerjee, M., Lee, J., Raymond Choo, K.-K.: A blockchain future for internet of things security: a position paper. Dig. Comm. Netw. **4**(3), 149–160 (2018). https://doi.org/10.1016/j.dcan.2017.10.006
15. Wazid, M., Kumar Das, A., Kumar, N., Vasilakos, A.V.: Design of secure key management and user authentication scheme for fog computing services. Future Gener. Comput. Syst. **91**, 475–492 (2019). https://doi.org/10.1016/j.future.2018.09.017

VIKAS: A Multimodal Framework to Aid in Effective Disaster Management

Gautham Manuru Prabhu[1]([✉]) [iD], Tanay Gupta[2]([✉]) [iD], Metta Venkata Srujan[3]([✉]) [iD],
A. R. Soumya[1]([✉]) [iD], Anshita Palorkar[2]([✉]) [iD], and Anurag Chowdhury[1]([✉]) [iD]

[1] Department of Computer Science and Engineering, Manipal Institute of Technology, Manipal
Academy of Higher Education, Manipal, Karnataka 576104, India
gauthamprabhu9@gmail.com, arsoumya21@gmail.com,
canurag18212@gmail.com
[2] Department of Data Science and Computer Applications, Manipal Institute of Technology,
Manipal Academy of Higher Education, Manipal, Karnataka 576104, India
tanay2502@gmail.com, anpalorkar@gmail.com
[3] Department of Information and Communication Technology, Manipal Institute of Technology,
Manipal Academy of Higher Education, Manipal, Karnataka 576104, India
mvsrujn@gmail.com

Abstract. In the event of a disaster, social media is often used to draw attention to affected areas and distressed people. The massive population and diversity in Indian languages warrant a novel real-time, big-data solution that can increase situational awareness, reduce special forces' response time, and expedite decision-making. The proposed solution, VIKAS, streams text, images, videos, and audio from posts on microblogging platforms using keywords. It then uses the Google Translate and Transliteration APIs to handle multilingual and macaronic hybrid text, including Hinglish. An Apache Kafka event pipeline processes the sheer volume of posts asynchronously. Duplicate, uninformative, or bot-posted data (checked using the Botometer machine learning algorithm) is discarded. Scraped data is also verified through Google's FactCheck Explorer API. Audio and video clips are processed leveraging speech-to-text methods. The solution incorporates a BERT pre-trained model and word embeddings for natural language processing tasks, including sentiment analysis and classification of textual data. Image classification and object identification are implemented using a ResNet deep learning model. This multimodal approach pinpoints locations using nearby landmarks, severity, and type of support needed, ranging from humanitarian aid and rescue relief to infrastructure damage. Easy-to-interpret visualizations on an accessible dashboard consolidate many details that can streamline resource distribution and personnel deployment. VIKAS was presented to the National Disaster Response Force at the national-level finals of the Smart India Hackathon 2022.

Keywords: Computer Vision · Natural Language Processing · Deep Learning ·
Disaster Management · Social Media · Information Security

© The Author(s), under exclusive license to Springer Nature Singapore Pte Ltd. 2023
S. Prabhu et al. (Eds.): ATIS 2022, CCIS 1804, pp. 279–289, 2023.
https://doi.org/10.1007/978-981-99-2264-2_22

1 Introduction

Over the last few years, social media platforms like Twitter have emerged as a crucial means of communication during the times of disaster [1]. Scaling of internet technologies has led to widespread usage of social media across all parts of the world. During disasters, platforms like Twitter are widely used by affected people to post situational awareness messages. These messages serve as crucial sources of information. Research demonstrates the importance and usefulness of this online information for humanitarian organizations working in disaster relief and management [2].

The information obtained can be used by organizations to facilitate faster decision making and assessment of disaster struck areas.

Since the solution acts as a bridge between people in distress and relief forces, it was named VIKAS ("Vipada Mein Aapke Saath", Hindi for "With you in disaster").

Consequently, we can summarise main contributions of our work as follows:

- We use the Google Translate and Transliteration APIs to handle multilingual and macaronic hybrid text, including Hinglish.
- Increased activity on social media is observed during a disaster, this leads to the generation of a large volume of posts. This is processed by an Apache Kafka event pipeline.
- Duplicate, uninformative and bot-generated text is discarded using the Botometer machine learning algorithm. Scraped data is also verified using Google's FactCheck Explorer API.
- We process audio and video clips through different speech-to-text methods.
- We employed CrisisNLP datasets for carrying out our experiments.
- Our approach pinpoints locations using nearby landmarks, severity, and type of support needed, ranging from humanitarian aid and rescue relief to infrastructure damage.

2 Related Work

Various implementations of assessing disaster characteristics from social media have been carried out in the past. Disaster related information from social media if processed timely and effectively may be significant in disaster mitigation. For example, classification and extraction of data based on relevancy [3]. Another approach involves text summarization to extract situational updates of a disaster from tweets [4] followed by the classification of the text into various informational categories. Another tool, AIDR (Artificial Intelligence for Disaster Response) [5], was designed to automate classification of crisis related messages on microblogging platforms. These messages were classified into a set of user defined categories of information. For this purpose, the system continuously ingests data from Twitter, processes it and leverages human participation in real-time. Collection of disaster related messages is done by AIDR, and a subset of these messages are labelled by a crowd. Based on these labels, an automatic classifier is trained.

Apart from text from messages and posts on social media platforms, images shared by users also provide critical information about a disaster. Some of the previous works on images include an image classifier [6]. In this approach, images from social media are first filtered using a filtering module. After checking for relevancy and duplication, the images are assessed and the training set for the specific classifier was built. Manual labelling of images was done to tag images based on its content. Based on the labelling, classification of images into various categories is carried out. Besides these, another research involves a complete system with a real-time image processing pipeline in place for analysing social media data at the onset of any emergency event [2]. The system involves two types of noise filtering (i.e., image relevancy and de-duplication) and the damage assessment classifier. Irrelevant images are removed by a transfer learning approach.

Another work involves classification of disaster related images as informative or non-informative [7]. Capsule networks were used for classification of images. The work demonstrated that capsule networks performed better than convolutional neural networks (CNN) in both in domain and cross domain settings.

A few multimodal strategies have also been researched in the past. A. K. Gautam, L. Misra et al. [8] involves analysis of multimodal data relevant to various types of natural calamities and proposes a novel decision diffusion technique to classify them into informative and non-informative categories. In this approach, classification of tweets containing different modalities is carried out in multiple steps. First the performance of various methods is evaluated on individual modalities, and then combined using a multimodal decision fusion technique.

3 Methodology

The workflow of the proposed framework is demonstrated in Fig. 1.

3.1 Scraping Multimodal Data in Real-Time

The online news, social networking, and microblogging site Twitter was chosen as the social media platform to extract data from in the scope of this project. Its extensive API documentation, convenient interface, and high amount of metadata offered made it ideal for experimentation.

A Twitter application was set up using a Developer account with Elevated Access to the Twitter Streaming API. The Python library Tweepy [9] allows the creation of a tweet streamer using the account's credentials to obtain real-time tweets and metadata. The streamed data included:

- Textual content
- Media URLs
- Timestamp of creation
- Username
- Location of the profile (set by the user, not always useful; Twitter's API does not provide geolocation or EXIF data)
- Hashtags

Apache Kafka [10] is an open-source distributed event streaming platform which can publish, subscribe to, store, and process streams of records in real time. Its scalability

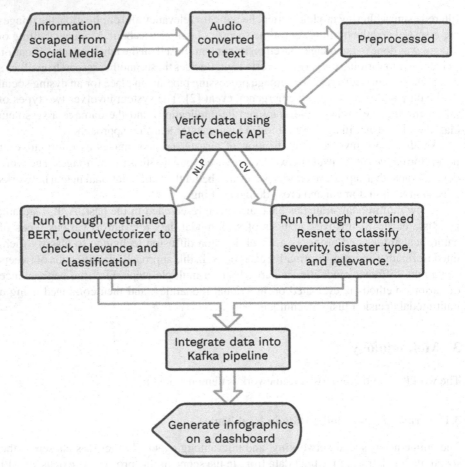

Fig. 1. Flow diagram for VIKAS

and high-performance abstraction of messages in order allows the creation of a robust big-data pipeline for extracted data. In Kafka, events are organized and durably stored in topics, which are partitioned over different Kafka brokers or servers together forming clusters.

Producers are client applications that publish (write) events to Kafka, and consumers are ones that subscribe to (read and process) these events. In Kafka, producers and consumers are fully decoupled and agnostic of each other. Producers never need to wait for consumers. The Twitter data was streamed in real-time through a producer-consumer Kafka module. Thus, streaming could be performed asynchronously.

The botometer machine learning algorithm uses the Botometer API [11] to extract features such as public tweets, mentions, friends, social network structure, temporal activity patterns, language, and sentiments, to classify whether a Twitter user account is a bot or not. The Python library botometer assigned each username in the extracted data with an overall score in the range of 0 to 1, as well as subscores for its likeliness to be a specific type of bot, including:

- fake_follower: Bots purchased to increase follower counts
- self_declared: Bots from botwiki.org
- astroturf: Manually labeled political bots and accounts involved in follow trains that systematically delete content
- spammer: Accounts labeled as spam bots from several datasets
- financial: Bots that post using "cashtags"
- other: Other miscellaneous bots obtained from manual annotation, user feedback, etc.

Tweets from accounts with an overall score higher than a threshold of 0.5 were discarded.

Normalization of the text involved case-folding and translation. The Google Transliterate API was used to handle macaronic hybrid text such as tweets in Hinglish, where Hindi words are written using English letters as opposed to Devanagari script. The Google Translation API Basic was then used to convert non-English text into English.

Cleaning and preprocessing included removal of the following using simple regular expression filters and stopword lists:

- Retweets (discard tweets beginning with 'RT')
- Emojis, special characters, and punctuation (discard non-alphanumeric words)
- Non-media URLs and emails (discard entities of the form abc@xyz.com or containing http)
- Common, non-informative words such as articles, prepositions, etc.

3.2 Natural Language Processing Pipeline

The Natural Language pipeline is an integral part of the proposed framework. The proposed solution employed techniques for validating and analysing the tweets using comprehensive models described below. The task of the pipeline was to perform:

i. Relevancy Check [12]
ii. Classification of the relevant tweets into nine categories described below.

The relevance model used a huge dataset of tweets marked as "Relevant" and "Not Relevant" from a Kaggle dataset [13].

The "Wikipedia 2014 + Gigaword 5" GloVe embeddings [14] were used, which contain 6 billion tokens, 400,000 vocab with uncased 100-dimensional vectors.

The data was initially converted into an intermediary form called a "token", the sequence of which were created from the text. In the next step, an embedding matrix was created from the tokenized words to effectively create a mapping between a word and its axis.

The framework employs 2 LSTM layers [15] consisting of dropout and recurrent dropout layers [16]. Two dense layers were added in the end, one using the activation function of ReLu [17] and ending with a layer using the sigmoid activation function

[18]. Ultimately, the model was trained with an Early Stopping [19] callback condition using validation loss as the monitored metric, as prescribed in the paper cited.

On testing the model on a subset of the dataset not trained, a minimum accuracy of 75% was observed in classification of relevant tweets against irrelevant tweets, on multiple training iterations. A minimum accuracy of 70% was also achieved when measured against the test dataset provided. An 80:20 validation split on the train data was employed. [20].

The next step involved using the obtained relevant data from the corpus and subsequent classification of the type of tweet into 9 categories namely: "Caution and Advice", "Displaced People and Evacuations", "Donation Needs or Offers or Volunteering Services", "Infrastructure and Utilities Damage", "Injured or Dead People", "Missing Trapped or Found People", "Not Related or Irrelevant", "Other Useful Information", "Sympathy and Emotional Support". The dataset used here contained tweets pertaining to floods [21]. The data was split into test and train components.

The first experiment involved the implementation of a Support Vector Machine (SVM) [22] where the data was first represented as vectors, and the model was subsequently fitted through a Linear Support Vector Classifier. The fitted model on testing returned an accuracy of around 67%.

Upon comparing the performance of the different classical machine learning models, the literature suggested the implementation of a BERT classifier [23] which returned a higher baseline accuracy of ~71% on the test dataset.

The proposed multimodal solution incorporates the modality of audio which can be extracted from uploaded videos on social media. The framework employs the use of the SpeechRecognition library [24] in Python to extract words from the given regional language. The text is passed through the googletrans library [25] and the given language is translated into English text, which can be passed through the framework described for a comprehensive multimodal analysis.

The working of the relevance classifier has been demonstrated in Fig. 2.

Fig. 2. The entered text in the classifier returns an output of "Disaster"

3.3 Computer Vision Pipeline

The computer vision pipeline is important for getting visual information which may not be acquired from textual or audio sources otherwise. This pipeline has three broad components:

i.   Relevance classifier into "Relevant" and "Not Relevant"

ii.   Damage Type classifier into four broad categories
iii. Severity classifier into "Mild" and "Severe".

The images and videos are passed through the relevance classifier first, after which the damage type and severity is analysed.

The Computer Vision Models used in this project were written using the Fast.ai library [26], a high-speed deep learning library that was built upon PyTorch. They were run on Google Colab, which provides an Intel(R) Xeon(R) CPU with two cores and a frequency of 2.30 GHz.

All the three classifiers used labelled data obtained from the Crisis MMD Dataset, consisting of labelled multimodal data from seven different disasters that occurred during the year 2017. [27, 28] Images were sampled from a pool of approximately 18,000 images, ensuring there was no redundancy.

The dataset was split into test and train parts with an 80:20 ratio [20], with a batch size of 192, and the images were resized uniformly. The models were then trained using PyTorch's pretrained ResNet50 [29] weights, with a validation split of 70:30 and 10 epochs.

The relevance model used a labelled dataset with images marked as "Relevant" and "Not Relevant". A training accuracy of ~91% was achieved.

The Damage type model was trained on a dataset which contains images labelled into four categories: 1) "Fire", 2) "Flood", 3) "Infrastructure" and 4) "Natural". The same methodology was used as the relevance model, except that the images were cropped instead of resized. Training for five epochs, an accuracy of ~86% was achieved.

In case of the Severity model, the dataset was composed of images from two categories of damage severity: 1) Mild and 2) Severe. Adopting similar strategies as before, after training for ten epochs, an accuracy of ~ 83% was obtained.

The training details for all the 3 classifiers have been shown in Table 1.

Table 1. Training Details for the Computer Vision models

Classifier	Dataset Size	Training Duration	Accuracy (in %)
Relevance	2800	170 min	91.25
Damage Type	1400	50 min	86.78
Severity	2000	150 min	83.25

To work with video data, a script that extracts frames from a video every specified few seconds was written. The extracted frames were then put into the same computer Vision pipeline that was used for image data.

All three classifiers have been deployed on HuggingFace and are available for public use. The working of the damage type and damage severity classifiers has been demonstrated in Figs. 3 and 4.

Fig. 3. Image input through the classifier returns the likelihood of the type of damage

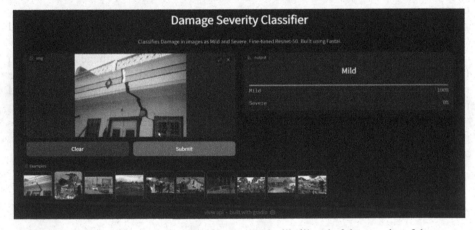

Fig. 4. Image input through the classifier returns the likelihood of the severity of damage

4   Results

The processed data is displayed in the form of helpful infographics on a dashboard as demonstrated in Fig. 5. Keeping in mind that the concerned user base will consist of people with various levels of technical knowledge, it was imperative to minimize the complexity of the dashboard. The final User Interface is clean and minimal, displaying only the most important and necessary data on the Home Page. To gather more insight about a certain infographic, the user can interact with it and view an in-depth analysis, if required. This ensures that the dashboard can be used by technical novices as well. Furthermore, the dashboard is also optimized to display information in multiple languages, to cater to the diverse population of India. These features are implemented to keep the technical aspects of the model tucked away and convey useful data to first responders in the quickest and easiest way possible.

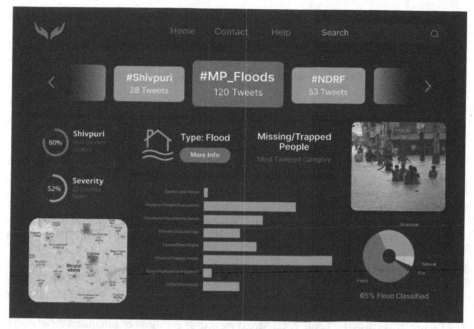

Fig. 5. Final dashboard which is viewed by first responders

5 Future Scope

Research into language processing, corpora collection for Indian languages can be integrated into the framework to extend the solution to work for a larger locality. Incorporating information regarding documentation of local landmarks can refine search space. Integration of data from other social media platforms can enhance the corpus and improve accuracy, reduce redundancy.

References

1. Said, N., et al.: Natural disasters detection in social media and satellite imagery: a survey. Multimed. Tools Appl. **78**(22), 31267–31302 (2019). https://doi.org/10.1007/s11042-019-07942-1
2. Alam, F., Ofli, F., Imran, M.: Processing social media images by combining human and machine computing during crises. Int. J. Human-Comput. Interact. **34**(4), 311–327 (2018). https://doi.org/10.1080/10447318.2018.1427831
3. Imran, M., Elbassuoni, S., Castillo, C., Diaz, F., Meier, P.: Practical extraction of disaster-relevant information from social media. In: WWW 2013 Companion – Proceedings of the 22nd International Conference on World Wide Web (2013). https://doi.org/10.1145/2487788.2488109
4. Rudra, K., Goyal, P., Ganguly, N., Imran, M., Mitra, P.: Summarising situational tweets in crisis scenarios: an extractive-abstractive approach. IEEE Trans. Comput. Soc. Syst. **6**(5), 981–993 (2019). https://doi.org/10.1109/TCSS.2019.2937899

5. Imran, M., et al.: AIDR: Artificial intelligence for disaster response. In: Proceedings of the 23rd International Conference on World Wide Web (2014)
6. Sindhu, S., Nair, D.S., Maya, V.S., Thanseeha, M.T., Vishnu Hari, C.: Disaster management from social media using machine learning. In: 2019 9th International Conference on Advances in Computing and Communication (ICACC), pp. 246–252 (2019). https://doi.org/10.1109/ICACC48162.2019.8986198
7. Dinani, S.T., Caragea, D.: Disaster image classification using capsule networks. Int. Joint Conf. on Neural Netw. (IJCNN) **2021**, 1–8 (2021). https://doi.org/10.1109/IJCNN52387.2021.9534448
8. Gautam, A.K., Misra, L., Kumar, A., Misra, K., Aggarwal, S., Shah, R.R.: Multimodal analysis of disaster tweets. In: 2019 IEEE Fifth International Conference on Multimedia Big Data (BigMM), pp. 94–103 (2019). https://doi.org/10.1109/BigMM.2019.00-38
9. Roesslein, J.: Tweepy: Twitter for Python!. https://github.com/tweepy/tweepy (2020)
10. Hiraman, B.R., Chapte Viresh, M., Karve Abhijeet, C.: A study of apache kafka in big data stream processing. In: 2018 International Conference on Information, Communication, Engineering and Technology (ICICET), pp. 1–3 (2018). https://doi.org/10.1109/ICICET.2018.853 3771
11. Sayyadiharikandeh, M., Varol, O., Yang, K.C., Flammini, A., Menczer, F.: Detection of novel social bots by ensembles of specialized classifiers. In: Proceedings of the 29th ACM International Conference on Information & Knowledge Management, pp. 2725–2732, October 2020
12. Duarte, N., Llanso, E., Loup, A.C.: Mixed messages? the limits of automated social media content analysis. In: FAT 106 (2018)
13. Howard, A., Guo, Y.: Natural Language Processing with Disaster Tweets (2019)
14. Pennington, J., Socher, R., Manning, C.D.: GloVe: Global Vectors for Word Representation (2014)
15. Hochreiter, S., Schmidhuber, J.: Long short-term memory. Neural Comput. **9**, 1735–1780 (1997). https://doi.org/10.1162/neco.1997.9.8.1735
16. Semeniuta, S., Severyn, A., Barth, E.: Recurrent Dropout without Memory Loss (2016)
17. Agarap, A.F.: Deep Learning using Rectified Linear Units (2018)
18. Han, J., Moraga, C.: The influence of the sigmoid function parameters on the speed of backpropagation learning. In: Mira, J., Sandoval, F. (eds.) IWANN 1995. LNCS, vol. 930, pp. 195–201. Springer, Heidelberg (1995). https://doi.org/10.1007/3-540-59497-3_175
19. Prechelt, L.: Early stopping - but when? In: Orr, G.B., Müller, K.-R. (eds.) Neural Networks: Tricks of the trade, pp. 55–69. Springer Berlin Heidelberg, Berlin, Heidelberg (1998). https://doi.org/10.1007/3-540-49430-8_3
20. Gholamy, A., Kreinovich, V., Kosheleva, O.: Why 70/30 or 80/20 relation between training and testing sets: a pedagogical explanation (2018)
21. Zahra, K., Imran, M., Ostermann, F.O.: Automatic identification of eyewitness messages on twitter during disasters. Inform. Process. Manag. **57**(1), 102107 (2020). https://doi.org/10.1016/j.ipm.2019.102107
22. Evgeniou, T., Pontil, M.: Support vector machines: theory and applications. In: Paliouras, G., Karkaletsis, V., Spyropoulos, C.D. (eds.) ACAI 1999. LNCS (LNAI), vol. 2049, pp. 249–257. Springer, Heidelberg (2001). https://doi.org/10.1007/3-540-44673-7_12
23. Devlin, J., Chang, M.-W., Lee, K., Toutanova, K.: BERT: Pre-training of Deep Bidirectional Transformers for Language Understanding (2018)
24. Zhang, A.: SpeechRecognition. https://github.com/Uberi/speech_recognition (2014)
25. Han, S.: Googletrans (2017)
26. Howard, J., et al.: "fastai" (2018)

27. Alam, F., Ofli, F., Imran, M.: CrisisMMD: multimodal twitter datasets from natural disasters. In: Proceedings of the 12th International AAAI Conference on Web and Social Media (ICWSM). Stanford, California, USA (2018)
28. Ofli, F., Alam, F., Imran, M.: Analysis of social media data using multimodal deep learning for disaster response. In: Proceedings of the 17th International Conference on Information Systems for Crisis Response and Management (ISCRAM). USA (2020)
29. He, K., Zhang, X., Ren, S., Sun, J.: Deep Residual Learning for Image Recognition (2015)

Discovery of Rare Itemsets Using Hyper-Linked Data Structure: A Parallel Approach

Goutham Yadavalli and Shwetha Rai[✉] [iD]

Department of Computer Science and Engineering, Manipal Institute of Technology, Manipal Academy of Higher Education, Manipal, Karnataka 576104, India
shwetha.rai@manipal.edu

Abstract. Pattern mining has been more important in the solution of various data mining jobs over the years. The extraction of common patterns was the primary focus of pattern mining research for a long period of time, with the mining of rare patterns being neglected. Rare pattern mining is becoming more popular as researchers recognize the importance of rare patterns. The hyper-linked data structure is suitable to store sparse data set in the main memory and enables dynamic adjustment of links during the mining process using recursion. However, a sequential approach to discovering rare patterns from a large dataset is inefficient. Hence a CUDA-based parallel algorithm has been implemented to discover rare itemsets. The algorithm is tested using dense and sparse datasets on a GPU. The GPU initialization time affects the time taken to discover rare itemsets. The time taken to transfer data between CPU and GPU is significantly large and the parallel implementation of an algorithm with a recursive approach is unsuitable.

Keywords: CUDA · Data mining · Parallel programming · Rare itemset · Tree data structure

1 Introduction

Data mining has gained popularity since the beginning of the digital revolution due to its application in various fields. Alan Turing introduced the idea of a universal machine in 1936, which was one of the first instances of data mining since it could do computations like those performed by modern computers [1]. Data mining is increasingly being used by businesses to enhance anything from sales operations to financial analysis for investment reasons. It involves analyzing huge quantities of data to discover business insights that may help companies solve problems, reduce risks, and take advantage of new opportunities [2]. It requires sifting through enormous amounts of data to discover hidden value from the dataset. To get the best results, data mining requires a range of tools and techniques such as artificial intelligence, association rule mining (ARM), clustering, classification, machine learning and regression [2].

© The Author(s), under exclusive license to Springer Nature Singapore Pte Ltd. 2023
S. Prabhu et al. (Eds.): ATIS 2022, CCIS 1804, pp. 290–301, 2023.
https://doi.org/10.1007/978-981-99-2264-2_23

Pattern mining, a technique in ARM, has played an important part in various data mining activities throughout the years. For a long time, pattern mining research focused only on the extraction of common patterns, ignoring the mining of rare patterns. Rare patterns have been shown to be useful in a variety of applications, including network anomaly detection, equipment failure, medicine, and fraud detection [3]. Given the importance of rare patterns, rare pattern mining research is gaining traction, and a significant amount of effort has already been done to extract these significant patterns [4].

The term "frequent itemset mining" focuses on locating itemsets that appear in groups frequently [5]. Rare itemsets mining uncovers previously unknown relationship among the less frequent itemsets. All the algorithms in place to extract rare itemsets are serial algorithms which will be time inefficient with the increasing volume of data. Due to the nature of the task of finding rare itemsets, a certain part of the process, which is time and resource-consuming, can be implemented in parallel hence reducing the time taken to discover the rare itemsets. The research aims to understand the nature of the hyperlink data structure in a parallel environment by implementing parallel mining with the assistance of the CUDA framework.

2 Literature Review

Different algorithms that have been developed in a similar field are discussed with its pros and cons. Liu et al. [7] implemented rare pattern mining and assigned minimum support threshold to each of the items separately, utilizing the Apriori-based method. The rare itemset mining algorithms, ARIMA [6] and the AfRIM [8], on the other hand, utilized a single minimum support value for all components. The use of Apriori-based algorithms has several limitations which led to the development of tree-based methods, such as the Compressed FP-Growth (CFP-Growth) which uses a multiple minimum support framework to extract rare patterns. For mining rare patterns, the Rare Pattern Tree (RP-Tree) Mining method described by Tsang et al. [9] is the most efficient pattern growth technique. Only transactions with at least one rare item are considered by the system, which employs two support criteria. Bhatt et al. implemented MCRP-Tree algorithm [10] that improves it even further by utilizing several support levels for improved performance. It dynamically assigns suitable minimum support to each item, allowing for more efficient extraction of frequent itemsets including rare items than current methods. Rare pattern mining methods as discussed by Borah et al. [4] collect patterns from databases in a horizontal style, with one column representing the transaction id. The other, on the other hand, indicates the total number of objects involved in the transaction with that specific id. The Apriori algorithm is the most often used algorithm in pattern mining.

Most rare pattern mining methods are based on frequent itemset mining techniques, resulting in time-consuming candidate creation or traversal of all frequent patterns. To address the aforementioned difficulties, the author offers a novel algorithm that is based on top-down and depth-first approaches. For each transaction, a negative itemset is created, which includes all the items that are not in the itemset. The method presented by Lu et al. [11], the Negative Infrequent Itemset tree miner (NIIMiner), was implemented in Java. The negative itemset in NIIMiner gets excessively big for sparse datasets, when there is only one item in a transaction, resulting in extremely lengthy calculations.

The RP-growth method outperforms all prior algorithms in terms of finding rare itemsets, but its performance degrades for sparse data, and memory consumption rises. Rare Pre-Post is a novel algorithm proposed by Darrab et al. [12] (RPP). By eliminating conditional trees at each stage of the RP growth, it saves spending time and resources on worthless candidate itemsets. The memory usage of RPP was lower than that of the RP-growth algorithm for certain minSup criteria. The threshold values chosen for both minSup and maxSup have an impact on the outcomes of rare itemset mining by Kanimozhi et al. [13]. However, when these numbers are changed, the results vary dramatically, allowing the discovery of intriguing patterns. The itemsets are divided into three groups in this method, and each group's threshold is generated independently. The itemsets over the suggested threshold in each group are then grouped back together.

By using the principles of fuzzy theory, the author introduces us to FRI-Miner by Cui et al. [14], a fuzzy-based mining method that helps us discover intriguing, rare itemsets from a quantitative database. FRI-Miner is described in detail in this article. It is necessary to perform certain pruning procedures in each step-in order to improve the performance of the algorithm and to make better use of the available resources. This algorithm is more concerned with discovering fewer rare itemsets that are qualitative in nature rather than finding numerous rare itemsets, which is what the Automated Apriori algorithm is concerned with doing. The method has been thoroughly tested by changing various factors such as the minSup value and the density of the dataset, and the results have been documented for the varied runtimes for the various values. The most significant disadvantage of this method is the difficulty in determining the right minSup value since it must be set manually.

Recent advancements in Graphics Processing Units (GPUs) have made it possible to achieve low-cost high-performance computing for a wide range of general-purpose applications. A programming paradigm based on Compute Unified Device Architecture (CUDA) offers programmers with sufficient C language-like APIs that allow them to better utilize the parallel capabilities of the graphics processing unit (GPU). Data mining is extensively utilized and has substantial applications across a broad range of industries and disciplines. Current data mining toolkits, on the other hand, are unable to satisfy the performance requirements of applications that use large-scale databases in terms of speed. According to this paper [15], the author proposes three techniques for speeding up fundamental problems in data mining algorithms on the CUDA platform. These techniques are scalable thread scheduling scheme for irregular pattern, concurrent distributed top-k scheme, and concurrent large-scale high dimension reduction scheme. Adil et al. [16] propose a new CUDA based approach for association rule mining what has a 18x speedup over the serial algorithm for association rule mining.

3   Methodology

Various terminologies that are used to describe the algorithm are discussed. Furthermore, the algorithm, and its implementation details are discussed in this section.

3.1   Basic Terminologies

- Itemset: An itemset is a collection of items in the database T_d and it is represented as I. A set of n items in an itemset I is represented as $I = i_1, i_2, \ldots, i_n$.
- Database: The database is a collection of m transactions represented as $T_d = t_1$, $t_2, \ldots, t_m$ where $t_1, t_2, \ldots, tm$ are transaction identifiers representing each transaction.
- Support: A support is a user-defined threshold to discover frequent and/or infrequent itemsets. The support of any itemset in a database with Td transactions is calculated as the total number of times it has appeared in the transaction database.
- Frequent Itemset: An itemset is said to be frequent if its occurrence in the database is greater than or equal to the user-defined threshold minfreq.
- Infrequent (or Rare) Itemset: An itemset is said to be infrequent if its occurrence in the database is between two thresholds minrare and minfreq. If the occurrence of the itemset is less than minrare then it is considered noise.

3.2   Efficient Hyper-Linked Rare Pattern Structure Algorithm

Algorithm 1 computes the header table which consists of the different items present in the database transactions and their support counts, this table can be further used to find our rare and frequent itemsets. Algorithm 2 is used to generate the projected databases after discarding the frequent itemsets at each step to discover rare itemsets.

Algorithm 1 : Efficient Hyper-Linked Rare Pattern Structure (EHLRPS)

Input: Complete original transaction database (DB), minrareSup, minfreqSup
Output: Complete set of rare itemsets
1 Create header table (HT) containing the following fields: itemid, supcount and hyperlink
2 for each item IT ∈ DB do
3   if item IT is in the HT then
4   support count(IT)←support count(IT)+1
5   Sort HT in ascending order of Sup_Count
6   else if item IT not in the HT then
7   create entry for item IT in HT
8   support count(IT)←1
9   hyperlink←NULL
10   end if
11   end for each
12   for each item IT in HT do
13:       if minrareSup < support count(IT) <minfreqSup
14   Rare←Rare U IT
15   for each transaction TR ∈ DB do
16   if ∃r| (minrareSup < r<minfreqSup) ∧ r∈TR then
17   RareItemTransaction ← TR
18   end if
19   end for each
20   Create different queues,Qj with following fields: itemid and hyper-link that stores the items of jth RareItemTransaction. Use a hyperlink to link all transactions with the same first item.
21 for each item x in HT
22   create rare item projections from x-projected database()
23 end for each

Algorithm 2: Create a x-projected database to mine rare itemsets:

Input: Main Header table HT, str
Output: Rare itemsets
1 for each item x in HT do
2   Traverse the queues attached through hyperlink
3   Create a sub-header HTsub with the items in the transaction queues and its corresponding support count.
4   Create a string 'str' to store the itemsets and its corresponding support
5   for each item in HTsub do
6   if minrareSup < HTsub. item_id.support < minreqSup
7   concatenate (x, HTsub.item_id)
8   concatenate (x, ": HTsub. item_id.support")
9   end if
10   end for
11   if HTsub.item.hyperlink is not NULL and if the item y in HTsub is Rare then
12   xy-projected database ()
13   end if
14 end for

The flowchart shown in Fig. 1 (a) describes the basic flow of the sequential algorithm. Initially, the data is read from the file and the transactions are copied into the main memory in a hyperlink data structure. In the next step, a support count map is created for the items in the transaction. This step is taken when the database is read once, to reduce multiple reads of the database. Next, the support count map is sorted based on the support count in ascending order. This sorted map is used to create the data structure HeaderTable, HT which contains the item, its support count, and a hyperlink which links to the transactions containing that item. The items are added to the results that have a support count which falls in the range of minSup and maxSup. In the next step, a sub HeaderTable is created for the items that have the support count in the required frequency. Further, a loop is run over these sub HeaderTables and this process is repeated for all the elements in the sub HeaderTable using a recursive function, and the rare itemsets are added to the results.

In the second algorithm, it can be noticed that the rare items are extracted for each entry of the HeaderTable HT in a loop, thus indicating that each entry in the HeaderTable can be processed separately. This is the main idea behind the design of the parallel algorithm. The initial preprocessing part which includes the algorithm -1 can be implemented in serial. We can process each entry of the HeaderTable in a different thread parallelly in CUDA. This process is done in the kernel code, and the further recursive calls made by each separate entry of the HeaderTable are executed on the same thread. All the results are collected in an array and displayed after the parallel execution is completed. The CUDA program can be divided into two parts, sequential instructions, and parallel instructions. In the sequential part, the input file is read and the initial HeaderTable is constructed. Then the contents of the HeaderTable are copied onto the GPU since the parallel part of the code cannot refer to the variables declared and initialized in the serial code The parallel execution of the code begins from when the __global__ function is

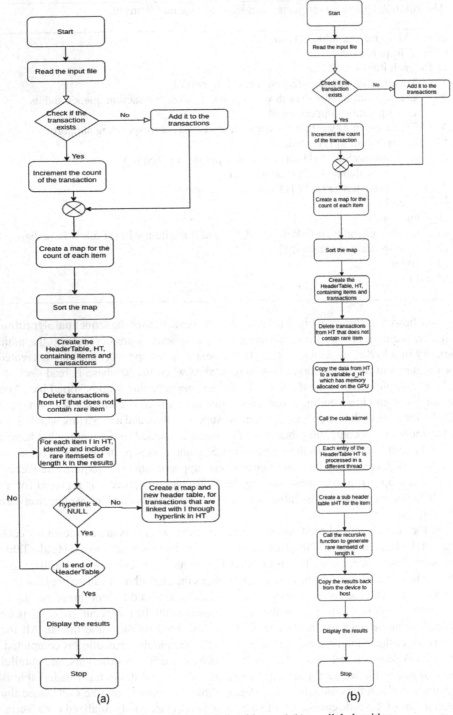

Fig. 1. Flowchart of (a) serial algorithm and (b) parallel algorithm

called. This function can only be called from the host code. Each of the items in the HeaderTable is used on a different thread to construct the sub header table and then process it recursively. This recursive process is done in a __device__ function which can only be called from the __global__ function. All the results are collected in an array and this array is copied back from the device to the host. The flowchart of the parallel approach is shown in Fig. 1 (b).

4 Result Analysis

The results are recorded by testing the algorithms against standard transaction databases used to test the performance of data mining algorithms. All the tests have been conducted on Chess and Connect datasets obtained from [17]. The number of transactions in chess data is 3,196 and tests have been conducted by varying the number of the transactions and the number of items in each transaction between 6 and 7. There are 67,557 transactions in the Connect dataset.

4.1 Performance of Sequential Approach

The serial algorithm is implemented in C++ and all the tests are conducted on a Linux machine running Intel(R) Core (TM) i5-7200U CPU @ 2.50GHz processor. The compiler used is g++, which is a GNU-based C++ compiler.

The experiments are conducted by varying the number of rows in the database and the size of the transactions in the database. In Tables 1 and 2, we summarize the results that are recorded after running the code 5 times and the average execution time is noted down.

The following observations can be made from the results obtained as shown in Tables 1 and 2:

1. The execution time increases as the length of the transaction increases, this is because it increases the depth of the recursion as we generate more sub header tables.
2. The execution time also increases as we increase the number of transactions, but this observation has a lot of irregularities in it. This is because, as we store only the unique transactions, an increase in the size of the database might not always lead to growth in the size of our data structure as the new transactions might already exist in it. Also, it depends on the items falling in the range of minSup and maxSup. If the items that are rare have only a few transactions linked to it through the hyperlink, the depth of the recursion decreases, and the runtime decreases substantially because of this.

4.2 Performance of Parallel Approach Using CUDA

The parallel code has been developed in C++ using the CUDA library. The experiments have been conducted on the Google Colab environment which provides a GPU for

Table 1. Execution time(milliseconds) for Chess dataset using sequential and parallel approach

# Transactions	Chess 6		Chess 7	
	Sequential	Parallel	Sequential	Parallel
500	4366	8501	5467	8917
1000	5677	8648	6668	8927
1500	4494	8764	6286	8841
2000	4855	8601	6738	8903
2500	4686	8662	7074	9018
3000	6435	8623	6020	8961

running our code. It provides a single 12GB NVIDIA Tesla K80 GPU. We have used the nvcc compiler to compile the CUDA code.

The results in Table 1 show initial observation from executing the parallel code. The execution time is much higher than the execution time of the serial code for the same data. On further investigation it is found out that this is due to the time taken to initialize the GPU as the GPU switches off whenever it is not in use. Most of the algorithms that are developed in CUDA are tested after running a warmup call to the kernel code. This warmup call initializes the GPU and all the setup that is required. Interesting results were found after timing the second call to the kernel function for the Chess dataset.

Table 2. Execution time(milliseconds) for Connect dataset using sequential and parallel approach

# Transactions	Connect 6		Connect 7	
	Sequential	Parallel	Sequential	Parallel
10000	2218	8440	3211	8956
20000	2713	8578	3072	9148
30000	2392	8535	3431	9278
40000	2885	8702	3050	8988
50000	2738	8561	3718	8863
60000	2985	8543	3334	8958

The execution times for the second run are much faster than any of the results. It has a 400 times speedup on the initial run of the parallel code and approximately 250 times speedup against the serial code. To make sure that the results are accurate, we have flushed the Cuda memory using cudaFree() API and copied the data back to the device again to test the algorithm before the second run. The execution time includes the cudamemcpy API as well. To make sure the results are accurate we have noted down the average execution times of multiple runs.

Table 3. Execution times for parallel code in after initiating the GPU for Chess data

#Transactions	500	1000	1500	2000	2500	3000
Execution time (ms)	16	21	20	32	21	20

Both the Chess and Connect datasets are dense datasets, experiments are also conducted against sparse data that are generated using the SPMF generator from [16]. This data set contains 1000 transactions with 5000 unique items having a maximum transaction length of 7. A real-life example may be any rare disease with multiple mimicking symptoms such as sarcoidosis. The sparse data utilizes more memory than the dense data because the number of items in the sparse data is much higher than that of the dense data, hence it was running out of space and time on the CUDA kernel. A parallel approach was implemented to analyze the performance to discover rare itemsets from dense and sparse dataset. Theoretically, one can assume that the parallel algorithm is faster than the serial code because of the nature of the code. But the parallel code takes longer time to execute, this is because of the time taken to initialize the GPU which was not accounted for beforehand. The same can be observed in Table 3 which contains the execution time after initiating the GPU for Chess dataset.

5   Conclusion and Future Scope

This is one of the first algorithms in the field of rare itemset mining that has been developed to execute in parallel. The execution time increases as the length of the transaction increases, this is because it increases the depth of the recursion as we generate more sub header tables. The execution time also increases as we increase the number of transactions, but this observation has a lot of irregularities in it. This is because, as we store only the unique transactions, an increase in the size of the database might not always lead to growth in the size of our data structure as the new transactions might already exist in it. Also, it depends on the items falling in the range of minSup and maxSup. If the items that are rare have only a few transactions linked to it through the hyperlink, the depth of the recursion decreases, and the runtime decreases substantially because of this. One of the limitations of the parallel and serial codes that have been implemented is memory consumption. Since it is a recursive process and due to the large sizes of the datasets the main stack memory might be full if we increase the size of the transactions or the size of the database. The memory that can be stored in the CUDA functions is even lesser. We can run the code in the latest NVIDIA GPUs which have a higher compute capability and thus allow us to store more data. Further optimizations can be made in the algorithms too to reduce memory usage. This limitation can be observed while running the algorithms on sparse datasets which consume more memory than the dense datasets like chess and connect data.

In the parallel code, only one level of parallelism is achieved i.e., the load on the main thread is reduced by only one-fold. After the initial kernel call, all the processing happens on the same thread for each item of the HeaderTable HT. Further developments can be made to increase the parallelism of the algorithm by making the algorithm run in parallel in the next level too. This can be done using dynamic parallelism in CUDA. A recursive method has been used in the kernel function to generate the itemsets of size k, where k = 1, 2, 3, ..., n where n is the size of the transaction. This algorithm is converted into an iterative algorithm by using a data structure to store all the necessary parameters for the next iteration since CUDA does allow recursion only up to one level. Further optimizations can be made in the algorithm by using tree-based approaches. Another optimization that can be done to the code is the usage of variable support values [13]. Only static minSup and maxSup values are used in the code. Using variable values for each itemset might lead to more accurate results. The memory that can be utilized on the CUDA device is little. Since the sparse data uses more memory than the dense datasets, it was not possible to execute the generated sparse dataset. This is a limitation of the parallel algorithm.

References

1. "Universal Turing Machine". https://en.wikipedia.org/wiki/Universal_Turing_machine
2. Padhy, N., Mishra, P., Panigrahi, R. The survey of data mining applications and feature scope. ArXiv, abs/1211.5723 (2012)
3. Han, J., Cheng, H., Xin, D., et al.: Frequent pattern mining: current status and future directions. Data Min. Knowl. Disc. **15**, 55–86 (2007)
4. Borah, A., Nath, B.: Rare pattern mining: challenges and future perspectives. Complex Intel. Syst. **5**(1), 1–23 (2018). https://doi.org/10.1007/s40747-018-0085-9
5. Borgelt, C.: Frequent item set mining. WIREs Data Mining Knowl. Discov. **2**, 437–456 (2012). https://doi.org/10.1002/widm.1074
6. Szathmary, L., Napoli, A., Valtchev, P.: Towards rare itemset mining. In: 2007 19th IEEE International Conference on Tools with Artificial Intelligence, ICTAI 2007, vol. 1, pp. 305–312. IEEE (2007)
7. Liu, B., Hsu, W., Ma, Y.: Mining association rules with multiple minimum supports. In: Proceedings of the Fifth ACM SIGKDD International Conference on Knowledge Discovery and Data Mining, pp. 337–341. ACM (1999)
8. Adda, M., Wu, L., Feng, Y.: Rare itemset mining. In: 2007 Sixth International Conference on Machine Learning and Applications, ICMLA 2007, pp. 73–80. IEEE (2007)
9. Cuzzocrea, A., Dayal, U. (eds.): LNCS, vol. 6862. Springer, Heidelberg (2011). https://doi.org/10.1007/978-3-642-23544-3
10. Bhatt, U., Patel, P.: A novel approach for finding rare items based on multiple minimum support framework. Proc. Comput. Sci. **57**, 1088–1095 (2015)
11. Lu, Y., Richter, F., Seidl, T.: Efficient infrequent pattern mining using negative itemset tree. In: Appice, A., Ceci, M., Loglisci, C., Manco, G., Masciari, E., Ras, Z.W. (eds.) Complex Pattern Mining. SCI, vol. 880, pp. 1–16. Springer, Cham (2020). https://doi.org/10.1007/978-3-030-36617-9_1
12. Darrab, S., Broneske, D., Saake, G.: RPP algorithm: a method for discovering interesting rare itemsets. In: Tan, Y., Shi, Y., Tuba, M. (eds.) Data Mining and Big Data: 5th International Conference, DMBD 2020, Belgrade, Serbia, July 14–20, 2020, Proceedings, pp. 14–25. Springer Singapore, Singapore (2020). https://doi.org/10.1007/978-981-15-7205-0_2
13. Kanimozhi Selvi, C.S., Tamilarasi, A.: Mining rare itemset with automated support thresholds. J. Comput. Sci. **7**(3), 394–399 (2011). https://doi.org/10.3844/jcssp.2011.394.399
14. Cui, Y., Gan, W., Lin, H., Zheng, W.: FRI-miner: fuzzy rare itemset mining. Appl. Intell. **52**, 3387–3402 (2021). https://doi.org/10.1007/s10489-021-02574-1

15. Jian, L., Wang, C., Liu, Y., et al.: Parallel data mining techniques on Graphics Processing Unit with Compute Unified Device Architecture (CUDA). J. Supercomput. **64**, 942–967 (2013)
16. Adil, S.H., Qamar, S.: Implementation of association rule mining using CUDA. Int. Conf. Emerging Technol. **2009**, 332–336 (2009). https://doi.org/10.1109/ICET.2009.5353149
17. "SPMF Datasets". http://www.philippe-fournier-viger.com/spmf/index.php?link=datasets.php

Author Index

© The Editor(s) (if applicable) and The Author(s), under exclusive license
to Springer Nature Singapore Pte Ltd. 2023
S. Prabhu et al. (Eds.): ATIS 2022, CCIS 1804, pp. 303–304, 2023.
https://doi.org/10.1007/978-981-99-2264-2

Printed in the United States
by Baker & Taylor Publisher Services

Printed in the United States
by Baker & Taylor Publisher Services